HOT TOPICS
IN THE
LEGAL
PROFESSION

•

2012

Benefit Tulane PILF Series

qp

Quid Pro Books

New Orleans, Louisiana

Hot Topics in the Legal Profession • 2012

The *Benefit Tulane PILF Series* of law books helps to fund the school's public interest organiza-tion and the placements it sponsors for the representation of indigent clients and public causes. More information is found in the Foreword.

Published in 2012 by Quid Pro Books.

ISBN: 1610271106 (pbk)
ISBN-13: 9781610271103 (pbk)
ISBN: 1610271114 (ePub)
ISBN-13: 9781610271110 (ePub)

Quid Pro, LLC

5860 Citrus Blvd., Suite D-101
New Orleans, Louisiana 70123
www.quidprobooks.com

Publisher's Cataloging-in-Publication

Childress, Steven Alan (ed.).

    Hot Topics in the Legal Profession - 2012 / edited by Steven Alan Childress.

      p. cm. — (Benefit Tulane PILF Series)

ISBN-13: 9781610271103 (paperback edition)

"A timely collection of student studies on current events in legal ethics and the U.S. legal pro-fession, discussing issues both important and changing during 2010-2011."

1. Lawyers—United States. 2. Attorney and client—United States. 3. Practice of law—United States. 4. Legal ethics—United States. I. Title. II. Series.

KF 302.C28 2012
174' 32'7388—dc20
      201253552

qp

CONTENTS

FOREWORD

Ethics and the Profession in a Time of Continuing Challenge and Change

In the predecessor volume, *Hot Topics in the Legal Profession 2010*, I noted the unsurprising observation that many issues of modern legal ethics and the structure of the U.S. legal profession move at lightning speed. Legal ethics and professional responsibility are not static mandates but rather use evolving concepts and rules. The years 2010–2011, most relevant to the current volume, confirmed this urgent reality yet again. And beyond the legal ethics rules, bar opinions, and lawyer disciplines that have been at issue in the past two years, the entire legal industry, as with the economy surrounding it, has seen even more evolution and transition lately.

Ethics rules and bar discipline tell only part of the story of legal ethics. Beyond rules of conduct and their enforcement by bar organizations and judges, there is a whole world of law governing lawyers that is simply not about bar discipline or sanctions. Moreover, that is just the changing world of professional regulation, governance, and liability. The matter gets much bigger, and the changes even more pronounced, when one considers the legal profession in all its structural, economic, and social upheaval during this time: law firm layoffs and deferments, major partner moves, the effect on legal education of reform proposals and fiscal reality (combined with mounting student debt), the shrinking of traditional law work and moving it in-house or abroad, and of course lawyer satisfaction and, in many situations, desperation. The professional picture expands even further when one ventures outside the United States and looks at changes the world over, in a time of economic downturn, national debt and austerity reform, legal outsourcing, and corporatizing of law firms — or looks beyond the *legal* profession to other professions and industries. These stories and more dominated the headlines of the law media and bloggers over the past two years, and they promise to continue to signal massive adaptation to come.

All of this is to say that there is a lot of "law of lawyering" out there, and even more economic and social issues in the legal profession beyond rules of ethics as such. For each specific example, one could write a book. I have not done so. However, I have collected fourteen excellent essays from Tulane law students written in 2011 about legal and judicial ethics, as well as the legal profession more broadly, and I have edited them into this book on current events. We offer it not as a survey of the entirety of the field of ethics and the profession, but rather as a "selected topics" book, though admittedly of some of the most pressing and fascinating topics over the past few years.

The students chose the topics independently, as part of the requirements to participate in an Advanced Legal Profession Seminar that I conducted in spring 2011. They performed independent research, discussed their topics with each other, shared editing ideas, and presented their findings in a formal presentation to the class (many using PowerPoint). I did not pick the topics for them, but I applaud their choices; they present some great topics, with current application and meaning, and I hope that lawyers, judges, and academics — as well as the general public interested in lawyers' roles and rules — will find them to be useful, as I have. Not every profound event in the profession is purported to be represented here, as it might in a comprehensive survey or yearbook, yet the topics explored here matter, and the students' research and views will prove interesting to a wide audience.

Anyone trying to keep up lately with the state of flux in legal ethics, and the profession writ large, will find some helpful tools in digital form, among them some daily-updated law blogs. In particular, the best sources for really current events in this field are *The Legal Profession Blog* and *Legal Ethics Forum*. Both blogs have been named to the *ABA Journal*'s "Top 100 Law Blogs" several times. And about these two blogs, *Capital Defense Weekly* once wrote, "as someone who is petrified of effing up and losing the bar card, these sites are tops of my RSS feeds." Not to slight the other editors of these blogs (including myself, writing for LPB), but as to hot topics, I would say that the standout and prolific work of Michael Frisch (LPB) and John Steele (LEF), in particular, will keep any lawyer or bar observer current as to the state of the profession, rules changes, and discipline reports. There are other sources out there that help keep readers updated, too, including general purpose law blogs featuring occasional reports on ethics, the *ABA Journal*'s own blog, and the quarterly newsletters of the AALS Section on Professional Responsibility. Teachers, scholars, and practitioners in the field are lucky to have these resources.

As to the selected topics in this volume, I recommend to you their diversity of focus and depth of analysis. The timely topics include: false guilty pleas and candor to the court, ethical considerations in keeping or returning the client's files as a digital record, legal outsourcing and occupational competition, the dilemma of student debt in a slowed legal economy (including recent, controversial bar character and fitness decisions affecting students with high debt), the practice of law by legal websites such as LegalZoom, the capital defense of Jared Lee Loughner and the autonomy of a client, Justice Antonin Scalia's constitutional seminar sponsored by conservative congressmembers, the need for the profession's sensitivity to "cultural competence," bar discipline for behavior outside the practice of law, the deregulation of ethics in ADR and negotiations, hybridized MDL settlements, prosecutorial relationships with key witnesses, and the advocate-witness rule. Its chapters are accessible to lawyers and also, since not bogged down with heavy legal jargon, to anyone interested in current topics of interest about the state of, and conflicts in, the legal profession and the justice system.

The student-authors of these chapters include current students who will graduate this spring (many of whom already write for and serve on one of Tulane's law journals or our moot court board), as well as several writers who graduated after the seminar was completed and have since gone on to become law firm associates, assistant district attorneys, public defenders, and judicial law clerks. Those already in the trenches of legal practice certainly know by now how *real* the kinds of ethical and professional issues they explored in the seminar truly are, on a day-to-day basis. The topics above include problems of autonomy, confidentiality, cultural disparity, and conflicts of interest that they surely recognize by now to be more than theoretical. And, unfortunately, the chapters on student debt and a shaky economic infrastructure in law are all too authentic to many as well.

As much as I hope that readers learn from their product, as I did, I must stress that the students' primary purpose in writing these papers was academic. They supported a secondary goal of compiling this volume for public distribution, but I emphasized to them their principal obligations to the course and to their classmates. The result is that their papers were written, first, for that purpose, and with no pretense of turning this into a "law review" experience (though my editorial work was made easier, I am grateful to say, because so many of the students had writing experience and were willing to share it with each other). I instructed them that they were to use a consistent and informative footnote style, but they were under no obligation to use a strict *Bluebook* format (indeed I told them to err on the side of more complete information or citations than they were required to give under the *Bluebook*). They were not asked to be sure that the style or formats they used were consistent among themselves (e.g., you will read entries described as "paper," "chapter," or "article" with no effort to pick one label for all students). Nor were they supposed to try to sound like a Spock-like neutral law review Comment; rather, I encouraged them to share opinions, make proposals, and even take stabs at tentative ideas. To the extent any contribution does not meet a reader's expectations about what typical law journal work by students should be, please blame me. This is not to suggest that the students do not succeed on such measures too; I could not possibly know, as the last time I saw a *Bluebook*, Al Gore had not yet invented the internet any more than *Harvard Law Review* editors like Barack Obama and Elena Kagan had ciphered a way to cite it. I was focusing on the substance. The students certainly met my expectations, and those of their colleagues. So their important production, both in substance and in presentation, ought to be read by more than just us. I am happy that, with the publication of this volume, it will be.

To that end, the students are not responsible for the reality of an inevitable lag time between their final drafts and the public publication to print and digital editions. In most instances, the work remains as current as any such publication can be (short of immediate online blogging), and it is fair to describe this book, as I do, as largely responsive to the current issues entering 2012, from looking over the period 2010–2011. I may have been using a car manufacturer's marketing ethics in putting the model year 2012 into the title (a decision by me, not the students), but I felt that was a fair statement of where we are now, and a title consistent with the timeframe and title of the previous volume in the series. These certainly remain the hot issues of ethics and professionalism that we identified, and they retain their relevance and analytical significance to this day. It would not be accurate to use a label that suggested their work was out of date when it hit the street. To the extent some current events have superseded small parts of the analysis in this volume, please blame me and not the students.

The students' work was accurate and supported at the time of the course, and I asked no more than that. (For example, chapter 6 on the defense of Jared Loughner, and chapter 7 on the tragedy of Henry Glover and the prosecution of police involved in his killing, both made reasonable assumptions based on information available by summer 2011, but should not be read as the last word on their factual backgrounds or procedural postures.) Indeed, by encouraging all the students to pick "hot" events, I made it even more likely that in a few instances they would be making factual summaries or making predictions while trying to board a moving train. (The newer metaphor is that sometimes you just have to go ahead and buy the iPhone 7, knowing that the iPhone 8 will come out after and fit on your charm bracelet.) Nonetheless, I am heartened that on hindsight so much of what they wrote has been validated, and the analysis is worth considering even where the train may arrive at an unexpected location. The students simply succeeded in the main purposes of this project.

There was another purpose as well. That is, this volume is the second work in the *Benefit Tulane PILF Series* — two I hope of many — and its net proceeds benefit our school's organization, the Public Interest Law Foundation (which is not, I must add, responsible for any content or errors). Tulane PILF is a non-profit whose student members work tirelessly to promote legal representation of indigent clients and public interest causes, throughout the United States, by funding internships of students in law jobs for that purpose. PILF members, among other fundraising activities, run a fantastic and entertaining auction each spring; and they perform many other labor-intensive services throughout the year. All just to help their classmates have great public interest work experiences, and to help clients who need representation by the brilliant and eager young minds Tulane Law School can offer them.

Those needs — clients needing legal help, public-minded students needing support for work — are more acute than ever. Yet PILF can only sell so much coffee and the loathsome Skittles (so looking like an M&M but so not). This book series, and the extra donations that may come from readers of PILF's web page, is offered in part to fund that need and remind people of the sacrifice and excitement for this cause that so many students at Tulane bring to bear when they volunteer for PILF. Whether the book succeeds on that level is entirely up to you.

Speaking for the student-authors of this book, thank you for purchasing it and considering their research, ideas, and opinions expressed in this volume.

Steven Alan Childress
Conrad Meyer III Professor of Law
Tulane University

New Orleans, Louisiana
January 2012

HOT TOPICS

IN THE

LEGAL PROFESSION

•

2012

PART ONE

Changes in the Legal Industry

"Common Legal Matters":
The Practice of Law and LegalZoom

Jason E. Corley

I. Introduction: LegalZoom and its Business

LegalZoom is an online legal service founded in 2001 by Brian Liu, Eddie Hartman, Brian Lee, and Robert Shapiro.[1] Brian Liu co-founded the company after working as a corporate attorney at the established and leading New York-based law firm Sullivan & Cromwell.[2] Eddie Hartman is not an attorney, but was rather a co-founder who brought technological expertise to the group acting as its Chief Technology Officer, integrating software for the development of LegalZoom.[3] Brian Lee is an attorney who co-founded LegalZoom after leaving the large firm Skadden, Arps, Slate, Meager & Flom, another leading firm that is based in New York.[4] He specialized in tax and accounting consultation.[5] Finally, Robert Shapiro is the famous California attorney who participated on the defense team in the *People v. O.J. Simpson* trial. He seems to be Legal-Zoom's primary spokesperson in the company's advertising campaigns.[6]

These three attorneys and one technology specialist founded a company in which its "founding vision was for an easy to use, online service that helped people create their own legal documents."[7] They claim that the result of this vision was the creation of the "nation's leading online legal document service."[8] LegalZoom also states on its website that "every year, Americans spend millions of dollars on routine legal needs, from incorporations to trademarks to last wills."[9] The company's website says that the founders, as attorneys, knew "there had to be an easier, more affordable way to take care of common legal matters."[10] Their goal, or at least what they claim to be their goal, is "putting the law within reach of millions of people."[11] LegalZoom, though based out of

---

[1] http://www.legalzoom.com/about-us (last visited April 12, 2011).

[2] http://www.legalzoom.com/about-us/management-team (last visited April 12, 2011).

[3] *Id.*

[4] *Id.*

[5] *Id.*

[6] *Id.*

[7] LegalZoom, http://www.legalzoom.com/about-us (last visited April 12, 2011).

[8] *Id.*

[9] *Id.*

[10] *Id.*

[11] *Id.*

Los Angeles, also states on its website that it provides legal services to "all fifty states" throughout the country.[12]

On December 14, 2010, Todd Jansen and others, on behalf of themselves and on behalf of all others similarly situated, filed a lawsuit against LegalZoom in the United States District Court for the Western District of Missouri.[13] The class action claimed that customers purchased legal documents from Legal-Zoom and that in doing so, LegalZoom engaged in unauthorized practice of law (UPL), violating the Missouri Merchandising Practices Act (MPA).[14] The plaintiffs alleged that LegalZoom's website, where customers are charged a fee for many types of legal services including trusts, wills, contracts etc., based upon how the customer answers certain questions in a decision tree, qualifies as practicing law.[15] LegalZoom argued in its defense that "its licensed attorneys create templates for legal documents and that a 'branching intake mechanism' on its website allows customers to skip inapplicable questions based on their prior answers."[16] LegalZoom also claimed that its employees "review the data file only for completeness, spelling, and grammar errors, and consistency of names, addresses and other factual information."[17] Moreover, LegalZoom stated that it was a firing offense to provide legal advice when communicating with a customer.[18]

This article was inspired by the class action lawsuit, though the focus of the article will not be on the legal action itself. Instead, this article first aims to examine the idea of unauthorized practice of law, a concept that has been frustratingly nebulous and unclear for years. Second, this article aims to evaluate LegalZoom's claim, namely the goal of "putting the law within reach of millions of people" regarding what LegalZoom cavalierly calls "common legal matters."[19] This article also aims to evaluate whether in attempting to achieve this goal LegalZoom has moved into the realm of practicing law. The company's success raises confounding ethical questions about the nature of the legal practice itself, including the costs associated with legal counsel and the obvious risks involved with self-help material, although these issues are also arguably only indirectly related to the question of whether or not LegalZoom is conducting unauthorized practice of law.

Furthermore, I argue that state bar associations need to accept a national standard developed by the ABA to meet this new development and to protect consumers as well as the legal community including the courts from a relatively modern phenomenon: the use of websites or software like LegalZoom instead of attorneys for a host of legal needs. This does not mean that LegalZoom should be eliminated or prevented from serving the public, but it does mean

---

[12]*Id.*

[13]*Jansen v. LegalZoom.com Inc.*, 271 F.R.D. 506 (W.D. Mo. Dec. 14, 2010).

[14]*Id.*

[15]*Id.*

[16]*Id.*

[17]*Id.*

[18]*Id.*

[19]LegalZoom, http://www.legalzoom.com/about-us (last visited April 12, 2011).

that changes need to be made in the law to protect consumers, perhaps even from themselves. Part IV will also analyze whether the standard of care to be applied to LegalZoom and other self-help companies in negligence actions needs to be made stricter and more demanding.

Finally, in Part V, I argue that stricter standards need to be set for the way LegalZoom markets itself and for how LegalZoom provides disclaimers to the public. It is not sufficient for LegalZoom to simply say that it is not a law firm. The goal of these changes should not be to protect lawyers who may or may not be losing business to LegalZoom, but rather the American public who may be wholly unaware of the differences between the services of an attorney on the one hand, and the services of LegalZoom on the other.

II. Defining Unauthorized Practice of Law (UPL)

The American Bar Association's (ABA) Model Rules of Professional Conduct do not provide much guidance on how unauthorized practice of law should be defined. Model Rule 5.5 focuses on protecting jurisdictions from unlicensed attorneys who may be attempting to conduct multijurisdictional practice in jurisdictions where they are not licensed.[20] Comment 2 to Rule 5.5 states that "[t]he definition of the practice of the law is established by law and varies from one jurisdiction to another."[21] This standard by the ABA leaves the possibility of fifty different definitions of what exactly a lawyer does. In 1995, the Commission on Nonlawyer Practice ("the Commission"), a group created by the ABA in response to "concern regarding nonlawyer engagement in the practice of the law," issued a report based on an investigation it conducted and made recommendations "on how states should address problems arising from non-lawyer involvement in legal-related activities."[22]

During 2002-2003, the ABA went one step further when its Task Force on the Model Definition of the Practice of the Law "provided a framework for defining the practice of the law and recommended that every jurisdiction es-tablish a definition for the practice of the law."[23] The Task Force also stated that "each state's judicial branch of government should abolish the traditional case-by-case approach to the practice of the law analysis and adopt a formal definition and a regulatory scheme that fosters consumer protection, access to justice and accountability."[24] The goal of achieving consumer protection would be achieved by limiting those who may practice the law to "individuals possess-ing the character and ability required for the proficient practice of law."[25] This

---

[20]ABA Model Rules of Professional Conduct, Model Rule 5.5 Unauthorized Practice of Law; Multijurisdictional Practice of Law, 2010.

[21]*Id.*, Comment 2.

[22]Michael S. Knowles, *Keep Your Friends Close and the Laymen Closer: State Bar Associations Can Combat the Problems Associated With Nonlawyers Engaging in the Unauthorized Practice of Estate Planning Through a Certification System*, 43 Creigh-ton L. Rev. 855, 859 (2010).

[23]*Id.*

[24]*Id.*

[25]*Id.* at 860-61.

goal needed to be accomplished while still allowing for access to the judicial system. This is not an easy task. In 2005 the Legal Services Corporation reported that up to eighty percent of "lower-income American's legal needs are not being fulfilled."[26] The third goal, accountability, is arguably the most important.

Law Professor Sande L. Buhai has shown that the public can run into legal difficulties when trying to recover damages from nonlawyers who were providing legal services. Professor Buhai argues that this is because there is not a set standard of care that courts throughout the nation have instituted.[27] According to Buhai, most jurisdictions have held nonlawyers to the same standard of care as lawyers when the nonlawyer is engaging in unauthorized practice of law.[28] There are some jurisdictions, however, that do not use this standard and instead hold the nonlawyers conducting unauthorized practice of the law to a simple standard of negligence.[29] In either case, this debate about the correct standard of care to be applied in cases against someone or something conducting unauthorized practice of law is secondary to the primary question of what is unauthorized practice of law, or even more precisely, what is the practice of law.

The ABA Task Force also attempted to provide a general definition to help achieve the goals discussed above. It read that "the practice of the law is the application or legal principles and judgment with regard to the circumstances or objectives of a person that require the knowledge and skill of a person trained in the law."[30] The rule made the presumption that "the definition was met when acting on behalf of another in: (i) giving advice or counsel to persons as to their legal rights or responsibilities or to those of others; (ii) selecting, drafting, or completing legal documents or agreements that affect the legal rights of a person; (iii) representing a person before an adjudicative body, including, but not limited to, preparing or filing documents or conducting discovery; or (iv) negotiating legal rights or responsibilities on behalf of a person."[31] This proposal was not pursued, however, after the Federal Trade Commission, the U.S. Department of Justice, and others attacked it for being too broad.[32]

Some have described unauthorized practice of law in the same fashion that Justice Potter Stewart once famously defined obscenity: the standard is

---

[26]*Id.* at 861.

[27]Sande L. Buhai, *Act Like a Lawyer, Be Judged Like a Lawyer: The Standard of Care for the Unlicensed Practice of Law*, 2007 Utah L. Rev. 87, 92-93 (2007).

[28]*Id.* at 97.

[29]*Id.*

[30]Gillian K. Hadfield, *Legal Barriers to Innovation: The Growing Economic Cost of Professional Control Over Corporate Legal Markets*, 60 Stan. L. Rev. 1689, 1707 (2008) (citing ABA Task Force on the Model Definition of the Practice of Law, Report to the House Delegates, Recommendation (2003), available at http://www.abanet.org/cpr/model-def/recomm.pdf (last visited April 12, 2011)).

[31]*Id.* at 1707-08 (citing ABA Task Force on the Model Definition of the Practice of Law, Report to the House Delegates, Recommendation (2003), available at http://www.abanet.org/cpr/model-def/recomm.pdf (last visited April 12, 2011)).

[32]*Id.* at 1708.

"knowing it when you see it."[33] This definition, however, is not currently an accepted legal standard nationally. *Black's Law Dictionary* defines unauthorized practice of law by relating it to its definition of the practice of the law. According to *Black's Law Dictionary*, unauthorized practice of law is "the practice of law by a person, typically a nonlawyer, who has not been licensed or admitted to practice law in a given jurisdiction."[34] *Black's Law Dictionary*, on the other hand, defines practice of law as "the professional work of a duly licensed lawyer, encompassing a broad range of services such as conducting cases in court, preparing papers necessary to bring about various transactions from conveying land to effecting corporate mergers, preparing legal opinions on various points of law, drafting wills and other estate-planning documents, and advising clients on legal questions."[35] Under this definition it is arguable that LegalZoom is conducting unauthorized practice of law. However, as previously stated, each state has a separate standard and it is these varied state standards that are enforceable in a UPL proceeding or bar discipline prosecution.

Oregon's courts, for example, have always struggled with a solid definition of "practice of law," let alone the unauthorized practice of it.[36] Oregon's UPL statute provides that "[e]xcept for the right reserved to litigants by ORS 9.320 to prosecute or defend a cause in person, no person shall practice law or represent that person as qualified to practice law unless that person is an active member of the Oregon State Bar."[37] This definition is still not particularly helpful when attempting to discern what activities are or are not the practice of the law being done in an unauthorized capacity.

The Texas Bar Association was the first state association to openly pursue UPL actions against the "self-help" software industry.[38] In 1998 the Unauthorized Practice of Law Committee of the Texas Bar Association sued Parsons Technology, Inc. (Parsons), the company that makes Quicken Family Lawyer, in an UPL action.[39] The district court concluded that Parsons was conducting UPL because its marketing language "creates an air of reliability about the documents which increases the likelihood that an individual user will be misled into relying on them."[40] Parsons appealed to the United States Court of Appeals for the Fifth Circuit, but it became unnecessary for a decision to be reached on appeal.[41] While the appeal was pending, the UPL Committee of the Texas Bar

---

[33]Justin D. Leonard, *Cyberlawyering and the Small Business: Software Makes Hard Law (But Good Sense)*, 7 J. Small & Emerging Bus. L. 323, 358 (2003) (citing Justice Potter Stewart concurring in *Jacobellis v. Ohio*, 378 U.S. 184, 197 (1964)).

[34]Black's Law Dictionary, Third Pocket Edition, 2006.

[35]*Id.*

[36]Leonard, 7 J. Small & Emerging Bus. L. 323, 363 (2003).

[37]*Id.* at 364.

[38]*Id.* at 369.

[39]*Id.*

[40]*Id.*

[41]*Id.* at 370.

Association began to make some aggressive moves against Nolo Press, a company that also provided self-help materials similar to that of Quicken Lawyer.[42] Lobbyists pushed the Texas State Legislature to amend the Texas UPL statute in order to protect the self-help companies, and the legislature responded.[43] The Texas UPL statute was changed to read that "the practice of the law does not include design, creation, publication, distribution, display or sale...of written materials, books, forms, computer software, or similar products if the products clearly and conspicuously state that the products are not a substitute for the advice of an attorney."[44] It is now obviously legal for companies to provide self-help materials in the state of Texas.

Nebraska, on the other hand, uses the criminal courts to monitor UPL. In Nebraska, it is a Class III misdemeanor to conduct UPL.[45] This method was found to be generally inept at protecting consumers in the area of transactional legal practice, so the Nebraska Supreme Court adopted rules in order to protect the public.[46] These rules adopted by the court can be likened to the method of preventing UPL adopted by Arizona. Arizona has no statute dealing with UPL.[47] Instead, the Arizona Supreme Court uses its inherent power to create rules regulating the practice of the law and broadly defines practice of the law as conduct that "involves furnishing legal services or advice for or to another person."[48]

It is apparent, at least on the surface, that LegalZoom seems to be legally providing services in some locations and it would therefore be incorrect to say that it is violating the law on a nationwide scale. The rules and laws controlling UPL are too varied and too general. Whereas in Texas it is quite obviously acceptable for LegalZoom to provide its self-help materials, the same cannot be said for a state like Arizona where a broad definition of legal practice is utilized. Instead of focusing on specific state rules and statutes, which is not the aim of this article, I ask the general question of whether or not LegalZoom is conducting practice of the law as a reasonable person would perceive it. The next question I address is how the legal community should respond to protect consumers. In each state, the standards are too fact-specific to reach a general conclusion. Before reaching this general conclusion, it is necessary to evaluate LegalZoom's, and LegalZoom's apologists', fundamental argument in defense of LegalZoom and others that provide self-help. As stated on LegalZoom's webpage, the company espouses the goal of providing legal services to millions who would otherwise not have access to those services, typically provided by attorneys. The implication of this is that legal representation is too expensive for many in the population to afford. In other words, the people using LegalZoom would not be using an attorney even if LegalZoom did not exist, or at the very

---

[42]*Id.*

[43]*Id.*

[44]Tex. Code Ann. § 81.101(c) (2003).

[45]Knowles, 43 Creighton L. Rev. 855, 869-70 (2010).

[46]*Id.* at 870.

[47]*Id.*

[48]*Id.* (citing Ariz. Sup. Ct. R. 31(a)(2)(A)).

least they are saving an enormous amount of money in using LegalZoom instead.

III. Costs and Perils: Issues Related to UPL

A. Costs of Legal Counsel

In 2005, a California survey asked over two thousand of its residents whether the costs associated with hiring an attorney prevented or might prevent them from using the justice system.[49] The response was disheartening. Sixty-nine percent of these residents agreed with the general proposition that costs would keep them or might keep them out of court.[50] Although this is only one locality, the fact remains that legal services are too expensive for most people and it is a trend that does not seem to be changing. This may be related to a change in the legal profession that is often overlooked. In 1992, individuals generally received "forty percent of lawyers' attention while businesses commanded fifty-one percent."[51] This is in stark contrast to the percentages just 25 years earlier, when "fifty-five percent of lawyer time was devoted to individuals and thirty-nine percent to businesses."[52] This is combined with the fact that in the past two decades, "the amount provided by the federal government to support legal services to the poor has declined by one third."[53] It is estimated that currently four out of every five lower-income individuals cannot afford their legal needs and these same costs affect three out of every five persons in the middle class.[54] Fifty-three percent of Americans describe themselves as middle class.[55] To say that it is difficult for many Americans to afford an attorney or legal representation is an understatement.

LegalZoom, and other websites and software, ostensibly fill the void. A will at LegalZoom can cost as little as $69, while incorporating a business can cost as little as $99.[56] It is unquestionably the more affordable alternative. LegalZoom should be credited and applauded for attempting to provide this service at such low cost. It is not only the lower-income individuals who seem to be supporting the use of LegalZoom or other self-help companies. Some observers have even advocated replacing tax lawyers and accountants "safely"

---

[49]Stephen Landsman, *The Growing Challenge of Pro Se Litigation*, 13 Lewis & Clark L. Rev. 439, 441 (2009).

[50]*Id.*

[51]*Id.* at 443.

[52]*Id.*

[53]*Id.*

[54]*Id.*

[55]Stephen Rose, *An Economist Takes a Look at the Numbers: The Myth of the Declining Middle Class* (2008), available at http://stats.org/stories/2008/myth_decline_middle_june9_08.html (last visited April 12, 2011).

[56]LegalZoom, http://www.legalzoom.com/index1g.html (last visited April 12, 2011).

with "cyberlawyering applications."[57] Moreover, some argue that the "rapid advances in computing technology" allow small businesses to have "access to a wide variety of legal resources that enhance, or even replace, the services typically provided by attorneys."[58] Clearly then, it is not only the lower-income population that LegalZoom is helping through its efficient and affordable methods.

The problem with focusing solely on costs as an argument in support of LegalZoom and other self-help companies is that it misses the primary purpose of UPL laws and rules. The issues of cost and the issues of UPL are separate and distinct. There is no doubt that something needs to be done about the costs of legal representation. It is unacceptable that four out of five lower income individuals have no access to the legal system because of the costs associated with hiring an attorney.[59] Those social issues, however, are only tenuously linked to the issue of UPL. Certainly UPL exists in some areas because of the costs of legal counsel, but that does not mean the costs of legal counsel should be used to justify UPL. The costs of legal counsel in America need to be rectified, but an analysis of LegalZoom's activities and whether or not those activities qualify as practice of law does not rely on a social analysis of the rising costs of attorneys. UPL often concerns itself with the perils associated with having nonlawyers conduct legal work.

B. Perils of Self-Help Materials

There are dangers that exist, in relying on self-help materials, that might not seem apparent to most customers. "Reliance on bad or incomplete information can cost a small business dearly in terms of the time and money required to resolve the additional problems created by such misinformation."[60] It has been noted that some self-help materials in the area of estate planning injured consumers "because such instruments are not tailored specifically to each individual consumer."[61] For example, the Supreme Court of Wyoming noted that plaintiffs in a particular case "had the misfortune to fall victim to an itinerant hawker of fill-in-the-blank, one-size-fits-all, trust forms."[62] The court also added that this material was not suited for the plaintiffs' needs and that the self-help material had managed to "squander a significant portion of their hard-earned life savings on legal proceedings and attorney's fees."[63] These perils have been explored and written about for years regarding self-help material, whether that self-help material was provided through books, floppy disks, CDs, or the internet. Again, though, the obvious risks associated with self-help are merely a by-product of UPL, or perhaps poor self-help manuals. These risks are not directly related to the fundamental issue of LegalZoom's

---

[57]Leonard, 7 J. Small & Emerging Bus. L. 323, 331 (2003).

[58]*Id.* at 323.

[59]Landsman, 13 Lewis & Clark L. Rev. 439, 443 (2009).

[60]Leonard, 7 J. Small & Emerging Bus. L. 323, 355 (2003).

[61]Knowles, 43 Creighton L. Rev. 855, 856 (2010).

[62]*Id.* at 856 (citing *Garwood v. Garwood*, 194 P.3d 319, 327 (Wyo. 2008)).

[63]*Id.*

services functioning as possible practice of law, in the same tenuous manner that costs associated with hiring legal counsel are not directly related to unauthorized practice of law.

The costs of legal counsel and the risks associated with using self-help materials are important issues, but they are not the focus here. They are by-products of UPL, self-help materials, and the shift in the legal profession to higher-end corporate work. They are not determinative on the issue of whether or not LegalZoom is conducting practice of law and the direct risks associated with that, whether or not any state jurisdiction would define it that way. Nevertheless, these issues are certainly relevant in determining whether or not a national standard should be employed in defining practice of law and the unauthorized practice of it.

IV. LegalZoom and Practice of Law

One of the primary difficulties of coming to a sound conclusion on whether or not LegalZoom is conducting practice of law, or the unauthorized practice of law, is because of the nature of the work it provides. Lawyers are not merely clerks who fill in specific answers in spaces; they are counselors who provide specific advice and prod their clients for unapparent desires, conscious to the client or not. In one sense, then, LegalZoom is not conducting practice of law because it does not provide that service. Its customer service technicians will openly tell a customer that he or she must seek a lawyer's advice on a legal matter; furthermore they allegedly do not advise customers on any legal matter whatsoever. The site also provides a disclaimer stating that it is "not a law firm" and that its services "are not a substitute for one."[64] On the other hand, Legal-Zoom is doing work and providing services typically provided by an attorney. Because of this, it is easy to imagine how many people are using LegalZoom in lieu of an attorney, rather than because they don't need an attorney. Some have advocated the use of LegalZoom as a model for law firms.

The LegalZoom model for law firms has been stated as a method in which "clients and perspective clients...will be able to enter the firm's website and be provided information (either for free or for a price) relating to services the firm provides" and then download these service which can later be reviewed by an attorney or multiple attorneys at the law firm.[65] Nevertheless, even this Legal-Zoom model for law firms will likely not result in law firms providing do-it-yourself options for clients, for fear of malpractice lawsuits.[66] The likely result is that in the near future, if not already, LegalZoom will still be providing a uniquely different service to the public from that of law firms, even the law firms who do adopt some of LegalZoom's online-based methods of service. With this in mind, the costs of using a law firm may diminish slightly, but since lawyers will still need to review the client's requests and proposals, the high

---

[64]LegalZoom, http://www.legalzoom.com/index1g.html (disclaimer available at bottom of page) (last visited April 12, 2011).

[65]Jonathan G. Blattmachr, *Looking Back and Looking Ahead: Preparing Your Practice for the Future: Do Not Get Behind the Change Curve*, 36 ACTEC J. 1, 60 (2010).

[66]*Id.*

hourly fees attorneys charge will result in LegalZoom maintaining its hold on the lower-cost marketplace. This continuing differentiation between what a law firm does, compared to what LegalZoom's services provide, works both for and against LegalZoom when the company is accused of UPL.

Despite the fact that some may argue that lawyers overstate their level of expertise, and while acknowledging that technology will improve, it is difficult to defend a system that provides a lay customer with legal services without the customer's knowledge of what he or she is not being provided. In other words, LegalZoom says that it is not a law firm, but then does not provide the customer with information about what that means or what a law firm can provide that LegalZoom cannot.

The legal system and the law are not merely a series of jigsaw pieces that need to be put together in order to create a desired outcome. In some cases the customer service representatives at LegalZoom walk the fine line of providing legal advice as opposed to providing effective customer service. In 2010, Jonathan Blattmachr, a trusts and estates attorney and a former Regent of the American College of Trust and Estate Council, published his personal experience with LegalZoom.[67] According to Blattmachr, he purchased a last will and testament from LegalZoom for the cost of $71.[68] For this price, LegalZoom allowed him to build a will from a document assembly service using a "decision tree" to put the pieces together.[69] Blattmachr, a respected trusts and estates attorney, "found some of the questions used by LegalZoom confusing."[70] At one point, he "was offered an option for a testamentary trust with advice that some people want to use such an arrangement until a certain point such as when the child became age 21."[71] At this point, Blattmachr responded that he wanted it "for life."[72] He was then called over the telephone by a customer service representative at LegalZoom named "Seth" who informed him that he could not have a trust for the life of his children. Blattmachr did not question whether this was because it was not legal, or it was because LegalZoom's system did not provide that type of service.[73] Seth then informed him that he would need a supplemental needs trust and that he would need to contact an attorney in order to complete that.[74] Blattmachr responded that he did not need a supplemental needs trust, without ever revealing that he was an attorney.[75] Seth with LegalZoom remained silent and Blattmachr thought he simply accepted that statement as true.[76]

---

[67] *Id.* at 21-22.

[68] *Id.* at 21.

[69] *Id.*

[70] *Id.*

[71] *Id.* at 22.

[72] *Id.*

[73] *Id.*

[74] *Id.*

[75] *Id.*

[76] *Id.*

This conversation is interesting for two reasons. First, at one point Seth with LegalZoom told Blattmachr he could not have a trust for the life of his children. Although it is unclear whether or not this was due to LegalZoom's software capabilities, a lay customer would likely presume it was because it was legally unavailable. This, at least from the customer's point of view, qualifies as legal advice despite the simplicity of it. It is irrelevant whether or not Seth from LegalZoom was correct that those types of trusts may be unavailable; the issue is that Seth provided this information without being able to prod and question the customer about why he might want that other service and find an amenable solution. A layperson might just assume that there were no available alternatives. Second, by omitting to respond to Blattmachr's statement that he did not need a supplemental needs trust, Seth at LegalZoom implied to the customer that the customer was correct and should proceed. It is interesting to note that Blattmachr found the will that he purchased from LegalZoom "lacking in many ways."[77]

Practice of law is not, and should not be defined as, limited to the simple process of filling in specific legalese where the gaps exist. Modern neurolinguistics, the study of the mechanisms in the human brain that control comprehension, production, and acquisition of language, has shown that "most brain functions are not conscious and rational, but are unconscious and nonrational."[78] Furthermore, neurolinguistic science has shown that the majority of human thought is subconscious and that this "cognitive unconscious" dominates most of our brain function.[79] Subconsciously, the brain effortlessly integrates intellectual and emotional information. "How a person subjectively perceives a situation becomes as powerful (or more powerful) as whatever objective rendition of the facts might present."[80] Because of this, effective attorneys create a client-attorney relationship in which the attorney can truly understand the client's desires in order for them to be legally achieved.[81] This is the goal most attorneys have in mind when they attempt to develop a professional rapport with their client. In other words, despite the tendency to believe that the raw facts of a case decide its outcome, there are no two cases that are the same because the illogical thought process and emotional attachments of two different people will differ in every single case. "Despite the Enlightenment credo, the same reason does not apply to all situations, regardless of personal values."[82]

In the area of alternative dispute resolution (ADR), questions are asked of the client which do not fit into the typical legal mold of bare facts, and this type of approach is being utilized more and more in other areas of legal practice. For example, attorneys in ADR proceedings such as mediation will often inquire

---

[77]*Id.*

[78]Phyllis E. Bernard, *The Lawyer's Mind: Why a Twenty-First Century Legal Practice Will Not Thrive Using Nineteenth Century Thinking (With a Special Thanks to George Lakoff)*, 25 Ohio St. J. on Disp. Resol. 165, 171 (2009).

[79]*Id.* at 172.

[80]*Id.*

[81]*Id.*

[82]*Id.*

what the client's underlying interests are, not just his or her position or what he or she is demanding.[83] The attorneys might also inquire into how the client perceives the relationship and whether or not the attorney is able "to meet the subjective and objective expectations."[84]

This type of approach is, or at least should be, utilized in all elements of the client-attorney relationship extending far beyond the realm of ADR and into trusts and estates practice, tax representation, civil litigation and more. This type of approach is also a technological impossibility for LegalZoom to provide, at least at the current level of technology available; it is difficult to envision a computer with a subconscious intuition driving at a certain issue to reveal more information. It is hard to imagine how, considering the attorney's role as advisor and counselor, some have advocated or somewhat predicted that many "Americans would get their legal advice from the legal equivalent of TurboTax."[85] Without exploring the social ambivalence about, or even antagonism against, attorneys in some circles, this belief is more likely the result of the public's lack of understanding of the complications involved in the law and its imprecise nature. This would lead some to genuinely believe that practicing the law is capable of such stringent and simple mechanics as those provided by LegalZoom.

Neurolinguistic science and recent trends in alternative dispute resolution are not the only evidence that the practice of law exists outside the bounds of mechanical functions. For ethical reasons, an attorney is required to act as an advisor and counselor to his or her clients. Model Rule 2.1 of the ABA Model Rules of Professional Conduct states that "[i]n representing a client, a lawyer shall exercise independent professional judgment and render candid advice. In rendering advice, a lawyer may refer not only to law but to other considerations such as moral, economic, social and political factors, that may be relevant to the client's situation."[86] The scope of this advice is broad, especially in situations where the client is inexperienced in legal matters. Comment 3 to Model Rule 2.1 states that if a client is experienced in legal matters and requests "purely technical" advice, the lawyer may grant that. [87] However, if the client is not experienced in legal matters, the attorney maintains his or her obligation to go beyond strictly legal answers to issues or questions posed.[88] Once again, LegalZoom does not have this burden and does not provide this service, so it can easily be argued that it is not practicing law. However, not providing the same services to clients or customers, but still leaving the indelible impression the services attain an equal outcome, are two different considerations entirely.

This could be called the "Fast-Food Chain Model" of law. When I go to a fast-food chain, I am almost immediately asked in the drive-through lane whether I would like to purchase some seasonal special for a specified amount

---

[83]*Id.* at 178.

[84]*Id.* at 179.

[85]Richard L. Marcus, *The Electronic Lawyer*, 58 DePaul L. Rev. 263, 275 (2009).

[86]ABA Model Rules of Professional Conduct, Rule 2.1 Advisor.

[87]*Id.*, Comment 3.

[88]*Id.*

of money. I always decline this offer and order one of the basic meals. When I do that, I am then asked whether I would like a meal that includes a soda and some other side item. I usually indulge in this offer and expand my meal. It is then usually followed by an offer from one of the fast-food chains to increase the size of the meal for ninety-nine cents more or for some other low price. Through this simple question and answer method I can get a cheap, efficient, but generally unappetizing meal. The making of the cuisine at fast-food joints is not the artistic and exploratory work of a trained chef working tirelessly to create the perfect filet mignon. It is the simple assembly line work of a fast-food chain's mixing the same ingredients repeatedly to provide a consistent but uncreative dining experience.

No one would compare the cooking at a fast-food chain to that of a five star restaurant. This is ultimately the major issue with LegalZoom. LegalZoom is the "Fast-Food Chain Model" of law. It is generally uncreative in individual cases using a system that cannot generate unique approaches to individualized problems. It uses a system of finite questions and answers that provides a finite number of solutions to the issue. In LegalZoom's defense, if a customer's desires require outside-the-box thinking or a special service not included in Legal-Zoom's software, LegalZoom will tell the customer to contact an attorney. But, unlike a customer at the fast-food chain who knows he or she is buying cheap but generally lower-quality food, it is debatable whether or not the customer at LegalZoom understands the alternatives that could be presented by meeting with an attorney. Or, on the other hand, the customer may think LegalZoom provides the same service, or at the least service of an equal quality or character. That is not to say that LegalZoom is providing a generally low quality of service, but in the field of law the stakes are much higher than a bad meal on a busy day.

Scientific study of the human brain shows that many human desires and emotions are not conscious, and a good attorney works to discover these desires, which are not apparent even to the client. Ethical considerations require attorneys to act as advisors and explore directions with the client not limited to the technical realm of legalese. For these reasons, it is arguable LegalZoom is not conducting practice of law because it simply cannot provide those services. However, the experience of some attorneys with LegalZoom, in this case Jonathan Blattmachr, leaves one dubious about LegalZoom's quality of product. Furthermore, it is highly debatable how a customer service representative without legal training can consistently provide services regarding legal documents without providing legal advice. Finally, LegalZoom is working in a field traditionally occupied by attorneys. LegalZoom is providing legal documents, without being able to provide the service provided by attorneys, though the cost of those attorneys is much higher. The market will reflect what the populace is and is not willing to pay for, and it is clear that at least a large amount of the population uses LegalZoom. The issues do not lie in simple supply and demand economics; rather, the issues lie in how LegalZoom portrays itself and how it seems to be perceived by the public.

As stated above, customers eating at a fast-food restaurant are generally aware it is not a substitute for a five star restaurant. LegalZoom advertises that "every year, Americans spend millions of dollars on routine legal needs, from incorporations to trademarks to last wills."[89] The implication of this type of statement is that the money is being spent needlessly, and that creating a will is as routine a decision as choosing between a fast-food chain and a five star restaurant for dinner. LegalZoom also advertises that "as attorneys [they] knew there needed to be an easier, more affordable way to take care of common legal matters."[90] Not only does this statement imply to the customer that attorneys are directly approving of each individual product developed by a customer through LegalZoom, it also implies that there is such a thing as a common legal matter. Any legal action that alters the rights of the parties involved is not a "common" matter. In fact, I would argue that there is no such thing as a "common legal matter." No work that is usually done by an attorney is "common" in the sense used by LegalZoom. This is the fundamental issue with LegalZoom, and the primary reason that I believe it has moved from the realm of document provider to conducting UPL. The legal community should not allow the implication to exist that the services of LegalZoom and those of an attorney attain the same results or are of a similar or equal character.

One can dance back and forth on a needle arguing about the semantics discussed above, including whether the nonexistence of an attorney-client relationship removes LegalZoom from being considered as a legal practitioner. It is undeniable, however, that the complications involved in LegalZoom's services discussed above are combined with other issues. LegalZoom has a tendency to play down the importance of the legal activity, especially when the site refers to working on "common legal matters." LegalZoom also simultaneously plays up the fact that the founders of the company are lawyers while informing the customer that LegalZoom is accepted in all fifty states. This creates an unsubstantiated and unjustified faith by the customer in the reliability of LegalZoom's product.

As discussed above in Part II, in 1998 the Unauthorized Practice of Law Committee of the Texas Bar Association sued Parsons Technology, Inc. (Parsons), the company that makes Quicken Family Lawyer, in a UPL action.[91] Before the legislature overruled him, Judge Barefoot Sanders concluded in that case that because the packaging of self-help software told the user that the software's forms were valid in 49 states, the software created "an air of reliability about the documents, which increases the likelihood that an individual user will be misled into relying on them."[92] Eleven years later, LegalZoom has conquered the self-help marketplace by advertising its low cost coupled with implications that it can be used in place of an attorney for legal needs, although the company denies that it is a law firm. This all occurs without any explanation to the customer of the differences between LegalZoom and law firms. These customers may or may not know what services the attorney can provide that LegalZoom cannot.

---

[89]LegalZoom, http://www.legalzoom.com/about-us (last visited April 12, 2011).

[90]*Id.*

[91]Justin D. Leonard, 7 J. Small & Emerging Bus. L. 323, 358 (2003).

[92]*Unauthorized Practice of Law Committee v. Parsons Technology Inc.*, 1999 WL 47235 at *6 (N.D. Tex. 1999).

V. Conclusion

LegalZoom, and other self-help materials and software, are providing a needed service at an affordable cost to a large portion of the community who otherwise may not be able to afford an attorney. The obvious risks associated with self-help materials are that information may be provided incompletely or incorrectly, and that the costs to correct the mistake may be severe. Instead of focusing on the rising costs of legal representation or the direct and obvious risks associated with using self-help material, this article has focused on the question of practicing law itself and the hidden dangers associated with the rise of companies like LegalZoom. This article has not aimed at attacking LegalZoom. Many of its objectives are admirable. This article is aimed at the ABA, which needs to create a national definition of practice of law that encompasses some elements of legal practice that are not concerned with technicalities or strict legal advice.

Attorneys do have a role as counselor and advisor in helping the client learn what his or her true desires and objectives are. This role needs to be used to distinguish attorneys from self-help software that advances in capabilities every day. The public, which may not be aware of the difference in these services, needs to be informed. State jurisdictions need to adopt a rigid and unforgiving standard of care for self-help companies operating in areas normally occupied by attorneys. Despite LegalZoom's statements, drafting a will is not "routine." These documents alter the rights of the parties involved and can have devastating results in cases where they are drafted incorrectly. Companies like LegalZoom should be held to the standard of care an attorney is held to when working in this field. This includes the possibility of being sued for malpractice. Like the ABA's Task Force on the Model Definition of the Practice of the Law concluded, accountability in the legal field is an objective that must be reached.[93] UPL enforcement nationwide needs to be guided by the words of Judge Sanders. Although it was not the focus of his opinion, he noted that one of the more dangerous elements of companies like LegalZoom is their apparent reliability to consumers who may be persuaded to avoid an attorney. This is the result of the confident and nonchalant attitude presented by LegalZoom regarding so-called "common legal matters."

As of this writing the class action lawsuit in Missouri against LegalZoom is ongoing, though the plaintiffs were successful in certifying their class.[94] In Missouri the practice of law is defined as "the appearance as an advocate in a representative capacity or the drawing of papers, pleadings or documents or the performance of any act in such capacity in connection with proceedings pending or prospective before any court of record."[95] The court will probably visit the issue of whether or not it was LegalZoom who drew up the legal documents, or whether the consumers were the drafters of those documents. That is not the real issue. The court should instead ask whether or not the plaintiffs used LegalZoom in lieu of an attorney because they were unaware and unin-

---

[93]*See* Knowles, 43 Creighton L. Rev. 855, 859 (2010).

[94]*Jansen v. LegalZoom.com Inc.*, 271 F.R.D. 506, 513 (W.D. Mo. Dec. 14, 2010).

[95]V.A.M.S 484.010, Practice of Law and the Law Business Defined.

formed by LegalZoom how they could be harmed by using LegalZoom rather than an attorney.

2

Developments in the Ethics of Legal Process Outsourcing

Nicholas Daum

Introduction

Outsourcing is a ubiquitous practice in the modern economy. Seeking to cut their expenses, businesses take advantage of the lower wages that are often available in foreign countries. Certain portions of a company's activities can be handled by third parties at substantially reduced cost. The practice is often associated with relatively unskilled labor such as manufacturing or customer relations. However, in a progressively globalized economy, advances in communications and information processing have allowed for the outsourcing of higher end, skilled services. Countries such as India or China that have a stable infrastructure, good educational systems, and widespread use of English have become major centers for this type of outsourcing. With the downturn in the U.S. economy, the ability to cut costs has become ever more crucial and these practices have become more and more common.

Legal process outsourcing (LPO) is one of the most recent incarnations of this trend. Law firms and corporate legal departments take advantage of the LPO industry which allows for time consuming, labor intensive tasks to be completed relatively cheaply and quickly. While legal work was being outsourced to India as early as 1996, the e-discovery laws established in 2006, which regulate the storage and management of electronic data for federal court actions, triggered a major increase in the practice of legal outsourcing.[1] Due to massive amounts of information that needed to be processed, attorneys in the United States needed an affordable solution to handle the load. Since then, the industry has expanded to include such things as research, document review, litigation support, and the drafting of contracts and patent applications. Rising costs for legal services will only continue to make outsourcing more attractive and practical.

India is one of the world's largest participants in legal process outsourcing, where it is considered a major growth industry. India is an attractive target for legal outsourcing because it shares a common law heritage from Britain and legal proceedings are conducted in English.[2] Hundreds of thousands of Indians enter law school each year, and the LPO industry provides an attractive career path for those that do not wish to practice in the overburdened legal system of

---

[1]*See* Rama Lakshmi, *U.S. Legal Work Booms in India,* Washington Post, May 11, 2008, at A20, *available at* http://www.washingtonpost.com/wp-dyn/content/article/2008/05/10/AR2008051002355_pf.html

[2]*Id.*

a country that that has about 13 judges for every one million citizens, and is characterized by backlogs and delays.[3] Likewise, many of the top law firms in India tend to be family oriented operations that offer limited opportunity for advancement to those lacking the proper connections. Moreover, Indian lawyers can work for as little as $10,000 a year while an American contract lawyer typically works for $30 an hour, and starting salaries can go as high as $160,000 annually.[4] This tremendous reduction in expense, sometimes by as much as a factor of ten, is becoming increasingly important to firms that have to reduce hiring and cut jobs in order to stay competitive. In addition, many LPOs are willing to hire recent law school graduates and will often provide the training necessary to work with United States law, further increasing their employment prospects. Forrester Research projections predict that the legal outsourcing industry in India may reach four billion dollars by 2015.[5]

There are several ethics rules, as exemplified by the Model Rules of Professional Conduct, that play a critical role in the context of legal process outsourcing. Rule 1.1 deals with an attorney's general obligation to render competent service. Rule 1.2(a) requires attorneys to abide by a client's decisions concerning the objectives of representation, and, in accordance with Rule 1.4, attorneys must consult with clients as to the means by which the objectives will be pursued. Rules 5.1 and 5.3 govern the responsibilities of supervisory lawyers as to themselves and to non-lawyer assistants. In accordance with Rule 5.5, these rules also serve to prevent the lawyer from engaging in or encouraging the unauthorized practice of law. Rules 1.7 through 1.11 come into play when there is potential for a conflict of interest. The fee arrangements permissible when outsourcing may be governed by Rules 1.5 and 5.4. Finally, Rule 7.5(d) states that lawyers must not make misrepresentations regarding practice in an organization or partnership.

Advisory Opinions

Legal outsourcing is no longer a novelty or an experimental practice; it is a reality. However, despite the economic reasons that make it attractive, questions still arise regarding the ethical obligations of American lawyers who outsource. In recent years, several influential bar associations have issued opinions stating that lawyers may offshore certain portions of their practice and still fulfill their professional responsibilities. The American Bar Association, as well as the bar associations in New York, Florida, San Diego, and elsewhere, have recognized the potential benefits of outsourcing. The ABA describes outsourcing as "salutary ... for our globalized economy."[6] The ABA applauded lawyers and firms to expand their services without the need to maintain human re-

---

[3]*Id.*

[4]*See* Anthony Lin, *Legal Outsourcing to India is Growing, But Still Confronts Fundamental Issues,* New York Law Journal, Jan. 23, 2008, *available at* http://www.law.com/jsp/ihc/PubArticleIHC.jsp?id=1201169145823.

[5]*Id.*

[6]ABA Comm. on Ethics and Prof'l Responsibility, Formal Op. 08-451 at 2 (2008).

sources on a constant basis.[7] Costs to both attorneys and clients can be reduced to the extent to which foreign service providers can furnish their services at lower rates than the attorneys themselves and their staff.[8] The relevant ethics opinions have provided guidelines for the lawyer who wishes to take advantage of outsourcing without violating any ethical rules.

While offshoring may seem like a recent phenomenon, it is important to realize that outsourcing has always, to a certain extent, been a part of the legal profession. Lawyers rely on paralegals, clerks, copy staff, and the like to handle the minutia of their practice while providing legal analysis and advice themselves.[9] Delegating tasks allows lawyers to render their services more economically and efficiently. Likewise, it is not uncommon for lawyers or law firms to bring on temporary contract lawyers to increase their output in certain matters. These established practices, which constitute simpler forms of outsourcing, provided a starting point for examining the ethical obligation related to outsourcing overseas, as much of the analysis regarding the unauthorized practice of law was developed in the context of paralegal work or the use of research firms staffed by non-lawyers.[10]

The ABA has concluded that there is nothing unethical about offshoring so long as the outsourcing lawyer ensures that the services are rendered by those with the "legal knowledge, skill, thoroughness and preparation necessary" for adequate representation.[11] Meeting the standards for competence in accordance with Model Rule 1.1 is the basic obligation for any provision of legal services. Whenever engaging the services of a non-lawyer, a lawyer must "make reasonable efforts to ensure that the person's conduct is compatible with the professional obligations of the lawyer."[12] In the context of offshoring, all the bar associations that have openly endorsed the practice have stated that supervision by the outsourcing lawyer is critical to ensure compliance with Model Rule 5.3.[13] The degree of supervision required will depend on the skill and experience of the person rendering the services, the amount of work involved in the particular matter, and the likelihood that ethical issues will arise during the course of the work.[14] Obviously, wholesale delegation is prohibited as it would constitute aiding in the unauthorized practice of law.[15] An attorney may not outsource work and then attempt to pass it off as his own. The supervising lawyer must independently verify that all services have been competently rendered.[16] In order for the supervision to be adequate, the supervising attorney

---

[7]*Id.*

[8]*Id.*

[9]Steven C. Bennett, *The Ethics of Legal Outsourcing,* 36 N. Ky. L. Rev. 479, 480 (2009).

[10]*Id.*

[11]ABA Comm. on Ethics and Prof'l Responsibility, Formal Op. 08-451 at 2 (2008).

[12]Model Rules of Prof'l Conduct R. 5.3(a) (2008).

[13]*See* Ass'n of the Bar of the City of New York Comm. on Prof'l and Judicial Ethics, Formal Op. 2006-3 (2006), *available at* http://www.nycbar.org/Ethics/eth2006.htm.

[14]*Id.*

[15]*Id.*

[16]*Id.*

must have the requisite expertise in the specific subject matter involved in the representation, otherwise the actions of the service provider will constitute the unauthorized practice of law.[17] However, if the degree of supervision and review is adequate, complex tasks such as the drafting of briefs may be allowed.[18]

The obligations regarding outsourcing begin before the outsourcing lawyer has even engaged a service provider. The ABA has stated that one of the initial challenges in outsourcing is to "ensure that tasks are delegated to individuals who are competent to perform them,"[19] and suggested several ways to do so. A lawyer who is outsourcing to lawyers trained in a foreign country should first determine whether or not that country's system of legal education is comparable to that of the United States.[20] Furthermore, in order to ensure ethical conduct, the lawyer should evaluate that country's disciplinary system to determine whether its principles of legal ethics are on par with those in this country.[21] The greater the degree of variance, the more important it will be for the lawyer to supervise and review the work that is being done.[22] Consideration of the country's "legal landscape" is also suggested in order to assess the risk of seizure of documents or loss of client information in judicial proceedings or in the event that a dispute arises between the lawyer and service provider.[23] While the ABA suggests the above evaluations, it does not provide clear criteria regarding how they should be made.

Electronic communications provide a method to "close [the] gap" in both distance and time zone that can complicate offshoring to far-off locales.[24] The lawyer should "consider conducting reference checks and investigating the background" of anyone that who will ultimately be providing service for a client.[25] Interviews with the service provider's principal lawyers should also be considered, along with an assessment of their educational background.[26] It may also be beneficial to inquire into their hiring practices to determine the quality and character of employees who may be granted access to a client's information. When dealing with sensitive information, the lawyer should even "consider investigating the security of the provider's premises, computer network, and perhaps even its recycling and refuse disposal procedures" in order to avoid risks regarding confidentiality.[27] While not stated as a definitive obligation, the ABA has stated that "it may be prudent" to inspect the service provider's facilities in person, regardless of the distances involved, in order "to get

---

[17] *Id.*

[18] *Id.*

[19] ABA Comm. on Ethics and Prof'l Responsibility, Formal Op. 08-451 at 3 (2008).

[20] *Id.*

[21] *Id.*

[22] *Id.* at 4.

[23] *Id.*

[24] *Id.* at 3.

[25] *Id.*

[26] *Id.*

[27] *Id.*

a firsthand sense of the professionalism" of the provider's personnel.[28] It is not uncommon for LPOs to carry liability insurance similar to that carried by law firms.[29] While insurance is not a requirement, as a practical matter outsourcing lawyers will probably take this into account when choosing a service provider.

As outsourcing becomes more common, it is likely that long term relationships will be formed between repeat players rendering this initial hurdle less burdensome. However, such relationships may give rise to further ethical challenges. Large or particularly attractive service providers who are engaged by multiple lawyers, law firms, or legal departments may give rise to the potential for conflicts of interest. Model Rule 1.10 states that conflicts of a single lawyer may be imputed to the rest of his firm. An earlier ABA opinion further suggests that even the conflicts of a temporary attorney may be imputed to the firm that engages him or vice versa when the temporary attorney has access to confidential information.[30] This creates the potential for difficulty in the outsourcing context. While the ABA opinion on outsourcing does not directly address conflicts of interest, the New York opinion provides further guidance. Prior to engaging a service provider, an outsourcing attorney should make inquiries into its conflict clearance procedures and whether or not it has performed work for parties adverse to the attorney's client.[31] The lawyer should try to ensure that the service provider is aware of the ethical rules regarding conflicts including Model Rules 1.7 through 1.12, and is capable of performing its services without violating them. It may be desirable for the outsourcing attorney to remind the service provider in writing of its obligations regarding confidentiality to current and former clients.[32] Furthermore, it is suggested that the attorney determine whether the service provider is capable of erecting "Chinese Walls" between various matters, or perhaps obtain written assertions of the absence of conflict.[33] The Florida ethics opinion suggests that additional inquiries should be performed as necessary.[34]

Model Rule 1.6 governing confidentiality is one of the most fundamental duties a lawyer will face. An outsourcing attorney must first obtain informed consent from a client before he can divulge any information about the representation to a service provider, as the implied consent of Rule 1.6(a) does not apply in the outsourcing context, whether onshore or offshore.[35] The information divulged should not be more than necessary to perform the delegated task, and written confidentiality agreements are highly recommended.[36] Such

---

[28]*Id.*

[29]*See* Anthony Lin, *Legal Outsourcing to India is Growing, But Still Confronts Fundamental Issues,* New York Law Journal, Jan. 23, 2008, *available at* http://www.law.com/jsp/ihc/PubArticleIHC.jsp?id=1201169145823.

[30]Steven C. Bennett, *The Ethics of Legal Outsourcing,* 36 N. Ky. L. Rev. 479, 485 (2009).

[31]*Id.*

[32]*Id.*

[33]*Id.*

[34]*Id.* at 486.

[35]ABA Comm. on Ethics and Prof'l Responsibility, Formal Op. 08-451 at 5 (2008).

[36]*Id.*

contracts help to fill gaps because the rules of ethics in the United States will not directly apply to offshore service providers. Some U.S. lawyers may go so far as to require the service provider to limit the internet access of its attorneys in order to avoid inadvertent disclosure of information.[37] Secure intranets can be used for the communication of sensitive materials. Other possible methods, such as stating research tasks in broad, hypothetical terms, may be less than foolproof and may also reduce the quality of the work product provided.

As stated above, informed consent must be obtained prior to divulging confidential client information. There are other circumstances when the client should be expressly informed that the lawyer is engaging the services of a third party service provider. In regards to any form of outsourcing, disclosure may be necessary depending on the degree of involvement in the particular matter and the significance of the work done.[38] Typically, disclosure is not required when the services performed are limited to simple research.[39] The client's expectations must be taken into account when determining whether or not it is necessary to inform the client of outsourcing.[40] If a service provider is performing significant document review or the client is being billed on a basis other than cost, then disclosure will be necessary.[41] The guidelines seek to ensure that the lawyer is fulfilling his obligations under Model Rule 1.4 to consult with the client as to the means to fulfill the objectives of the representation. Additionally, in accordance with Rule 7.5(d), the lawyer cannot imply that a third party service provider is associated with the lawyer or firm when that is not the case. Proper disclosure, when necessary, requires that the client be informed that the service provider is an independent third party hired by the lawyer.

Model Rule 5.4 forbids a lawyer from sharing legal fees with non-lawyers. Since offshoring typically involves the services of non-lawyers, the lawyer cannot bill it as the provision of legal services.[42] The client should be billed no more than the cost required and a reasonable allocation for overhead.[43] As always, the fees charged must be reasonable in accordance with Rule 1.5. However, the rules regarding fees may vary between jurisdictions. The Los Angeles Bar Ethics Committee requires that the attorney accurately disclose the basis on which any cost is passed on to the client.[44] On the other hand, the ABA committee states that depending on the expectations within the attorney client relationship, it is not always strictly required that the client be informed of the

---

[37]*See* Anthony Lin, *Legal Outsourcing to India is Growing, But Still Confronts Fundamental Issues,* New York Law Journal, Jan. 23, 2008, *available at* http://www.law.com/jsp/ihc/PubArticleIHC.jsp?id=1201169145823.

[38]Ass'n of the Bar of the City of New York Comm. on Prof'l and Judicial Ethics, Formal Op. 2006-3 (2006), *available at* http://www.nycbar.org/Ethics/eth2006.htm.

[39]*Id.*

[40]*Id.*

[41]*Id.*

[42]Steven C. Bennett, *The Ethics of Legal Outsourcing,* 36 N. Ky. L. Rev. 479, 485 (2009).

[43]*Id.* at 486.

[44]*Id.*

specific personnel assigned to the representation, though it may become desirable.[45] When formal fee arrangements are made between the attorney and client prior to the commencement of the representation, disclosure may be necessary.[46] Nevertheless, the general consensus is that when outsourcing, the costs may not be marked up; the client can only be charged the cost plus a reasonable surcharge or allocation of overhead.

Ongoing Considerations

The endorsement of legal outsourcing by influential bar associations, which have provided guidelines for lawyers using LPOs, has created rapidly growing confidence in the legal outsourcing industry. However, there may still be concerns regarding the ethical standards. While guidelines do exist, it should be noted that the disciplinary system in the United States is largely self-enforcing. State bar associations are not directly looking over the shoulders of lawyers or law firms who offshore portions of their services. It would be up to the clients or the attorneys themselves to try to ensure that there are no ethical violations in regards to outsourcing. Furthermore, the LPO service providers themselves are not directly bound by the United States ethics rules. The Model Rules themselves are advisory guidelines to the state bars, so are not particularly potent in and of themselves. Even if offshore service providers were made to be directly bound by the state ethics rules of the lawyer who engages them, there would be practical problems because they are likely to accept work from multiple jurisdictions.[47] The ethics rules of their home bars are similarly deficient because they are likely to be different from the rules in the United States.[48] This would also place a greater burden on outsourcing attorneys, who would have to familiarize themselves the ethical regulations of multiple jurisdictions if they engaged LPOs from multiple different countries.[49]

The outsourcing attorneys themselves will bear ultimate responsibility for whatever work they choose to outsource. The only visible means of reaching offshore service providers in order to impose standards would be through their contracts with the attorneys who engage their services.[50] This is not entirely impractical, because some major LPOs have their headquarters in the United States despite most of the work being done overseas. One major example is Pangea3, which is headquartered in New York despite employing primarily attorneys working in India. This would make the LPO more easily available to suit in the case of a suit for breach of contract. As stated above, contracts regarding confidentiality or written guarantees regarding the absence of conflict

---

[45]*Id.*

[46]*Id.* at 489.

[47]Darya Pollack, *I'm Calling My Lawyer...in India!: Ethical Issues in International Legal Outsourcing*, 11 UCLA J. Int'l L. & Foreign Aff. 99, 143 (Spring 2006).

[48]*Id.* at 142.

[49]*Id.*

[50]*See* Anthony Lin, *Legal Outsourcing to India is Growing, But Still Confronts Fundamental Issues*, New York Law Journal, Jan. 23, 2008, *available at* http://www.law.com/jsp/ihc/PubArticleIHC.jsp?id=1201169145823.

are necessary to compensate for the fact that LPOs are not directly bound by the rules of ethics. Only the lawyers who engage their services would be subject to disciplinary actions or suits for malpractice. This approach makes sense in certain ways. While critics of outsourcing may take issue with the fact that ethical standards are not directly applicable to the service providers, it is undeniable that outsourcing attorneys must bear responsibility. Otherwise, the "anonymous, fungible, overseas attorney [would be] the perfect scapegoat for ethical questions arising in the United States."[51]

Thus far, there have not been any major disciplinary actions or malpractice suits arising from legal process outsourcing. However, it is possible that a major incident such as a breach of confidence would raise a public outcry. Is the legal outsourcing industry just one malpractice suit away from a major upheaval? At this point it is unclear.

Action in Connecticut

Aside from ethics considerations and standards of competence, there is yet another reason that some are opposed to legal process outsourcing. In the current U.S. economy, the supply of lawyers and prospective lawyers outstrips the demand. Furthermore, given the high costs associated with an American legal education, law school graduates expect to be paid an amount that will ensure a reasonable return on their investment and allow them to pay back their student loans. However, under the current economic conditions, unemployment for law school graduates is becoming increasingly common. This is only exacerbated by the trend to shift legal services overseas.

Connecticut may take a stand against the practice of legal outsourcing. State Representative Patricia Dillon has proposed Bill Number 5083 which will serve to curb the practice of sending legal services overseas.[52] The bill seeks to accomplish this by redefining what constitutes the practice of law, aiming in particular at legal document review. The bill defines legal document review as drafting, reviewing, or analyzing legal documents for clients in Connecticut and researching or analyzing the law of the state and advising clients in that regard.[53] These services would constitute the unauthorized practice of law if practiced by a person not licensed in the state of Connecticut. It is plain on the face of the statute that, if enacted, it would effectively prohibit lawyers from outsourcing any of their services. Dillon has stated that the reason behind the proposed bill is that "there is a quality issue here and also a jobs issue. The licensure of teachers and health professionals is often not portable across state

---

[51]Darya Pollack, *I'm Calling My Lawyer...in India!: Ethical Issues in International Legal Outsourcing*, 11 UCLA J. Int'l L. & Foreign Aff. 99, 147 (Spring 2006).

[52]*See* Christian Nolan, *Conn. Bill Would Regulate Offshoring Document Review*, Connecticut Law Tribune, Jan. 19, 2001, *available at* www.law.com/jsp/lawtechnologynews/PubArticleLTN.jsp?id=1202478394479&src=EMC-Email&et=editorial&bu=LTN&pt=Law%20Technology%20News&cn=20110119_ltnda&kw=Conn.%20Bill%20Would%20Regulate%20Offshoring%20Document%20Review&sl return=1&hbxlogin=1.

[53]*Id.*

lines in this country, yet some legal work is being done abroad with no quality oversight."[54]

The bill has been met with some criticism. Some prominent U.S. attorneys have stated that the bill is "sloppily drafted" and ignores the substantial body of analysis in regards to legal outsourcing.[55] It has also been said to fail to address the real issues the industry is facing and will fail to solve the problems faced by unemployed lawyers in Connecticut, being little more than facile "protectionism."[56] It is true that the bill does not address the increasing number of law schools and law school applicants, nor the rising costs of legal education or the swelling burden of debt faced by law school graduates.[57] Legal blogger Lisa Solomon has commented that the loss of legal jobs in this country is due to the flagging economy, stating that the reason firms are restricting hiring and cutting jobs is not due to the fact that legal work is being shipped overseas.[58]

The Connecticut State Bar Association has not yet released an ethics opinion on the topic of outsourcing, but the relevant rules in Connecticut related to outsourcing are substantially the same as the Model Rules. Therefore it is unlikely that this state's bar would take a different position from that of the ABA. Nevertheless, the bill has been referred to the Connecticut joint committee on the judiciary, as of January 6, 2011. The actual text of proposed Bill Number 5083 is as follows:

> Be it enacted by the Senate and House of Representatives in General Assembly convened: That section 51-88 of the general statutes be amended to provide that the practice of law includes (1) drafting, reviewing or analyzing legal documents for clients in this state, and (2) researching and analyzing the law of this state and advising clients in this state of the status of such law, and that any person who has not been admitted as an attorney in this state who performs such activities commits the offense of the unauthorized practice of law.

> *Statement of Purpose:*
> To provide that outsourcing of legal document review to non-attorneys constitutes the unauthorized practice of law.

It is unlikely that the bill could be enacted in its current form. One clear problem is that it is overly broad. While it may be aimed at the offshoring of legal work, a plain reading of the bill would seem to indicate that it would also eliminate jobs in Connecticut. If legal document review, as defined in the bill, were deemed to be the unauthorized practice of law it is likely that there would be unintended consequences. The bill is aimed at a certain type of work, rather than the people engaged in it. Paralegals or law students working as clerks

---

[54]*Id.*

[55]*US State introduces Bill to stop law firms from off-shoring work to Indian LPOs*, Bar and Bench News Network, Feb. 03, 2011, *available at* http://barandbench.com/brief/2/1271/us-state-introduces-bill-to-stop-law-firms-from-off-shoring-work-to-indian-lpos.

[56]*Id.*

[57]*Id.*

[58]*Id.*

within the state, who are unlicensed and therefore the same as lawyers overseas, would suddenly be engaged in the unauthorized practice of law. This is the type of work that virtually all law students will engage in over the course of their schooling, typically in their summer jobs or in clinics. This bill would severely limit the opportunities of law students in Connecticut.

Nevertheless, if the bill were altered it would still be problematic. In order to fulfill the goal of prohibiting the offshoring of legal services, it would need to be aimed at types of people rather than types of activity. One method would be to prohibit legal document review by unlicensed persons outside of Connecticut. This would affect foreigners and out of state people equally, but could create a risk of retaliatory measures by other state bar associations. In order to avoid domestic retaliations, the bill could be amended to target only foreign unlicensed personnel. However, if this were the case, it would be difficult to see it as anything other than protectionism. Supervision by a licensed attorney is often considered the key element that prevents the activity of paralegals from becoming the unauthorized practice of law. The ethics rules do not provide grounds for differentiating between paralegals based on location. Stephen Gillers of NYU School of Law has commented that even if the service provider is unlicensed and in a foreign country, supervision and review by an American attorney "sanitizes" the process.[59] Likewise, Geoffrey Hazard, Jr. of the University of Pennsylvania School of Law has similarly commented that as long as the foreign service providers are under the supervision of U.S. attorneys, it should not make a difference where they are.[60] Given this, it is not clear that proposed ban on legal process outsourcing has any basis in the current ethical regulations and precedent.

There is the additional issue that the proposed bill may run afoul of the 1994 General Agreement on Trade in Services (GATS). GATS was one of the agreements signed as part of the creation of the World Trade Organization (WTO).[61] It was created in recognition of the growing importance of trade in services in the growth and development of global economies. All WTO members are signatories to the agreement. However, not all members have agreed to abide by GATS nor do all of them recognize the agreement as covering legal services.[62] Signatories are allowed to exempt their existing regulations from their commitments under GATS. Therefore, the situation under GATS is not a liberalization of trade in legal services, but one in which most members have agreed not to pass regulations more restrictive than those already in existence.[63] There is no requirement that members recognize foreign licensed attor-

---

[59]See Ellen L. Rosen, *Corporate America Sending More Legal Work to Bombay*, N.Y. Times, Mar. 14, 2004.

[60]Jennifer Fried, *Change of Venue; Cost-Conscious General Counsel Step up Their Use of Offshore Lawyers, Creating Fears of an Exodus of U.S. Legal Jobs*, The American Lawyer (Dec. 2003).

[61]Darya Pollack, *I'm Calling My Lawyer...in India!: Ethical Issues in International Legal Outsourcing*, 11 UCLA J. Int'l L. & Foreign Aff. 99, 110 (Spring 2006).

[62]*Id.*

[63]*Id.* at 111.

neys.[64] Bar associations continue to determine the standards for licensing, and may do so to the exclusion of foreign attorneys. The GATS provision on domestic regulation merely requires that "regulatory measures, such as admission, licensing, and discipline measures, be administered in a reasonable, objective, and impartial manner and that qualification requirements be not more burdensome than necessary to ensure the quality of the service."[65]

These requirements allow members to determine their own domestic regulations on the requirements to practice in a given jurisdiction. However, outsourcing as contemplated by the ABA is not an issue of licensure or of the unauthorized practice of law. As stated above, as long as best practice guidelines are met, the outsourcing providers may be unlicensed when providing legal support services. If the Connecticut bill were amended to only restrict document review by foreign personnel, it would look less like domestic regulation and more like a simple barrier to trade. GATS requires members to "provide for adequate procedures to verify the competence of professionals of any other Member,"[66] which should not be more burdensome than necessary. A blanket restriction on foreign outsourcing would likely fall short of this requirement.

Failure to comply with obligations under GATS would not necessarily be the death knell for the Connecticut bill. Trade agreements operate at a national level while regulation of the legal sector operates at the state level. WTO dispute resolution procedures require governments to enforce the terms of GATS, not private individuals.[67] A nation such as India would have to bring the issue to the U.S. federal government, which would then have to enforce its obligations on Connecticut.[68] This creates procedural complexities in addition to the fact that the state bar associations are usually allowed to regulate their own practice unmolested by the federal government.[69] Whether or not a foreign government would be willing to take such steps would likely be determined by the market impact of the statute and the lobbying power of the LPOs whose businesses are affected. Likewise, compliance is not guaranteed regardless of the outcome of a WTO proceeding.

The Bar Council of India generally insists on reciprocity.[70] It does not allow foreign firms to practice in India just as the United States does not allow foreign firms to practice in the United States.[71] However, LPOs technically are not engaged in the practice of law under the Indian rules, which is why LPOs such as SDD Global, which has its headquarters in New York and London, can

---

[64]*Id.* at 112.

[65]*Id.* at 111.

[66]General Agreement on Trade in Services, 33 I.L.M. 28 (1994).

[67]Darya Pollack, *I'm Calling My Lawyer...in India!: Ethical Issues in International Legal Outsourcing,* 11 UCLA J. Int'l L. & Foreign Aff. 99, 111 (Spring 2006).

[68]*Id.*

[69]*Id.*

[70]Akshaya Mukul, *UK Wants India to Act on Legal Firms Issue,* Times of India, Bangalore, Dec. 30, 2009.

[71]Raju Ramachandran, Professional Ethics: Changing Profession, Changing Ethics 84-86 (New Delhi, LexisNexis Butterworths, 2004).

set up shop in India.[72] Nevertheless, India's tendency towards reciprocity may reduce the ability of American legal professionals to work in India should the outsourcing of legal work from the United States be banned. Violation of GATS may generally make it difficult for U.S. lawyers to be hired as foreign legal consultants. While it is unlikely that the actions of Connecticut could spark legal services trade wars on their own, if this type of legislation became widespread, retaliation could become a possibility.

Conclusion

As knowledge and skilled services cross borders at an increasingly rapid pace, the practice of legal process outsourcing will become more and more frequent. Developments in technology and business models occur at a greater rate than the rules of ethics can adapt. As attorneys, clients, and bar associations struggle to keep up, uncertainty is prevalent and improvisation becomes necessary. Although there are currently best practice guidelines in the form of ethics opinions, the method by which they will be enforced remains unclear. Perhaps a single disciplinary action or malpractice suit will trigger a paradigm shift in the practice of legal process outsourcing. Regardless of whether or not that is the case, the rapid growth in the industry makes it unlikely that the practice will ever disappear entirely. Efforts like the one in Connecticut are unlikely to yield any tangible results. The best course of action for attorneys who wishes to engage in outsourcing is to exercise caution and diligence in choosing an LPO service provider and to thoroughly review the work product they receive. The lawyer must become knowledgeable regarding the technologies and business practices that make outsourcing possible, as well as the potential ethical pitfalls of outsourcing.

As interactions between attorneys, clients, and third party service providers become increasingly more complex, forthright discussion about the client's objectives and the means by which they will be achieved is crucial. While the continued expansion of the legal outsourcing industry may seem like a dismal affair to unemployed lawyers and prospective lawyers within the United States, it is likely that the value clients receive, dollar for dollar, when engaging legal services will increase. The medieval, guild-like structures of the law firms of the past have given way to more client-oriented models. The diffusion of legal services across international boundaries has led to a more competitive market, hopefully leading to cheaper, higher quality services.

---

[72]*See* Maya Karwande, *Legal Process Outsourcing: Efficient and Ethical?*, Immigration Daily (2008), *available at* http://www.ilw.com/articles/2008,0926-karwande.shtm.

3

Reaching Total Digitization: Ethical Issues Regarding the Client's Electronic Records

Rebecca Lasoski

I. Introduction

When it comes to client files, lawyers should have a few goals in mind: (1) to fulfill the ethical obligation and fiduciary duties owed to the client regarding record retention and return requirements of client records; (2) to preserve the client's confidentiality and confidence; and (3) to enable effective risk management through planning and a properly trained staff.[1] After many years of enthusiastically advocating the benefits of the paperless office, most law offices now operate with electronic record retention systems and minimized physical file retention.[2] The almost total exchange of physical records for electronic records has not altered these three goals for the lawyer. However, the increased use of technology in the law office, specifically in relation to client records, poses interesting challenges as lawyers and ethics boards attempt to define the permissible boundaries of electronic record storage and retention.

Although there is a growing sophistication concerning the types of electronic records that exist and a lawyer's ability to store them, many lawyers and ethics boards lack an adequate understanding of the risks of electronic record retention. The ethics boards' lack of understanding may mean that state bars will impose either vague standards of protection for the upkeep of client's electronic records or unreasonable demands on record preservation and accessibility. As technology advances at lightning speed, lawyers and their clients will have innumerable choices about how to store and preserve the client's records. These choices each have their own individual consequence on the lawyer's fiduciary duty to protect the client's information. Therefore, to understand the fiduciary duties and ethical implications, lawyers and ethics boards must understand how electronic files are currently created, stored, and, ultimately, returned to the client.

First, every lawyer should be aware that the Model Rules of Professional Conduct still apply to the electronic version of client records and that the lawyer's obligation to maintain and safeguard client records remain despite the

---

[1]*See, e.g.*, American Bar Ass'n, Model Rules of Prof'l Conduct, Rule 1.15 (2007) (retaining client property); *id.*, Rule 1.6 (confidentiality); and *id.*, Rules 5.1 and 5.3 (responsibility for office staff). Such ethics rules are discussed in detail below.

[2]*See* Adam M. Spence, *A Paperless Office in Five Easy Steps*, 40-AUG Md. B.J. 16, 18 (Aug. 2007) ("[E]xplaining the benefits of a paperless office is a bit like explaining the joys of children to people who have none: to truly appreciate the enormous gains, you have to do it.").

fact that these files no longer exist in a physical form. This obligation is rooted in Rule 1.15, which states "(a) A lawyer shall hold property of clients or third persons that is in a lawyer's possession in connection with a representation separate from the lawyer's own property. [P]roperty shall be identified as such and appropriately safeguarded. Complete records of such ... property shall be kept by the lawyer and shall be preserved for a period of [five years] after termination of the representation."[3] However, as the word "property" is not defined in the Model Rules, it is ambiguous as to what type of electronic information falls under this duty. Additionally, the rules require that client records be "safeguarded" while under the care of the lawyer. Innovations in online file storage services have abated the lawyer's fears that the client's paper records will be destroyed. In place of these fears are worries regarding risks associated with electronic records, such as exposing the client's confidential information on the internet and the loss of records due to cloud server outages.

Furthermore, the lawyer must take steps to properly hire and train competent staff.[4] Advancing technology has meant that previous employees with little to no training in electronic media may now be a liability for a firm that is trying to achieve efficient and secure electronic record retention.[5] The lawyer must decide who will be responsible for electronic record maintenance and whether those files will be safe from corruption and manipulation. Last but not least, although technology has created a more economical and simplified system to store data, a lawyer must decide whether or not electronic record retention is in the best interest of the client.

This article offers an overview of ethical issues associated with recent technological advances that push the boundaries of the paperless law office. This article begins with an overview of the Model Rules of Professional Conduct or their state-implemented versions that are most cited by ethics boards in regards to electronic record retention. The article then explains the importance of ethical considerations in the context of defining and storing client electronic records, retaining a competently trained staff to handle electronic records, and, ultimately, returning electronic records to the client. In addition, this article offers some practical suggestions for lawyers seeking to ethically navigate the digital workplace.

II. Balancing Ethical Duties with the Pursuit of Being Paper Free: Applicable Model Rules

There are several Model Rules of Professional Conduct that correspond to client records in electronic form. However, the rules do not distinguish between electronic and physical forms of a record. A number of state opinions issued over the past ten years make it clear that electronic records are included under

---

[3]Model Rules of Prof'l Conduct R. 1.15 (2007).

[4]*See* Model Rules of Prof'l Conduct R. 5.1, 5.3 (2007) (requiring law firm partners to take steps to ensure that the firm has in effect measures that give reasonable assurances that both the firm's lawyers and staff comply with the rules of professional conduct).

[5]*See* Nancy Beauchemin, *The New Role of Records: Is Your Law Firm Properly Staffed to Manage Records in the E-Mail Era*, Legal Management, May-June 2007, at 38.

the umbrella term of "client files."[6] In addition, the ethics opinions have noted concern regarding whether maintaining and storing files through technology compromises the lawyer's obligation to protect the client's interest and property. Lawyers who are attempting to convert their physical files to electronic format and lawyers who wish to maintain the majority of their documents in electronic format must examine these rules to successfully streamline their records management without violating any fiduciary duty owed to the client.

Primarily, every lawyer should be aware of the basic ethical guidelines that originate in the Model Rules and govern client files. There are three main categories of Model Rules that touch upon client files. The first category involves Rule 1.1 and Rule 1.4 of the Model Rules, and gives the lawyer direction regarding the amount and type of information that must be retained in the client's file. Under Rule 1.1, the lawyer has a duty to competently serve his or her client by providing the client with information or documents sufficient to ensure competent representation. Correspondingly, Rule 1.4 requires lawyers to keep clients adequately informed about the client's representation. In relation to client files, these rules advocate communication between lawyer and client. In terms of the client's file, documents such as letters, emails, phone records, text messages, and chat transcripts are often stored in the client's file to insulate the lawyer from later claims that the lawyer failed to adequately communicate with the client. Also, these rules encourage that the lawyer retain all records that would be considered essential to the case. The term "reasonably necessary for the representation" is often interpreted broadly as to avoid any possibility of ethical misconduct.[7]

The second category requires keeping the client's file safe, secure, and confidential so that it may be returned to the client. Safeguarding the property of the client is addressed in Rule 1.15. Additionally, Rule 3.4 instructs the lawyer to preserve client documents that may have potential evidentiary value, and Rule 1.16 addresses the steps a lawyer must take at the end of the representation to protect a client's interest including returning client files. Furthermore, Rule 1.6 requires the lawyer to protect confidential information concerning the client's representation. These three rules together send a clear message that, to maintain confidentiality, it is necessary to segregate, protect, and safeguard the client's file. The obligation of keeping the client's file organized, up-to-date, and indexed so that a lawyer may swiftly account for and produce the file upon request is inherent in the duty of confidentiality and Rule 1.15. The failure to safeguard or retain documents in the file could consist of a breach of any of the above mentioned rules. Thus, the principles of maintaining loyalty and fidelity to the client are so fundamental to the practice of law that these rules operate collectively to avoid even the risk of a breach of these principles.

---

[6]*See, e.g.,* Va. State Bar Comm. on Legal Ethics, Op. 1818 (Sept. 2005) (stating that lawyers may maintain client files in electronic format only provided that original paper documents are not necessary for the client's representation); Me. Prof'l Ethics Comm., Op. 183 (Jan. 2004) (finding that a lawyer may store client records in electronic format without keeping a paper copy but must retain them in a way that permits both client and lawyer access).

[7]Model Rules of Prof'l Conduct R. 1.1 (2007).

The third category involves the lawyer's liability for the negligence of others in regards to the treatment of the client's file. The ordinary principles of *respondeat superior* apply in actions for professional negligence.[8] As a consequence, a lawyer may be held liable for injuries caused by a negligent legal secretary, law clerk, paralegal, or other non-lawyer employee who is acting within the scope of employment.[9] Under Rule 5.1, lawyers are required to take steps to ensure that their firms have in effect measures giving reasonable assurances to clients that all employees of the firm are complying with the rules of professional conduct. The responsibilities of ensuring that client files are maintained according to the state's ethical rules belong to both the lawyer and non-lawyer employees associated with the client's representation. Thus, the lawyer is responsible for ensuring that the firm's employees follow all ethical rules when handling client files.

The rules demonstrate the need for every lawyer to be cautious regarding client file retention. Before a lawyer deletes his or her emails or sends another document to the virtual recycling bin on the computer's desktop, the lawyer should consider the risk of an ethics violation for not sufficiently protecting client information. If a lawyer is willing to invest the time and money on new technology for his or her law office, the lawyer should also be willing to consider the ethical consequences the technology may have on his or her legal practice if caution and preparation are not undertaken at the outset.[10]

III. Defining the Documents that Constitute the Client's Electronic File

Even before paperless offices gained popularity, determining the make-up of the client's file was a difficult task. Questions were often raised regarding whether the client owned all documents associated with his or her representation or only those that were considered the final work-product of the lawyer.[11] Courts and ethics boards in many states tried to address the ambiguousness of the rules in regards to a lawyer's obligation to his or her client's files.[12] A majority of states apply the approach that the client owns the entire

---

[8]*See* Therese A. Cannon, Ethics and Professional Responsibility for Paralegals 29 (2008) (explaining that under the principle of *respondeat superior* or vicarious liability, employers can be held responsible for the actions of their employees if these actions are carried out in the course and scope of his or her employment).

[9]*See id.*

[10]*See An Indiana Case Study in Paperless File Management*, 26 No. 21 Law. PC 7, 7 (Aug. 2009) (noting "digitization of a litigation matter requires planning, time and expertise").

[11]*See, e.g.,* Brian J. Slovut, *Eliminating Conflict at the Termination of the Attorney-Client Relationship: A Proposed Standard Governing Property Rights in the Client's File*, 76 Minn. L. Rev. 1483, 1486 (1992) (explaining the two different standards applied by state ethics opinions: one that allocates ownership of the entire file to the client and the other that gives lawyers ownership in their work-product).

[12]*See id.* at 1488 n.18 (comparing the ABA Comm. on Ethics and Prof'l Resp., Informal Op. 1376 (1977), which adopted an end product standard, with the State Bar of Mich., Informal Op. CI-722 (1982), which adopted the entire file standard). Some states have

file, including the attorney's work-product, subject to limited exceptions.[13] Under this view, the lawyer may have a duty to include all internal communications, drafts of documents, and notes in the client's files and maintain these documents in an accessible format to be available at the client's request.[14] The minority view is that the attorney owns the file and only end products belong to the client (such as pleadings, correspondence, final versions of contracts, wills, and other documents prepared for the client's use).[15] The minority views internal memoranda and preliminary drafts as work-product of the lawyer, and, therefore, these documents do not have to be maintained in the client's official

---

decided not to address the issue and either have expressed no opinion regarding the type of documents that must be released when returning client files or dismissed the issue as out of the ethics board's jurisdiction. *Id.* at 1490 (citing the Prof'l Ethics Comm. of the State Bar of Tex., Op. 395 (1980) and the Ethics Comm. of the Ky. Bar Ass'n, Op. E-300 (1985)).

[13]*See, e.g.,* Ala. Off. Of the Gen. Couns., Ethics Op. 2010-02 (2010). This state takes the "entire file" approach, stating "the materials in the file furnished by or for the client are the property of the client. Therefore, Rule 1.15 imposes an ethical and fiduciary duty on the lawyer to properly identify a client's file as such, segregate the file from the lawyer's business and personal property, as well as from the property of other clients and third persons, safeguard and account for its contents, and promptly produce it upon request by the client." *Id.* Other jurisdictions that support the view that the client owns the file include Louisiana, New York City, California, Ohio, Pennsylvania, Maryland, Georgia, Texas, South Carolina, New Jersey, Alaska, North Dakota, New Hampshire, and Oregon. *See* La. State Bar Ass'n Rules of Prof'l Conduct Comm., Public Op. 05-RPCC-003 (2005); N.Y. City Bar Ass'n Comm. on Prof'l & Jud. Ethics, Formal Op. 1986-4 (1986); Cal. Standing Comm. on Prof'l Resp. & Conduct, Formal Op. 1992-127 (1992); Ohio Sup. Ct. Bd. of Comm'rs on Grievances and Discipline, Op. 92-8 (1992); *Maleski v. Corporate Life Ins. Co.,* 641 A.2d 1, 6 (Pa. 1994); *Att'y Grievance Comm'n of Maryland v. Potter,* 844 A.2d 367, 384 (Md. 2004); *Matter of Kaleidoscope, Inc. v. Powell, Goldstein, Frazer & Murphy,* 15 B.R. 232, 241 (Bankr. N.D. Ga. 1981); *Grand Jury Proceedings v. United States,* 727 F.2d 941, 944 (10th Cir. 1984); *Resolution Trust Corp. v. H,* 128 F.R.D. 647, 648 (N.D. Tex. 1989); S.C. Bar Ethics Advisory Comm., Ethics Advisory Op. 02-17 (2002); N.J. Advisory Comm. on Prof'l Ethics, Op. 445 (1979); Alaska Bar Ass'n Ethics Comm., Ethics Op. 2003-3 (2003); N.D. Att'y Gen., Op. L-174 (1995); *Averill v. Cox,* 761 A.2d 1083, 1092 (N.H. 2000); Or. Formal Ethics Op. 2005-125 (2005). *See also* Anthony E. Davis & David J. Elkanich, *The Risk Management Challenges of Record Retention and Destruction: Developing Record Management Policies that Protect Both Law Firms and Their Clients,* 19 Prof. Law. 1, 5 (2008); John M. Naber & Juan R. Balboa, *Client Records: Whose Files Are They Anyway?,* 86-JAN Mich. B.J. 24, 26-27 (2007).

[14]*See* John M. Naber & Juan R. Balboa, *Client Records: Whose Files Are They Anyway?,* 86-JAN Mich. B.J. 24, 26-27 (2007) (noting New Hampshire's view that the client's file includes electronic communication and other computer based writings (citing *Averill v. Cox,* 145 N.H. 328, 339-400, 761 A.2d 1083, 1092 (2000))).

[15]Minn. Lawyers Prof'l Resp. Bd., Op. 13 (1989). Other jurisdictions that support the view that the lawyer owns the file include New York State, Michigan, Arizona, Illinois, North Carolina, and Rhode Island. *See* N.Y. Bar Assoc. Comm. on Prof'l Ethics, Op. 780 (2004); State Bar of Mich., Ethics Op. R-19 (2000); Ariz. Comm. on the Rules of Prof'l Conduct, Formal Op. 98-07 (1998); Ill. State Bar Ass'n, Op. 94-13; N.C. State Bar Ethics Comm., RPC 178 (1994); R.I. Supp. Ct. Ethics Advisory Panel, Op. 92-88 (1993).

file.[16] Depending on the jurisdiction, the lawyer is required to be aware of which documents, emails, and drafts must be included in the client's file. Electronic files further complicate the situation as the amount of information generated electronically, especially in regards to metadata, vastly exceeds what normally appears on a printed page.[17]

Aside from determining the type of documents that should be retained in the file, finding and viewing the contents of the client's file was much easier before the introduction of technology to the law office. The physical file was created by a secretary who labeled and sorted all the documents. Any letter sent to the client, any communication from the court, and all official documents were neatly assembled within file folders. Finding the file simply meant walking over to the filing cabinet and pulling open a drawer. Opening the physical file, the lawyer would find many subfiles with headers such as: Correspondence; Court Documents; Drafts; Notes; Memoranda and Legal Research; and Client Relations. The office secretary or paralegal was often in charge of keeping the subfiles separate, and documents were kept only if they created a meaningful history as to events that took place during the representation.

Today's lawyers communicate with their clients in writing almost entirely via email.[18] Also, lawyers now compose, revise, and file briefs and motions on a computer. Word processing developments such as "track changes," email, and document-sharing applications like "Google Documents" allow edits and suggestions to be made entirely on the computer. Furthermore, the popularity of electronic filing with the court system means that many important documents related to the representation of the client are never converted to a physical form. With all this electronic information, lawyers and their secretaries must become adept at searching online network systems to locate the correct documents. Even then, if the "record" is not in its designated repository, it is difficult to know whether the lawyer is looking at the complete file. As one author put it, "[C]lient files today are more sprawling repositories of disparate items relating to the representation of clients."[19]

Today's technological advancements have blurred the lines between the once easily distinguishable subfile categories. Correspondence is often made through a variety of communications tools, many of which create data that can and should be stored. Emailing and group chatting can quickly create a lengthy electronic paper trail. The sheer volume of correspondence regarding the client's

---

[16]*See* Minn. Lawyers Prof'l Resp. Bd., Op. 13 (1989). However, it should be noted that some jurisdictions that have adopted the view that the lawyer owns the file still require the lawyer to return documents such as memoranda and internal notes to the client upon request. *See* State Bar of Mich., Ethics Op. R-19 (2000).

[17]*See* Gary Marchionini, Information Seeking in Electronic Environments 163 (1997) (noting that "electronic information will eventually far exceed paper-based information in quantity").

[18]For example, a 2009 American Bar Association Legal Technology Survey Report found that 93% of lawyers send written communications to clients through email during the course of a year.

[19]Allison D. Rhodes & Robert W. Hillman, *Client Files and Digital Law Practices: Rethinking Old Concepts in an Era of Lawyer Mobility*, 43 Suffolk U. L. Rev. 897, 901-02 (2010).

case has increased exponentially.[20] Email and chat correspondence present a difficulty for lawyers as they are stored automatically in email systems, but are often automatically deleted after a predetermined amount of time as many email providers delete contents every ninety days or so.[21] Also, emails are generally not coded with the file name and, thus, must be saved to the lawyer's hard drive or shared network and renamed as to facilitate the record's retrieval. For email and chat correspondence to be saved, often a lawyer must make the extra effort both to convert the record to a portable document format or "PDF" and to save the record under a corresponding case name so that all client records can be grouped in a single, accessible location.

Even if a lawyer successfully saves all the client's electronic records in one place for convenient locating, a lawyer also must be aware of metadata that is generated by word processing documents.[22] Metadata is often defined as "data hidden in documents that is generated during the course of creating and editing such documents. It may include fragments of data from files that were previously deleted, overwritten or worked on simultaneously."[23] Often, the lawyer creates metadata as he or she develops, edits, and manipulates the electronic document. This information, often referred to as "substantive metadata," is most applicable to the client's file as this metadata reflects any changes to a document made by a user or creator of the document.[24] For those lawyers in jurisdictions that adopt the view that nearly all documents, including notes, memos, and revisions, are the property of the client, the lawyers must both be careful when sending documents that may contain metadata to opposing counsel and not delete metadata from electronic documents if doing so could be viewed as destroying the attorney's work-product and disadvantaging the client.[25]

---

[20]It has been estimated that office employees sent 2.8 billion emails a day in the year 2000. Dana Hawkins, *Office Politics in the Electronic Age*, US News and World Report Online, Feb. 28, 2000. Additionally, lawyers tend to be less guarded in statements made in emails than those made on paper. As a result, more off-the-cuff statements tend to be made in emails, statements that many lawyers later regret were recorded. Bruce E. Jameson, *Document Retention and Electronic Discovery*, 15-No. 5 Prac. Litigator 45, 45-47 (2004).

[21]*See* N.Y. City Bar Ass'n Comm. on Prof'l & Jud. Ethics, Formal Op. 2008-1 (2008). In this opinion, the Committee discusses saving emails and states that a lawyer is not under an ethical obligation to organize electronic documents in any particular manner, "as long as the lawyer ensure[s] that the manner of organization and storage does not (a) detract from the competence of the representation or (b) result in the loss of documents that the client may later need and may reasonably expect the lawyer to preserve." *Id.* The Committee goes on to suggest tips on saving documents, such as saving emails to prevent them from being inadvertently deleted by email providers. *Id.*

[22]Me. Prof'l Ethics Comm., Op. 196 (2008).

[23]N.Y. Bar Assoc. Comm. on Prof'l Ethics, Formal Op. 782 (2004).

[24]The Sedona Principles-Second Edition: Best Practices Recommendations and Principles for Addressing Electronic Document Production Cmt. 4 (Sedona Conference Working Group Series 2007), *available at* www.thesedonaconference.org/content/miscFiles/TSC_PRINCP_2nd_ed_607.pdf.

[25]Metadata has the potential to cause major damage to a client's case if the metadata is exposed to opposing counsel. *See, e.g.*, Stephen Shankland, *Hidden Text Shows SCO*

Furthermore, questions remain regarding why a more inclusive view of the client's file is not adopted in light of the popularity of electronic records. Previously, some ethics boards opposed the "keep everything" policy in relation to client's files because of the unreasonable obligation it put on lawyers to permanently preserve all files remotely related to client representation.[26] These boards reasoned that lawyers had limited storage space available and the added cost associated with such storage was burdensome.[27] However, electronic records are quick and easy to create, inexpensive to maintain, take up no physical storage space, and require little extra upkeep for the lawyer. Thus, a lawyer should re-evaluate whether the benefits of preventing the premature or inappropriate destruction of client electronic records outweigh the costs associated with maintaining the electronic records.

These ethical issues surrounding the digitization of client records become apparent when lawyers realize that records that should belong to a client's file are scattered in different locations on the lawyer's computer, with some located in personal email archives, some saved in word processing documents and formats, and some saved as a desktop icon. Of course, physical documents still exist as well that must be scanned into the computer to join their electronic counterparts.[28] From an ethical standpoint, the lawyer must somehow merge both electronic records and physical records belonging to the client's file so that all records are easily accessible in one location.[29] In addition to leaving the lawyer with a headache, it quickly becomes clear that to duly protect the client's interest and safeguard the client's property, preparation and training must be conducted before the client's engagement letter is even signed. Successful cli-

---

Prepped Lawsuit Against BofA, CNET News, Mar. 4, 2004, http://news.com.com/Hidden+text+shows+SCO+prepped+lawsuit+against+BofA/210 0-7344_3-5170073.html.

[26]See Ala. State Bar Ethics, "Retention, Storage, Ownership, Production and Destruction of Client Files," Op 2010-02.

[27]See id. See also D.C. Bar Legal Ethics Comm., Op. 206 (1989); ABA Comm. on Ethics & Prof'l Resp., Informal Op. 1384 (1989).

[28]That is, if the record is deemed acceptable to store in such a format, as some records are not. See N.Y. State Bar Assoc. Comm. on Prof'l Ethics, Formal Op. 758 (2002) (noting that trust account documents must be retained in original physical form); Me. Prof. Ethics Comm., Op. 183 (2004) (explaining that an attorney is not obligated to keep a paper copy of the lawyer's correspondence if it is kept in electronic format); N.Y. State Bar Assoc. Comm. on Prof'l Ethics, Op. 680 (1996) (noting that items such as checkbooks and bank statements must be retained in their paper form in the client's file).

[29]N.H. Bar Assoc. Ethics Comm., Op. 2005-06/03 (2006). The Opinion states:

> While not adopted by New Hampshire, the ABA rules reflect that, with increased reliance on electronic communications and records in the practice of law, it is reasonable to assume that a client's file can include electronic communications, such as emails, as well as electronic versions of documents filed on behalf of a client. Thus, the mere existence of a paper file does not necessarily allow a firm to automatically exclude from the client's file electronic communications and other computer-based writings. Therefore, if a client requests a copy of her file, the firm has an obligation to provide all files pertinent to representation of that client, regardless of the burden that it might impose upon the firm to do so.

ent representation generally requires that the lawyer have access to the client's file. And, from the principle that a client may discharge his or her lawyer at any time, it follows that the client should also have the ability to retrieve his or her files from the lawyer promptly. Therefore, if a lawyer wishes to take advantage of technological advancements, the lawyer "must evolve with technology in order to avoid breaching the standard of care owed to clients."[30]

IV. The Modern Filing Cabinet

Aside from defining which electronic documents must be grouped inside the client's file, the lawyer must also tackle the issue of electronic storage. Computers are, for the most part, the modern version of the lawyer's filing cabinet. This change was spurred by economic savings and efficiency, although lawyers tended to tout environmental friendliness and convenience to the client.[31] Statistics showed almost all these selling points were true. When previously a lawyer at a large law firm might consume up to one-half ton of copy paper a year, today's digitization of files has reduced that amount of paper printed at a savings of $10,000 in paper costs and $120,000 in office space costs for law firms.[32] Advocates of converting filing cabinets to electronic databases in law offices also often point out how efficient electronic filing systems are for office personnel attempting to locate files, compared to a physical search for paper files in filing closets and storage spaces.[33] Furthermore, the amount of time staff must spend organizing and filing the physical copies is greatly decreased resulting in fewer hours billed or perhaps even one fewer office personnel needed.[34]

Now that the amount of physical storage space is no longer an issue, lawyers must select the most suitable type of electronic storage device for their firm. These devices, much like any other piece of technology on the market today, seems to be in a constant state of flux. A lawyer, whose storage system was top of the line one year, could find the system used to be almost obsolete the next year. For example, at the very beginning of the paperless office trend, floppy disks and CDs were the preferred storage technique of electronic documents. Then, external hard drives and flashdrives took over with their speed and increased storage capacity. Next came the internal network drive that could be shared through an office and saved on one central server. Now, the newest rage is storing all electronic documents on the "cloud."

Cloud computing is the ability to store documents on a service provider's computer over the internet. "Service providers operate a group of computer servers that are connected to each other and function as a single 'cloud' of

---

[30]Rhodes & Hillman, *supra* note 19, at 903.

[31]Seth S. Gomm, *Ethical Considerations of Client File Retention in a Technological Age*, 38 Colo. Law. 103, 105-06 (Sept. 2009).

[32]*Id.*

[33]Masters, *Setting Up the Paperless Office*, GPSolo Magazine, Dec. 2003, *available at* www.abanet.org/genpractice/magazine/2003/dec/setuppaperless.html.

[34]Spence, *supra* note 2, at 18 (noting that "[s]tudies show that professionals spend nearly 150 hours a year searching for files, lost or otherwise").

resources."[35] The cloud operates by separating the responsibility of storing the data into small segments and assigning them to different servers. For those who are computer illiterate, the technicalities of cloud computing can be difficult to comprehend. However, the theory behind cloud computing is more easily understood as an electronic storage method that operates over the internet. In fact, the term "cloud" is used because it is difficult for users to pinpoint exactly where the documents are going and where they are being stored.[36] Thus the image of the cloud works well because files that are stored on these servers seemingly disappear into thin air and reappear again when needed.[37]

The evolution of cloud computing was driven by a few factors. First, internet access has increased in speed and availability throughout the United States. Second, a programming method called AJAX created webpages that function much like today's current computer desktop applications. Additionally, the widespread use of email and document host sites like Gmail and Google Docs made the public more at ease with storing its documents online.[38] The popularity of cloud computing seems to be catching on in the legal world, as the ABA reported a steady increase in use of online services from 2008 to 2009.[39]

The rampant evolution in the technology used to store electronic files has left state ethics boards scrambling to keep up. Many jurisdictions have yet to broach the subject of storing client files on the cloud. However, some more advanced jurisdictions have addressed the technology; they have indicated that this type of file storing is acceptable "as long as the lawyer [takes] appropriate steps to safeguard the information from inadvertent or unauthorized disclosure."[40] Most ethics opinions that address cloud computing discuss the risks

---

[35] William J. Robison, *Free at What Cost?: Cloud Computing Privacy Under the Stored Communications Act*, 98 Geo. L.J. 1195, 1199 (2010).

[36]*Id.* Those in the industry are even having difficult on agreeing as to the meaning of the term "cloud computing." *Id.* Robison notes that in October 2009, the National Institute of Standards and Technology (NIST) released its fifteenth draft of the proposal for a definition of this term (citing Peter Mell & Tim Grance, Nat'l Inst. of Standards and Tech., *The NIST Definition of Cloud Computing* (15th Ver. 2009)).

[37]Dennis Kennedy, *Working in the Cloud: Tips on Success with Online Software Services*, 95-Aug. ABA J. 31 (Aug. 2009).

[38]*Id.*

[39]In ABA's 2009 Legal Technology Survey Report, 16 percent of respondents reported using online software services, compared with 13 percent in the 2008 survey. *See id.*

[40]Richard Acello, *Get Your Head in the Cloud Despite Ethics Questions: Law Firms Are Storing Client Data on the Net*, 96-Apr. ABA J. 28, 28-29 (Apr. 2010). *See also* Az. State Bar's Comm. on the Rules of Prof'l Conduct, Op. 09-04 (2009) (concluding that a law firm may use an online file storage and retrieval system that enables clients to access their files over the internet as long as the firm takes reasonable precautions to safeguard the security and confidentiality of the client's information); N.Y. State Bar Assoc. Comm. on Prof'l Ethics, Formal Op. 842 (2010) (concluding "[a] lawyer may use an online data storage system to store and back up client confidential information provided that the lawyer takes reasonable care to ensure that confidentiality is maintained in a manner consistent with the lawyer's obligations under Rule 1.6. A lawyer using an online storage provider should take reasonable care to protect confidential information, and should exercise reasonable care to prevent others whose services are utilized by the lawyer from disclosing or using confidential information of a client. In addition, the lawyer should

associated with the potential breach of client confidentiality when storing client files other than at the law firm or a secure storage facility.[41] The American Bar Association, in a Formal Opinion, has also recognized the increased use of developing technology that allows lawyers to store data through the use of service providers, and suggests that reasonable efforts must be taken to prevent the unauthorized disclosure of client information.[42]

Another concern is the lawyer's duty to safeguard client files and the lawyer's responsibility to take "reasonable precautions" to prevent information from being intercepted by unintended recipients.[43] The difficulty with cloud computing and these responsibilities is that the lawyer is putting the files on a server that is run by an independent provider. The service providers would be considered non-lawyer assistants under Rule 5.3. Thus, if the files are lost or unintentionally deleted, the provider is generally held responsible contractually.[44] However, the lawyer's ethical duty to the client cannot be contractually signed away. Therefore, ethics boards place the burden on the lawyer's shoulders to select a cloud provider that is as competent as possible.

A reasonable precaution that a lawyer should take if utilizing cloud computing technology is to carefully read over the cloud provider's terms of service agreement and privacy policy.[45] The provider should expressly limit its access to the law firm's files for the sole purpose of providing computer storage and nothing else.[46] Furthermore, lawyers should be aware of the general security and confidentiality policies the cloud provider has in place for the provider's employees.[47] Richard Acello suggests that the provider's contract should be

---

stay abreast of technological advances to ensure that the storage system remains sufficiently advanced to protect the client's information, and the lawyer should monitor the changing law of privilege to ensure that storing information in the 'cloud' will not waive or jeopardize any privilege protecting the information."); N.J. Sup. Ct. Comm. on Prof'l Ethics, Op. 701 (2006) (stating that lawyers must take reasonable care to protect the confidentiality of client files stored electronically with a third party outside the lawyer's offices); Nev. State Bar Standing Comm. on Ethics and Prof'l Resp., Formal Op. 133 (2006) (stating that law firms may store electronically formatted client information on off-site third party servers, as long as the attorney takes reasonable steps to ensure the confidentiality of the client information and to prevent unauthorized access to that information).

[41]*See* Az. State Bar's Comm. on the Rules of Prof'l Conduct, Op. 09-04 (2009); *see also* N.Y. State Bar Assoc. Comm. on Prof'l Ethics, Formal Op. 842 (2010).

[42]ABA Comm. on Ethics & Prof'l Resp., Formal Op. 95-398 (1995).

[43]Model Rules of Prof'l Conduct R. 1.6 cmt. 17 (2009).

[44]*See* Acello, supra note 40, at 28-29.

[45]*See* Robison, *supra* note 35 (explaining that the privacy protections available to a cloud user will be determined by the cloud provider's terms of service agreement and privacy policy). Robison goes on to explain that "[o]nly when a cloud provider expressly limits its access to a customer's data for the purposes of providing computer storage or processing functions" will the customer be protected from liability. *Id.*

[46]*Id.*

[47]In particular, the fact that client data and work-product are stored somewhere outside the direct control of the law firm raises potential ethics concerns about whether the

worded so that the provider acts as a fiduciary for the law firm and the provider's employees are considered agents of the law firm.[48] Also, a lawyer should be aware of the risk of provider outages and should have contingency plans in place should the cloud provider go out of business.[49]

V. Competence Means a Properly Trained Staff

A paperless office has yet one more hurdle to conquer before it is in the ethical all-clear zone. Lawyers that have chosen to implement new technology that creates and stores digital client files must employ office staffers that are competent in electronic record retention. As discussed above, a lawyer's secretary was usually responsible for maintaining and locating a client's file.[50] Most secretaries were able to locate a client's file by using a card index system in which the client's name, file number, and location were written.[51] However, a secretary in today's techno-savvy workplace must have the skill set required for handling electronic records.[52] Office personnel must be adept at searching network systems and must communicate with firm lawyers to determine whether the personnel will have access to the lawyer's emails so that these records can be properly retained for the client's file.[53] Furthermore, the lawyer must ensure that office personnel can recognize the different formats of electronic data and any metadata that may be associated with it.[54]

Once personnel are hired with the proper skill set, these employees can assist the lawyer by developing and maintaining a record management policy to avoid potential problems, such as client records saved in a variety of locations in the network or losing emails due to an auto-delete function of the lawyer's email provider. There are several guides on the internet advising office staff on how to best manage electronic files.[55] Some authors have suggested that office staff in charge of client files be given a checklist of questions that

---

confidentiality and security of the information is adequately protected within the mandates of professional conduct rules for lawyers. Acello, *supra* note 40, at 28.

[48] A law firm should also focus on its relationship with the cloud provider's employees. A contract should be drawn up so the employees at the cloud provider act as a fiduciary for the law firm, similar to common contracts between IT personnel and the law firms they work for. *Id.* at 29.

[49] A question all lawyers should ask themselves, if using a cloud computing service, is what would happen to you, your clients, and your practice if a cloud provider went out of business? Recently, even big-name data storage providers like Gmail have experienced some outages. Dennis Kennedy, *Working in the Cloud: Tips on Success with Online Software Services*, 95-Aug. ABA J. 31, 32 (Aug. 2009).

[50] Beauchemin, *supra* note 5, at 38.

[51] *Id.*

[52] *Id.*

[53] *Id.*

[54] *Id.*

[55] *See* American Bar Association, *FYI: Records Management/Document Retention*, http://www.americanbar.org/groups/departments_offices/legal_technology_resources/resources/charts_fyis/rm.html (last visited Apr. 16, 2011).

should be answered in relation to every electronic file. Checklist questions include whether or not the file is active or inactive; whether the lawyer disclosed the electronic file management policy in the client's engagement letter; and whether the firm has any hardcopy files to accompany the electronic files.[56] Other authors stress the importance of creating a formal policy regarding file-naming, as while "digitizing documents is a fairly easy process, finding them again usually isn't."[57]

File-naming is an essential issue for all lawyers with electronic records, especially in instances where the lawyer is unable to locate a record because either the record was improperly named or the lawyer simply cannot remember in what location on the computer the record was saved. Non-standard filing names may mean the document is virtually undetectable on the lawyer's computer without opening every document and reading the contents. Furthermore, if the file-naming technique used by office personnel is not easily discernable, anyone else outside those employees would be unable to find the files. Authors suggest that firms implement a file-naming convention that is used by the entire firm.[58] Software that consists of document management systems can be purchased to create a file-naming convention that uniformly labels all documents, to prevent lawyers or other office personnel from creating their own name.[59]

VI. Returning the Electronic File

The most common ethical issue involving client files is returning the files to the client when the lawyer's representation is terminated. Under Rule 1.16 (d), the lawyer must return the client's property after termination or withdrawal. Unfortunately, the rule does not discuss in which form the files must be returned. Because the majority of client files now either originate in or are converted to electronic format, lawyers question whether this rule imposes an obligation on the lawyer to pay for printed copies of the electronic file or instead the rule permits the file to be returned electronically. The ethics boards grapple with this issue by attempting to weigh the client's interest and capabilities to access the technology and the lawyer's economic and efficiency interests in utilizing the cost-friendly electronic version.

There are ethic opinions that stand on either side of the issue. North Carolina has stated that lawyers may return electronic files to the client in an electronic format, such as a computer disk.[60] The ethics board notes that, "[i]n light of the widespread availability of computers, this standard is met if Attor-

---

[56]*See, e.g.*, Raymond P. Micklewright, *Understanding File Retention: Developing an Ethical Policy and Plan—Part 1*, 30-Oct. Colo. Law. 147, 150 (2001).

[57]JoAnn L. Hathaway, *Paperless Perils!*, 88-Feb. Mich. B.J. 46, 46 (Feb. 2009).

[58]*Id.*

[59]Examples of these systems include: WORLDOX, www.worldox.com (last visited on Apr. 16, 2011); Interwoven, www.interwoven.com (last visited on Apr. 16, 2011); DOCSOpen, www.opentext.com (last visited on Apr. 16, 2011); NetDocuments, www.netdocuments.com (last visited on Apr. 16, 2011). *Id.*

[60]N.C. State Bar Ethics Comm., Formal Op. 5 (2002).

ney provides Client with a computer disk containing the retained email communications or otherwise transmits them to Client in an electronic format."[61] The ethics board in California takes a more lenient view, allowing files to be returned to the client electronically but requiring the format of the file to be one that the client is able to access.[62] Missouri takes a more cautious view that the lawyer is allowed to give the file back to the client electronically if the lawyer and client had a previous agreement that the files would be returned to the client electronically.[63] The ethics board in Maine takes the opposite approach to that of North Carolina, stating the board's concern is that technology is not yet universal in its application and, thus, a lawyer should print out copies to the client if that is what the client desires.[64]

While many lawyers view printing out paper copies of electronic files as unnecessary, wasteful, and expensive, others view the duty as a proper one in light of the economic means of many of their clients. If the goal of the legal profession is to serve our client, should not our number one concern be our client's interest with our other concerns of increasing economic efficiency and promoting environmental awareness coming in second? Bruce Cameron, author of "The Rural Lawyer," posed a similar question on his blog about the ongoing law firm obsession with new technology and client relations:

> Do we, as a profession, know enough about our clients (the "raw materials" of our practice) to choose the technology that will produce an optimal experience for them, or are we choosing technology based on our personal biases and hoping that, through the miracle of "new and improved," it will produce a better (perhaps that should read "non-traditional" or "different") experience for the client and provide a mark of distinction that will elevate our practice above the herd?[65]

Cameron raises a valid point that a lawyer's obsession with employing the latest technology stems more from the lawyer's laziness and vanity than from the lawyer's desire to help his or her clients. Technology sometimes acts as a shield for the lawyer's insecurities. Aside from the fact that email is less expensive and more efficient than a telephone call, a letter, or an in-person meeting, lawyers are more apt to email the client with bad news if the lawyer wants to avoid the emotional reaction of the client. Also, lawyers are drawn to the ease of creating and saving electronic documents as compared to the previous labors that were involved when producing physical copies. An electronic document is easily manipulated, edited, and redacted. Multiple versions can be saved in case they are needed at a later time or due to changed circumstances. Cloud computing now allows the lawyer to forget his or her worries about physical storage space and the risk of a natural disaster to his or her office building or storage facility.

---

[61]*Id.*

[62]Cal. Standing Comm. on Prof'l Resp. & Conduct, Formal Op. 2007-174 (2007).

[63]Advisory Comm. of the Sup. Ct. of Mo., Scanning Client Files, Formal Op. 127 (2009).

[64]Me. Prof. Ethics Comm., Op. 183 (2004).

[65]Bruce Cameron, *Rural Technocracy*, The Rural Lawyer Blog (Sept. 3, 2010), http://rurallawyer.com/2010/09/03/rural-technocracy/#more-410.

With all the benefits to the lawyer, it comes as no surprise that even the slightest negative aspect of electronic record retention causes the lawyer to go running to the ethics boards. The cost associated with printing out the client's file is minimal compared to the amount of money the lawyer has saved by creating and storing his or her documents electronically. Perhaps the distaste comes more from the fact that a client asking for the return of his or her documents usually means that the lawyer has either been fired or representation was no longer possible. In this case, the lawyer should recognize that she cannot have her cake and eat it too.

VII. Conclusion

The digitization of client files and the advancements in internet technology have allowed lawyers to increase communication with their clients, quickly produce and file documents with courts, and decrease the need for expensive storage facilities and office personnel dedicated to copying and filing papers. With all the benefits of the new technology it is easy to overlook the ethical risks that must also be addressed. Lawyers should be aware of the fiduciary duty owed to the client and the client's property, even if that property no longer exists in a physical form.

4

The Perfect Storm: How Rising Tuition, Non-Dischargeable Loans, and a Struggling Job Market Created a Whirlwind of Problems for Law School Graduates

Lee Rudin

Introduction

Americans have felt the daily impact of the "Great Recession" across the United States at all economic levels and in all social spheres. The current economic downtown has not spared any industry, including the legal one. This article will address a major issue further exacerbated by the depressed economy and more apparent in the midst of it — the "perfect storm" of law student debt. Bloggers are yelling about it at the top of their proverbial lungs, writers are chronicling it in *The New York Times,* and law journals across America are dedicating ample space for its discussion. There is a significant problem with the current state of law school — in its cost, in its expectations of students, and its effects it on society.

The first section of this article will provide a brief overview of the recession's effects on the legal market. Section Two will describe the evolution of the American student loan process and its faults and failings. The third section will address the culpability of law schools in saddling law students with insurmountable debt and promises of employment grandeur. In Section Four, the article will identify additional culprits responsible for the law student debt fiasco and evaluate their contributions to it. Lastly, Section Five will outline potential solutions to combat the problem before it can further damage law students and society in general.

I. The Legal Field Is Not Recession-Proof

When the current economic recession hit the United States in December 2007,[1] it felt like a blow to the gut of young Americans envisioning law school followed by high-paying legal jobs on the horizon. For U.S. college students, "being well-off financially is now the most important life goal[.] Three-quarters rate it as essential or very important, a figure that has doubled over the past quarter century."[2] The recession should have dashed the dreams of believers in the

---

[1]Press Release, Nat'l Bureau of Econ. Research, Determination of the December 2007 Peak in Economic Activity, Dec. 11, 2008, *available at* http://www.nber.org/dec2008.pdf .

[2]Deborah L. Rhode, *The Profession and Its Discontents*, 61 Ohio St. L.J. 1335, 1341 (2000).

fairy tale that law school represented a three-year, get-rich-quick scheme where mere graduation guaranteed a $160,000 a year salary. As recently as November 2010, 2.4 million people possessing a B.A. or advanced degree were without work — so lawyers are not alone.[3] This harsh economic shift resulted in what Brian Tamanaha, Professor of Law at Washington University Law in St. Louis, described as the "worst recession in the legal market in at least two decades."[4] According to *The New York Times*, citing a Northwestern Law study, the recession has eliminated 15,000 attorney and legal-staff jobs since 2008.[5] Other estimates paint a far drearier picture. Data compiled by the Bureau of Labor Statistics indicates that legal industry jobs declined by 42,000 from November 2008-2009.[6] Further, between June 2007 and January 2011, the number of legal services positions decreased by approximately 93,000.[7]

The tough economic times have not discriminated — they have affected firms of all sizes, in all geographic regions and in all practice areas, resulting in a decrease in "virtually all key financial performance metrics."[8] For law stu-

---

[3]Mary Kate Sheridan, "Law School Isn't a Game—It's a Serious Investment," Vault.com, Jan. 10, 2011, *available at* http://www.vault.com/wps/portal/usa/blogs/entry-detail?blog_id=1260&entry_id=12389 ("In fact, in September 2010, the unemployment rate for 'management, business and financial' industries reached its highest point since 2000. But other graduate programs aren't receiving the same attention.").

[4]Brian Tamanaha, "The Irresponsibility of Law Schools," Balkinization, Oct. 18, 2010, *available at* http://balkin.blogspot.com/2010/10/irresponsibility-of-law-schools.html; "Brian Z. Tamanaha," WULS: Faculty Profiles, Washington University Law in St. Louis, *available at* http://law.wustl.edu/faculty_profiles/profiles.aspx?id=7287.

[5]David Segal, "Is Law School a Losing Game?," New York Times, Jan. 8, 2011, *available at* http://www.nytimes.com/2011/01/09/business/09law.html?pagewanted=1.

[6]American Bar Association, *Statement by the Commission on the Impact of the Economic Crisis in the Profession and Legal Needs* at 1, *available at* www.abanet.org/op/lamm/docs/accomplishments-for-website.pdf. "The current recession is the hardest to hit the United States since the Great Depression. The unemployment rate in October 2009 surpassed ten percent, the highest rate in twenty-six years." Maulik Shah, *The Legal Education Bubble: How Law Schools Should Respond to Changes in the Legal Market*, 23 Geo. J. Legal Ethics 843, 844 (Summer 2010) (citing Bob Willis, U.S. Recession Worst Since Great Depression, Revised Data Show, Bloomberg.com, Aug. 1, 2009, *available at* http://www.bloomberg.com/apps/news?pid=20601087&sid=aNivTjr852TI; Peter S. Goodman, *U.S. Unemployment Rate Hits 10.2%, Highest in 26 Years,* New York Times, Nov. 7, 2009, *available at* http://www.nytimes.eom/2009/11/07/business/economy/07jobs.html).

[7]Debra Cassens Weiss, *Law Schools Grow As Jobs Shrink, Producing Irate Unemployed Lawyers*, ABA Journal, Oct. 28, 2010, *available at* http://www.abajournal.com/news/article/law_schools_grow_as_jobs_shrink_producing_irate_unemployed_lawyers/. The definition of a legal service position is broad and includes additional employment positions beyond attorneys, such as legal assistants, paralegals, file clerks, and legal secretaries. "Legal Services Jobs," Monster.com, *available at* http://jobsearch.monster.com/Legal-Services_3?pg=2.

[8]Steven C. Bennett, *When Will Law School Change?*, 89 Neb. L. Rev. 87, 111 (2010) (citing Press Release, Incisive Legal Intelligence, *Incisive Legal Intelligence Survey: FY 2008 Per Lawyer Revenues Drop, Reflecting Flat Billing Rates and Decline in Billed Hours* (Sept. 14, 2009), *available at*

dents, a reduction in firm business has had a significant trickle-down effect. Not only did employed lawyers face layoffs, but prospective lawyers and summer associates, namely law students, saw their opportunities greatly altered. Many small and mid-size firms discontinued summer programs for law students, electing to divert resources to hiring more experienced attorneys.[9] In addition, numerous large, reputable law firms "disappeared entirely through bankruptcies and mergers," leading to a decrease in hiring and retention of law students.[10]

Those fortunate enough to receive employment offers believed the nightmare to be over, but they were wrong. In 2009, the deferral phenomenon encompassed legal hiring. The National Association for Legal Professionals (NALP) reported that "between 3,200 and 3,700 graduates had the start dates for their jobs with law firms deferred beyond Dec. 1, 2009. Eventually a number of offers of employment were terminated outright."[11] There have been signs of an uptick in the legal industry, though the conditions remain difficult. NALP Executive Director James Leipold issued a revealing statement about the current situation:

> For the class of 2009, the largest impact was the deferral [on being hired] phenomenon. By now, some of those who were deferred have actually started work, but others remain deferred at this time. For the class of 2010, there were many fewer offers for full-time employment.... For the class of 2011 — those who went through the on-campus interview process last fall — there were many fewer 2010 summer positions available. That is a situation that we expect to persist for the class of 2012. I don't think anyone expects recruiting volumes to pick up significantly during 2010, though the worst does now seem, we hope, to be behind us.[12]

Leipold's idealism is admirable; however, it contrasts with the reality that the legal market may have changed permanently. To illustrate this point, summer programs in 2010 consisted of approximately half the number of positions as in previous years, and, furthermore, firms offered only sixty-nine percent of summer associates positions, whereas generally ninety percent received offers

---

http://www.alm.com/pressroom/2009/09/21/incisive-legal-intelligence-survey-fy-2008-per-lawyer-revenues-drop-reflecting-flat-billing-rates-and-decline-in-billed-hours/).

[9]Daniel Thies, *Rethinking Legal Education in Hard Times: The Recession, Practical Legal Education, and the New Job Market*, 59 J. Legal Educ. 598, 607 (May 2010) (citing Press Release, Robert Denney Associates, Inc., *What's Hot and What's Not in the Legal Profession* (July 2008), *available at* http://www.robertdenney.com/pdf/comm-legal-hot-not-july2008.pdf).

[10]Bennett, *supra* note 8, at 112.

[11]NALP, *Market For Law Graduates Changes With Recession: Class of 2009 Faced New Challenges* at 1, Jul. 22, 2010, *available at* http://www.nalp.org/uploads/Class_of_09_Jobs_and_JDs_Report_Press_Release.pdf.

[12]Geoff Yuda, *Is Law School Still Worth It? Law Students are Facing a Convergence of Rising Costs, Debt and Lackluster Job Prospects that Makes the Question Uncomfortably Relevant*, 32-JUN Penn. Law. 18, 20 (May/June, 2010).

in the past.[13] In addition, "with corporations scrutinizing their legal expenses as never before, more entry-level legal work is now outsourced to contract temporary employees, both in the United States and in countries like India. It's common to hear lawyers fret about the sort of tectonic shift that crushed the domestic steel industry decades ago."[14]

Changes at law firms are not the only ones affecting law students. The recession has also struck law schools, which in turn has filtered down to their students. The floundering economy has limited the means of individuals, institutions, and governments. As a result, the funding normally afforded to law schools has decreased. Most public law schools exist as parts of larger state universities to which their respective state governments have reduced funding.[15] For private schools, enormous drops in endowment funds have significantly hamstrung their economic viability. According to University of Chicago Law School Dean Saul Levmore, "[R]eliance on funding from endowments varies, but generally makes up a quarter to a half of the operating budget at private schools."[16] Besides a decrease in funding from endowments, donations to law schools have diminished as well.[17]

It has been a "perfect storm" for law students in recent years.[18] Prior to the current recession, law schools graduates were often all but assured of securing employment and earning a comfortable living while repaying their debts. However, since the economic downturn, jobs have disappeared, law schools have suffered funding losses, and consequently they have passed their burden along to students through higher tuition costs. This continues to result in many students incurring enormous loans to pay for school without a foreseeable way of repaying them post-graduation.

II. Bursting the Student Loan Bubble: A Mortgage-Like Crisis?

Before delving into the current student loan mess, it is imperative to acknowledge that student loans in their most basic sense are good. They enable those without the means of affording an education to do so by borrowing against their potential. Granting student loans sounds like an altruistic endeavor on behalf of lenders; however, a closer look indicates there is something altogether devious going on. What may have once been an admirable venture has evolved

---

[13]Debra Cassens Weiss, *As 'Troubling Indicators' Mount for 2010 Law Grads, An ABA Expert Issues a Warning*, May 6, 2010, *available at* http://www.abajournal.com/news/article/as_troubling_indicators_mount_for_2010_law_grads_an_aba_expert_issues_a_war/.

[14]Segal, *supra* note 5. [Outsourcing of legal jobs overseas is discussed in chapter 2.]

[15]Karen Sloan, *Law Schools Dealing with Budget Cuts*, Nat'l L.J., Jan. 19, 2009, *available at* http://www.law.com/jsp/nlj/PubArticleNLJ.jsp?id=1202427496279&slreturn=1&hbxlogin=1.

[16]*Id.*

[17]Shah, *supra* note 6, at 846.

[18]*See generally* Bennett, *supra* note 8, at 108.

into a harmful practice burdening thousands of young Americans because of government changes to loan forgiveness policies.

The Higher Education Act (HEA), signed in 1965 by Lyndon Johnson as part of his 'Great Society' plan, enabled students to afford higher education by utilizing federally guaranteed loans and scholarships.[19] Evidence revealed that some doctors and lawyers "gamed the system" by filing for bankruptcy immediately following graduation to discharge their student debt.[20] The United States government responded to this when it enacted the Bankruptcy Reform Act in 1978.[21] This Act disallowed former students from discharging their student loan debt until five years after they made their first payback payment.[22] Congress extended this period to seven years in 1990.[23] In 1998, Congress took a further step to eliminate the discharge of student debt in bankruptcy — removing the ability to do so entirely,[24] though very limited exceptions remained.[25] Congress continued this trend in 2005 by amending the Bankruptcy Code to include non-discharge protection to private student loan lenders.[26] These amendments made all student loans — government and private — nearly impossible to discharge.[27] Most recently, President Barack Obama claimed to have overhauled the student loan program, calling it "one of the most significant investments in higher education since the G.I. Bill," but the problems for students remain.[28]

---

[19]College Scholarships.org, *The Student Loan Scheme: A Gateway Drug to Debt Slavery — 2nd Edition*, *available at* http://www.collegescholarships.org/research/student-loans/.

[20]*Id.* The enactment of this Act may have been a little harsh or at least a little hasty considering the "actual discharge rate at the time was less than 1%." *Id.*

[21]*Id. See* Bankruptcy Reform Act of 1978, P.L. 95-598, Nov. 6, 1978.

[22]College Scholarships.org, *The Student Loan Scheme: A Gateway Drug to Debt Slavery — 2nd Edition*, *available at* http://www.collegescholarships.org/research/student-loans/.

[23]*Id.*

[24]*Id.* The same inability to discharge debt applies to limited circumstances including debt from criminal acts (i.e., debt incurred from a civil suit following a criminal act) and debt from fraud. *Id.*

[25]One of the few exceptions enabling students to discharge education debt is the Undue Hardship Standard, codified in the United States Bankruptcy Code. *See* 11 U.S.C. § 523(a)(8); Moderator, "Undue Hardship," National Bankruptcy Forum, *available at* http://www.nationalbankruptcyforum.com/tag/undue-hardship/.

[26]Moderator, "Undue Hardship," National Bankruptcy Forum, *available at* http://www.nationalbankruptcyforum.com/tag/undue-hardship/.

[27]*Id.*

[28]*Id.* President Obama failed to mention that this overhaul benefited the government and taxpayers, but not those most affected by the loans — students. The changes in student lending limited the role of private lenders like Sallie Mae by eliminating the government subsidies they received. Without these subsidies, now the federal government recoups loan profits that once belonged to private lenders by replacing for-profit collection agencies like GRC with non-profit agencies like EdFund, though their jobs remain the same.

"Loans for education are the only type of loan that has [a] Federal 'no-escape' clause."[29] In addition, the "harshest collection methods are reserved for student loans," including wage garnishment without a court order, suspension of state professional licenses, garnishment of social security or disability income, and withholding of IRS tax refunds.[30] Elizabeth Warren, Harvard Law Professor and Chair of the TARP Congressional Oversight Panel, when discussing the startlingly few consumer protections that exist for student loan borrowers, stated: "Student-loan debt collectors have power that would make a mobster envious."[31] However unlikely it may be, Professor Warren's comments should certainly put students on notice of the unyielding commitment and burden of student debt.

Some compare the structure of the student loan industry to the mortgage industry structure responsible for creating the housing bubble. According to *The Value Proposition of Attending Law School*, a report issued by the ABA Commission on the Impact of the Economic Crisis on the Profession and Legal Needs, law school tuition has risen twice as fast as inflation over the last twenty-five years.[32] This rise has equated to an average in-state tuition cost of $16,836 for public law schools.[33] For private law schools, average annual tuition totaled $34,298 — a striking total when considering that ten years earlier the average private school tuition was $9,650 per year.[34] The ABA Commission's report concluded:

> When one adds books and living expenses to tuition, the average public law student borrows $71,436 for law school, while the average private school student borrows $91,506. Many students borrow far more than $100,000, and these numbers do not even include debt that students may still carry from their undergraduate years.[35]

According to the "2010 Best Law School Rankings" released by *U.S. News and World Report,* students from Thomas Jefferson Law School graduated with the highest debt of any school in its rankings — $131,800 on average — and ninety-five percent of students graduating from the school graduated with

---

[29]*Id.*

[30]College Scholarships.org, *supra* note 19.

[31]Lurie Daniel Favors, "Student Loans: Gateway Drug to Debt Slavery," NYC Debt and Bankruptcy Law, Jan. 10, 2011, *available at* http://www.nycdebtandbankruptcylaw.com/student-loans-gateway-drug-to-debt-slavery/.

[32]American Bar Association, The ABA Commission on the Impact of the Economic Crisis on the Profession and Legal Needs, *The Value Proposition of Law School* (Nov. 2009) (hereinafter, ABA Commission), *available at* http://www.americanbar.org/content/dam/aba/migrated/lsd/legaled/value.authcheckdam.pdf.

[33]*Id.*

[34]*Id.*; Leslie Kwoh, "Irate law school grads say they were misled about job prospects," The Star-Ledger, Aug. 15, 2010, *available at* http://www.nj.com/business/index.ssf/2010/08/irate_law_school_grads_say_the.html.

[35]ABA Commission, *supra* note 32.

at least some debt.[36] These astronomical totals are shocking, especially considering estimates by Dean David Van Zandt of Northwestern University Law School conclude the average salary needed "for the investment in a law school education to provide law graduates with a positive return over that from an alternative career" is $65,315.[37] Dean Van Zandt estimates that students must earn at least this amount to overcome the cost of attending law school and that forty percent of law school graduates earn starting salaries below this amount — that is, if they are earning salaries at all.[38]

Critics have analogized the present student loan situation to the recent mortgage crisis, equating a law degree to a "toxic asset."[39] Given the current state of the economy and its effects on the legal field and law schools, it is not surprising that irresponsibility has reared its ugly head in the educational loans business like it did with mortgages — this time in the form of shouldering naïve students, unaware that the promises of law schools are mirages in the legal job-market desert, with insurmountable debts.

III. Point the Blame: Holding Schools Responsible for Student Debt

So where do law schools stand in all of this? How much of the responsibility belongs to them for the runaway train that law student debt has become? The answer is not clear, but what is certain is that law schools deserve some blame for what a 2009 *Forbes* article described as "an unfolding education hoax on the middle class that's just as insidious, and nearly as sweeping, as the housing debacle."[40] Critics of attributing blame to schools exist and they say that students should be responsible for the loans they signed up for. The argument is not without merit (and this article will discuss it further in Section IV), yet "[m]uch like the mortgage crisis, [it is] difficult not to assign blame to the parties that appear to be profiting the most from the drunken free for all, and in the current situation, that's not the students."[41] Further, there are two specific reasons to blame schools. First, law schools owe a duty to their students to be

---

[36]"The great law school 'rip-off': By the numbers," The Week, Jan. 11, 2011, *available at* http://theweek.com/article/index/210930/the-great-law-school-rip-off-by-the-numbers.

[37]Thomas A. Donovan, *A Mind is a Terrible Thing to Waste,* 58-JAN Fed. Law. 4 (Jan. 2011) (citing ABA Commission, *supra* note 32).

[38]*Id.* This total did not include the "opportunity costs of spending three years in law school instead of earning a normal income[.]" *Id.* "Dean Van Zandt's calculation assumes the student would earn $60,000 per year in an alternative occupation, that law school tuition is $30,000 per year, that the student works for 30 years as a lawyer and that the discount rate is 5 percent." *Id.* at *5 note 9.

[39]Kelly Francis, "Law School Debt and the Mortgage Meltdown," Minnesota Lawyer, Sep. 21, 2010, *available at* http://minnlawyer.com/jdr/2010/09/21/law-school-debt-and-the-mortgage-meltdown/.

[40]Kathy Kristof, "The Great College Hoax," Forbes, Feb. 2, 2009, *available at* http://www.forbes.com/forbes/2009/0202/060.html.

[41]Francis, *supra* note 39.

honest and forthcoming with information necessary for students to make reasonable decisions regarding enrolling. Second, and related to the first, despite being for-profit entities, it is unethical and for schools to utilize, as Law Professor William Henderson of Indiana University contends, "Enron-type accounting standards" to skew their statistics positively to increase enrollment.[42]

A. ABA Standards Impose Duties on Law Schools to Admit Students Suitable for Bar Admission

The American Bar Association delineates the necessary standards for law schools to earn accreditation. Accreditation is extremely important in the law school business and schools therefore take the required steps to obtain accreditation. Chapter Five of the ABA Standards for Approval of Law Schools, entitled "Admissions and Student Services," is the relevant one for the purposes of this article.[43] The chapter includes numerous standards that, if followed, would alter law school behavior in a way that could lessen the damaging effects of law student loans.

Standard 501, part (b), dictates that schools "shall not admit applicants who do not appear capable of ... being admitted to the bar."[44] This standard relates directly to Standard 504 regarding character and fitness.[45] Because admittance to every state bar requires the passage of a character and fitness examination, it is imperative that every applicant be capable of fulfilling this requirement. As a result, in both advising prospective students of its existence and counseling them on their ability to pass it, schools have an obligation to ensure that those it admits, who hope to join a state bar association in the future, are capable of passing the character and fitness portion of the examination. A school that enrolls a student incapable of passing this portion of the exam, and thereby incapable of being admitted to the bar, is shirking its responsibility under Standard 501(b). This is particularly important because debt load and a student's plan to pay it off are factors considered during the character and fitness determination. Given the growing debt issue amongst law students, the character and fitness hurdle becomes quite problematic.

Take the case of Hassan Jonathan Griffin. Griffin graduated from Ohio State University's Moritz College of Law in 2008 with $170,000 of student loan debt and approximately $16,500 in credit card debt.[46] Upon applying for ad-

---

[42]Segal, *supra* note 5.

[43]American Bar Association, *2010-2011 ABA Standards for Approval of Law Schools*, *available at* http://www.americanbar.org/content/dam/aba/migrated/legaled/standards/2010-2011_standards/2010-2011abastandards_pdf_files/chapter5.authcheckdam.pdf.

[44]*Id.* at 35.

[45]*See id.* at 37.

[46]*In re Application of Griffin*, Slip Opinion No. 2011-Ohio-20, at ¶ 4, *available at* https://www.supremecourt.ohio.gov/rod/docs/pdf/0/2011/2011-ohio-20.pdf. Griffin's student loan debt consisted of "$20,000 for his undergraduate studies [at Arizona State University] and $150,000 for law school." *Id.*

mission to the Ohio bar and its examination in February 2010, the Columbus Bar Association's Admissions Committee reviewed Griffin's applications and recommended approval for his admission.[47] However, Ohio's "Board of Commissioners on Character and Fitness *sua sponte* instituted an investigation of [Griffin's] debt" and instead recommended Griffin be disapproved for admission.[48] The Board based this decision upon his sizeable debt, his inability to meet his credit card obligations, the fact that he could only discharge his credit card debt (and not his student loan debt) in bankruptcy, and that he only worked part-time at the Public Defender's office earning $12 per hour.[49]

The Ohio Supreme Court issued a *per curiam* opinion regarding Griffin's denial of admission to the Ohio bar.[50] The Ohio Supreme Court agreed with the Board's decision and upheld its denial of Griffin's bar admission. The most troubling aspect of this decision is present in paragraph nine of the opinion. After accepting the Board's findings of fact, the Ohio Supreme Court concluded that Griffin

> neglected his personal financial obligations by electing to maintain his part-time employment with the Public Defender's Office in the hope that it will lead to a full-time position upon passage of the bar exam, rather than seeking full-time employment, which he acknowledges would give him a better opportunity to pay his obligations[.][51]

For these reasons, the court held that Griffin "failed to prove he possesse[d] the requisite character, fitness, and moral qualifications for admission to the practice of law."[52] In effect, under the guise of enforcing a character and fitness requirement, the court made its own determination that Griffin's choice of work was insufficient to pay off the loans he had accrued and this made him unfit to be a lawyer. To the court, Griffin's choice to pursue work that would not immediately enable him to repay his debts was a negative reflection of his character, which therefore made him unsuitable to practice law. The court's reasoning discounts or disregards the fact that Griffin *was* working and his employer was someplace that would evolve into a full-time position following his bar passage, and that he was working in a neglected area of law — public interest. The court insinuated that Griffin was required to accept employment that would enable him to pay off his debts, or else the court would continue to deem him unfit to practice law. This certainly sounds as though the court is promoting indentured servitude.[53]

---

[47]*Id.* at ¶ 2.

[48]*Id.* at ¶¶ 3 and 7.

[49]*Id.* at ¶¶ 5 and 6.

[50]*Id.* at ¶ 8. Griffin was denied admission because he "did not possess 'the requisite character, fitness, and moral qualifications for admission to the practice of law' based upon his debt." *Id.*

[51]*Id.* at ¶ 9.

[52]*Id.* at ¶ 10.

[53]Elie Mystal, "Character & Fitness Fail for Graduate With 'No Plan' To Pay Off His Debts," Above The Law, Jan. 12, 2011, *available at*

To make matters worse, Griffin's debts — at least those of most concern to the court — were non-dischargeable as they were student debts, the majority of which he incurred for his legal education. So because the government would not allow Griffin to discharge this debt via bankruptcy and because the court believed the area of the law Griffin chose would be insufficient to pay off his debts, it prevented him from obtaining a license to practice law altogether. Yet the very schools that allowed him to enroll to obtain his legal education had an *obligation* under ABA Accreditation Standards 501 and 504 to inform him of the possibility that the debt he incurred to become a lawyer could be his undoing — the sole fact that would prevent him from achieving that goal.[54] After assessing all of that, I conclude that schools deserve some responsibility for the insurmountable debt befalling law students such as Hassan Jonathan Griffin throughout the country.

Besides Standards 501 and 504, two other standards enable attributing responsibility to law schools for the enormous debt of their students. Standard 509 requires schools to "publish basic consumer information ... in a fair and accurate manner reflective of actual practice," including placement rates and bar passage data.[55] In addition, Standard 510 mandates that schools take "reasonable steps to minimize student loan defaults."[56] In sum, these standards mandate transparency, honesty and disclosure, yet this area is where most law students find themselves in trouble.

B. Law Schools Prevent Students from Making Educated Decisions by Providing Distorted Statistics

The problem with the data provided to most students prior to attending law school is the source. Generally, the information law students base their decisions upon comes directly from the schools or via *U.S. News and World Report*, which gets most of its information from the schools. Therefore, since the problem surrounding law student debt is a result of misinformation leading to enrollment under false pretenses, the providers of the information ought to be held responsible, and in this case, the guilty parties are law schools. The problem is simple — schools are fudging the numbers. *The New York Times* reported that, "[i]n reality, and based on every other source of information, ... a generation of J.D.'s face the grimmest job market in decades," but judging "from data that law schools collect, [which] is published in the closely parsed *U.S. News and World Report* annual rankings, the prospects of young doctors

---

http://abovethelaw.com/2011/01/character-fitness-fail-for-graduate-with-no-plan-to-pay-off-his-debts/.

[54]Elie Mystal of the legal blog *Above The Law* emphatically criticized the Ohio Supreme Court: "Why don't they force Moritz to put up a warning on its website that reads: WARNING: Inability to pay off our ridiculous tuition in the middle of a recession could result in a character and fitness failure." *Id.*

[55]American Bar Association, *supra* note 43, at 38-40.

[56]*Id.* at 40. Standard 510 indicates that the accreditation committee will consider student loan default rates in assessing school compliance.

of jurisprudence are downright rosy."[57] Since the ABA does not explicitly define its expectations for basic consumer information, "schools can manipulate or distort the information" — and they do.[58]

For example, Dean Roger J. Dennis of Drexel University's Earle Mack School of Law explained that when reporting employment, the NALP determines the number by dividing the number of students working in *any* capacity by those students of known status.[59] In order to determine a more meaningful number, Drexel computes its employment by dividing the number of students working in full- or part-time legal jobs plus students pursuing an LL.M. degree by students whose status is known plus those not seeking work.[60] Drexel's computation uncovered an employment rate seven percentage points lower than the NALP's total.[61]

After seeing the difference in the NALP and Drexel employment calculations, it is not difficult to understand how *U.S. News and World Report* can boast employment statistics of ninety-three percent during a recession, while over ten years earlier, average employment totaled only eighty-four percent.[62] Dissecting these statistics further makes the manner of their portrayal even worse. According to the NALP, the Class of 2009 had the lowest employment rate since the mid-1990s.[63] Worse even, of those jobs reported, just below one quarter of them were temporary, many of which the law schools created for their students to enhance their employment data.[64] In addition, a large proportion of those reporting employment were not working in jobs requiring the practice of law.[65] According to *The New York Times*, "[a] law grad, for instance, counts as 'employed after nine months' even if he or she has a job that doesn't require a law degree. Waiting tables at Applebee's? You're employed. Stocking aisles at Home Depot? You're working, too."[66] Further, nearly half of those that

---

[57]As cited in Segal, *supra* note 5.

[58]Shah, *supra* note 6, at 853-54.

[59]Yuda, *supra* note 12, at 20, 27.

[60]*Id.* at 27.

[61]*Id.* For the Drexel Class of 2009, the NALP determined employment to be 82.31 percent, whereas Drexel found it was 75.34 percent. *Id.*

[62]Segal, *supra* note 5. The recent statistics mentioned were from the 2010 report and the earlier statistics are from 1997.

[63]NALP, *supra* note 11.

[64]*Id.* "This data is entirely self-reported by schools and should be treated as essentially fiction," said University of Chicago law professor Brian Leiter, a well-known expert on law school rankings. "In addition, we know nothing about the nature of the employment — it could simply be as a research assistant, which is what Northwestern did a few years ago for its unemployed grads." Mark Grabowski, "Opinion: Are Law Schools Scamming Students?," Oct. 15, 2010, *available at* http://www.aolnews.com/2010/10/15/opinion-are-law-schools-scamming-students/.

[65]NALP, *supra* note 11, at 2.

[66]As discussed in Segal, *supra* note 5.

were practicing law were doing so as solo practitioners.[67] Just because law professors and deans report that "number-fudging games are endemic"[68] does not make it acceptable or ethical; in fact, it makes the behavior more abhorrent because of its widespread effect.

Law professors, despite their institutional affiliations, are adamantly opposed to schools' dishonesty. Professor William Henderson of Indiana University Law says he "feel[s] dirty" every time he looks at his school's employment data.[69] The "pipe dreams" that schools are selling students bothers New York University Law Professor Samuel Issacharoff, too.[70] He supports providing transparent statistics that would enable students to "discern which schools are guilty."[71] Issacharoff is likely hoping more schools follow the lead of Washington and Lee Law School, to provide more informative, though potentially less flattering, numbers.[72] Professors are not the only ones appalled by the law schools' behavior. Law School Transparency, a non-profit group formed by two Vanderbilt law students, states that it is "dedicated to encouraging and facilitating the transparent flow of law school employment information."[73] A like-minded group, Down by Law, is comprised of attorneys who advocate for greater transparency in law school admissions.[74]

Furthermore, the ABA is not oblivious to the problem. It issued its warning to students about the current economics of law school,[75] and, as of December 2010, it was "making the case to persuade college students not to go to law

---

[67]NALP, *Class of 2009 Faced New Challenges With Recession; Overall Employment Masks Job Market Weakness* at 2, *available at* http://www.nalp.org/uploads/09SelectedFindingsPressRelease.pdf.

[68]Segal, *supra* note 5. Unfortunately, not all of the misinformation available to students is a result of schools intentionally fudging their numbers — a practice they could correct. Even schools with no intention to mislead potential students may be doing so because they gather employment data through voluntary surveys, which subjects their data to the effects of non-response and self-selection biases. *See* TRC, "Non-Response Bias in Survey Sampling," GreenBook, Dec. 7, 2009, *available at* http://www.greenbook.org/marketing-research.cfm/non-response-bias; "Selection Bias, Psychology Wiki," *available at* http://psychology.wikia.com/wiki/Selection_bias.

[69]As quoted in Segal, *supra* note 5.

[70]Larry Reibstein, "How Law Schools are Ripping Off Students, Enron-Like," Forbes.com, Jan. 9, 2011, *available at* http://blogs.forbes.com/larryreibstein/2011/01/09/how-law-schools-are-ripping-off-students-enron-like/.

[71]*Id.*

[72]*See* Mary Kate Sheridan, "The Future of Legal Education: Stop Resisting and Get Creative," Vault.com, Mar. 2, 2011, *available at* http://www.vault.com/wps/portal/usa/blogs/entry-detail/?blog_id=1260&entry_id=12815.

[73]*See* Law School Transparency website, *available at* http://www.lawschooltransparency.com.

[74]Sergei Lemberg, "Why Law School Grads are Getting Collection Calls," Stop Collector Blog, Jan. 10, 2011, *available at* http://www.stopcollector.com/blog/2011/01/why-law-school-grads-are-getting-collection-calls/.

[75]*See* ABA Commission, *supra* note 32.

school."[76] It seems the ABA is beginning to realize the truly influential role that misleading employment figures play in student choice to attend law school. Also in December 2010, the ABA held a two-day meeting to discuss the collection of job placement data and "whether it should refine the questions in its surveys in order to get more realistic and useful statistics for the *U.S. News* rankings,"[77] a question to which of course the answer is emphatically yes.

It is not surprising that schools are "remarkably resistant to change,"[78] considering that Secretary of Education Arne Duncan describes them as "cash cows."[79] In law schools, the Socratic Method style of teaching enables the increase of class sizes without schools incurring additional expenses.[80] A recent law graduate described the law school business as one "big Ponzi scheme," in which schools are "cranking kids out for $45,000 a year."[81] Of course, tuition hikes during a recession are insensitive and irresponsible, but the economics of supply and demand dictate that law schools, as businesses, are behaving the way they should be. Schools have no incentive, at least economically, to charge lower tuition as long as students continue to enroll in increasing numbers.[82] The dean of the University of Baltimore School of Law, Philip Closius, acknowledged the dilemma for law schools: "There are millions of dollars riding on students' decisions about where to go to law school, and that creates real institutional pressures."[83] In addition, the increase in student demand to attend

---

[76]Stephanie Landsman, "Getting Schooled in Law Loans," CNBC.com, Dec. 31, 2010, *available at* http://www.cnbc.com/id/40863598/Getting_Schooled_in_Law_Loans.

[77]Segal, *supra* note 5; *see also* Kwoh, *supra* note 34 ("The ABA, which is in the middle of a three-year review of its accreditation process, last week appointed a committee to study how schools can more accurately report their job placement and salary figures, said Donald Polden, who is heading the effort.").

[78]Sheridan, *supra* note 72.

[79]Jessica Rettig, "Law School Grads Face Tougher Economic Times," U.S. News & World Report, Apr. 15, 2010, *available at* http://www.usnews.com/education/best-graduate-schools/top-law-schools/paying/articles/2010/04/15/law-school-grads-face-tougher-economic-times.

[80]Segal, *supra* note 5. "'If you're a law school and you add 25 kids to your class, that's a million dollars, and you don't even have to hire another teacher,' says Allen Tanenbaum, a lawyer in Atlanta who led the American Bar Association's commission on the impact of the economic crisis on the profession and legal needs. 'That additional income goes straight to the bottom line.'" *Id.*

[81]Kwoh, *supra* note 34. A former clerk to Supreme Court Justice Ruth Bader Ginsberg and legal commentator, David Franklin, described the situation as such: "Law schools ... are profit centers.... Overhead costs are low, financial aid is the exception rather than the rule.... The Socratic method allows law schools to maintain a high student-to-teacher (tuition-to-salary) ratio." Jason M. Dolin, *Opportunity Lost: How Law School Disappoints Law Students, the Public, and the Legal Profession*, 44 Cal. W. L. Rev. 219, 231-32 (Fall 2007) (quoting David Franklin, "Trials of Socrates," Slate, July 31, 1997, *available at* http://www.slate.com/id/3133/).

[82]Rettig, *supra* note 79; *see also* Donovan, *supra* note 37 ("The nation's law schools continue to enroll an increasing number of students. In 2010, the number of J.D. degrees granted by law schools was 11.5 percent higher than in 2000.").

[83]Segal, *supra* note 5.

law school has lead to new law school openings, which further compounds the debt problem by increasing the number of students attending law school (and paying dearly to do so).[84]

On a more positive note, not all schools are continuing to behave immorally and irresponsibly. In 2011, two New York law schools have committed to reduce their class sizes by ten students.[85] Dean of Touro Law Lawrence Raful explains the decision: "I don't think the [job] placement situation is going to turn around for a number of years and I think we are concerned about the ethics of turning out quite so many students in debt when we know that not everyone can get a job to pay off that debt."[86] It is inconceivable to absolve law schools of any blame for the insurmountable debt their students graduate with after three years of legal education. The legal profession prides itself on the tenets of "knowing-and-intelligent waiver, informed consent, and full disclosure of all material facts (including avoiding the omission of facts required to make the facts disclosed not misleading)."[87] It would be counterintuitive for schools seeking to groom lawyers to practice these foundational principles to ignore the same principles when enticing students to enroll. Accordingly, schools must take some responsibility for their deception in providing unrealistic economic data to prospective attendees and, as such, should be forced to change this behavior or bear some responsibility for the consequences.

IV. Others to Blame: Law Schools Are Not Alone

Law schools are not the only ones to blame: state bar associations, the United States government, *U.S. News and World Report,* and law students themselves deserve to shoulder a portion of the responsibility for the large post-graduation student debt totals. First, state bar associations mandate that prospective legal practitioners earn a degree from an ABA-accredited law school before sitting for the bar exam.[88] Initially, this mandate served as a barrier to entry to limit the number of lawyers, but recently it has instead driven up the cost of legal education, placing it in high demand — and, in turn, has heightened the cost of legal services.[89] The requirement that students attend law school, instead of being able to apprentice for a number of years before sitting for the bar exam, creates a continuing subsidy to the legal education system while simultaneously imposing burdensome debt upon students with no alternative way of entering the legal profession.

---

[84]Dolin, *supra* note 81, at 227.

[85]Mary Kate Sheridan, "Reducing Law School Class Size," Vault.com, Mar. 4, 2011, *available at* http://www.vault.com/wps/portal/usa/blogs/entry-detail?blog_id=1260&entry_id=12835.

[86]*Id.*

[87]Donovan, *supra* note 37.

[88]George Leef, "Re: Law Schools Imitate Enron," National Review Online, Jan. 10, 2011, *available at* http://www.nationalreview.com/phi-beta-cons/256773/re-law-schools-imitate-enron-george-leef.

[89]*Id.*

The United States government is another institution that deserves some responsibility for the student debt mess. As mentioned in Section II, changes to loan forgiveness policies in the past, and a failure to act during the current recession, have further exacerbated student loan problems.[90] Few, if any, consumer protections exist to protect students from themselves. Critics against these sorts of policies may argue the government has no right to intervene with who can attend school; however, the government intervenes in many other areas for which its involvement is for the betterment of society and its citizens, and higher education represents another area that needs assistance. If the federal government intervened and changed loan policies by requiring lenders to impose similar standards for school loans like small business loans, then many students would not be burdened with astronomical debt.[91] If a student had to sit before a banker and explain his plan to repay the loans, he may rethink the decision altogether or have it made for him by banks refusing to lend. The U.S. government has the power to get involved and, for the betterment of society, it should.

This article has mentioned *U.S. News and World Report* numerous times because its rankings represent an integral part of the decision-making process for many, if not all, prospective law students. Furthermore, because of the importance of the *U.S. News* rankings, schools feel the need to "keep up with the Joneses" to maintain or improve their position. *The Wall Street Journal* asserts that "[p]rospective students are voracious readers of the annual *U.S. News* rankings" and rely on them as influential forces dictating their law school decisions.[92] Critics of the rankings do not discount their appeal. Observers describe the rankings as "a quick and convenient way to get a good part [of the story] and to see how law schools compare to one another with respect to important relevant criteria."[93] Despite the widespread discussion about the unreliability of some of its statistics, the rankings remain in high demand.

U.S. News is a business seeking to sell magazines. Despite the importance of the information it provides, the magazine will continue to cater to its audience and tailor the information to what customers, in this case prospective students, want to read — and that is generally the rosy kind, portraying a positive outlook. One of the problematic aspects of the rankings is that they correlate heavily to cost-related inputs by schools, such as per-student expenditures, student-faculty ratio, and library resources, none of which are indicative of future employment prospects.[94] Despite all of the benefits the rankings

---

[90]*See* Section II, Bursting the Student Loan Bubble: A Mortgage-Like Crisis?, *supra*.

[91]Elie Mystal, "Now That the New York Times Acknowledges the Perils of Law School Debt, the Next Question is How to Recover From the Ruin," Above the Law, Jan. 10, 2011, *available at* http://abovethelaw.com/2011/01/now-that-the-new-york-times-acknowledges-the-perils-of-law-school-debt-the-next-question-is-how-to-recover-from-the-ruin/.

[92]Amir Efrati, "Law School Rankings Reviewed to Deter 'Gaming,'" Wall St. J., Aug. 26, 2008, *available at* http://online.wsj.com/article/SB121971712700771731.html.

[93]Mitchell Berger, *Why the U.S. News and World Report Law School Rankings are Both Useful and Important*, 51 J. Legal Educ. 487, 498 (2001).

[94]Yuda, *supra* note 12, at 24. (Critic Jeffrey Evans Stakes of Indiana University Law School explained in an essay for the *Indiana Law Journal* in 2006 that "[t]he *U.S. News*

present to law schools and the magazine, neither party encourages prospective students to rely solely on the magazine rankings when making an enrollment decision.[95] Nevertheless, it is clear that students rely heavily upon the rankings. As a result, if the law schools will not change their reporting of statistics, *U.S. News*, in order to meet the desires of its student consumers, must demand different information to provide a more accurate picture, or else it also is culpable for the egregious student debt fiasco. *U.S. News* editor Brian Kelly recently sent a letter to law school deans explaining his support for advocate group Law School Transparency and its goal of making accurate employment data more widely available. Kelly wrote, "[I]t is not in anyone's interest — especially that of prospective students — to have less than accurate data being put out by law schools. It's creating a crisis of confidence in the law school sector that is unnecessary and we think could be easily fixed."[96]

The last group that deserves to bear responsibility for the student debt crisis is, of course, the students. Despite the tone of this article, in no way does it contend that students do not deserve a portion of the blame. In fact, students deserve most of the blame.[97] Aspiring lawyers should be intelligent and analytical — and if taking every piece of information at face value is an indication of these students' future prowess then perhaps the legal field is not for them. One critic equates law school admissions offices with the leasing office of an apartment rental company, challenging students to delve deeper beyond the numbers offered on their face: "Why take their numbers at face value when they may have an agenda."[98]

---

rankings have created incentives for schools to teach to the bar exam, spend money on glossy publications, raise tuition, increase the number of transfer students and admit students according to their bubble ability (their aptitude for taking multiple-choice standardized exams) rather than their prospects for contributing to the learning environment at the law school or their prospects for becoming effective and responsible lawyers." *Id.*).

[95]Shah, *supra* note 6, at 853 (citing U.S. News & World Report, "How to Use Our Lists Wisely," Apr. 22, 2009, *available at* http://www.usnews.com/articles/education/best-graduate-schools/2009/04/22/how-to-use-our-lists-wisely-2010.html; and Law Deans' Statement, *available at* http://www.lsac.org/choosing/deans-speak-out-rankings.asp).

[96]David Lat, "Quote of the Day: Well, it might be in *some* people's interest...," Above the Law, Mar. 11, 2011, *available at* http://abovethelaw.com/2011/03/quote-of-the-day-well-it-might-be-in-some-peoples-interest. Kelly continued, "Specifically, employment after graduation is relevant data that prospective students and other consumers should be entitled to. Many graduate business schools are meticulous about collecting such data, even having it audited. The entire law school sector is perceived to be less than candid because it does not pursue a similar, disciplined approach to data collection and reporting." *Id.*

[97]Certainly, schools should not provide prospective students with misleading information, and *U.S. News* should demand more accurate data from these schools. Yes, state bar associations should allow aspiring lawyers alternative routes into the profession (i.e., bypassing law school), and the federal government should support additional loan forgiveness policies. Nevertheless, students still must take responsibility for their own actions and that includes willingly incurring burdensome debts.

[98]Broke Professionals, "3 Things to Do Before Deciding to Further Your Education," Jan. 10, 2011, *available at* http://brokeprofessionals.com/2011/01/10/3-things-to-do-before-deciding-to-further-your-education/.

Too often, students resort to finger-pointing or rely on entitlement, naïveté, and ignorance as excuses as to why they are swimming in debt. These excuses are unacceptable. ABA President Carolyn Lamm instructs prospective law students to "look at the numbers and envision how their future might be before going to law school, not after."[99] Professor Herwig Schlunk of Vanderbilt University blames students for failing to research the true economic costs and benefits of a law degree,[100] information that exists throughout the internet, including the blogosphere. Professor Schlunk criticizes, "It's kind of blindly accepted that education in general, and legal education in particular, is always worth the money."[101] *Vault* editor Mary Kate Sheridan echoes this sentiment, proclaiming that "[l]aw school provides an education, not a golden ticket to a corner office and six-figure salary."[102] Law school graduate and blogger Kimber Russell points to a "not me" attitude as a reason for student debt: "Even if you tell them the bottom has fallen out of the legal market, they're all convinced that none of the bad stuff will happen to them. It's a serious, life-altering decision, going to law school, and you're dealing with a lot of naïve students who have never had jobs, never paid real bills."[103]

Again, the information is available. It may not be the easiest to find, but the number of anti-law school blogs increase daily, offering information to aid prospective students in making attendance decisions. The blogs are not hiding their intentions with names like *Exposing the Law School Scam, The Jobless Juris Doctor, Law School Must be Debunked,* and *Shilling Me Softly.*[104] The ball is in students' courts. They can no longer sit idly by and let schools paint the picture for them. Students must be active in seeking out the information to aid their decision making, because ultimately it is their lives that insurmountable debts will affect, not those of law school deans or administrators.

V. A Cry for Help, A Call to Arms: What Can Law Students Do?

So what can students do? An important response is to keep talking and get the information out there. Bloggers are doing their parts. Current students must confront their administrations to provide better information. If every dean across the country would consider it unethical to graduate students with enormous debts and meager job prospects to pay off these obligations[105] — and then affect change by acting upon this feeling — then perhaps the country could

---

[99]Kwoh, *supra* note 34.

[100]Rettig, *supra* note 79.

[101]*Id.*

[102]Sheridan, *supra* note 3.

[103]Lemberg, *supra* note 74.

[104]On the Net, "Anti-Law School Blogs Multiplying," KEYTLaw, Mar. 27, 2010, *available at* http://www.keytlaw.com/blog/2010/03/anti-law-school-blogs-multiplying/. Other blogs include *Big Debt, Small Law; But I Did Everything Right; Subprime JD; Rose Colored Glasses; Third Tier Reality; Waitress J.D.;* and *Shit Law Jobs.*

[105]*See* Sheridan, *supra* note 85.

begin to limit student debt, which seems to be spiraling further out of control. Additionally, professors and practicing lawyers must continue to advocate for future generations of lawyers because, in the end, if students can graduate law school without having to resort to indentured servitude to pay off egregious loan sums, the legal field will be better off. Young lawyers will be able to pursue public interest careers without stressing about how to pay the next loan installment.

If schools refuse to provide the appropriate information, then what should students do next? One response may be a lawsuit. Some critics believe that "[s]ooner or later the lawyers will file class action lawsuits against the law schools for misrepresentation, failure to disclose material facts and other possible causes of action."[106] Of course, this is not the ideal solution, but it may be the last resort beyond boycotting attendance. If the ABA revises Standard 509 to more explicitly address employment data, such as providing the number of jobs in the "private sector, public interest, business, and government jobs"[107] and their salary amounts, then students will have a more accurate picture upon which to base their decisions. With this information, students will have even less of an excuse for incurring large debts.

The argument for informational transparency is not new. Two decades ago, the MacCrate Report acknowledged, "Law school administrators know the strengths and weaknesses of their own institutions and should be candid in discussing them with applicants."[108] If schools will not do this willingly, then students must scream and shout until they do. If students will not fight for themselves, then no one will ... and that would be the biggest shame of all.

---

[106]On the Net, "Irate Law School Grads Say They Were Misled About Job Prospects," KEYTLaw, Aug. 16, 2010, *available at* http://www.keytlaw.com/blog/2010/08/irate-law-school-grads/. There has been at least one prior case of a student suing law schools for providing misleading data. *See Bank v. Brooklyn Law School*, 2000 WL 1692844 (E.D.N.Y. 2000). Recently, a Boston College third-year law student wrote an open letter to the school's dean asking for his tuition money back. Jessica Heslam, "BC Law student asks for money back," Boston Herald, Oct. 20, 2010, *available at* http://www.bostonherald.com/news/regional/view/20101020bc_law_student_asks_fo r__back/srvc=home&position=3.

[107]Shah *supra* note 6, at 854.

[108]Thies, *supra* note 9 (citing ABA Section of Legal Educ. & Admissions to the Bar, *Report of the Task Force on Law Schools and the Profession: Narrowing the Gap*, at 228 (1992)).

5

The Impending Student Debt Crisis: Reducing the Size of a Looming Bubble

Anastasia Caton

I. Introduction: The Looming Student Debt Crisis

From grade school forward, Americans are trained to believe in the American Dream. Every American has the potential to succeed with a little elbow grease and hard work. The fruits of success include home ownership and a college education. Even if an American cannot afford to purchase something outright, he can set up a repayment plan with his bank and eventually own that minivan for transporting his kids to soccer practice and that home in the suburbs with the white picket fence. After all, he has worked hard to support his family and he deserves something to show for it.

By late 2008, Americans were abruptly forced to understand the realistic implications of financing something that they could not afford. The sub-prime mortgage crisis, characterized by a tangled web of credit default swaps and mortgage-backed securities, is complicated. But the reason for the mortgage bubble bursting is relatively simple and intuitive, regardless of which way the facts are presented: Americans were taking out loans they could not possibly afford to pay back; lenders and real estate agents were handing out loans to people who would undoubtedly default. When people began defaulting on loans en masse, the bubble burst and banks began foreclosing on homes. Within months, the entire economy, which as it turns out was inextricably interwoven with these toxic loans (thanks to the credit default swaps and mortgage-backed securities), crumbled to its knees in the worst recession since the Great Depression.

Suppose that thousands of American college graduates began plunging into the exact same situation as did their parents and their parents' peers: borrowing money they may never be able to afford to pay back. Suppose this debt, unlike the relief of a foreclosure, survives bankruptcy. Suppose, also, that the lender was not a predatory mortgage company, but was instead the federal government. And finally, suppose that the career these students chose to pursue had erected bars to entering the field with massive quantities of debt. These young people are simply pursuing their own American Dream: an *education*, not some McMansion in Dallas. This is a path to a career, and a lucrative one at that. But what happens when the profession these students chose dries up and they cannot leverage the education for increased income? What happens if all of these debtors default en masse?[1]

---

[1]Numerous bloggers and journalists compare the impending student loan crisis with the sub-prime mortgage crisis. This is a useful comparison because student loan lenders, like mortgage companies, are dishing out mortgage-sized loans to young, vulnerable

This is the looming student debt crisis. Contrary to what some critics assert, it will not unfold in the same way as the sub-prime mortgage crisis[2] for at least two of the reasons suggested above: (1) student debt is non-dischargeable;[3] and (2) the federal government is the lender.

Recently, the news has been filled with the woes of recent law school graduates who have taken on $100,000 or more in debt[4] to fund a professional education that trains them to work in a market in which demand has plummeted.[5] Countless blogs are devoted to imputing responsibility to a wide cast of characters: law schools for manipulating employment numbers; *U.S. News and World Report* for not holding law schools accountable for their numbers; the American Bar Association for accrediting too many schools when demand is down; state bar associations for withholding licenses from recent graduates as a result of their massive amounts of debt; law professors for making too much money; law students themselves for not doing their homework; the federal

---

people so that those eager students may pursue the American dream of obtaining higher education. Unfortunately, the economy has contracted to the point where recent college and professional school graduates cannot find employment. The sub-prime crisis was characterized by homes that were vastly overpriced when initially purchased, and real estate agents who targeted people they were certain had no way of repaying the loan. When a mortgagee could only afford to make minimum payments, he had no shot at owning a home, much less avoiding default within his lifetime. Along the same lines, although the proposition of financing an education *seemed* worthwhile at the outset, a freshly minted college graduate entering a bleak economy with no or very low income cannot possibly be expected to repay his student loans. The college graduate will either default or never repay the loan within his lifetime.

[2]One blogger has also likened the law student debt crisis to General Motors' bankruptcy. This is another useful comparison for at least grabbing the attention of taxpayers, who bore the burden of bailing out GM. The comparison is also useful because it targets law and other professional schools specifically. Law school is a means to ultimately a profitable career, as opposed to an end in and of itself, like a college education, a house, or a car. In that sense, according to this author, borrowing for law schools is analogous to GM's issuing bonds to reinvest in an effort to turn a profit. Although the GM comparison is helpful, I chose the sub-prime crisis here because the looming bubble of student debt is not confined to only lawyers; college graduates coming out of elite institutions cannot find jobs. Although college students borrow in smaller proportions and less money than law students, the fact of their debt and bleak employment prospects makes this issue salient to many more Americans. *See Law Student Debt and the GM Bankruptcy*, Law School Labyrinth (www.lawschoollabyrinth.com).

[3]11 U.S.C. § 523(a)(8)(B). Under the bankruptcy code, student loan debt is one of only 19 forms of non-dischargeable debt. Some scholars refer to student loan debt as "conditionally dischargeable" because the debt can in fact be discharged if the debtor is able to meet the high threshold of showing "undue hardship" would result from continued payment on the debt. *See* Rafael L. Pardo & Michelle R. Lacey, *Undue Hardship in the Bankruptcy Courts: An Empirical Assessment of the Discharge of Educational Debt*, 74 U. Cin. L. Rev. 405 (2005).

[4]Transcript, *Panel Discussion: The Cost of Law School and the Burden of Law School Debt* 2 (Apr. 27, 2004), New York City Bar Association (*available at* http://www.abcny.org/pdf/report/PanelDiscussionABCNYMeeting-42704.pdf).

[5]David Segal, *Is Law School a Losing Game?*, New York Times, Jan. 8, 2011 (*available at* http://www.nytimes.com/2011/01/09/business/09law.html).

government for continuing to lend money to students to attend "third" and "fourth tier" law schools. But the blame game with student debt, like the blame game with the sub-prime mortgage crisis, is inappropriate, counterproductive, and confusing.

This chapter is dedicated to understanding the heart of this problem and proposing options for managing the problem. Part II analyzes the development of law student lending as it relates directly to changing costs of education. Part III describes how the law, and bankruptcy courts in particular, handle the issue of student debt. Part IV describes the legal profession's response to rising law student debt as graduates are evaluated in the character and fitness portion of bar exams. Part V is an analysis of future issues that will arise for the profession and proposes options for the profession to manage the reality of its members practicing with extreme levels of debt.

II. Bills, Bills, Bills:
The Skyrocketing Cost of Education

Four years of college is expensive. Tacking on three more years of education at the end of that experience not only means foregoing three years of income (incurring what economists describe as an "opportunity cost") but also means paying even more money for the additional education.[6] If parents or savings will not cover the cost of professional school, the student must take out loans that he or she will eventually have to repay because student debt is non-dischargeable. The only rational reason for doing such a thing is either that the additional education is free or largely subsidized or because the additional education will reap benefits far beyond its costs. Most students applying to law school take on this burden for the latter reason — in essence, investment. For many years before 2007, this was a rational decision. Not only was law school cheaper than it is now, but the legal market was lucrative.[7] Accredited law schools were fewer in number and demand was high. Taking out a loan to cover tuition and cost of living was a reasonable decision under the circumstances because such a career would eventually pay off. Even if the legal market dipped and a law graduate could not find employment in the profession, the loan payments would not be unmanageable on a non-lawyer salary.

The average price of private law school education between 1990 and 2003 increased 118%; for out-of-state public law schools the figure was 173%; for in-state public law schools the figure was 234%.[8] Perhaps law schools saw how extravagantly the upper echelons of the profession were living. Perhaps legal academia wanted a piece of the pie; the average starting salary in private prac-

---

[6]*See* Herwig Schlunk, *Mamas Don't Let Your Babies Grow Up To Be...Lawyers*, Working Paper No. 09-29, at SSRN No. 1497044 (2009) (comparing the earnings of a student who did not attend law school with his J.D. counterpart).

[7]From the 1980s until the present, the cost of law school has increased at between double and triple the rate of inflation. Maimon Schwarzschild, *The Ethics and Economics of American Legal Education Today*, Research Paper No. 08-032, 5 (July 2008).

[8]John A. Sebert, *Cost and Financing of Legal Education*, Syllabus, Vol. 35, No. 2, Table A (Feb. 2004).

tice rose 80% over the same period.[9] But during the 1990s and 2000s, the cost of legal education skyrocketed, far outpacing consumer prices.[10] Whatever the explanation for the exponential rise in tuition costs, it is likely unrelated to the costs associated with running a law school. The total expenditures of law schools between 1990 and 2003 increased by only 70%.[11] As David Segal posits in his *New York Times* article, large lecture halls and no lab or other expensive equipment to purchase or maintain keep costs low for law schools.[12] Maimon Schwarzschild adds that increased scholarship by professors, facilitated by reduced teaching loads, leads to greater expenditures on professor salaries.[13]

Whatever the cause of rising costs, the result was that the total volume of law school loans grew threefold.[14] This was most likely a function of an increase in four areas: (1) the number of students forced to take out loans; (2) the amount of tuition the loans covered; (3) the number of students choosing to attend law school; and (4) the number of ABA accredited law schools.[15] The latter two phenomena will be addressed later in the chapter with regard to the impact of debt on the legal profession and proposed solutions for coping with this unavoidable problem. The data on the first two is more recent than the rise in tuition data, which dates through 2003.

According to the ABA, in 2008 the average student attending a public law school took on around $71,436 in debt to finance his or her legal education; that same figure for private law schools was $91,506.[16] It comes as no surprise that, in light of the recession, data from 2009 will be even bleaker. The ABA predicts that more students will borrow more money as a result of increasing tuition and less parental contribution during the recession.[17]

These numbers are significant, but as any economist knows, they mean nothing unless they can be compared alongside the alternative of not attending law school. This alternative of not attending law school, as mentioned previously, is called the "opportunity cost," and it reflects the lost earnings of a student during the three years that he or she attended law school. In a recent economic analysis, Herwig Schlunk questioned the profitability of attending

---

[9]Between 1991 and 2001, starting salaries in private practice grew 80%, from $50,000 to $90,000. Adele Waldman, *In Debt from Day One*, Christian Science Monitor (Mar. 9, 2004) (*available at* http://www.csmonitor.com/2004/0309/p11s01-legn.html).

[10]During the 13-year period between 1990 and 2003, the Consumer Price Index rose by 41%. Sebert, *supra* note 8, at Table A.

[11]Sebert, *supra* note 8, at Table B.

[12]David Segal, *Is Law School a Losing Game?*, New York Times, Jan. 8, 2011 (*available at* http://www.nytimes.com/2011/01/09/business/09law.html).

[13]Schwarzschild, *supra* note 7, at 7.

[14]Sebert, *supra* note 8, at Table C.

[15]Between 2000 and 2009, law schools awarded 11.5% more J.D.s. During that same period, the number of ABA accredited law schools grew by 9%. Annie Lowrey, *A Case of Supply v. Demand*, Slate (Oct. 27, 2010) (www.slate.com).

[16]*The Value Proposition of Attending Law School*, ABA Commission on the Impact of the Economic Crisis on the Profession and Legal Needs (Nov. 2009).

[17]Most public law schools were raising tuition by 10-25% in the year of the study. *Id.*

law school.[18] Using mathematical figures, Schlunk examined three hypothetical law students. The analysis considered factors such as what these students would have made in the non-legal job market during their three years in law school, the total cost of attendance of law school (including living expenses), money earned at summer associate positions, estimated salary figures (taking into account the great disparity between Biglaw positions and all other legal jobs), and future earnings based on an assumption of increasing productivity with experience. Schlunk's conclusion, as the title of the article suggests, was "Mamas Don't Let Your Babies Grow up to Be ... Lawyers." In other words, law school is not a profitable proposition unless the stars align.

Schlunk suggests that the undergraduate English major who is able to attend law school at Harvard and secure a Biglaw job upon graduation is economically sound in the long run because this student would likely not have earned very much with only an English degree. At the same time, this presumption does not account for the type of student who would earn admission to Harvard and how she or he would fair in the non-legal job market. Schlunk acknowledges that the study cannot account for individual differences such as these and encourages individuals to do their own cost-benefit analyses according to their particular circumstances. Moreover, he acknowledges that the study omits any valuation on the "prestige" of earning a law degree because, according to Schlunk, "you can't eat prestige."[19]

Schlunk's study is useful for at least highlighting the hidden costs of attending law school. Add three years of lost earnings to the cost of tuition and the price of law school increases dramatically, although an engineer's costs would rise more than those of a public policy studies major. Financing a legal education is no small feat. With most graduates entering the profession with at least $100,000 in debt and small chances of making a six-figure salary to repay that debt,[20] what happens when graduates default under the weight of the loans?

III. A Fresh Start: Student Loan Debt in Bankruptcy

Earlier, I asked what would happen if a law graduate could not find a job to repay the overwhelming burden of student loans. Now I will address how the world of bankruptcy and debtor-creditor law handles default student loan debt. This section will focus on overall student loans rather than specifically on law school loans. Bankruptcy law lumps all student debt as one because, for the

---

[18]Herwig Schlunck, *Mamas Don't Let Your Babies Grow Up To Be...Lawyers,*Working Paper No. 09-29, at SSRN No. 1497044 (2009).

[19]*Id.*

[20]According to a survey by the National Association of Legal Placement (NALP), among the graduating law school class of 2008, only 23% started with a salary of $160,000. Within that same cohort, 42% started with salaries of $60,000 or less. Thus, the smaller percentage of graduates clustered around the higher salary mark raise disproportionately the average salary of all law school graduates to around $100,000. The reality of this bimodal pay structure is that most starting lawyers barely earn above half of six figures. *See* NALP, *Jobs & JD's: Employment and Salaries of New Law Graduates*, 18-19 (2009).

most part, no functional difference exists between loans. In addition, many students enter graduate school already saddled with some amount of debt from undergraduate education loans.[21]

Unsurprisingly, student loans defaults rose as the recession hit. According to the United States Department of Education, between 2007 and 2008, the student loan default rate rose 22%, from 6.7% to 7.0% of all borrowers who entered repayment in 2008 defaulting on their loans.[22] In so doing, the rate inched closer to the national credit card loan default rate of 8.8% and mortgage default rate of 9.1%.[23] For those weighed down by credit card debt or an unmanageable mortgage, federal bankruptcy court is a place to seek relief. Typically, unsecured debt incurred from credit cards can be discharged in a bankruptcy.[24] This means that when a debtor gets his or her "fresh start," the credit card debt is wiped clean with the major consequence being that the debtor will have difficulty obtaining credit cards and other forms of finance in the future. Depending on the debtor's assets and income, he or she may be required to repay a portion of this debt in a payment plan lasting no more than five years. However, student loan debt is one of the very few forms of debt that survives bankruptcy to continue burdening the debtor. When the average student is taking out almost $100,000 in loans, this is hardly a fresh start.

A. The History: The Abusive Student Debtor

With the passage of the Higher Education Act of 1965, the federal government began guaranteeing on behalf of students the interest and principal on private

---

[21]This treatment does not take into account the fact that a law school loan is more like leverage than is a college loan (although presumably both will yield returns on investment). As described *supra*, at note 1, a law school loan is made almost exclusively in anticipation of a particular increase in returns in the form of a higher salary than a non-legal career. However, in the world of bankruptcy, the risk and expected pay-off undertaken by the lender yields to considerations such as giving the debtor a fresh start and the debtor's ability to pay. All student loan debt is non-dischargeable presumably because, unlike a car or home loan, the lender cannot reclaim any tangible capital from the debtor to satisfy the debt. The standard for the rare instance of discharging student debt focuses on the debtor's hardship and the subject matter of the loan rather than the lender's risk assessment. For this reason, my legal analysis of student debt will focus on student debt generally rather than the particularized instance of law student debt.

[22]United States Department of Education, *Student Loan Default Rate Increases* (Sept. 13, 2010) (www.ed.gov).

[23]*Student Debt Crisis Threatens U.S. Economy*, International Business Times (Dec. 28, 2010) (www.ibtimes.com).

[24]Student loan debt is also unsecured, meaning that if the debtor defaults, the creditor has nothing to seize in return for payment. Unlike a home, which is a secured form of debt that can be foreclosed upon and resold by the bank, the information and experiences captured in a college graduate's mind and memory can never be taken away. *See* Kevin C. Driscoll, Jr., *Eradicating the 'Discharge by Declaration' for Student Loan Debt in Chapter 13*, 2000 U. Ill. L. Rev. 1311, 1315 (2000); *see also* Steven Jackson, *Heavy Backpacks: Res Judicata and Appropriate Notice to Creditors During a Student Loan Discharge in Bankruptcy*, 12 U. Pa. J. Bus. L. 235, 238 (2009).

student loans.[25] As a result, loans were made readily available for many people who could not afford higher education.[26] The purpose underlying this action was to expand access to education. Until 1976, student loan debt was dischargeable in bankruptcy.[27] Although at the time less than one percent of federally insured student loans were discharged in bankruptcy, Congress revised the Higher Education Act to exempt federally guaranteed student loans from the forms of dischargeable debt in bankruptcy.[28] The purpose was to prevent abuse of the system.[29] Proposals for the new Bankruptcy Code (passed in 1977) included a provision that would repeal the non-dischargeability amendment in the Higher Education Act.[30] Ultimately, the proposal was defeated by opponents in Congress who feared abuse of the system: students would graduate from college and immediately file for bankruptcy to absolve the debt before starting out. Creditors would be left without recourse because, unlike a car or boat, an education cannot be reclaimed or liquidated.[31] The resulting Bankruptcy Code demarcated that the only way a debtor with student loans can have her or his loans discharged is by showing, in an adversarial proceeding against the creditor, that continuing payment on the loans would result in "undue hardship."[32] Despite subsequent revisions to other portions of the student debt provision, Congress has never defined undue hardship in the context of student loan discharge, leaving the courts responsible for crafting a definition.[33]

---

[25]Kevin C. Driscoll, Jr., *Eradicating the 'Discharge by Declaration' for Student Loan Debt in Chapter 13*, 2000 U. Ill. L. Rev. 1311, 1313 (2000).

[26]4 Collier on Bankruptcy ¶ 523.14[1] (Alan N. Resnick & Henry J. Sommers, eds., 15th ed. rev. 2009).

[27]Rafael L. Pardo & Michelle R. Lacey, *Undue Hardship in the Bankruptcy Courts: An Empirical Assessment of the Discharge of Educational Debt*, 74 U. Cin. L. Rev. 405, 420 (2005).

[28]*Id.* at 420.

[29]*Id.*

[30]*Id.* at 423.

[31]*See id.* at 423-27 (describing the contentious legislative history behind the student loan debt provision in the Bankruptcy Code).

[32]Courts have held that there is one way in which a debtor may avoid an adversarial proceeding. In a Chapter 13 bankruptcy, which includes a repayment plan, a debtor may include in the plan language indicating that confirmation of the plan constitutes an adjudication on the issue of "undue hardship." Thus, when the plan is confirmed, the debtor is entitled to discharge of some or all of the student loan debt. Student loan creditors, challenging on due process grounds the denial of an adversarial proceeding, usually lose. *See* Driscoll, 2000 U. Ill. L. Rev. at 1312-13 (describing the process for discharging student loan debt by petition rather than adversarial proceeding).

[33]Pardo & Lacey, 74 U. Cin. L. Rev. at 427-28. The last part of this section will discuss how Congress recently defined "undue hardship" in a context other than student loan discharge.

B. Judicial Treatment of Dischargeability:
The Circuits Split

Courts employ an ad hoc approach when answering the question of undue hardship. Depending upon the combination of given facts, the bankruptcy court determines whether the debtor is attempting to abuse the bankruptcy system or whether the debtor is truly unable to repay the debts.[34] The circuit courts do not all agree on a single factual situation that will lead to a finding of undue hardship, but most courts follow the Second Circuit's *Brunner* test.[35] Under *Brunner*, the debtor must show "(1) that she cannot maintain, based on current income and expenses, a minimal standard of living for herself and her dependents if forced to repay the loans; (2) that additional circumstances exist indicating that this state of affairs is likely to persist for a significant portion of the repayment period of the student loans; and (3) that the debtor made a good faith effort to repay the loans."[36] All three prongs must be fulfilled to meet the standard.

The Eighth Circuit, on the other hand, applies a "totality of the circumstances" test that is more flexible. The Eighth Circuit considers "(1) the debtor's past, present, and reasonably reliable future financial resources; (2) a calculation of the debtor's and her dependents' reasonable necessary living expenses; and (3) any other relevant facts and circumstances."[37] In *Long v. Education Credit Management Corp.*, the Eighth Circuit expressly rejected the *Brunner* test for undue hardship, finding it too restrictive.[38] The court explained that the vagueness contained in the bankruptcy code justified a flexible totality-of-the-circumstances test and held that it would consider carefully each debtor's special circumstances in making the undue hardship determination.[39] Thus the primary difference between *Brunner* and the Eighth Circuit's standard is that the Eighth Circuit does not require that a debtor have made a good faith effort to repay her loans.[40]

In the eight years since the Eighth Circuit decided *Long*, the Supreme Court has yet to resolve the circuit split as to whether the standard should be ad hoc or bright-line for determining undue hardship. The major practical difference in the circuit split is that a student loan debtor who has not made any payments on the loan and is attempting to have his student loan debt discharged would be automatically disqualified from relief in all circuits but the Eighth Circuit. If the Supreme Court were to settle the split, thereby signaling what significance should be given to good faith attempts to repay the debt, the impact on undue hardship determinations would likely be minimal. Recent

---

[34]Driscroll, 2000 U. Ill. L. Rev. at 1318.

[35]Jackson, 12 U. Pa. J. Bus. L. at 239.

[36]*Brunner v. New York State Higher Education Services Corp.*, 831 F.2d 395, 396 (2d Cir. 1987).

[37]*Long v. Educ. Credit Mgmt. Corp.*, 322 F.3d 549, 554 (8th Cir. 2003).

[38]*Long*, 322 F.3d at 553.

[39]*Id.* at 554-55.

[40]Jackson, 12 U. Pa. J. Bus. L. at 240.

data suggest that the great majority of debtors attempting to discharge student loan debt in bankruptcy fit the model of someone who has been out of school for almost two decades and has attempted to repay his loans or made efforts to relieve the debt by other means, such as deferment, forbearance, and negotiating a repayment plan with the creditor.[41] Moreover, the rate of finding undue hardship under the *Brunner* test is around 49%; the rate of finding undue hardship under the Eighth Circuit totality-of-the-circumstances test is 46%.[42] This difference is not statistically significant.

A study by Rafael Pardo and Michelle R. Lacey comparing debtors whose student loan debt was discharged with debtors whose student loan debt was denied discharge by bankruptcy courts found few significant statistical differences between the groups.[43] Both the median and average age of all debtors in the study (including those who were denied and those who were granted discharge) was around 40 years old.[44] On one hand, this seems to debunk the myth that recent college graduates are the ones abusively seeking recourse from the system. On the other hand, it is difficult to determine how the demographics would change if the bankruptcy law allowed for discharge. However, the Pardo study did include a comparison with a GAO study conducted prior to the 1976 amendment to the Higher Education Act. The House of Representatives used the GAO study as evidence of lack of abuse of the student loan dischargeability provision of the Higher Education Act prior to its amendment. Pardo and Lacey found that their analysis of debtors in the non-dischargeability regime yielded remarkably similar results to the GAO analysis of debtors in the dischargeability regime.[45] These data suggest that legislators' fears over abuse of the system had little basis in reality and that the designation of student loan debt as non-dischargeable has had little effect on the types of debtors seeking relief from such debt.

C. What is Undue Hardship?

A consideration of where the two groups differ would give some insight into what exactly constitutes "undue hardship" for the purposes of student loan debt discharge. The Pardo study attempts to do just this by analyzing charac-

---

[41]Pardo & Lacey, 74 U. Cin. L. Rev. at 477. Eighty-four percent of debtors in the study sought relief prior to filing bankruptcy, including deferral, forbearance, and negotiating a repayment plan with the creditor. From this data, the authors concluded that bankruptcy is a last resort for those seeking to get out from under student loan debt.

[42]*Id.* at 487.

[43]This section considers all student debt, not merely law school debt. However, the study contained an interesting finding with regard to the legal profession. Those with legal occupations comprised 6.41% of the group debtors whose student loan debt was discharged. Compare this with the fact that those with legal occupations comprised 15.56% of the group of debtors whose student loan debt was denied discharge. The difference between discharge and denial is starker between members of the legal occupation than any other occupation in the study. Pardo & Lacey, 74 U. Cin. L. Rev. at 483, T.5.

[44]*Id.* at 442-45.

[45]*Id.* at 477-78.

teristics of both debtors and court opinions. As described earlier, Pardo and Lacey found few statistically significant differences between the debtors whose student loans were discharged and those whose debt was not discharged. According to factors such as age, gender, marital status, number of dependents, occupation, median monthly disposable income, median level of educational debt, and educational debt to household income ratios, the debtors who received discharges were no worse off than those who did not.[46] However, both the median monthly household income and expenses of debtors whose student loans were discharged were lower than the corresponding median amounts for debtors who did not receive discharges.[47] Moreover, debtors who received discharges suffered from work-limiting illnesses or cared for unhealthy dependents at higher rates than debtors who were denied discharges.[48]

The final portion of Pardo and Lacey's study attempts to delve into the reasoning for courts either granting or denying discharge. The authors concluded that three factors were, for the most part, dispositive for courts: "(1) the debtor's current inability to repay; (2) the debtor's future inability to repay debt; and (3) the debtor's good faith effort to repay," with future inability to pay being the most important.[49] Because health problems also appeared to correlate with discharge, Pardo and Lacey compared courts' findings on future inability to pay as to debtors suffering from work-limiting health problems or debtors who were caring for ill dependents.[50] The findings were unsurprising: debtors who suffered from work-limiting health problems or who cared for ill dependents were usually deemed unable to repay the debt in the future.[51]

Because health seems to bear on future ability to repay, which was the most dispositive factor among those cited by bankruptcy and appellate courts, the reasoning follows that health may be the one thread that ties the complex and confusing undue hardship standard together. However, health cannot be the only thread. The study only asserts that future inability to pay is the *most* dispositive of any other factors. The results will vary based on the bankruptcy court's views on dischargeability of debt and the myriad of other factors presented by each individual debtor. What is clear is that the results will likely not vary between circuits applying the *Brunner* test and the Eighth Circuit's totality-of-the-circumstances test.

D. BAPCPA Provides a Hint

A final issue relating to student loan debt in bankruptcy that cannot be overlooked is the Bankruptcy Abuse Prevention and Consumer Protection Act of 2005 (BAPCPA). Although Congress never crafted a definition for undue hardship as it relates to dischargeability of student loan debt, Congress did provide

---

[46]*See id.* at 481-84 (modeling the study's findings in graphic tables).

[47]*Id.* at 483-85.

[48]*Id.* at 485-86.

[49]*Id.* at 496.

[50]*Id.* at 496.

[51]*Id.* at 503-05.

an objective way of calculating undue hardship in the reaffirmation context in BAPCPA. Reaffirmation is the process by which a debtor, in exchange for retaining certain property (often a car), continues paying on a debt that would have normally been discharged in a bankruptcy. BAPCPA creates a presumption of undue hardship in the reaffirmation context when the debtor's disposable income exceeds the amount of payment specified in the reaffirmation agreement.

The analogous comparison in the student loan debt context would require the court to determine whether, based on debtor's current disposable income, he can afford to pay off the balance on loan. However, this analogy creates problems on either side of its balance. The first problem with this calculation is on the income side of the balance. The reason the debtor's current disposable income is a useful figure in a determination of undue hardship for a reaffirmation agreement is that reaffirmations tend to be for smaller ticket items than student loans and thus do not last as long. On the other hand, if a student loan is not discharged in bankruptcy, the debtor will have to make payments toward that loan for many years to come. Thus, a more useful figure for educational debt would be the debtor's total future disposable income, which necessarily includes consideration of a number of other factors.

The second problem with the reaffirmation undue hardship standard is on the loan side of the balance. In order to have a value against which to measure disposable income, the court must disaggregate the educational loan. While a reaffirmation explicitly contains a payment that the debtor must continue making to retain the property through the course of a bankruptcy, a loan repayment contract is not tied to the retention of certain property that can be reclaimed by the creditor and the exact monthly payment amount is not explicitly pinned down in a way for the court to evaluate. Thus, the variable against which disposable income is measured is essentially a moving target that is not secured by property. For these reasons, a better test for undue hardship in the student loan context would be a measure of the debtor's total future disposable income against the balance on the loan, including future interest. This measure would be consistent with BAPCPA and would necessarily take into account a whole host of factors such as future earnings, work-limiting disabilities, and caring for dependents.

The one thing this calculation leaves out is a consideration of the debtor's good faith and past behavior, which necessarily seeks to hold the debtor responsible for his bankruptcy. A look at the debates surrounding the Bankruptcy Code and amendments to the Higher Education Act, as well as the factors mentioned by bankruptcy and appellate courts in undue hardship opinions, indicates that the debtor's past behavior, and good faith in particular, are not overlooked. As described above, neither *Long* nor *Brunner*, which both take into account the debtor's past conduct, has been overruled or considered by the Supreme Court. Thus, a bankruptcy court will usually either apply a totality-of-the-circumstances test or the three-pronged *Brunner* test, which both include debtor conduct considerations, rather than looking exclusively to the future-oriented "undue hardship" definition in the reaffirmation provision of BAPCPA. On one hand, the tests developed by the courts in *Brunner* and in *Long* are more nuanced and tailored to the unique situation of conditionally dischargeable debt that is not secured by tangible property. However, these tests were also developed prior to the adoption of BAPCPA, which provides a statutory framework for undue hardship that excludes pre-bankruptcy debtor conduct and, as a result, tends to deprive the court from making moral judgments (because moral judgment is irrelevant to the reaffirmation context).

However, the actual text of the Bankruptcy Code provides better clues as to congressional intent. As Pardo and Lacey point out, the Bankruptcy Code merely requires the court to consider whether *continued payment* on the loan would result in undue hardship, thus taking into account only current facts and their bearing on the future.[52] Moreover, Congress has explicitly specified in other provisions of the Code when good faith is to be taken into account; the statutory interpretation assumption follows that, if Congress intended good faith to be considered in undue hardship for student loan discharge, it would have explicitly said so. Finally, debtor culpability and causation are generally not elements of bankruptcy law.

In conclusion, this section was not intended to be an extensive treatment of student loan dischargeability. However, the major issues covered provide a backdrop for the rest of the discussion. Student loan debt must be seen through the lens of a confused and inconsistent bankruptcy system. Until courts decide to start applying the prospective definition of undue hardship laid out in BAPCPA, students seeking to have their educational debt discharged in bankruptcy will likely be forced to justify their past actions and prove that they acted in good faith in taking out student loans. Bankruptcy courts do not ask the same for consumers who charge outrageous amounts to credit cards, or for the home buyer who mortgaged a house that cost more than she would make in the course of ten years. On the one hand, the objects of these debts are tangible and the creditor can reclaim them; the same is not true of a student loan. Moreover, the courts have an easier time believing that credit card and mortgage companies are predatory. Courts have not been made aware of the arguably predatory practices of law schools in luring students in with promises of six-figure jobs and charging them increasingly outrageous tuition, *U.S. News and World Report* for not holding schools accountable for their employment figures, and perhaps even the federal government for dishing out loans without holding schools accountable for returns on investment. Highlighting these practices might cause the bankruptcy courts, and Congress, to take pause and recognize that the potential for abuse is not with the students, but is instead with the facilitators.

IV. Catch-22: The Legal Profession Responds to the Student Debt Crisis

This section explores the recently developing conundrum that faces aspiring lawyers who take out loans to fund their astronomical education costs. State bar associations have begun to consider debt as a legitimate impediment to the "character and fitness" they require of an applicant to receive a license to prac-

---

[52]*See* Pardo & Lacey, 74 U. Cin. L. Rev. at 514-16 (describing how good faith has been explicitly included in other parts of the Code, and its absence indicates congressional intent that good faith not be considered, especially considering the fact that causation and culpability are not elements in bankruptcy law).

tice law. Some courts and bar associations have denied bar admission based on student and other debt. Although financial responsibility is a key component of ethical lawyering,[53] the fact of having amassed a huge amount of debt in pursuit of what was promised to be a lucrative career does not seem to have much bearing on financial responsibility. However, courts and bar associations, the members of which likely did not pay the astronomically high levels of tuition that students today shell out, believe that debt incurred in pursuit of an education is potentially a bar to leveraging that education for a higher salary to repay the debt.

This section will discuss three recent cases in which bar associations have decided to withhold licenses from law school graduates because of the applicant's debt. Each one highlights different issues present when the bar association gets in the business of delving into graduates' finances without an adequate understanding of the costs of law school education and the trade-offs that students must make. All three stories have been reported in major news sources as well as heavily covered in the legal blogosphere.

The first case involves a law graduate of Ohio State University named Jonathon Griffin who was denied admission to the Ohio state bar as a consequence of having accumulated $170,000 in student debt and $16,500 in consumer credit card debt.[54] As noted in Part II, the average student at a public law school in 2008 took out $71,436 to finance a legal education. These numbers are pre-recession and do not include debt from undergraduate education. Mr. Griffin took out $150,000 to finance law school, on top of an additional $20,000 to finance his undergraduate education.[55] In deciding to preclude Griffin from receiving his law license, the court relied on the fact that Griffin had accepted a low-paying, part-time job as a public defender although prior to attending law school he had worked as a high-paid stockbroker.[56] Moreover, the court explained that although Griffin had promised to file for bankruptcy in order to have his consumer credit card debt discharged, he had not done so at the time of sitting for the bar[57] (perhaps, the court might have considered, because he was studying to pass the bar). The court added that the majority of the debt would not be discharged by the bankruptcy anyway.[58] Finally, the court cited Griffin's lack of a "plan" to repay his debt, in combination with the facts recited above, as a significant factor in the decision.[59]

The moral of Mr. Griffin's story is, implicitly, threefold. First, bar associations expect students to make the Schlunk calculation before attending law school. Had Mr. Griffin chosen to stick with his high-paying job in the financial industry, rather than attending law school and then serving under-served

---

[53]*See* Model Rules of Professional Conduct, Rule 1.15 (governing the safekeeping of property and prohibiting the commingling of client funds).

[54]*In re Application of Griffin*, 2010 WL 115541, ¶4 (Ohio 2011).

[55]*Id.*

[56]*Id.* at ¶5.

[57]*Id.* at ¶6.

[58]*Id.*

[59]*Id.*

clients as a public defender, he would not have been in this situation.[60] Second, the bar association can withhold a license if it determines that a student's career choice is not prudent. Here, the bar association decided that working part-time as a public defender in hopes that the position would lead to a full-time job was not satisfactory and that Mr. Griffin should have instead sought out full-time employment.[61] Third, the bar association wants to discourage students with too much debt from pursuing practice in the field of public interest. If this is the case, the legal profession is expected to pass on its higher costs to its clients, thereby freezing out an even larger majority of the population that cannot afford lawyers' fees from obtaining legal representation.

The second case involves an applicant named Robert Bowman who was denied admission to the New York state bar because he was $430,000 in debt.[62] The New York Supreme Court Appellate Division[63] decision disposing of Bowman's case is just one paragraph long. The court determined that Bowman was unfit to practice law based upon (1) the size of his debt; (2) the fact that his loans covered a 20-year period; (3) the fact that he had not made any payments on the loans; and (4) a finding that Bowman was inflexible in his discussions with loan servicers (i.e., debt collectors).[64] The court apparently rejected Bowman's contentions that he possessed good faith intent to repay the loans and that he had not been paying the loans because of the "downturn in the economy and bad faith negotiations on the part of some of the loan servicers."[65]

A recent *New York Times* article detailed Mr. Bowman's woes.[66] Bowman suffered from serious medical problems that caused him to go through years of rehabilitation and delayed his pursuit of an undergraduate degree.[67] Bowman claimed that he was denied a deferral from Sallie Mae after a physically debilitating injury and had difficulty communicating with the lender.[68] He documented with "obsessive intensity" his communications with his lender, Sallie Mae, and later the debt collectors to whom Sallie Mae sold his debt.[69] Bowman claims that before his loans were sold to the debt collectors, he owed about $230,000.[70] When the debt collectors tacked on a 25% fee, the amount due on

---

[60]*See id.* at ¶9 (expressing "concerning about [Griffin's] neglect of his financial responsibilities").

[61]*Id.*

[62]*In re Anonymous*, 875 N.Y.S.2d 925, 925 (N.Y. App. Div. 2009).

[63]Although Bowman lost in lower court, his appeal was dismissed by New York's highest court. *In re Anonymous*, 14 N.Y.3d 763 (N.Y. 2010).

[64]*In re Anonymous*, 875 N.Y.S.2d 925, 925 (N.Y. App. Div. 2009).

[65]*Id.*

[66]Jonathan Glater, *Aspiring Lawyer Finds Debt is Bigger Hurdle Than Bar Exam*, N.Y. Times, Jul. 1, 2009 (http://www.nytimes.com/2009/07/02/business/02lawyer.html).

[67]*Id.*

[68]*Id.*

[69]*Id.*

[70]*Id.*

the loans jumped up to $400,000.[71] According to Sallie Mae representatives, Bowman presented an extraordinary case as he had taken out 32 separate loans over a 26-year period.[72] The New York State Board of Law Examiners called Bowman's "persistence remarkable" and recommended his approval; Bowman had relentlessly pursued both a J.D. and LL.M. in spite of serious injuries and took the bar examination four times before finally passing.[73] Despite the law examiners' recommendations, and the fact that courts usually follow law examiner conclusions, the Appellate Division denied Bowman his ability to repay his loans by denying him a license to practice law.

Mr. Bowman's story signals to future lawyers that perhaps they should give up at the first sign of an obstacle. The facts of Bowman's case are extreme; but his persistence is extraordinary. Overcoming adversity is apparently not a quality valued by the New York state bar association. Funding an education that he could not otherwise afford is a characteristic that could render a person ineligible to pursue his career path. Considering the astronomical cost of funding a legal education, I conclude that this opinion is out of touch with reality.

The third case deals with an anonymous applicant named G.W. who was denied admission to the New Hampshire bar as a consequence of several factors, including multiple criminal convictions, 20 years of unemployment, and non-payment on his $140,000 in law school loans since graduating from law school.[74] The criminal convictions included reckless conduct, six violations of a restraining order in one year, criminal threatening, and two DWIs.[75] The criminal conduct was disconcerting for the bar association but of equal concern was the fact that G.W. had outstanding debts.[76] G.W. refused to take responsibility for his criminal convictions, explaining to the Committee on Character and Fitness that he lacked the requisite *mens rea* for several of the acts in question.[77] Moreover, the Committee found that G.W. had not been completely candid by failing to disclose a DWI charge in his most recent application for admission.[78] After describing in depth G.W.'s criminal history, the court transitioned to his debt, bluntly stating that "the applicant's debts are equally of concern."[79] The court emphasized that the criminal record combined with the inability to repay debts resulted in the decision to find G.W. unfit to practice law.[80]

The moral of G.W.'s story for future lawyers is found in a key phrase used by the court, perhaps unintentionally, but nonetheless the language sends a

---

[71]*Id.*

[72]*Id.*

[73]*Id.*

[74]*In re G.W.*, 2011 WL 261722, *1 (N.H. 2011).

[75]*Id.*

[76]*Id.*

[77]*Id.* at *2.

[78]*Id.* at *5.

[79]*Id.*

[80]*Id.*

signal: "[T]he applicant's debts are equally of concern."[81] By this, $140,000 of educational debt is of equal concern as a long criminal rap sheet, for a committee evaluating moral fitness. This is the same ironic theme from the stories above: the court and bar association reject an aspiring lawyer because he incurred debt to attend law school, among other factors. Now that he is seeking a law license to be able to practice law and eventually repay the debt, the court and bar association step in, determine the debt is outrageous, and preclude the aspiring lawyer from fulfilling his debt obligation.

How do courts expect J.D.'s who are denied law licenses to repay their loans? State supreme courts and character and fitness committees are clearly aware that the debt is non-dischargeable in bankruptcy.[82] If the gatekeepers of the bar want to limit the number of people entering the practice, they could certainly start by accrediting fewer law schools, or petitioning the government to hold law schools accountable for the money the government lends to students. Most importantly, bar associations can get the word out to those undergraduates considering attending law school and explain to them the risk of taking on that level of debt. All of this would be significantly more responsible on the part of the bar, and more useful to creditors, than depriving students of a livelihood once they have already incurred crippling quantities of debt.

V. Economics 101: Cleaning Up the Mess

In concluding this somber review of debt and despair, I propose a few solutions for the legal profession to deal with the student debt crisis accruing among the newest members of its ranks. Clearly starting from the roots is ideal: educating prospective law students; encouraging law schools to be more candid with prospective students; petitioning the government to request accountability from schools for the loans it provides to students; ending the practice of self-reporting by law schools to *U.S. News and World Report*; raising the standards for ABA accreditation. However, a large cohort of students, saddled with massive amounts of debt, have already and will soon be entering the profession. This segment of the profession is of greatest concern at the moment.

In most industries, when costs rise, the industry passes on the costs to its customers. This is one option for the legal profession. However, this would ultimately freeze out large sectors of the population from obtaining legal services. Moreover, in a slumping economy where the legal market has taken a major hit, raising prices for clients is not a viable option.

A second, more challenging, option is to create demand. When the Great Depression hit, FDR's New Deal created a mass of legal jobs for young lawyers in Washington, D.C.[83] The profession can petition the government to address the student debt crisis by creating federal jobs for recent graduates. This request can be pitched as something much broader than a special interest: the fact that the federal government guaranteed these loans means that the federal

---

[81]*Id.*

[82]*See Griffin*, 2010 WL 115541 at ¶6.

[83]Jerold S. Auerbach, *Unequal Justice: Lawyers and Social Change in Modern America*, Ch. VII: The New Deal: A Lawyer's Deal (Oxford University Press 1976).

government and taxpayers have an interest in seeing that the loans are repaid. Unfortunately, the federal government moves slowly — especially with Congress, the holder of the purse strings, in a hyper-partisan stalemate on most issues.

The third option, along the same line as the second option, is to work to come up with a more extensive loan repayment assistance program (LRAP) that at the same time generates demand for legal services. Although the federal government does allow for loan repayment assistance for graduates employed in federal positions and the military Judge Advocate General's Corps (JAG), these positions are, understandably, highly competitive and coveted.[84] Many states[85] as well as the ABA[86] also provide LRAPs for recent law school graduates to pursue careers in public interest law. Law schools also often provide public interest law subsidies for students and graduates. These programs are meaningful and worthwhile opportunities for students who are passionate about public interest law but are limited by the cost of their education. However, nothing exists along the lines of a "legal job corps" that mobilizes to provide legal services to underserved communities and includes a generous loan forgiveness program; the medical profession does benefit from such a program. Considering the caseloads of public defenders, this program would be enormously helpful toward improving the quality of legal aid by reducing the quantity borne by each public defender.

VI. Conclusion

In summary, the challenges faced by law graduates come in all shapes and sizes. In order to afford a legal education, students must take on mortgage-sized amounts of debt that will saddle them for a lifetime, perhaps even prevent some of them from becoming a licensed attorney. And once they do become attorneys, they will likely be forced to repay the debt on half the salary they were expecting with few options for loan forgiveness. Without extensive efforts from law schools, the ABA, state bar associations, and the federal government, the student debt crisis threatens to burst under the sagging legal market. And again this time, the government and taxpayers, rather than the private sector, will be left feeling the pain of toxic loans.

---

[84]*Loan Forgiveness, Legal and Medical Studies* (www.finaid.org/loans/forgiveness).

[85]*Loan Repayment Assistance Programs: Summary*, November 2010 (www.americanbar.org).

[86]*Legal Aid and Indigent Defendants: Loan Repayment Assistance Programs* (www.americanbar.org).

PART TWO

Changes in the Practice of Law

6

Jared Lee Loughner:
The Unabomber Trial, Part II? The Unsolved
Ethical Dilemma of Who Controls the Defense

Ashley Martin

I. Introduction

They are a well-known group of criminal defendants: a mother accused of drowning her children; a man accused of detonating bombs at an abortion clinic, gay bar, and the 1996 Olympics; a mathematician accused of sending a series of bombs through the mail; and a man accused of participating in the terrorist attacks of September 11, 2001. These individuals, Susan Smith, Eric Rudolph, Ted Kaczynski, and Zacarias Moussaoui, reside across the country and have never met. However, they have all been indicted with numerous counts of criminal acts. They all inflicted tragedy upon lives of innocent victims. They faced their day in court. They pled not guilty. They were defendants in capital cases. They were all spared the death penalty and sentenced to life imprisonment. And, most significantly, they were all represented by one federal public defender: Judy Clarke.

This list of well-known defendants, represented by an individual who members of the legal community refer to as "the One-Woman Dream Team" who saves lives, recently increased from four to five.[1] As a result of her reputation for success in capital cases, the Phoenix Public Defender's Office recently appointed Judy Clarke to serve as defense counsel for Jared Lee Loughner, the criminal defendant accused of firing into a crowd of innocent civilians attending a political gathering on January 8, 2011.[2] Loughner, who has pled not guilty to the numerous criminal charges filed against him, will almost certainly face the death penalty.

However, Clarke's most notable performance in a capital defense case occurred fourteen years ago during her representation of Unabomber Ted Kaczynski, when numerous ethical concerns surfaced pertaining to the representation of the defendant. Coincidentally, the cases of Loughner and Kaczynski possess many striking similarities that raise the question of whether these same ethical concerns have the potential to resurface in Clarke's latest case. The ethical dilemma, concerning competing interests between Kaczynski and his lawyers, proved burdensome for the defense as his attorneys struggled to balance their own paternalistic tendencies with their client's autonomy in exer-

---

[1]Marisol Bello, *Loughner's Lawyer is a 'One-Woman Dream Team,'* USA Today, Jan. 11, 2011, *available at* http://www.usatoday.com/news/washington/2011-01-11-lawyer11_ST_N.htm (last visited Apr. 17, 2011).

[2]*Id.*

cising decision-making authority. More importantly, the ethical complications presented to the Kaczynski court, regarding control of the defense strategy, remain unresolved. Specifically, the allocation of decision-making authority between the lawyer and the client concerning the assertion of a mental status defense remains uncertain. Further, the Kaczynski court never received the opportunity to fully resolve the issue of whether a client suffering from a mental impairment or diminished capacity should control and is able to competently exercise such decision-making authority — or whether counsel is justified in overriding the client's decision, especially in a capital trial where the outcome is one of life or death.

This paper will examine these unanswered ethical questions that may arise in the representation of a capital defendant by examining the context in which they surfaced in the Unabomber case and hypothesizing the manner in which they may reappear in the Loughner trial. This paper will first explore, in Part II, the most fundamental similarity between the two defendants: defense attorney Judy Clarke. Part III will focus on Clarke's representation of Kaczynski and the ethical complications that emerged throughout the 1998 proceeding. In an effort to compare the two cases and predict the manner in which the Loughner proceedings may progress, this paper will then focus on the events that occurred leading up to the arrest and indictment of Jared Loughner. After discussing factual similarities that exist between the two cases and the potential for similar ethical conflicts to arise, Part IV will address the failure of the Model Rules of Professional Conduct to serve as an effective source of guidance in resolving the ethical dilemmas at issue. Finally, having demonstrated the necessity for a clear authoritative source on the issue of who controls the defense strategy when the client is of an impaired mental state, Part IV will also suggest modification of the Model Rules to include an unambiguous set of requirements and guidelines to resolve these ethical concerns as they apply specifically to capital cases. Ultimately, this paper seeks to address the likelihood that the unsolved ethical dilemmas raised in the Unabomber case may reappear at any given time and require a sense of urgency from the legal community in seeking a solution. An immediate solution is required because, for those clients affected by these lingering ethical questions, the result is one of life or death. The Loughner case, with Judy Clarke serving as counsel, may provide the opportunity to finally address these issues.

II. Judy Clarke: The One-Woman Dream Team

Judy Clarke, also referred to as the "patron saint of criminal defense attorneys," is known for her passion for justice, understanding of the law, and deep-seated opposition to the death penalty.[3] Her commitment to ensuring that no individual is sentenced to death fuels her willingness to take capital cases and serves as a source of motivation that contributes to her success in the courtroom.[4] Clarke believes that "legalized homicide is not a good idea for a civilized

---

[3]*Id.*

[4]Dan Webster, *Judy Clarke to Defend Susan Smith*, The Spokesman-Review, Jan. 29, 1996, *available at* http://www.spokesman.com/stories/1996/jan/29/judy-clarke-defend-susan-smith/ (last visited Apr. 17, 2011).

nation," and it is this belief that enables the defense attorney to empathize with all of her clients regardless of their alleged criminal offenses.[5] Clarke's staunch opposition to capital punishment, and her ability to "reach into people and find the human being inside, no matter how the rest of the word looks at them," contributes to her success in practice and her reputation as a unique force in the courtroom.[6] During trial, Clarke does not focus on her client's innocence, but rather she is able to successfully appeal to the emotions of the jurors.[7] Quinn Denvir, who served as Clarke's co-counsel in the Susan Smith murder trial, spoke of Clarke and stated that by demonstrating "a 'mitigating social history' — a narrative of abuse, violence or mental illness that the defendant may have suffered" — she is able to defeat the death penalty.[8]

After completing her legal studies at the University of South Carolina, Clarke assumed a position as a public defender in Richland County, California.[9] Upon completing one year of service in the Richland County office, Clarke began to pursue her career as a federal public defender on the West Coast and practiced in both California and Washington.[10] During this time, she established a positive reputation for herself, and in 1996, she became the president of the National Association of Criminal Defense Lawyers.[11] While serving as a federal public defender in Spokane, Washington, she was contacted by a law school classmate, David Bruck, who at the time assumed the position of acting defense counsel for Susan Smith.[12] Bruck, familiar with Clarke's reputation and work, requested that she join him as counsel in his representation of Smith, a mother accused of the murder of her two children in South Carolina.[13] Clarke agreed, and in 1995 assumed the position of defense counsel in her first capital case.

Clarke began her journey as an advocate for clients facing capital punishment when she offered to participate as a member of the defense team for Susan Smith. Smith faced a possible death sentence for criminal charges relat-

---

[5]*Id.*

[6]Beau Friedlander, *The Legendary Lawyer Who Will Defend Loughner: Judy Clarke*, Time, Jan. 12, 2011, *available at* http://www.time.com/time/nation/article/0,8599,2041943,00.html#ixzz1H1JujB11 (last visited Apr. 17, 2011).

[7]Joseph Goldstein and Marc Lacey, *To Defend the Accused in a Tucson Rampage, First a Battle to Get Inside a Mind*, New York Times, Feb. 12, 2011, *available at* http://www.nytimes.com/2011/02/13/us/13tucson.html (last visited Apr. 17, 2011).

[8]*Id.*

[9]Clif LeBlanc, *Tucson Suspect's Lawyer has South Carolina Ties*, The State, Jan. 14, 2011, *available at* http://www.thestate.com/2011/01/14/1645123/suspects-lawyer-has-sc-ties.html (last visited Apr. 17, 2011).

[10]*Id.*

[11]Bello, *supra* note 1.

[12]LeBlanc, *supra* note 9.

[13]Dennis Wagner, *Jared Loughner Case: Defense Attorney Gets Juries to See Other Side*, The Arizona Republic, Jan. 24, 2011, *available at* http://www.azcentral.com/news/articles/2011/01/24/20110124gabrielle-giffords-loughner-judy-clarke.html (last visited Apr. 17, 2011).

ing to the death of her two sons.[14] In October 1994, Smith contacted local police and informed officers that an alleged perpetrator hijacked her car and killed her children.[15] Several days later, Smith revealed to authorities that she fabricated the story, and that she herself had secured her two sons into their car seats and rolled the vehicle containing her children into a lake in South Carolina.[16] Both children, unable to escape, drowned in the lake.[17] Smith was arrested for their murder.[18] Clarke and Bruck, aware of the strong evidence against Smith and the likely reactions of jury members given the heinous nature of the crime, made every effort to save their client's life by portraying her "as a victim of sexual abuse at the hands of her stepfather, a woman with an unfaithful husband, and a woman whose lover rejected her to avoid the complications associated with becoming a father-figure."[19] With her client's life in the hands of the jury, Clarke succeeded in sparing Smith from the death penalty. Clarke and her co-counsel successfully convinced the jury that Smith was undeserving of execution. In Clarke's closing argument, she instructed the jury by saying, "This is not a case about evil. This is a case about despair and sadness. [Smith] had choices and decisions to be at the lake that night. She made that decision with a confused mind and a heart without hope. Confusion is not evil, and hopelessness is not malice."[20] This instruction is reflective of the powerful case that Clarke presented to force jury members to see beyond their visceral reactions and to perceive Smith as a victim herself, incapable of malice. As a result, the jury concluded that given Smith's severe emotional problems, sentencing her to death would not serve justice.[21] Ultimately, Smith received a sentence of life in prison, and Clarke won, in a sense, her first capital case. In addition to her representation of Smith, Clarke further demonstrated her commitment and opposition to the death penalty when she donated $83,000, all of her earnings generated from the case, to South Carolina's capital indigent defense fund.[22]

Following Clarke's successful representation of Susan Smith, she began to gain momentum in establishing her reputation as a "master strategist in death penalty cases."[23] In 1998, Clarke represented Unabomber Ted Kaczynski, who faced criminal charges and a potential death sentence for mailing a series of

---

[14]Elizabeth M. Reza, *Gender Bias in North Carolina's Death Penalty*, 12 Duke J. of Gender L. & Pol'y 179,187 (2005).

[15]Rick Bragg, *Arguments Begin in Susan Smith Trial*, New York Times, July 19, 1995, *available at* http://www.nytimes.com/1995/07/19/us/arguments-begin-in-susan-smith-trial.html?src=pm (last visited Apr. 17, 2011).

[16]*Id.*

[17]Reza, *supra* note 14, at 187.

[18]*Id.*

[19]*Id.*

[20]Webster, *supra* note 4.

[21]Reza, *supra* note 14, at 187-88.

[22]LeBlanc, *supra* note 8.

[23]*See id.*

bombs across the United States over the course of several years.[24] Despite the egregious nature of Kaczynski's crimes and a series of complications that arose concerning Clarke's representation of her client, she successfully arranged a plea deal with the prosecution.[25] Kaczynski pled guilty, agreed to life imprisonment with no chance of parole, and avoided execution.[26] Once again, Clarke's client, eligible for death, was spared from execution. (The details of the Kaczynski case will be explained in Part III.) Following her representation of the Unabomber, Clarke assumed the role as counsel for white supremacist Buford Furrow. Furrow, charged with opening fire outside of a Los Angeles Jewish Community Center and injuring several innocent victims, was eligible for the death penalty.[27] Clarke successfully arranged a plea deal that spared Furrow the death penalty and resulted in a sentence of life in prison.[28]

Clarke further demonstrated her commitment to representing capital defendants, and her inordinate ability to appeal to the jury, when she accepted a position on the defense team for Zacarias Moussaoui in 2001.[29] Moussaoui, the only individual indicted in the United States for crimes in connection with the terrorist attacks of September 11, 2001, stood trial for criminal charges that carried a sentence of death.[30] Despite Moussaoui's admitted allegiance to Osama bin Laden, his pledge to kill Americans, and his alleged participation in the most heinous terrorist attack to take place on American soil, the defense proved victorious in its efforts to avoid capital punishment.[31] The jury considered the mitigating social factors submitted by the defense, which revealed Moussaoui's unstable childhood and troubles with his violent father.[32] After deliberation, a majority of jurors concluded that these factors did not support execution of the defendant, and ultimately Moussaoui was sentenced to life in prison.[33]

Clarke's list of capital defendants who were spared execution further increased when she assumed the position of lead defense attorney for Eric Rudolph. Rudolph, accused of committing the 1996 Olympic Park bombing in Atlanta, and a pair of bombings in 1997 and 1998 at a gay bar and an abortion

---

[24]*Id.*

[25]Friedlander, *supra* note 6.

[26]*Id.*

[27]Joseph Goldstein and Marc Lacey, *To Defend the Accused in a Tucson Rampage, First a Battle to Get Inside a Mind,* New York Times, Feb. 12, 2011, *available at* http://www.nytimes.com/2011/02/13/us/13tucson.html (last visited Apr. 17, 2011).

[28]*Id.*

[29]Jerry Markon and Timothy Dwyer, *Jurors Reject Death Penalty for Moussaoui,* The Washington Post, May 4, 2006, *available at* http://www.washingtonpost.com/wp-dyn/content/article/2006/05/03/AR2006050300324.html (last visited Apr. 17, 2011).

[30]Online NewsHour, *Judge Rejects Guilty Plea in Moussaoui Case,* Public Broadcasting Service, July 18, 2002, http://www.pbs.org/newshour/updates/moussaoui_07-18-02.html.

[31]Markon and Dwyer, *supra* note 29.

[32]*Id.*

[33]*Id.*

clinic in Atlanta, caused the death of two innocent victims and inflicted injuries upon 150 people.[34] Rudolph remained at large for five years hiding in the woods of North Carolina, and federal agents finally captured the defendant in 2003.[35] With the help of Clarke, Rudolph avoided execution and received four consecutive life sentences without parole as a result of a plea agreement reached between his attorney and the prosecution.[36] Clarke once again succeeded in keeping her client alive. As the list of clients Clarke continued to save from execution increased, her reputation and popularity throughout the legal community as one of the most successful capital defense attorney also increased. This reputation for success, and ability to portray defendants accused of extremely heinous crimes as victims, led to Clarke's most recent appointment. Aware of her renowned success in the courtroom, the Phoenix Public Defender's Office in Arizona recently appointed Clarke to represent Jared Lee Loughner with the understanding that through her representation, he would receive the best defense possible and chance at avoiding execution.[37]

III. Loughner: The Sequel to Kaczynski?

A. Introduction to the Ethical Dilemmas

Clarke's success as a criminal defense attorney in capital cases is evident given her track record of preventing the execution of her clients. However, amidst her many successes in the courtroom, she is arguably most notable for her representation of the Unabomber, Ted Kaczynski. While representing Kaczynski, Clarke found herself confronted with an ethical dilemma when her client challenged her ability to control the defense strategy.[38] That dilemma, which specifically concerned the ability to assert a mental status defense in the presence of competing interests between the lawyer and client, although brought to the attention of the judge, the legal community, and the general public,

---

[34]Bernard Troncale, *Rudolph Pleads Innocent to Abortion Clinic Bombing*, USA Today, The Associated Press, June 6, 2003, *available at* http://www.usatoday.com/news/nation/2003-06-03-rudolph_x.htm (last visited Apr. 17, 2011); Sheila Dewan, *Bomber Offers Guilty Pleas, and Defiance*, New York Times, Apr. 14, 2005, *available at* http://www.nytimes.com/2005/04/14/national/14rudolph.html?ref=ericrobertrudolph (last visited Apr. 17, 2011).

[35]Sheila Dewan, *Bomber Offers Guilty Pleas, and Defiance*, New York Times, Apr. 14, 2005, *available at* http://www.nytimes.com/2005/04/14/national/14rudolph.html?ref=ericrobertrudolph (last visited Apr. 17, 2011).

[36]*Id.*

[37]Friedlander, *supra* note 6.

[38]*See* Jonathon Barker and Matthew Cosentino, *Who's in Charge Here? The Ethics 2000 Approach to Resolving Lawyer-Client Conflicts*, 16 Geo. J. Legal Ethics 505, 510 (2003) (discussing the "struggles between Kaczynski and his paternalistic lawyers for control in his defense, [which] raise the most fundamental moral issue with regard to lawyers, clients, ethics, and power").

remains unresolved. Today, Clarke finds herself back in the courtroom representing her newest client, Arizona shooting suspect Jared Lee Loughner, and although fourteen years later, the same ethical dilemmas that troubled Clarke and the legal community in the Unabomber case have the potential to resurface and finally demand a solution.

Several striking similarities exist between the two defendants, Loughner and Kaczynski, and the acts for which they were criminally indicted, which provide a foundation for the emergence of similar ethical concerns. Loughner, like Kaczynski, faces a series of criminal charges in federal court. A federal public defender, Judy Clarke, was appointed as representative counsel for both defendants. Like Judge Burrell in the Kaczynski case, Judge Larry Burns, who will preside over the Loughner case, serves in a United States District Court in California. Both defendants reportedly experienced periods of alienation prior to commission of their crimes. The two suspects were allegedly motivated to commit their offenses in order to pursue personal agendas and to communicate messages related to views they espoused in opposition to those generally held by society. Both took the lives of several innocent victims; both inflicted multiple injuries on others. Loughner, like Kaczynski, left written evidence suggesting that he intended to commit the crimes for which he is charged, demonstrating premeditation of his actions. Both defendants pled not guilty at the initial stage of their legal proceedings. Each defendant yielded to a court-ordered mental examination and hearing to determine whether or not he was competent to stand trial. Loughner's mental state, like Kaczynski's, will undoubtedly be an issue raised in trial. The United States Department of Justice will likely seek the death penalty for Loughner as it did for Kaczynski. Finally, and most importantly, the issue remains as to whether or not Loughner, like Kaczynski, will refuse to accept the defense strategy set forth by his counsel, thus raising ethical concerns identical to those presented to the legal community in Clarke's 1998 representation of Kaczynski.

In her attempt to effectively represent Kaczynski, Clarke and her co-counsel, Quinn Denvir, faced an ethical dilemma that many criminal defense attorneys are forced to confront during the course of representation: *who controls the defense?*[39] In her efforts to zealously advocate for her client, a criminal defendant in a capital case, Clarke's primary interest focused on saving her client's life — sparing him from execution. Despite objections from Kaczynski regarding the defense strategy, Clarke continued to forcefully pursue this interest, and the irreconcilable views between Clarke and her client led to a polarized attorney-client relationship.[40] As a result of the conflicting interests between Kaczynski and his counsel, he challenged his representation and several ethical questions emerged.[41] These concerns fueled discussion on a number of ethical questions that applied not only to the Kaczynski case, but are relevant to many criminal cases in determining the allocation of authority between the client and the attorney. Is the assertion of a mental status or dim-

---

[39]Joel S. Newman, *Doctors, Lawyers, and the Unabomber*, 60 Mont. L. Rev. 67, 67-70 (1999).

[40]*Id.*

[41]*Id.*

inished capacity defense a strategy controlled by the lawyer or the client?[42] If a lawyer abandons the only defense strategy that he or she believes will prevent the client from being sentenced to death, because the client demands that the lawyer pursue an alternative strategy, is the lawyer's conduct in violation of the rules of ethics? If a court finds that when the lawyer and client disagree on the defense strategy, the decision is the client's to make, how can the lawyer determine whether or not the client is sufficiently competent to make such decisions?[43] Further, if a client is found competent to stand trial, yet diagnosed with a mental illness or condition causing a diminished capacity, is the attorney justified in overriding the client's decision? Or must the attorney defer to the client's decisions regardless of whether or not the client is decisionally competent and further, whether the client may make a decision that will result in execution through the enforcement of the death penalty?

These questions, although raised in Clarke's representation of the Unabomber, were not fully answered by the Kaczynski court, and, accordingly, the task to address and resolve these issues remains for some future court. Given Clarke's involvement in both the Kaczynski and Loughner proceedings, and the presence of an alarming number of similarities between the two cases, it is possible that the above-mentioned ethical concerns will materialize once again. By examining the Kaczynski and Loughner proceedings in detail, the remainder of this paper will discuss similarities between the two cases which demonstrate that it is conceivable that Clarke will confront similar ethical complications concerning the control of the defense in a capital case. An analysis of the Model Rules of Professional Conduct will then disclose the ambiguity and lack of authority provided by the rules which are designed to guide practicing attorneys. Specifically, this paper will address Model Rules 1.2, 1.3, and 1.14. Finally, after addressing the inadequacies and inconsistencies that flourish throughout the flawed but indispensible sources of authority which lawyers are supposed to consult, this paper will make recommendations to define the lawyer's scope of decision-making authority in capital cases.

B. The Kaczynski Case: Background Information

On January 8, 1998, Ted Kaczynski, also known as the Unabomber, entered a courtroom in the United States District Court for the Southern District of California to stand trial for a series of alleged criminal offenses.[44] Kaczynski, a Harvard graduate and former mathematics professor at the University of California at Berkeley, relocated to Montana in 1971, after resigning from his position as a professor.[45] While in Montana, Kaczynski isolated himself in a cabin located in the hills where he resided with no electricity and became

---

[42]*Id.* at 69-70.

[43]*See id.*

[44]Online NewsHour, *Restless Defense,* Public Broadcasting Service, Jan. 8, 1998, http://www.pbs.org/newshour/bb/law/jan-june98/unabomber_1-8.html (last visited Apr. 17, 2011).

[45]Newman, *supra* note 39, at 70.

known around town as somewhat of a recluse.[46] Over time, he developed anti-technology sentiments and became convinced that technology directly contributed to the destruction of civilization.[47] Specifically, he believed that "[t]he Industrial Revolution and its consequences have been a disaster for the human race"[48] and that such consequences "made life unfulfilling ... subjected human beings to indignities ... led to widespread psychological suffering ... and ... inflicted severe damage on the natural world."[49] With these views serving as his source of motivation, Kaczynski retaliated against society's acceptance of technological advancement by engaging in a 17-year crusade of bombings.[50] During his crusade against technology, he mailed at least 16 bombs to locations across the country, and, consequently, three individuals lost their lives and 23 others suffered serious injuries.[51] While the FBI continued to search for the Unabomber, ultimately Kaczynski's brother provided federal agents with the information necessary to lead to his capture.[52] Kaczynski had entered into a negotiation with the *New York Times* and the *Washington Post,* in which he offered to promise to discontinue his practice of mailing bombs in exchange for a pledge from each newspaper to publish an unedited copy of his full "Manifesto."[53] The "Manifesto" contained Kaczynski's writings concerning his beliefs about technology, and from these writings, now published for the national community to read, the Unabomber's brother, David Kaczynski, recognized the writing style and contacted federal agents to reveal his brother's identity.[54] As a result, two decades of hunting the Unabomber came to an end in 1996 when agents seized Kaczynski at his Montana residence.[55]

C. The Kaczynski Case: The Ethical Complications Arising out of the Struggle to Control the Defense

During Clarke's representation of Kaczynski, several ethical concerns arose regarding the defense strategy. Clarke and her team of attorneys, knowing that evidence weighed heavily against their client because federal agents had obtained a large amount of irrefutable evidence after they searched Kaczynski's

---

[46]George Lardner and Lorraine Adams, *To Unabomb Victims, a Deeper Mystery*, The Washington Post, Apr. 14, 1996, *available at* http://www.washingtonpost.com/wp-srv/national/longterm/unabomber/bkgrdstories.victims.htm (last visited Apr. 17, 2011).

[47]Newman, *supra* note 39, at 70-73.

[48]Ted Kaczynski, *The Unabomber Manifesto: Industrial Society and Its Future, available at* http://www.time.com/time/reports/unabomber/unifesto1.html#1.

[49]*Id.*

[50]*See* Newman, *supra* note 39, at 70.

[51]Lardner and Adams, *supra* note 46.

[52]Richard Uviller, *Calling the Shots: The Allocation of Choice Between the Accused and Counsel in the Defense of a Criminal Case,* 52 Rutgers L. Rev. 719, 730-731 (2000).

[53]*Id.* at 730.

[54]*Id.* at 720, 730.

[55]Newman, *supra* note 39, at 72.

cabin, believed that it would be very difficult to convince a jury that he was not guilty by reason of insanity.[56] Accordingly, Clarke and her co-counsel, Quinn Denvir, chose not to assert an affirmative defense of not guilty by reason of insanity; rather, they chose to argue in the guilt phase that their client suffered from an impaired mental status.[57] If the jury found Kaczynski guilty, Clarke and Denvir intended to pursue a defense strategy where the assertion of an impaired mental state would serve to negate the *mens rea* required for the commission of the offense and in essence, mitigate punishment.[58] Although his attorneys believed this to be his strongest defense and saw no alternative to ensuring that their client was not sentenced to death, Kaczynski expressed forceful opposition to the assertion of any psychiatric defense because he did not want to appear "insane."[59] Kaczynski maintained that he was sane and, having developed an understanding that a mental impairment defense would bring to reality his "fear that his political and social protest would be dismissed as the ranting of a 'sickie,'" he informed his attorneys that he would prefer to receive a sentence of death than to be perceived as mentally ill.[60] He wanted his views to be respected and knew that the actualization of this goal required him to be recognized as free from any sort of mental illness. Kaczynski desired to use the trial as a forum to further communicate his anti-technology views that he so devoutly espoused, regardless of the risk of death.[61] Despite her client's repeated demands, Clarke and her team continued to pursue the mental status defense — what they believed to be the only hope of saving Kaczynski's life.[62]

This departure between the client's demands and the defense strategy to be pursued by the attorney, which emerged because of competing views pertaining to Kaczynski's best interest, provided the foundation for the ethical dilemma for which the Kaczynski case is known. After doctors determined that Kaczynski suffered from paranoid schizophrenia, Clarke and Denvir believed that the applicable rules of professional conduct required that they submit evidence of this mental impairment if necessary to spare him the death penalty.[63] After learning that his attorneys planned to assert a mental status defense to mitigate punishment and that they intended to present psychiatric evidence to support this position, Kaczynski appeared before the court in 1998 and requested the discharge of his current counsel and replacement by attorney Tony Serra.[64] Serra had agreed to present the defense in the manner that Kaczynski requested: the use of his trial as a forum for anti-technology beliefs absent of

---

[56]Uviller, *supra* note 52, at 730.

[57]Newman, *supra* note 39, at 68.

[58]*Id.*

[59]*See* Jonathon Barker and Matthew Cosentino, *Who's in Charge Here? The Ethics 2000 Approach to Resolving Lawyer-Client Conflicts*, 16 Geo. J. Legal Ethics 505, 510-11 (2003).

[60]Uviller, *supra* note 52, at 731.

[61]Newman, *supra* note 39, at 90.

[62]*Id.* at 68-70.

[63]Barker and Cosentino, *supra* note 59, at 510; Newman, *supra* note 39, at 78-79.

[64]Newman, *supra* note 39, at 73.

any mental status defense.[65] Judge Burrell, who heard the case, denied Kaczynski's request and "expressed the opinion that the decision whether to present a defense of mental impairment was the lawyer's not the client's choice."[66] Judge Burrell then appointed Kevin Clymo as the defendant's attorney for purposes of conflict.[67] Clymo quickly convinced Kaczynski that any attorney serving as his counsel would assert a mental status defense, and feeling left with no source for recourse, Kaczynski withdrew his request for change of counsel.[68] Ultimately, Kaczynski requested the right to represent himself without counsel because he believed this to be the only way in which he might avoid being portrayed as mentally ill.[69]

Kaczynski's challenges made with respect to his counsel and their defense strategy raised several questions of first impression for the court to consider. The first of these questions pertained to whether or not the ability to assert a mental status defense belonged to the client or the attorney. Clarke, on behalf of her defense team, acknowledged that the law does not provide clear instruction regarding who controls the assertion of a mental status defense. She then addressed the court:

> [W]e believe ... it is the lawyer's professional obligation to make strategic decisions and present the case in a way that the lawyer professionally believes is accurate and appropriate. And I think to say otherwise to counsel would pit a lawyer against his or her oath, professional oath....
>
> [Kaczynski's] present counsel intend to present him in a light of mental illness and intend to present to the jury his case in a way that he has for his entire life a deep and abiding fear that he would be presented.[70]

In essence, Clarke and her defense team maintained that as counsel, they possessed the authority to determine whether or not to present a mental status defense as a strategic means to negate *mens rea* and mitigate punishment despite their client's wishes.[71] Further, Clarke informed the court that to require the capital defense lawyer to substitute the client's strategy in place of the attorney's, where the client's will surely lead to execution, would place the lawyer in conflict with ethical obligations to serve the best interest of the client and to advocate as a zealous representative.[72] Clarke, sympathetic to the concerns of her client, maintained that she and her defense team were in compliance with the governing ethical restrictions.[73] Despite Kaczynski's objections to his coun-

---

[65]*Id.*

[66]Uviller, *supra* note 52, at 733.

[67]Newman, *supra* note 39, at 73.

[68]*Id.* at 73-74.

[69]*Id.* at 75-76.

[70]*Id.* at 76.

[71]*See id.* at 75-76.

[72]*Id.*

[73]*See id.*

sel and the manner in which they sought to defend him, Judge Burrell denied his motion to proceed pro se because the request had not been filed in a timely manner.[74]

Following his failure to avoid the assertion of a mental status defense in trial, given his rejected requests to change counsel and proceed without counsel, Kaczynski believed that he had one remaining option to pursue in order to avoid appearing mentally ill: he entered a plea bargain with the prosecution and received a sentence of life imprisonment.[75] Kaczynski succeeded in avoiding a trial in which members of the jury and the world observing would have the opportunity to perceive his actions as those of a severely ill individual.[76] Additionally, Clarke and her defense team succeeded in defeating the death penalty.

However, many individuals have regarded the Unabomber case as anything but a success. The ethical complications cultivated in the Kaczynski case have caused many legal scholars and practitioners to ponder whether or not Clarke's defense counsel should have been ordered to adhere to Kaczynski's requests and whether they were justified in refusing to do so on the grounds that it might violate their professional obligations. Further, because Kaczynski finally surrendered and chose to enter a plea agreement, the court was able to avoid responding to a very important question that poses significant uncertainty and is not adequately addressed in the Model Rules, case law, or other sources of authority discussing legal ethics: if Kaczynski had been declared as suffering from a mental illness or diminished capacity, would his defense counsel then be justified in overriding his decision pertaining to the assertion of a mental status defense because of his condition? This question, which the court failed to answer, remains ripe and has the potential to arise in Clarke's latest case — that of Jared Lee Loughner.

D. The Loughner Case: Background Information

Eight days into the new year, January 8, 2011, a series of gunshots were fired outside of a supermarket in Tucson, Arizona, where United States Representative Gabrielle Giffords engaged in a dialogue her with constituents at a scheduled event known as "Congress on Your Corner."[77] Eighteen individuals were unable to escape the line of fire and fell victim to the attack.[78] Among those who were shot, six individuals lost their lives and the remaining twelve suffered serious injuries.[79] Victims included Chief Judge John M. Roll of the

---

[74]*Id.* at 79.

[75]*Id.*

[76]*See id.*

[77]Marc Lacey and David M. Herszenhrown, *In Attack's Wake, Political Repercussions,* New York Times, Jan. 8, 2011, *available at* http://www.nytimes.com/2011/01/09/us/politics/09giffords.html?ref=jaredleeloughner r (last visited Apr. 17, 2011).

[78]*Id.*

[79]*Id.*

U.S. District Court for Arizona and Representative Giffords, whom authorities believe the gunman targeted in the attack.[80] Roll was fatally wounded, and Giffords was immediately placed in critical condition. The alleged shooter, 22-year-old Jared Lee Loughner, was taken into custody immediately and currently awaits trial.[81]

Loughner is charged with 49 counts of criminal activity.[82] Federal prosecutors will attempt to proceed with a novel argument that seeks to charge the defendant as if he committed the shootings on protected federal grounds.[83] This argument, therefore, resulted in a higher number of charges because no distinction will be made between federal employees and civilians who were in attendance at the event.[84] These charges consist of numerous counts of murder, attempted murder, murder of two federal officials, numerous weapons charges, causing the deaths of participants in a federal activity, and violation of civil rights laws.[85]

Following his arrest, Loughner exercised his Sixth Amendment right to receive an appointed defense counsel.[86] The Arizona Federal Public Defender's Office, however, recused itself from representing Loughner because of the alleged murder of their colleague Chief Judge Roll.[87] Additionally, Roll's colleagues seated on the federal bench recused themselves from the case.[88] Accordingly, both an outside defense counsel and trial judge have been appointed to serve in the case.[89] The Arizona Federal Public Defender's Office appointed Judy Clarke, who was working in private practice and providing consultation on death penalty cases, to represent Loughner.[90] Further, Judge Larry Burns, of the U.S. District Court for the Southern District of California, received an appointment to preside over the proceedings.[91]

---

[80]*Id.*

[81]*Id.*

[82]Sari Horwitz, *Jared Loughner Indicted on Dozens More Charges in Arizona Shootings*, The Washington Post, March 4, 2011, *available at* http://www.washingtonpost.com/politics/federal-grand-jury-indicts-loughner/2011/03/03/ABYOPsN_story.html (last visited Apr. 17, 2011).

[83]*Id.*

[84]*Id.*

[85]*Id.*

[86]Laurence Hammack, *Low-Key W&L Professor Judy Clarke Takes on Tucson Shooting Suspect Jared Loughner's Case*, The Roanoke Times, Jan, 3, 2011, *available at* http://www.roanoke.com/news/roanoke/wb/275512 (last visited Apr. 17, 2011).

[87]*Id.*

[88]Horwitz, *supra* note 82.

[89]*Id.*

[90]Marisol Bello, *Loughner's Lawyer is a 'One-Woman Dream Team,'* USA Today, Jan. 11, 2011, *available at* http://www.usatoday.com/news/washington/2011-01-11-lawyer11_ST_N.htm (last visited Apr. 17, 2011).

[91]Horwitz, *supra* note 82.

E. Comparison of Kaczynski and Loughner

The ethical dilemma that Clarke confronted in the courtroom throughout the Kaczynski case, which demonstrated a clash between an instrumentalist and paternalistic approach of representation, has the potential to occur yet again in her representation of Jared Loughner. The existence of this mere potential reveals the urgent need to clarify boundaries for acceptable decision-making authority afforded to an attorney attempting to assert a specific defense strategy — especially the attorney representing a client whose trial is a matter of life or death. Clarke's client in the Unabomber case, Ted Kaczynski, was a candidate for execution, and although the Justice Department as of this writing has not yet confirmed whether prosecutors will seek the death penalty for Loughner, reports indicate that it is almost certain that Attorney General Eric Holder will announce that the department is seeking execution.[92] Accordingly, Clarke's agenda once again will apparently entail serving as a zealous representative for her client by working relentlessly to save his life.

In pursuing this agenda, Clarke will likely construct a defense that will lead to the rise of ethical complications identical to those that existed in the Kaczynski case. At the outset of the Kaczynski trial, Clarke and her defense team advised their client to plead not guilty, yet given the insurmountable evidence against Kaczynski, they knew that it would be very difficult to convince a jury that he was not guilty by reason of insanity.[93] Rather than asserting the affirmative defense, Clarke felt that the use of an impaired mental status defense to negate *mens rea* and mitigate punishment in the guilt phase of trial would afford the best strategy available to save her client's life.[94] Here, where Jared Loughner will almost certainly face a potential sentencing of death for 49 alleged charges, it is likely that an assertion of a mental status defense will, like Kaczynski, be the only viable means of sparing his life. The evidence available against Loughner, like Kaczynski, suggests that he consciously committed the offenses charged and premeditated his actions and decisions to execute them.[95] According to the criminal complaint initially filed against Loughner, the suspect left written statements that imply the presence of "premeditation, intent, and a specific target."[96] Therefore, as eloquently stated by Ron Kuby, a criminal defense attorney familiar with Clarke's work, "The insanity defense would not work. He knew the nature of his action. His mental condition should be instrumental in mitigating punishment and that's where Judy Clarke comes in."[97]

---

[92]Benjamin Weiseer, *Legal Strategy Could Hinge on Mental Assessment*, New York Times, Jan. 11, 2011, *available at* http://www.nytimes.com/2011/01/12/us/12legal.html (last visited Apr. 17, 2011).

[93]Newman, *supra* note 39, at 72-73.

[94]*Id.* at 73.

[95]Andrew Cohen, *Jared Loughner's Trial: Previewing the Tucson Massacre*, Politics Daily, Jan. 10, 2011, *available at* http://www.politicsdaily.com/2011/01/10/ready-jared-loughners-federal-trial-previewing-the-tucson-m/ (last visited Apr. 17, 2011).

[96]*Id.*

[97]Friedlander, *supra* note 6.

Many of Clarke's former colleagues have publicly reported that she will likely seek to allege and confirm that Loughner suffered from some sort of impaired mental state.[98] In addition to predictions made by Clarke's peers, Clarke's recent objections to the prosecution's request for a psychiatric evaluation of her client, in order to determine whether he is mentally competent to stand trial, further indicates that she will likely assert an impaired mental status defense.[99] Despite Clarke's objections, Judge Burns ordered a competency hearing for Loughner scheduled for May 25, 2011.[100] Her objections to the competency evaluation and hearing, however, are significant because they further imply her defense strategy. Clarke's objections likely arose out of a concern that confronts defense attorneys: jurors, having learned that medical examiners at one time found the defendant competent to stand trial, are less likely to be sympathetic to a claim of an impaired mental status or mental illness asserted later at trial.[101] Although the criteria used to determine whether a defendant is competent to stand trial are entirely different from the criteria used to determine whether a defendant suffers from a mental illness, jurors sometimes experience difficulty separating these standards.[102] Clarke's request to vouch for her client's competency and proceed to trial without a formal hearing on the issue further indicates that she intends to assert a mental status defense similar to that offered for Kaczynski.

Although Judge Burns did ultimately order a competency hearing, it is possible that Loughner, like Kaczynski, will eventually be found competent to stand trial. In order to assert a claim of diminished capacity or impaired mental status, Clarke will need to confirm from medical experts that Loughner suffers from a mental illness. She will likely have her client examined by medical professionals to confirm a diagnosis. In the Unabomber case, the defense sought examination of Kaczynski, and when it was determined that he suffered from a mental illness, Clarke intended to use this information to proceed with the defense.[103] Here, it is highly likely that Loughner will be diagnosed with an impaired mental condition or diminished capacity. This potential diagnosis is evidenced by Loughner's behavior and symptoms of psychosis, signs of paranoia, interest in conscious dreaming, and previous

---

[98]*See id.*

[99]Julie Watson, *Defense Opposes Mental Exam of Tucson Suspect*, Charlotte Observer, Charlotteobserver.com, Mar. 10, 2011, http://www.charlotteobserver.com/2011/03/10/2128650/defense-opposes-mental-exam-of.html (last visited Apr. 17, 2011).

[100]*Id.*

[101]*Id.*

[102]*See* J.C. Oleson, *Swilling Hemlock: The Legal Ethics of Defending a Client who Wishes to Volunteer for Execution*, 63 Washington & Lee L. Rev. 147, 168-170 (2006) (discussing the standard for competency to stand trial as defined by the Supreme Court of the United States in *Dusky v. United States* to involve a test to determine whether a defendant has "capacity to appreciate his position and make a rational choice with respect to continuing or abandoning further litigation or on the other hand whether he is suffering from a mental disease, disorder, or defect which may substantially affect his capacity ... low thresholds for a defendant to clear").

[103]Newman, *supra* note 39, at 72-73.

commitment to an Arizona mental hospital.[104] Several psychiatrists have suggested that Loughner's strange behavior and symptoms exhibited in recent years prior to the attack indicate that it is highly likely that Loughner suffered from severe mental illness.[105] Accordingly, having established that Loughner, like Kaczynski, will almost certainly be eligible for capital punishment and yet receive a medical diagnosis confirming a mental illness, and that defense counsel Judy Clarke will likely attempt to assert that her client suffered from an impaired mental status to mitigate punishment (assuming that he eventually will be tried, upon a finding of competency), the question remains as to whether Loughner, like Kaczynski, will oppose the strategy set forth by his attorney — the strategy that she believes is the only means available to prevent the death of her client.

Kaczynski fiercely opposed Clarke's strategy to use a mental status defense in order to avoid a conviction of death because of his apprehension towards being perceived as crazy.[106] Kaczynski believed that he was brilliant and refused to allow a jury to find him otherwise.[107] He engaged in his crusade against technology in order to communicate a message to society about the dangers and destruction that it would cause, and he refused to allow any defense strategy to undermine this message even if it meant he would lose his life.[108] Loughner, like Kaczynski, who descended into madness during the days before his attack, also appears to have committed his outrageous acts of violence in an attempt to communicate a set of strong beliefs that he held in opposition to those held by society.[109] For Kaczynski, his crusade of violence was one against technology, and for Loughner, his attack appears to have been committed to express his opposition to government.[110] His frustrations with the government are evidenced by several writings and online videos that have surfaced since his arrest. Specifically, authorities located a letter found inside Loughner's home, which contained the language, "I planned ahead ... my assassination ... Giffords."[111] The lack of sincerity resonating from this writing and the strong assertions made in his online rants and videos reveal that Loughner, like Kaczynski, may object to any defense strategy that would undermine his

---

[104]Sal Gentile, *Jared Loughner May be Mentally Ill, But Does That Matter?*, Public Broadcasting Service, Jan. 13, 2011, http://www.pbs.org/wnet/need-to-know/health/jared-loughner-might-be-mentally-ill-but-does-that-matter/6291/.

[105]*Id.*

[106]Newman, *supra* note 39, at 68-73.

[107]*Id.* at 68-70.

[108]*See id.*

[109]*See* Andrew Cohen, *Jared Loughner's Trial: Previewing the Tucson Massacre*, Politics Daily, Jan. 10, 2011, *available at* http://www.politicsdaily.com/2011/01/10/ready-jared-loughners-federal-trial-previewing-the-tucson-m/ (last visited Apr. 17, 2011).

[110]*See id.*

[111]Elisa Roupenian, *Exclusive: Jared Loughner Radically Changed Before Alleged Shooting, Friend Says*, ABC News, http://abcnews.go.com/Blotter/jared-lee-loughner-suspected-gabrielle-giffords-shooter-school/story?id=12575278&page=3 (last visited Apr. 17, 2011).

beliefs, discount the message that he sought to communicate, or inherently lead the world to perceive him as a mentally unstable individual. As a psychiatrist who has worked with Clarke in previous cases, Michael First, informed the *New York Times* in March 2011, Clarke's ability to assert a mental status defense "could go many different ways. He [Loughner] could be totally acknowledging he's mentally ill, or he could be the Kaczynski type and be absolutely adamant that there's nothing wrong with him."[112]

As proceedings progress, Loughner has the potential to agree with the defense strategy that Clarke chooses to pursue, but if he believes that he suffers from no diminished capacity and that the assertion of a mental status defense will undermine the message he intended to communicate through the attack, he, like Kaczynski, may disagree with the strategy set forth by his defense counsel. Accordingly, if Loughner is eventually found competent to stand trial, diagnosed with a mental illness, and expresses opposition to any attempt to convince a jury that he suffered from an impaired mental state even though such an assertion is likely the only way to avoid death, where does this leave Clarke? She may find herself confronted with the same pressures and constraints that she experienced in her representation of Kaczynski due to an ethical dilemma for which there appears to be no clear answer: must she accede to the wishes of her mentally impaired client, or may she refuse and continue to pursue the course that she feels is in his best interest and ultimately save his life?

IV. Lack of Guidance Available to the Criminal Defense Attorney

A. The Model Rules

The ethical dilemma that Clarke once found herself confronted with, and may find herself at odds with in the future, is one that has not yet been resolved. More importantly, this dilemma is one in which the Model Rules of Professional Conduct remain ambiguous and provide little guidance. Three Model Rules govern the discussion of the attorney's decision-making authority in his or her representation of a client: 1.2 - *Scope of Representation and Allocation of Authority Between Client and Lawyer*, 1.3 - *Diligence*, and 1.14 - *Client with Diminished Capacity*. These rules, as will be examined, are largely unclear; lawyers, therefore, "are ultimately left to exercise their discretion in determining ethical conduct, weighing up the values of autonomy against paternalism and using their own idiosyncratic belief systems as decision heuristics."[113]

Model Rule 1.2 serves as a source of guidance for attorneys when deciding the "Scope of Representation and Allocation of Authority Between Lawyer and Client." The rule, in part, gives the following instructions:

---

[112]Marc Lacey, *To Defend the Accused in a Tucson Rampage, First a Battle to Get Inside a Mind*, New York Times, Feb, 12, 2011, *available at* http://www.nytimes.com/2011/02/13/us/13tucson.html (last visited Apr. 17, 2011).

[113]Oleson, *supra* note 102, 63 Wash. & Lee L. Rev. 147 at 183.

> [A] lawyer shall abide by a client's decision concerning the objectives of representation and, as required by Rule 1.4, shall consult with the client as to the means by which they are to be pursued. A lawyer may take such action on behalf of the client as is impliedly authorized to carry out the representation. A lawyer shall abide by a client's decision whether to settle a matter. In a criminal case, the lawyer shall abide by a client's decision, after consultation with the lawyer, as to a plea to be entered, whether to waive jury trial and whether the client will testify.[114]

The text explicitly provides that the client in a criminal case, not the attorney, has complete decision-making authority concerning whether or not to enter a plea agreement. Accordingly, the decision to plead guilty, not guilty, or not guilty by way of insanity is clearly a decision reserved solely for the client.[115] During the Kaczynski trial, Judge Burrell, in responding to the defendant's request for dismissal of counsel, asserted that the Model Rules clearly articulate that Kaczynski had the right to decide whether or not to enter a guilty plea by way of insanity.[116] Although Judge Burrell's assertion was accurate, the dispute in the Kaczynski trial did not concern a plea agreement, but rather the presentation of a mental status defense. It is important to distinguish between the two. Model Rule 1.2 provides explicit instructions for who controls the former but not the latter. Further, Judge Burrell acknowledged that the Model Rules did not provide clear guidance on whether Kaczynski or his defense team should have the authority to decide whether to present a mental status defense.[117]

The text of Model Rule 1.2 also informs readers that while the client is to control the objectives or ends of the representation, the lawyer is to have authority with respect to the means pursued to achieve those objectives.[118] The Kaczynski case, however, reveals further inadequacies of Model Rule 1.2 by demonstrating the difficulty that can arise in attempting to distinguish a line between the objectives of representation and the means to pursue those objectives. While Kaczynski defined his objective of representation as the use of trial to serve as a forum to communicate his anti-technology views and to appear as a sane individual while doing so, Clarke and her defense team, following Kaczynski's initial plea of not guilty, believed that the objective of representation was to obtain the lightest punishment possible. Accordingly, having established what she believed to be her client's objective, Clarke viewed the mental status defense and all other techniques to be used at trial as a means to pursue this objective and therefore within her control. Although the comment to Model Rule 1.2 provides that "clients normally defer to the special knowledge and skill of their lawyer with respect to the means to be used to accomp-

---

[114]ABA Model R. Prof. Conduct 1.2 (2010); *see* ABA Model R. Prof. Conduct 1.4 (2010) (Model Rule 1.4 provides guidance on communication that must take place between the lawyer and the client).

[115]*Id.*

[116]Newman, *supra* note 39, at 87.

[117]*Id.*

[118]ABA Model R. Prof. Conduct 1.2 (2010).

lish their objectives, particularly with respect to technical, legal, and tactical matters,"[119] when there is a fundamental disagreement as what is an objective and what is a means, the Model Rules prescribes no clear guidance on how to resolve such a discrepancy. In her representation of Loughner, it is likely that Clarke will continue to act in accordance with her belief that she, as counsel, has the authority to assert whatever means necessary to achieve her client's objective. Further, given the potential for capital punishment, it is likely that she will again define the client's objective as limited to avoiding death and obtaining the lightest possible punishment.[120] Ultimately, little guidance is provided to resolve the question of whether the defense strategy is a means or an objective, and this will lead to a conflict when the lawyer and client both believe that they are in the position to make that determination.[121]

Yet perhaps the most significant deficit in Model Rule 1.2 which emerged in the Kaczynski case is its failure to "inform the lawyer when a client's decisions about matters likely to arise when the client is mentally disabled must be followed."[122] Kaczynski, having been found to suffer from paranoid schizophrenia, was arguably mentally disabled. Model Rule 1.2 provides that, "[i]n a case in which the client appears to be suffering from a mental disability, the lawyer's duty to abide by the client's decision is to be guided by model rule 1.14."[123] Model Rule 1.14, which provides the authority for working with a client of diminished capacity, states that:

> (a) When a client's capacity to make adequately considered decisions in connection with a representation is diminished, whether because of minority, mental impairment or for some other reason, the lawyer shall, as far as *reasonably* possible, maintain a normal client-lawyer relationship with the client.[124]

In essence, Model Rule 1.2, which concerns the allocation of authority in the lawyer-client relationship, refers readers to Model Rule 1.14 when a client suffers from a diminished capacity; but Model Rule 1.14 instructs readers to maintain, to the greatest extent possible, a normal lawyer-client relationship as described in Model Rule 1.2. This cross-reference provides very little guidance and reveals a lack of clarity, definiteness, and consistency inherent within the Model Rules. Accordingly, when representing a client who, like Kaczynski or Loughner, is found to suffer from some form of diminished capacity, the question remains as to whether the client is decisionally capable of and competent in exercising the decision-making authority proscribed in Rule 1.2, especially when the effect of that decision is one of life or death.

---

[119]*Id.*

[120]*See* Jonathon Barker and Matthew Cosentino, *Who's in Charge Here? The Ethics 2000 Approach to Resolving Lawyer-Client Conflicts*, 16 Geo. J. Legal Ethics 505, 510-12 (2003).

[121]*Id.*

[122]*Id.* at 509 (quoting Christopher Slobogin, *The Criminal Defense Lawyer's Fiduciary Duty to Clients with Mental Disability*, 68 Fordham L. Rev. 1581, 1612 (2000)).

[123]ABA Model R. Prof. Conduct 1.2 (2010).

[124]ABA Model R. Prof. Conduct 1.14 (2010) (emphasis added).

Model Rule 1.3, which requires the lawyer to act diligently in representing a client, is often referenced with respect to attorney-client decision-making allocation in support of a paternalistic approach that favors giving more power to the attorney to make decisions if such decisions are within the client's best interest.[125] Specifically, Comment 1 to Model Rule 1.3 provides that "a lawyer must also act with commitment and dedication to the interests of the client and with zeal in advocacy upon the client's behalf."[126] While addressing Judge Burrell pertaining to Kaczynski's request for dismissal of counsel, Clarke argued that to require defense counsel to assert anything less than its best defense, a defense which provided the only hope of saving Kaczynski's life, would be to ask the counsel to violate his or her ethical obligations.[127] Those ethical obligations to which Clarke referred stem from Model Rule 1.3. It is likely that Clarke will again reference Rule 1.3 as justification for her decisions if similar ethical concerns arise in her representation of Loughner. Believing that zealous advocacy requires her to pursue all means necessary to prevent her client's death, she may argue, "[h]ow can you defend your client competently when you abandon your best defense before you start? How can you represent your client zealously — going all out — if you start the fight with one hand tied behind your back?"[128] Model Rule 1.3, read in isolation, arguably favors a paternalistic approach that gives the attorney more control in the decision-making process. This basic rule, however, should not be followed in isolation, but rather in conjunction with all other Model Rules. This attempt to resolve the extent to which lawyers may rely on Rule 1.3 presents further inadequacies inherent within the Model Rules, because those attorneys believing that zealous representation is a guiding principle in the ethics of criminal defense may construe the rule to grant significant decision-making discretion to the attorney even where such discretion may conflict with other Model Rules.

B. Recommendations for Improving Guidance Provided by the Model Rules of Professional Conduct

The inadequacies inherent within the Model Rules have resulted in a lack of guidance to criminal lawyers who work with clients possessing a diminished capacity and require, therefore, further clarification. Furthermore, the failure of authorities addressing legal ethics to provide unambiguous guidance for the attorney working with a client who suffers from diminished capacity or mental illness is unacceptable.[129] More specifically, the status quo is unacceptable

---

[125]*See* ABA Model R. Prof. Conduct 1.3 (2010).

[126]ABA Model R. Prof. Conduct 1.3 (2010).

[127]Newman, *supra* note 39, at 95-97.

[128]*Id.* at 96.

[129]The American Bar Association's Criminal Justice Standards also fail to adequately address the scope of decision-making authority in determining who controls the defense. Standard 4 of the Criminal Justice Standards address *Defense Function*, and Standard 4-5.2 specifically addresses *Control and Direction of the Case*. This standard, like the Model Rules, allocates certain decisions to the client and others to the attorney. Specifically, Standard 4-5.2 reserves to the accused the right to decide (i) what pleas to

because for some clients, those facing capital punishment, the allocation of authority between the attorney and client can have a significant impact on whether the client lives or dies. Kaczynski and Loughner not only suffered from a mental impairment, but both defendants faced the possibility of potential execution. The client confronting a trial that may determine his fate is under further stress that may contribute to a diminished capacity even without the presence of an already existing psychiatric condition.[130] This raises specific questions for the capital attorney that other lawyers may not confront: "What factors can capital lawyers consider in deciding to substitute their judgment for that of disabled clients?"[131] Can the stress, anxiety, or simple fear inherent in the possibility of a conviction of death provide sufficient justification for a lawyer to override her client's decision, especially if that decision is one that will save the client's life?[132]

These concerns, pertaining to additional stress experienced by the capital defendant due to the nature of the potential execution itself, along with the potential for the presence of a diminished capacity proven through psychiatric evidence, present a unique set of considerations for the capital lawyer. Accordingly, given the extreme situation that capital defense attorneys experience regarding representation — the life or death of their client — a separate set of guidelines and requirements should be created for these attorneys.[133] The ability of a client to potentially accomplish his or her own death under the current ambiguous set of Model Rules further compels the need to create clear guidelines. Had Judge Burrell in the Kaczynski case, after acknowledging the lack of guidance afforded by the Model Rules, informed Clarke that she must accede to her client's wishes, Kaczynski in essence would have determined his fate — death.

---

enter; (ii) whether to accept a plea agreement; (iii) whether to waive a jury trial; (iv) whether to testify in his or her behalf; and (v) whether to appeal. Unlike the Model Rules, Standard 4-5.2 addresses allocation of responsibility concerning defense strategy. The standard provides that "[s]trategic and tactical decisions should be made by defense counsel after consultation with the client where feasible and appropriate." Accordingly, pursuant to this standard, it would appear that the defense attorney has the authority to control the assertion of a mental status defense as a strategic decision. However, the standard urges "consultation with the client where feasible and appropriate." Although the standard initially appears to favor a paternalistic model of decision-making allocation, it provides inadequate guidance for the attorney whose client does not agree with the strategic and tactical decisions he or she chooses to pursue. The standard simply provides, "If a disagreement on significant matters of tactics or strategy arises between defense counsel and the client, defense counsel should make a record of the circumstances." In the event of a disagreement between the client and attorney on the strategy to be employed, the instruction to make a record provides very little guidance and is not helpful for the attorney wanting to comply with ethical standards. The standard does not clarify whether the attorney should proceed with the strategy after making a record or whether he or she must accede to a client's wishes. ABA, Standards for Criminal Justice 4-5.2, Second Edition, Vol. I (1980).

[130]Oleson, *supra* note 102, 63 Wash. & Lee L. Rev. 147 at 180.

[131]*Id.*

[132]*See id.*

[133]*Id.*

The severity of this issue requires a serious attention that it has not yet been afforded by the current Model Rules. Clear guidelines should be created that establish to what extend the capital defendant is able to control decisions regarding representation and at what point the individual facing death row is incapable of making coherent decisions when they boil down to those that will affect their very existence. Given the severity of the outcome and potential for the defendant to lose his or her life, perhaps such a set of guidelines specifically for the capital defense attorney should favor a paternalistic approach to the extent that the defendant is in a diminished capacity or suffers from a mental illness that inhibits his or her decision-making abilities. However, such an approach would require explicit guidelines defining when a client is in a diminished capacity and to what extent that impairment must affect the defendant.

V. Conclusion

In 1998, during the trial of Unabomber Ted Kaczynski, the court had the opportunity to provide answers to several ethical dilemmas that continue to plague criminal defense attorneys today. At that time, Judy Clarke, Kaczynski's representative counsel, found herself at odds with her client, who maintained that he should control whether or not his lawyers could assert a mental status defense in court in an effort to prevent his execution. Believing that she was merely pursuing the best interest of her client, Clarke attempted to proceed with the defense, which required the presentation of psychiatric evidence despite her client's objections. She believed this to be the only way in which she could discourage jurors from condemning her client to death.

This disagreement between Clarke and her client escalated to a point that required intervention from the court. The court found itself confronted with questions pertaining to allocation of decision-making authority with respect to the ability to control the assertion of the defense, and whether or not a capital defendant who suffered from a mental impairment or a diminished capacity could competently exercise the decision to control the defense strategy. Before the court received the opportunity to answer these questions, however, Ted Kaczynski pled guilty.

Both the Kaczynski court and the Model Rules have failed to adequately resolve these issues. However, the tragedy that struck in Tucson, Arizona in January 2011 has created a situation in which Clarke may once again find herself subject to an ethical dilemma in the representation of her client, Jared Loughner. The similarities between the Kaczynski and Loughner proceedings reveal the potential for the Loughner court to find itself confronted with identical ethical issues concerning the representation of Clarke's latest client in a capital case.

7

Prosecutors Wearing Dual Hats: The Tragic Tale of Henry Glover

Alexander Liu

In the legal profession, we often talk about lawyers wearing dual hats or taking on other roles besides that of an advocate. However, when a lawyer plays a dual role, special duties arise and impose restrictions on the scope of the dual hat activities. Generally, a lawyer is prohibited from participating in the dual role of lawyer and witness in the course of a trial;[1] however, there are exceptions to the rule. There are times when prosecutors have to put on duals hats and act as both prosecutor and witness. This paper looks at the concerns when a prosecutor acts as both a prosecutor and witness. As Peter Parker's uncle Ben once said in Stan Lee's *Spider-Man*, with great power comes great responsibility.

I. Overview of ABA Model Rule 3.7

The American Bar Association's Model Rules of Professional Conduct are rules that, when implemented by state bars and courts, govern lawyer conduct. Forty-nine states have adopted the Model Rules' numbering system and most of the rules or language contained in the rules.[2] The Model Rules are rules on how lawyers should conduct themselves. It should be noted that the ABA Model Rules of Professional Conduct are, in themselves, non-binding.[3] They act as guidance for states to enact their own rules and how respective states ought to regulate the legal profession.

The courts of each state adopt their jurisdiction's rules of professional conduct, and apply them through their state's bar disciplinary system. It should be noted that the American Bar Association is a voluntary, private organization, which means that it has no power to discipline lawyers and no control over each state's respective rules of professional conduct besides the power of persuasion.[4] It should also be noted that no state has adopted all of the ABA Model Rules verbatim.[5] There are many variances with the Model Rules and states have their own respective rules. No two states have adopted exactly the same ethics rules.[6] The Model Rules are, some put it, "merely a starting point

---

[1]*See* ABA Model Rule 3.7 - Advocate Witness Rule.

[2]Stephen Gillers, Roy D. Simon, and Andrew M. Perlman, *Regulation of Lawyers: Statutes and Standards* 3 (2010).

[3]*Id.* at 3.

[4]*Id.*

[5]*Id.*

[6]*Id.*

for discussing the rules of legal ethics and represent only one of many possible approaches to the regulation of lawyers."[7]

ABA Model Rule 3.7 guides the process of when a lawyer acts as both advocate and witness. The rule states:

> (a) A lawyer shall not act as advocate at a trial in which a lawyer is likely to be a necessary witness unless:
>   (1) the testimony relates to an uncontested issue;
>   (2) the testimony relates to the nature and value of legal services rendered in the case; or
>   (3) disqualification of the lawyer would work substantial hardship on the client.
> (b) A lawyer may act as advocate in a trial in which another lawyer in the lawyer's firm is likely to be called as a witness unless precluded from doing so by Rule 1.7 or Rule 1.9.[8]

In certain criminal cases, prosecutors are called as witnesses. In these cases, they play dual roles, one as a prosecutor and one as witness. The capacity in which the prosecutor plays a witness usually involves testifying about some part of the investigation that led to litigation.[9] For example, the prosecutor may need to testify about prior statements made by a witness. Although there are no rules that prohibit prosecutors from doing this,[10] there are ethical considerations that need to be addressed. This paper addresses the ethical considerations that follow when a prosecutor plays a dual role in a criminal proceeding.

Some jurisdictions allow prosecutors to take on dual roles as both prosecutor and witness, and address it in their version of the advocate witness rule. Most jurisdictions are silent on whether prosecutors can assume dual roles. These jurisdictions apply the advocate witness rule to all lawyers, including prosecutors. For example, Wisconsin's Rule 20:3.7 - Lawyer as Witness states:

> (a) a lawyer shall not act as advocate at trial in which the lawyer is likely to be a necessary witness unless:
>   (1) the testimony relates to an uncontested issue;
>   (2) the testimony relates to the nature and value of legal services rendered in the case; or

---

[7]*Id.*

[8]American Bar Association, Model Rules Prof'l Conduct R. 3.7 (2010), *available at* http://www.americanbar.org/groups/professional_responsibility/publications/model_rules_of_professional_conduct/rule_3_7_lawyer_as_witness.html.

[9]Christine M. Wiseman & Michael Tobin, *Criminal Practice and Procedure: Wisconsin Practice Series* §6:3 Prosecutors as witnesses (2010).

[10]There are limitations placed on what prosecutors can and cannot do when they play both prosecutor and witness. *See United States v. McKoy*, 771 F.2d 1207, 1210-11 (9th Cir. 1985) (holding that a prosecutor who is called as a witness "may not vouch for a witness, or state their personal opinion on the defendant's guilt or the strength of the case against him").

(3) disqualification of the lawyer would work substantial hardship on the client.[11]

Prosecutors in Wisconsin can use one of these exceptions such as claiming that what they are about to testify to is an uncontested issue.[12] The drafters were aware of this issue and delineated the situations as to when a defendant has a proper objection to a prosecutor acting in a dual capacity. The drafters stated that a proper objection exists where "the combination of roles may prejudice that party's rights in the litigation. A witness is required to testify on the basis of personal knowledge, while an advocate is expected to explain and comment on evidence given by others. It may not be clear whether a statement by an advocate-witness should be taken as proof or as an analysis of proof."[13] As long as the witness meets the basic requirements of the rules of evidence, namely that the testimony is relevant and is not hearsay, the witness should be allowed to testify.

Both Louisiana and Wisconsin have adopted an identical version of Model Rule 3.7 - Advocate Witness Rule.[14] However, unlike their counterparts in Wisconsin, the drafters in Louisiana did not add comments the Louisiana advocate witness rule. The state courts in Louisiana tend to follow the lead of other jurisdictions interpreting when a prosecutor takes on a dual role.[15] In *State v. Miller*,[16] the Supreme Court of Louisiana stated, "[D]istrict attorneys should avoid the dual role of prosecutor and witness. The general rule, governing all lawyers, prohibits testimony by attorneys who are engaged in the trial of the case, except in isolated circumstances."[17] The court went further by stating that "even stronger reasons weigh against testimony by a prosecutor."[18] Louisiana falls in line with most jurisdictions and the courts highlight the same concerns in terms of prosecutors having dual roles.

Some federal courts have analyzed the concerns addressed in the Wisconsin drafters' comments. The Seventh Circuit addressed this issue in *United States v. Johnston*,[19] stating that, "as a general rule, the government prosecutor is not to be automatically disqualified as a witness or as trial advocate after testifying at a pretrial suppression hearing, but testifying and continuation as coun-

---

[11]*See* Wisconsin Rules of Prof'l Conduct R. 20:3.7 (2010), *available at* http://legis.wisconsin.gov/rsb/scr/5200.pdf.

[12]Model Rule 3.7 addresses the concept of an advocate which includes prosecutors.

[13]*See* Wisconsin Rules of Prof'l Conduct R. 20:3.7, cmt 2 (2010), *available at* http://www.wisbar.org/AM/Template.cfm?Section=Lawyer_Regulation_and_Discipline&template=/CM/ContentDisplay.cfm&contentid=62720.

[14]*See* Louisiana Rules of Prof'l Conduct R. 3.7 (2010), *available at* http://www.ladb.org/Publications/ropc.pdf.

[15]*See State v. Miller*, 391 So.2d 1159 (La. 1980) (holding that prosecutor may act as a witness as long as she is a competent witness).

[16]*State v. Miller*, 391 So.2d 1159, 1161 (La. 1980).

[17]*Id.* at 1163.

[18]*Id.*

[19]*See United States v. Johnston*, 690 F.2d 638, 640 (7th Cir. 1982).

sel shall be subject to the sound discretion of the trial judge...."[20] The court explained the dangers that occur by giving four reasons. The court stated:

> First, the rule eliminates the risk that a testifying prosecutor will not be a fully objective witness given his position as an advocate for the government.

> Second, there is fear that the prestige or prominence of a government prosecutor's office will artificially enhance his credibility as a witness.

> Third, the performance of dual roles by a prosecutor might create confusion on the part of the trier of fact as to whether the prosecutor is speaking in the capacity of an advocate or of a witness, thus raising the possibility of the trier according testimonial credit to the prosecutor's closing argument.

> Fourth, the rule reflects a broader concern for public confidence in the administration of justice, and implements the maxim that "justice must satisfy the appearance of justice.[21]

These concerns expressed by the court in *Johnston* address the dilemmas faced by a prosecutor acting in a dual capacity. The first concern that the court addresses is the danger that the prosecutor will skew his testimony for the sake of winning his case as an advocate for the government. The fear is that the prosecutor will forget about ABA Model Rule 3.8 and the rules that govern a prosecutor's duties.[22] This concern is one that addresses the adversary nature of litigation and how lawyers are trained in an adversarial environment. Lawyers are taught to win for their clients.

The second concern is the danger of too much weight given to the credibility of the prosecutor just because she works for the government. The fear is that jurors will give great credence to what a prosecutor is testifying to just because he is associated with the government, and this upsets the notion of fairness in a criminal proceeding. For example, if a prosecutor assumed a dual role and claimed that a respective defendant was responsible for murder and the jury was evenly split on guilt, jurors might place great weight on this claim by the prosecutor just because the prosecutor is associated with the government. Essentially, the prosecutor would get the benefit of the doubt in proving his case rather than the defendant getting the benefit of doubt. The assumption that we have to make is that the jurors believe that the government is good and that if the government is good, then anyone working for the government is automatically good and therefore credible.

The third concern that is addressed by the court is very similar to the second concern. The third concern addresses the dangers that jurors might develop when a prosecutor takes on a dual role. Here, the court is concerned with the fact that an ordinary juror might not be able to separate the different

---

[20]*Id.* at 646.

[21]*Id.*

[22]*See* American Bar Association, Model Rules of Prof'l Conduct R. 3.8, *available at* http://www.americanbar.org/groups/professional_responsibility/publications/model_rules_of_professional_conduct/rule_3_8_special_responsibilities_of_a_prosecutor.html.

roles of when a prosecutor acts as a prosecutor and when a prosecutor acts as a witness. The court assumes that the ordinary juror who is untrained in the legal field might not be able to differentiate when the prosecutor switches hat and acts as a witness. For example, imagine a prosecutor playing both roles. The prosecutor first acts as a witness testifying to what a defendant or witness had said previously. Next, the prosecutor is giving his closing argument and highlights the testimony he just presented. An ordinary juror might place great weight on the prosecutor's case believing that the prosecutor was actually there as a witness and therefore adding more credibility to the prosecutor. The danger here is that the ordinary juror will not be able to distinguish what to give more weight or less weight in terms of evaluating the evidence, and this upsets our fundamental notions of fairness in criminal proceedings. The juror essentially gets confused as to when the prosecutor is playing the role of a prosecutor and as to when she is playing the role of a witness.

The last concern that the court addresses is one of appearance. The court is particularly concerned with its public image and how the public perceives how the judicial system operates. As Justice Felix Frankfurter once stated, "for they concern the ingredients of what constitutes justice ... justice must satisfy the appearance of justice."[23] The public acts as the final arbiter by giving an unspoken the seal of confidence on the verdict. If the courts lose the confidence from the public, then the criminal system will cease to be perceived as fair. Without public support, the criminal justice system will be perceived as unfair and verdicts rendered will lose the public's confidence in a just result.

The Third Circuit has also examined this issue in *United States v. Birdman*.[24] There the court stated that "federal courts have almost universally frowned upon the practice of a Government prosecutor testifying at the trial of the case he is prosecuting, whether for or against the defendant, and have stated that the practice should be permitted only in extraordinary circumstances or for compelling reasons."[25] Most of the federal circuits tend to follow the Third and Seventh Circuits. They tend to allow prosecutors to take on a dual role, but only under limited circumstances.

II. Henry Glover Story

Days after Hurricane Katrina, New Orleans was in turmoil. A majority of the city had been evacuated and those who stayed faced uncertainty and unrest. A New Orleans Police Officer had been severely wounded by being shot by a suspected looter. These events had the entire police department on high alert.[26] Amidst the chaos, on September 5, 2005, Henry Glover was shot and killed by

---

[23]*Offutt v. United States*, 348 U.S. 11, 13 (1954). *See also* Richmond Newspapers, Inc. v. Virginia, 448 U.S. 555, 571 (1950) (stating, "[t]o work effectively, it is important that society's criminal process "satisfy the appearance of justice, and the appearance of justice can best be provided by allowing people to observe it").

[24]*United States v. Birdman*, 602 F.2d 547, 549 (3d Cir. 1979).

[25]*Id.* at 553.

[26]*See* New Orleans Police Report: Shooting Report Item #L-01447-05, *available at* http://media.nola.com/crime_impact/other/Henry%20Glover2.pdf.

New Orleans Police Department Officer David Warren. Two other New Orleans Police Department Officers, Greg McRae and Lt. Travis McCabe, were also found guilty in the subsequent burning of Glover's remains and obstructtion of justice.[27]

What exactly happened that fateful post-Katrina day?[28] According to the first NOPD police report,[29] Officer David Warren and Officer Linda Howard were assigned to guard the Fourth District Detective Officer at 3751 General De Gaulle. The office had been severely damaged by Hurricane Katrina and contained many vital police records. While they were assigned at this location, they were also assigned to guard the adjacent businesses from looters. Around 11:00 a.m., Officers Warren and Howard positioned themselves on the second floor balcony, adjacent to the Detective Office. The officers then heard a loud engine noise and proceeded to investigate.[30]

Officer Howard walked across the courtyard balcony to get in a better position to observe the oncoming vehicle. Officer Howard observed a white truck and two unknown black males exiting the vehicle. She further observed the two men approach the rear gate of the building. During this time, Officer Howard was in a different position on the balcony and was unable to observe what Officer Warren had seen before he fired a single fatal shot.[31]

According to Officer Warren, he had walked across the courtyard balcony to a position where he could observe the approaching truck. He noted that he saw the oncoming truck had a "Firestone" company logo on the truck and that alerted him because the Firestone Company down the road was closed due to hurricane. This created his suspicion that the truck might have been looted.[32] Suddenly, two black males exited the truck while the engine was still running and ran towards the rear courtyard entrance. Officer Warren then identified himself and told the suspects to get out. At this point, the men looked at Officer Warren and continued towards the building. Officer Warren claimed that he saw one suspect holding what he believed to be a weapon in his right hand.

---

[27]See Department of Justice, *Three New Orleans Police Officers Found Guilty in the Post-Katrina Shooting and Burning of Henry Glover*, (2010) *available at* http://www.justice.gov/opa/pr/2010/December/10-crt-1420.html.

[28]Henry Glover's mysterious death was not investigated until three years after the fact when A.C. Thompson investigated and wrote on his death. This drew public attention to his mysterious death. *See* A.C. Thompson, *Katrina's Hidden Race War* (2009), *available at* http://www.thenation.com/article/katrinas-hidden-race-war. *See also* Laura Maggi, *Missing-person report on Henry Glover shooting got no timely follow-up, NOPD records show* (2010), *available at* http://nola.com/crime/index.ssf/2010/05/missing-person_report_on_henry.html.

[29]See New Orleans Police Report: Shooting Report Item #L-01447-05, *available at* http://media.nola.com/crime_impact/other/Henry%20Glover2.pdf. (This police report is the original police report that later led to the federal investigation and the unraveling of the cover-up of Henry Glover's death.)

[30]New Orleans Police Report: Shooting Report Item #L-01447-05, *available at* http://media.nola.com/crime_impact/other/Henry%20Glover2.pdf.

[31]*Id.*

[32]*Id.*

Fearing for his safety, he fired one shot.[33] The suspects then fled the scene, leaving the truck behind.

According to the police report, Officer Warren notified his superiors as to what had happened and a subsequent investigation was conducted. The original police report noted that Officer Warren believed that he had missed and that there were no subjects found.[34] Officer Warren's superiors concluded that, based on his statements, Officer Warren's use of force was proper. This is where stories start to diverge, which led to the subsequent investigation and prosecution of Mr. Warren.

It was later revealed that, after Henry Glover had been shot, a passing motorist took him and his friend to a nearby makeshift police station to seek help.[35] When the three men reached the makeshift police station, they were greeted by police officers with their guns drawn and directed at them. The men were then handcuffed, and, meanwhile, Mr. Glover was left to die in the back seat of the car.[36] Once the two uninjured men were handcuffed and removed from the scene, Officer McCrae drove off with the car containing Mr. Glover and burned both the body and the car with a traffic flare.[37]

The outcome of this tragic incident led to a federal investigation that revealed several NOPD police officers had committed civil rights violations in the cover-up of Mr. Glover's death.[38] David Warren was charged in an eleven-count federal second superseding indictment along with four co-defendants, Dwayne Scheuermann, Gregory McRae, Robert Italiano, and Travis McCabe.[39] Mr. Warren was charged with one count of deprivation of rights under color of law for shooting Mr. Glover without legal justification, in violation of Title 18, United States Code, Section 242. He was also charged with one count of use of a weapon during a crime of violence in violation of Title 18, United States Code, Section 924(c) and (j).[40]

During the trial, the Government presented its case by claiming that Mr. Warren fired his personally-owned .233 caliber rifle at Henry Glover as he was running away. The Government claimed that Mr. Glover did not possess any

---

[33]*Id.*

[34]*Id.*

[35]*See* Department of Justice, *Three New Orleans Police Officers Found Guilty in the Post-Katrina Shooting and Burning of Henry Glover*, (2010), *available at* http://www.justice.gov/opa/pr/2010/December/10-crt-1420.html.

[36]*Id.*

[37]*Id.*

[38]It needs to be noted that, although Mr. Warren was already tried and found guilty, at the time of this writing the appeals process is currently underway and the full trial transcript is not ready yet. My recount of the Henry Glover story and analysis is based on both government and defense pleadings, my interview with a non-partisan attendant at the trial, and news excerpts courtesy of the *Times-Picayune* newspaper of New Orleans.

[39]Government's Response and Incorporated Memorandum in Opposition to Defendant's Post-Verdict Motions for Judgment of Acquittal, New Trial and/or Alternatively Arrest of Judgment at 1, *United States* v. *Warren*, No. 10-154 (E.D. La. Jan. 19, 2011).

[40]*Id.*

weapon and posed no risk to either the officers or civilians.[41] The jury decided in favor of the Government's presentment of the case and found Mr. Warren guilty of using a firearm in the commission of a crime.[42] The jury also convicted Officer McRae of willfully using fire to destroy a civilian's property by burning and destroying Tanner's car[43] and willfully depriving Glover's family members of their right to seek redress of his death.[44] Lastly, the jury convicted Officer McCabe of obstructing justice by writing and submitting a false report about the shooting of Henry Glover. He was also convicted of lying to the FBI and committing perjury by lying to a federal grand jury that was convened to investigate Mr. Glover's death.[45]

At trial, the defense alleged that they were not notified by the Government prior to trial that the Government's key witness, Officer Linda Howard, had given conflicting stories as to what she observed during the shooting of Mr. Glover. The defense asserted that Officer Howard originally told investigating agents that during the shooting she and Warren were on the second floor balcony, and then later recalled that they were actually behind a locked gate on the second floor.[46] The defense tried to discredit Officer Howard's testimony on cross-examination by impeaching her on her inconsistent statements.[47] The defense contended that Officer Howard's statements had changed multiple times and asserted that Officer Howard could not have seen Mr. Warren shoot Mr. Glover because the balcony where Officer Howard claimed to have observed all of this had a lock on the first and second floor.[48] The defense claimed that the only way for Officer Howard to have observed all that she claimed she observed, she would have had to been on the balcony of the second floor during the incident. However, if the stairs leading to the balcony had been locked, as Officer Howard first claimed, then there would have been no possible way for

---

[41]*Id.* at 2.

[42]Sentencing for the defendants has not started yet and the record will not be ready until April 26, 2011.

[43]Mr. Tanner is the individual who was determined to be with Mr. Glover at the time when Mr. Glover was shot and killed. *See* Laura Maggi, *Missing-person report on Henry Glover shooting got no timely follow-up, NOPD records show* (2010), *available at* http://nola.com/crime/index.ssf/2010/05/missing-person_report_on_henry.html.

[44]*See* Department of Justice, *Three New Orleans Police Officers Found Guilty in the Post-Katrina Shooting and Burning of Henry Glover,* (2010), *available at* http://www.justice.gov/opa/pr/2010/December/10-crt-1420.html.

[45]*Id.*

[46]Government's Response and Incorporated Memorandum in Opposition to Defendant's Post-Verdict Motions for Judgment of Acquittal, New Trial and/or Alternatively Arrest of Judgment at 7, *United States.* v. *Warren,* No. 10-154 (E.D. La. Jan. 19, 2011).

[47]*Id.*

[48]Memorandum in Support of Defendant Warren Motion for Judgment of Acquittal, New Trial, and Arrest of Verdict Under F.R.C.P. 29 33 and 34 at 8, No. 10-154 (E.D. La. Jan. 6, 2011).

her to get on the second floor balcony to observe the situation.[49] The defense stated that if the second floor gate was locked, then there could have been no possible way for Officer Howard to see Officer Warren shoot Mr. Glover.[50] The issue at trial was whether Officer Howard had actually seen Officer Warren shoot Mr. Glover. This led Special Agent Ashley Johnson to testify why the defense did not receive Officer Howard's different statements under *Brady* and *Giglio*.[51]

Special Agent Johnson testified during the Government's rebuttal about Officer Howard's inconsistent statements and stated that Officer Howard had indeed made inconsistent statement.[52] Agent Johnson stated that Officer Howard did make inconsistent statements, and that Officer Howard's attorney called back later and "corrected" her statement.[53] During Agent Johnson's cross-examination by the defense team, she was asked why a 302 form was not generated in connection with Officer Howard's inconsistent statements or why this change was not recorded by the prosecution. There was much confusion as to this issue, and the only cure was by having the prosecutor who commenced the investigation to testify to this error.[54] The prosecutor explained that, "adding to the confusion of the information given to the defense was Agent Johnson's statement that her 302 on Howard on May, 15, 2009 cited the wrong date."[55] The defense claimed that the Government knew of these inconsistent statements made by Officer Howard. Furthermore, whether the change in her story was written down or not, the Government knew of these changes, and should have notified the defense.[56] The Government responded to this by having the Assistant United States Attorney explain about the confusion, having the Assistant United States Attorney testify to the inconsistencies of Officer Howard's

---

[49]Government's Response and Incorporated Memorandum in Opposition to Defendant's Post-Verdict Motions for Judgment of Acquittal, New Trial and/or Alternatively Arrest of Judgment at 7, *United States* v. *Warren*, No. 10-154 (E.D. La. Jan. 19, 2011).

[50]*Id.*

[51]*See* Brady v. Maryland, 373 U.S. 83, 92 (1963) (holding that prosecution must give to the defense any exculpatory evidence); Giglio v. United States, 405 U.S. 150 (1972) (holding that prosecution's failure to inform the jury that a witness had been promised not to be prosecuted in exchange for his testimony was failure to fulfill the duty to present all material evidence to the jury, and constituted a violation of Due Process).

[52]Government's Response and Incorporated Memorandum in Opposition to Defendant's Post-Verdict Motions for Judgment of Acquittal, New Trial and/or Alternatively Arrest of Judgment at 8, *United States* v. *Warren*, No. 10-154 (E.D. La. Jan. 19, 2011).

[53]*Id.*

[54]I must note again that the issue that I highlighted was based on interviewing the defense counsel, interview with non-partisan trial attendant, and through the pleadings by both the prosecution and the defense counsel. The trial transcript will not be ready until after the defendants have been sentenced. There might be some discrepancies with my factual recount of the events, but without a trial transcript, I must rely on the pleadings, journalistic recount of the events, and trial attendant description.

[55]Memorandum in Support of Defendant Warren Motion for Judgment of Acquittal, New Trial, and Arrest of Verdict Under F.R.C.P. 29 33 and 34 at 8, No. 10-154 (E.D. La. Jan. 6, 2011).

[56]*Id.*

story, and by allowing the Assistant United States Attorney to testify as to why the 302 report was not written or filed.[57] This was the same Assistant United States Attorney who began the investigation of Mr. Glover's death and aided in the prosecution of Mr. Warren. The court decided to allow the Government to use the Assistant United States Attorney as a witness.

III. Analysis

The prosecutor in the Henry Glover case was allowed to serve both as prosecutor and as a witness. The court overruled vehement objections by the defense team, but still allowed the Government to proceed. The crucial question, then, is whether the court overstepped its boundary or violated the advocate witness rule?

As indicated above, there is no rule that prohibits a prosecutor from acting as a witness and as a prosecutor. Many states and federal circuits agree on the advocate witness rule and generally frown on such practices, but nevertheless allow it.[58] When we apply the standard Model Rule 3.7, we have to keep in mind the exceptions that allow advocates to act as both an advocate and a witness. Here, in the Henry Glover case, we have a very similar situation as to what happened in *United States v. Kenney*.[59] Both cases involve the situation where an Assistant United States Attorney who investigated and helped prepare the case for prosecution was called on by the Government as a witness. In *Kenney*, the court concluded that the testimony given by an Assistant United States Attorney "was not a contested matter as the jury was aware."[60] This would allow the Assistant United States Attorney's testimony to fall under the exception of Model Rule 3.7(a)(1) which allows an advocate to serve as a witness as long as it related to an uncontested matter.

In the Henry Glover case, the Assistant United States Attorney's testimony could have fallen under the uncontested issue exception, however the issue is a little more complex. The defense alleged that the Government violated *Brady* and *Giglio* obligations by not timely handing over exculpatory evidence or Officer Howard's inconsistent statements made to the FBI during the investigation. Due to the fact that the defense raised this issue, the matter on which the Assistant United States Attorney testified becomes material and no longer an uncontested matter under Model Rule 3.7(a)(1). However, the Assis-

---

[57]*See* note 38, *supra*.

[58]*See* United States v. Kenney, 911 F.2d 315, 320 (9th Cir. 1990) (holding that Assistant United States Attorney who assisted in the investigation and preparation of the case and was called by the government as a witness was proper). *See also* Lukas v. State, 194 Wis. 387 (Wis. 1927) (holding that there is no rule that prohibited a prosecutor from testifying as a witness).

[59]United States v. Kenney, 911 F.2d 315, 318 (9th Cir. 1990).

[60]*Id.* at 320.

tant United States Attorney testified to the confusion of why the 302 form was not properly filled out and why the date on the 302 form was incorrect.[61]

A the Assistant United States Attorney's testimony as to what caused the confusion might seem harmless at first, the fact that the defense alleged a *Brady/Giglio* violation makes the issue a bit more difficult. Going back to the four concerns addressed in *Johnston*, the first concern should be apparent. Although the government was trying to clarify confusion, the Assistant United States Attorney still runs the risk that "a testifying prosecutor will not be a fully objective witness given his position as an advocate for the government."[62] The very fact that the defense alleged a *Brady/Giglio* violation, which can ultimately lead to dismissal of the charges, turns the matter on which the Assistant United States Attorney is testifying into a contested matter. The defense raised the point that regardless of whether the Government was trying to withhold *Brady/Giglio* evidence, by having the Assistant United States Attorney explain this, the court would neglect the very concerns that were addressed in *Johnston*. It would be like asking the cat, who just ate the canary, whether he had seen the canary.

On the other hand, the Government asserted that this confusion was caused by human error and that the Government was not intentionally withholding *Brady/Giglio* evidence. The Government kept asserting its position that having the Assistant United States Attorney testify should be allowed under Rule 3.7(a)(1) to clear the confusion. The Government insisted that it was not withholding *Brady/Giglio* evidence, and that the error was a simple human error. After all, the Government claimed mere human error was the cause of the confusion, and the easiest way to clarify the confusion was to have the Assistant United States Attorney testify. Further bolstering the Government's claim is the fact that even if this issue is appealed and found to be error, it will quite possibly be considered to be harmless error.[63] It will quite possibly found to be harmless error because the Government met its *Brady/Giglio* obligations, and the defense was given Officer Howard's inconsistent statements in a timely fashion.[64]

IV. Conclusion

In the end, the court took great caution and care by allowing the Assistant United States Attorney to testify in order to clarify the confusion. The court

---

[61]Government's Response and Incorporated Memorandum in Opposition to Defendant's Post-Verdict Motions for Judgment of Acquittal, New Trial and/or Alternatively Arrest of Judgment at 8, *United States* v. *Warren*, No. 10-154 (E.D. La. Jan. 19, 2011).

[62]*Johnston*, 690 F.2d at 638.

[63]*See* United States v. Hosford, 782 F.2d 936 (11th Cir. 1986) (holding that prosecutor's participation as both prosecutor and witness at most constituted harmless error with the overwhelming evidence against the defendant). *See also* State v. Miller, 391 S.2d 1159 (La. 1980) (holding that prosecutor's dual role in a murder trial amounted to harmless error).

[64]Government's Response and Incorporated Memorandum in Opposition to Defendant's Post-Verdict Motions for Judgment of Acquittal, New Trial and/or Alternatively Arrest of Judgment at 8, *United States* v. *Warren*, No. 10-154 (E.D. La. Jan. 19, 2011).

made sure to excuse the jurors when both sides were debating this very issue, and when the jurors returned, the court gave the jurors extra instructions on how to weigh the evidence.[65] Further, even if this issue is appealed, the court could find that this issue is harmless error or even that there was no *Brady* or *Giglio* violation because the defense was given all of Officer Linda Howard's inconsistent statements. The defense was able to use and present to the jury all of Officer Howard's inconsistent statements.[66]

What happened in the Henry Glover case is something that is often permitted in criminal trials, but must be done with great care. What the court allowed is also in line with most jurisdictions including Louisiana.[67] What happened to Henry Glover is a tragedy and, while the process of justice continues on, the defense still has another bite at the apple through the appeals process. Once the appeals process is over, we may be able to determine whether or not the prosecutor's dual role was proper.

---

[65]There might be some discrepancies on how this advocate witness rule issue played out in the Henry Glover case. I am recounting the events through sources that attended the trial. Until the trial transcript is ready, it is impossible to recount with certainty what occurred during the trial. As I have said before, this paper addresses the concerns of the advocate witness rule and the special exceptions that prosecutors have when they take on dual roles. The analysis is also written from a time when the case as a whole is continuing and in flux, and events after this writing may supersede some aspects.

[66]Government's Response and Incorporated Memorandum in Opposition to Defendant's Post-Verdict Motions for Judgment of Acquittal, New Trial and/or Alternatively Arrest of Judgment at 8, *United States* v. *Warren*, No. 10-154 (E.D. La. Jan. 19, 2011).

[67]*See* State v. Miller, 391 So.2d 1159, 1161 (La. 1980) (holding that prosecuting attorney is a competent witness; however, noting that there is a danger inherent in allowing prosecuting attorney to assume the role of a witness).

8

The Advocate Witness Rule Expanded: The Relationship Between Attorneys and Their Witnesses and the Potential Conflicts of Interest

John Matthew Thomas

On a hot, muggy New Orleans summer night, a veteran of the New Orleans Police Department answers a call from dispatch. The words coming from the other end are all too common: "Shots fired in the 1200 block of Rampart Street, witness seen fleeing in black or dark blue vehicle on Rampart to Esplanade Avenue."[1] The officer, lucky to be nearby, races to the scene in time to get a glimpse of the shooter's vehicle driving away. After a brief high-speed chase, the shooter makes an attempt to evade the officer by foot. The officer follows. As he is chasing the suspect, the officer witnesses the suspect throw his gun and several other items by the wayside. The suspect suddenly makes a wrong turn and is met by an insurmountable fence; he is caught and arrested.

After his apprehension, the suspect is taken and booked at the Orleans Parish Prison. From here, the suspect's legal case begins. Prosecuting the case is one of Orleans Parish's ninety or so Assistant District Attorneys.[2] As it turns out, this prosecutor is the wife of the arresting officer. It is plain to see that this situation could possibly present a conflict of interest with the prosecutor.

The integrity of the legal system plays an integral part in the amount of confidence the public has in our government.[3] Being the most visible participant in the criminal justice system, a prosecutor giving even the appearance

---

[1]For this hypothetical situation I used the description of a tragic shooting occurring on Sunday March 20, 2011. Katie Urbaszewski, *Man found shot dead on South Front Street, available at* http://www.nola.com/crime/index.ssf/2011/03/man_found_dead_uptown/1952/comments-2.html (last visited April 15, 2011).

[2]The number of Assistant District Attorneys is taken from an Amicus Curiae Brief in the matter of *Harry F. Connick, in his official capacity as District Attorney; Eric Dubelier; James Williams, in his official capacity as Assistant District Attorney; Leon Cannizaro, Jr., in his official capacity as District Attorney; Orleans Parish District Attorney's Office versus John Thompson*, 09-571 (June 14, 2010).

[3]Kara S. Donahue, *Prosecutorial Ethics: The Case for the Per Se Rule*, 18 Fordham Urb. L.J. 407 (1990-1991), *available at* http://heinonline.org/HOL/LandingPage?collection=journals&handle=hein.journals/frdurb18&div=20&id=&page= / (last visited April 15, 2011). In this article, Donahue is citing, *inter alia*, the Model Code of Professional Responsibility. While those rules are no longer in general use, the language used here still holds true with regard to how the public views attorneys and the legal system.

of impropriety damages the trust that the public holds in the system.[4] The prosecutor has a responsibility as a minister of justice, not simply that of an advocate, a responsibility carrying with it the specific obligation to see that the defendant is accorded justice.[5] In achieving these duties, the prosecutor must act in a manner balancing his goal to convict with his duty to achieve justice and truth.

The Model Rules of Professional Conduct contain several different rules that come close, but do not quite address the situation in which a prosecutor holds a relationship with a witness. First, there is Model Rule 3.7, sometimes called "the advocate witness rule," which governs the attorney who desires to act as both advocate and witness.[6] And second, there is Model Rule 1.7, which is the code's general conflict of interest policy.[7] While both rules contain highly valuable information, neither, on its own, hits the proverbial nail on the head.

This paper examines the relationship between attorneys, specifically prosecutors, and the witnesses they examine. In Part I, I will introduce relevant statutes and ethical rules from which we can draw analogies. In Part II, I will lay out the various possible relationships between a prosecutor and a witness. In Part III, I will explore the ethical dilemma presented by these relationships through the examination of several hypothetical situations. And finally, in Part IV, I conclude that, if at all possible, the prosecuting attorney who is likely to examine a necessary witness with whom he holds a close relationship should withdraw from the case.

I. Statutory and Ethical Rules

Because there is not one specific rule regarding the ethical situation presented when a prosecutor is in some sort of relationship with a witness, we will examine several rules and statutes from which we can analogize. It is my contention throughout this paper, given the right level of relationship between a witness and a prosecutor, that the witness can act as a "stand-in" for an attorney with regards to the advocate witness rule. By this I mean that in reading the Model Rules of Professional Conduct regarding this situation, when the rules mention an attorney acting as a witness, the relationship between the prosecutor and the testifying witness is so great that this witness will ignore his own goals and values and act in a manner in which he believes the prosecutor would want him to act. Because a version of the Model Rules has been enacted in nearly every state, these rules will serve as our guide.

A. Model Rules of Professional Conduct — Rule 3.7

Model Rule 3.7 reads as follows:

---

[4]*Id.*

[5]Model Rules of Professional Conduct Rule 3.8, cmt. 1.

[6]Model Rules of Prof. Cond. Rule 3.7. Full analysis of rule to be discussed *infra*.

[7]Model Rules of Prof. Cond. Rule 1.7. Full analysis of rule to be discussed *infra*.

(a) A lawyer shall not act as advocate at a trial in which the lawyer is likely to be a necessary witness unless:
    (1) the testimony relates to an uncontested issue;
    (2) the testimony relates to the nature and value of legal services rendered in the case; or
    (3) disqualification of the lawyer would work substantial hardship on the client.
(b) A lawyer may act as advocate in a trial in which another lawyer in the lawyer's firm is likely to be called as a witness unless precluded from doing so by Rule 1.7 or 1.9.[8]

I. Analysis of the Rule

Except for the three enumerated circumstances, a lawyer shall not act as an advocate at a trial in which the lawyer is likely to be a necessary witness. The first logical step in this analysis is to determine what is and what is not a necessary witness. In a North Carolina State Bar Journal Ethics Opinion Article, bar counsel Deanna S. Brocker described the criteria to be a "necessary witness" under North Carolina's Revised Rule 3.7, which is based upon Model Rule 3.7. She wrote, "Certainly, if the client's case would fail but for the lawyer's testimony, the attorney must abandon the role of advocate. Moreover, if an attorney's testimony would be deemed by a 'disinterested attorney' likely to be important to the client's success, the attorney should withdraw as advocate and testify instead."[9] Ms. Brocker adds that "an attorney should be permitted to continue representation at trial if the proposed testimony is merely cumulative or is obtainable from another source."[10] Finally, Ms. Brocker arrives at the conclusion that "the trial court is vested with discretion to determine issues of 'necessity' while balancing the interests of expediency and fairness in ruling upon motions to disqualify."[11]

When a witness is being examined by an attorney with whom he holds some sort of relationship, there is the possibility that the witness will act in a manner in which he believes the attorney would like him to act, rather than in a manner in which the entire truth is presented. When a witness conducts himself this way, he is stepping into the shoes of the attorney, and Model Rule 3.7 provides an outline of how to deal with this analogous situation. With this guideline, the court could use the same standard in determining whether the witness was a necessary witness as it does when it determines whether an attorney would be a necessary witness. After a determination that a witness is necessary, the analysis of the rule turns to the situations in which a lawyer is permitted to act as both an advocate and a witness. Once it has been determined that the witness is necessary, the only way the prosecuting attorney will

---

[8] MRPC Rule 3.7 - Lawyer As Witness.

[9] Deanna S. Brocker, *"Advocate or Witness?,"* Ethics Opinion Articles — N.C. State Bar Journal, *available at* http://www.ncbar.gov/ethics/eth_articles_2,4.asp. (last visited April 15, 2011).

[10] *Id.*

[11] *Id.*

avoid disqualification is by meeting one of the three exceptions enumerated below.

Important to a prosecutor seeking to act as both an advocate and a witness, or in the situation at hand, a prosecutor seeking to examine a witness with whom she is in a close relationship, are the three exceptions to Rule 3.7's general rule that an attorney may not act as an advocate in a case in which he is a necessary witness. As these exceptions indicate, there are three scenarios in which an attorney is permitted to act as both advocate and witness, or for our case, in which a prosecuting attorney will be able to examine a witness with whom he holds a close relationship: (1) if the testimony relates to an uncontested issue; (2) if the testimony relates to the nature and value of the legal services rendered in the case; or (3) if qdisqualification of the lawyer would work substantial hardship on the client.[12] Since our hypothetical witness would not be testifying to the nature and value of the legal services provided, the only two relevant exceptions are numbers one and three.

In my opinion, exception number one would work itself out through the natural flow of the legal process. If the testimony is uncontested then all parties will know that it is uncontested and, as such, the prosecutor will be permitted to act as a witness, or, in our case, examine a witness with whom he has a close relationship.

Given the nature of the third exception, it appears that this is where many potential issues will occur. Will the disqualification of a prosecutor, based on his close relationship with a necessary witness, work substantial harm on the client — the general public? This balancing test is best answered through a series of hypothetical situations, which I will discuss below.

II. Policies Behind the Rule

Essential to analogizing Model Rule 3.7 to the situation being discussed in this paper is an examination of the policies behind the rule. As the first comment to this rule states, "combining the roles of advocate and witness can prejudice the tribunal and the opposing party and can also involve a conflict of interest between the lawyer and client."[13] In an article for the New York Professional Responsibility Report, Professor Roy Simon of Hofstra University School of Law identifies the policies underlying why an attorney is not permitted to act as both a witness and advocate, as laid out by the Second Circuit as follows:

> We have identified four risks that rule 3.7(a) is designed to alleviate: (1) the lawyer might appear to vouch for his own credibility; (2) the lawyer's testimony might place opposing counsel in a difficult position when she has to cross-examine her lawyer-adversary and attempt to impeach his credibility; (3) some may fear that the testifying attorney is distorting the truth as a result of bias in favor of his client; and (4) when an individual assumes the role of advocate and witness both, the line between argument and evidence may be blurred, and the jury confused. These concerns matter because, if

---

[12]MRPC Rule 3.7.

[13]MRPC Rule 3.7, cmt. 1.

they materialize, they could undermine the integrity of the judicial process.[14]

Although the New York Rules of Professional Conduct are slightly different from the Model Rules of Professional Conduct, the fact remains that when a witness takes the stand who has a close relationship with the attorney who is examining her, several of these same policy concerns will arise.[15]

Of these policy concerns, three seem to be relevant when talking about a witness who has a relationship with the prosecutor. The first related policy issue lies in the concern that some may fear that the testifying attorney might be distorting the truth as a result of bias in favor of his client. This issue raises a great deal of concern. It is easy to see the correlation between the two scenarios. On one hand, there is the attorney testifying and potentially distorting the truth to favor his client — and on the other hand there is the person who holds the close relationship with the attorney testifying and distorting the truth in favor of the person with whom he holds a close relationship, which in turn is distorting the truth in favor of the client. If these concerns materialize in the case of a witness testifying before an attorney with whom he has a close relationship, the integrity of the judicial process could be undermined.

The second concern arises when an individual assumes the role of both advocate and witness, leaving the line between argument and evidence blurred, and the jury confused. In the situation here, the concern would arise when the witness with whom the prosecutor holds a close relationship begins his testimony. The judge and jury, aware that the prosecutor and witness maintain a relationship, could be confused by the "team" that they are listening to. Because of the relationship, it is quite possible that the jury could become lost in what is argument and what is evidence. A witness is required to testify on the basis of personal knowledge, while an advocate is expected to explain and comment on evidence given by others.[16] It might not be clear to the jury whether a statement by a witness maintaining a relationship with a prosecutor should be taken as proof or as an analysis of the proof.[17]

Although the Second Circuit lists this concern first, I believe the third concern flows logically from the second. In the case where an attorney is exam-

---

[14]Roy Simon, *A Flurry of Decisions Under the Advocate-Witness Rule (Rule 3.7)*, New York Professional Responsibility Report, May 2010. The above quote taken from Simon is a direct quote from *Murray v. Metropolitan Life Ins. Co.*, 583 F.3d 173 (2d Cir. 2009), known in the district court as *In re MetLife Demutualization Litigation*.

[15]The case being discussed by Professor Simon involved New York Rules of Professional Conduct, Rule 3.7.New York has adopted a version of the Model Rules similar to the rules drafted by the American Bar Association. Outside of a few phrasing changes, the only difference is two additional instances where a lawyer shall not act as both an advocate and a witness. The first says that a lawyer may not act as an advocate before a tribunal in a matter in which the lawyer is likely to be a witness on a significant issue of facts unless the testimony will relate solely to a matter of formality, and there is no reason to believe that substantial evidence will be offered in opposition to the testimony; and the second allows for the attorney to act as an advocate and as a witness when the testimony is authorized by the tribunal.

[16]MRPC Rule 3.7, cmt. 2.

[17]*See* MRPC Rule 3.3, cmt. 2.

ining a witness with whom she has a close relationship, it could appear to the court that the prosecutor is vouching for the credibility of her witness. Prosecutorial vouching can occur in two ways: first, "the prosecution may place the prestige of the government behind the witness by personal assurances of the witness' veracity," and, second, the prosecution "may indicate that information not available to the jury supports the witness' testimony."[18] Although I have not suggested that a prosecutor would be explicitly vouching for the witness' veracity, it seems that by examining a witness with whom the prosecutor holds a close relationship, she would be implicitly vouching for the witness. This problem raises the same concern raised when analyzing the policy behind Rule 3.7.

B. Model Rules of Professional Conduct — Rule 1.7

In determining whether it is permissible to act as an advocate in a trial, or in our situation where a prosecutor would like to act as an advocate in a trial in which he maintains a relationship with a necessary witness, the lawyer must also consider whether there are any potential conflicts of interest which will require compliance with Rule 1.7.[19] Even if a lawyer is not disqualified by Rule 3.7, he still must clear the hurdle of Rule 1.7.

A general rule governing conflicts of interest, Model Rule 1.7 reads in its entirety as follows:

Rule 1.7 Conflict of Interest: Current Clients

(a) Except as provided in paragraph (b), a lawyer shall not represent a client if the representation involves a concurrent conflict of interest. A concurrent conflict of interest exists if:

(1) the representation of one client will be directly adverse to another client; or

(2) there is a significant risk that the representation of one or more clients will be materially limited by the lawyer's responsibilities to another client, a former client or a third person or by a personal interest of the lawyer.

(b) Notwithstanding the existence of a concurrent conflict of interest under paragraph (a), a lawyer may represent a client if:

(1) the lawyer reasonably believes that the lawyer will be able to provide competent and diligent representation to each affected client;

(2) the representation is not prohibited by law;

(3) the representation does not involve a claim by one client against another client represented by the lawyer in the same litigation or proceeding before a tribunal; and

(4) each affected client gives informed consent in writing.[20]

---

[18]William B. Johnson, Annotation, *Use of plea bargain or grant of immunity as improper vouching for credibility of witness in federal cases*, 76 A.L.R. Fed. 409 (originally published in 1986).

[19]MRPC Rule 3.7, cmt. 5.

[20]MRPC Rule 1.7.

I. Analysis of Rule

Rule 1.7 is the general conflict of interest rule. Pertinent to our discussion, Rule 1.7(a)(2) states that "except as provided in paragraph (b), a lawyer shall not represent a client if the representation involves a concurrent conflict of interest."[21] A concurrent conflict of interest exists if there is a significant risk that the representation of one or more clients will be materially limited by the lawyer's responsibilities to another client, a former client or a third person, *or by a personal interest of the lawyer.*[22]

It is a distinct possibility that a prosecutor who calls to the stand someone with whom she holds a close relationship will encounter a concurrent conflict of interest as a result of the examination of this witness. Family ties and personal relationships can present situations in which a material-limitation conflict arises.[23] In fact, the State Bar of Arizona has previously dealt with a situation quite similar to the one being discussed in this paper.[24] In that case, an assistant public defender was involved romantically with a police officer who had been an investigating, arresting, or witnessing officer on several occasions involving the clients of the Public Defender's Office.[25] The Committee said, "It is not difficult to imagine a situation where the Officer takes the stand to testify against the accused, followed by cross examination of the APD, followed by redirect examination in which the prosecutor uses the romantic relationship to either bolster the Officer's testimony or weaken the cross-examination."[26] Unwilling to draw a bright line rule, the Committee issued several factors to consider in determining whether representation would be adversely affected by the relationship: "(1) the nature and duration of the relationship; (2) the nature of the charges at issue; and (3) the nature of the anticipated testimony of the Officer, including the materiality of the issue to which the Officer is expected to testify, and whether the anticipated testimony is disputed."[27] When a jury hears testimony from a witness and that testimony being taken by someone in a personal relationship with that witness, there is a chance that this testimony could be seen as tainted and swing in favor of the defendant. This would be an adverse effect on the representation of the people.

Subsection (b) of Rule 1.7 lays out the instances in which an attorney could represent her client, despite the conflict of interest.[28] One key aspect of these exceptions is getting informed consent, in writing from the client, regarding the conflict of interest. Jurisdictions around the country have differing opinions on whether a government entity may waive its counsel's conflict of

---

[21]*Id.*

[22]*Id.* (emphasis added).

[23]*See* ABA, Annotated Model Rules of Professional Conduct, Rule 1.7 (2010).

[24]Ariz. Ethics Op. 2001-12 (2001).

[25]*Id.*

[26]*Id.*

[27]*Id.*

[28]MRPC Rule 1.7.

interest.[29] Some of these jurisdictions adhere to a per se government-cannot-consent rule, relying on the public interest and reasoning that a government lawyer may use his or her position to secure consent improperly.[30] Other jurisdictions, on the other hand, have chosen to reject this rationale and permit government entities, such as a district attorney's office, to give consent.[31]

II. Types of Relationships

After a close examination of the analogous rules that could potentially govern a situation in which the attorney has a relationship with the witness she is questioning, we must take a deeper look into the types of potential relationships that could be encountered.

A. Friendship

To start, we can look at how a friendship between a prosecutor and her witness can present a potential conflict of interest. In *Hot Topics in the Legal Profession 2010*, Daniel Meyer breaks down friendship as a legally cognizable term. First, he provides a broad definition for friendship, stating that friendship is a relational term which signifies something about the quality and character of the relationship involved."[32] Building upon this definition with the words of Plato, Meyer says that the quality and character of a friendship is a kind of love where people generally assist each other.[33] As the next building block, Meyer uses a definition provided by Professor Charles Fried: a "friend is described as one who acts in the interest of another over his own."[34] And finally, the most poignant definition given in Meyer's article comes from a dictionary: "a friend [is] one well known to another and regarded with affection and loyalty; an intimate supporter."[35] After quoting a host of philosophers and professors alike, Meyer arrives at the concise conclusion that friendship implies loyalty and that this loyalty implies partiality.[36] This partiality — the desire of a witness to assist his friend, to act in his friend's interest instead of his own, to remain loyal and support his friend — could very well play out when the prosecutor is examining a witness who is her friend.

---

[29]ABA, Annotated Model Rules of Professional Conduct, Rule 1.7 (2010).

[30]*Id.*

[31]*Id.*

[32]Daniel Meyer, *"Friends," Episode 2: The Wisdom of Discretionary Recusal and Judge as Actual Friend,* Hot Topics in the Legal Profession 2010. Meyer is quoting from Ethan J. Lieb, *Friendship and the Law,* 54 UCLA L. Rev. 631, 638 (2007).

[33]Meyer, paraphrasing Jeremy M. Miller, *Judicial Recusal and Disqualification: The Need for a Per Se Rule on Friendship (Not Acquaintance),* 33 Pepp. L. Rev. 575 (2006).

[34]*See id.* (Meyer discussing Professor Fried's concept of "the lawyer as friend").

[35]*Id.*

[36]*Id.*

B. Spousal Relationship

The logical progression of an argument based on a conflict of interest arising out of a friendship between a prosecutor and a witness is the conflict of interest presented when there is a spousal relationship between prosecutor and witness. It has been said time and again that marriage is the cornerstone of society.[37] With marriage comes family. And the "strength of a family, like the strength of an army, is in its loyalty to each other."[38] The bond between a married couple is an indication of loyalty to the highest degree. To an even greater extent than in the friendship situation described above, a wife questioning her husband, and a husband questioning his wife, will definitely find it hard to leave loyalties aside and act in a way that does not prejudice the tribunal and the opposing party. Even if they could find it within themselves to act properly, it will be very hard for anyone in the jury or outside the legal field to come to the same conclusion.

Whether the relationship is a spousal relationship, merely a friendship, or somewhere in between, it is clear that, should a situation arise in which a prosecutor is questioning someone with whom she holds a personal relationship, there is at least a chance of impropriety.

III. Hypothetical Situations

A. Heroic Arrest in New Orleans

It is now time to revisit the opening hypothetical situation. Officer Tom Smith, an upstanding member of the New Orleans Police Department, responds to a call indicating that shots have been fired and a victim is down. Officer Smith arrives to the scene in time to witness the vehicle screech away. Fortunately for the citizens of New Orleans, Officer Smith began pursuit of the suspect. After a brief high-speed chase, the suspect decided to try his luck in a footrace. Unbeknownst to the suspect, Officer Smith was a former state champion in track at the Isidore Newman School in Uptown New Orleans. Once on foot, it only took a brief second for the suspect to make a mistake, which allowed Officer Smith to apprehend the suspect and place him under arrest for a variety of charges including murder and possession of marijuana.

The next day, a 15-year veteran of the Orleans Parish District Attorney's Office is assigned to prosecute this case. As luck would have it, the Assistant District Attorney was Mrs. Meagan Smith, the officer's wife. Mrs. Smith, being the zealous advocate that she is, did not want to pass up the opportunity to prosecute this case.

---

[37]A Google search for the phrase "marriage cornerstone of society quote" yielded 265,000 results in .24 seconds. The search is available at: http://www.google.com/search?hl=en&safe=off&q=necessary+witness&btnG=Search#s client=psy&hl=en&safe=off&q=marriage+cornerstone+of+society+quote&aq=f&aqi=&a ql=&oq=&pbx=1&bav=on.2,or.r_gc.r_pw.&fp=9e7e71450ecd8df6.

[38]Mario Puzo, The Family 9 (2001).

As she began to prepare for the trial, it became apparent that Officer Smith would be required to testify, as he was the only person who saw the suspect's vehicle leave the scene, he was the only officer in pursuit, and he was the only officer to witness the suspect attempt to ditch the murder weapon and drug stash.

I. Rule 3.7

Before trial, the Honorable Judge Greg LeBlanc was presented with both the Defendant's Motion to Disqualify Counsel and the prosecution's Opposition to Motion to Disqualify Counsel. After reviewing the defense's pleading and memorandum containing the analogy of Model Rule 3.7 to the situation, Judge LeBlanc granted Defendant's Motion to Disqualify. Without any specific rule regarding the situation, Judge LeBlanc reviewed Rule 3.7 and agreed with defendant's counsel, deciding that this is the best starting point. Judge LeBlanc began the application of counsel's analysis by looking at the relationship between Officer Smith and ADA Smith. As a married couple, it was apparent that the prosecutor and witness could be extremely loyal to each other. In light of this, Judge LeBlanc decided to go forth with the analysis of Rule 3.7, with it on his mind that, given the situation, the prosecutor and the witness were basically the same person.

Judge LeBlanc first determined that Officer Smith was a necessary witness. Judge LeBlanc noted that but for the testimony, the state's case would fail. Further, Judge LeBlanc believes that Officer Smith's testimony would be deemed by a disinterested attorney likely to be important to the state's success, and, as such, ADA Smith should have withdrawn.

Because Judge LeBlanc has determined that Officer Smith is a necessary witness, the only way ADA Smith would be able to testify (if she were the witness) is if her testimony fits into one of the three exceptions. The only exception this situation could possible fall under is exception number (3). This exception says that a lawyer shall not act as advocate at a trial in which the lawyer (here, again treating the witness and prosecutor to be one and the same) is likely to be a necessary witness unless disqualification of the lawyer would work substantial hardship on the client.[39]

Next Judge LeBlanc applied the balancing test to determine whether or not ADA Smith would be disqualified. Whether the tribunal is likely to be misled, or the opposing party is likely to suffer prejudice, depends on the nature of the case, the importance and probable tenor of Officer Smith's testimony, and the probability that the officer's testimony will conflict with that of witnesses.[40] Even if there is a risk of prejudice, in determining whether the lawyer should be disqualified, due regard must be given to the effect of disqualification on the lawyer's client.[41] It is relevant that one or both parties could reasonably foresee that the lawyer would probably be a witness.[42]

---

[39]MRPC Rule 3.7.

[40]See id., cmt. 4.

[41]Id.

[42]Id.

Taking all of this into account, Judge LeBlanc decided to disqualify ADA Smith as prosecuting attorney from this case. He determined that the jury could become confused by the relationship between Officer Smith and ADA Smith and the trial could become prejudiced. Further, it was highly foreseeable that as the arresting officer, Officer Smith would be called as a necessary witness. Given all of the information provided in the hypothetical, Judge LeBlanc made the correct call. The state's case will not miss a beat; as soon as ADA Smith is out of the case, the District Attorney will assign one of his other ninety ADAs to the case.

II. Rule 1.7

Even if Judge LeBlanc had not disqualified ADA Smith on the basis of Rule 3.7, she should have been aware of the potential conflict of interest under Rule 1.7. This rule provides that a lawyer shall not represent a client if there is a significant risk that the representation of one more clients will be materially limited by a personal interest of the lawyer. Despite this ban, attorneys can still represent their clients if they have met the requirements of subsection (b). Subsection (b) lists four factors that must be met, chief among them is the requirement that a lawyer must reasonably believe that the lawyer will be able to provide competent and diligent representation to her client.[43]

In my opinion, ADA Smith should not have taken representation in this case. In a large district, such as New Orleans, an Assistant District Attorney is not suffering from a lack of work. It would have been prudent of ADA Smith to pass the case along to another ADA and pick up the next file on her desk. My opinion remains the same even if ADA Smith contends that she reasonably believed she could provide competent and diligent representation to the state. There is no reason to give the judge and jury any reason to think that there is any impropriety in the case. Even if ADA Smith was completely clear of any conflict of interest in her mind, she should have recognized that it would be extremely hard for a jury to see that her relationship with the witness would not affect the case. I believe that, given the situation, there is a significant risk that the jury will view the relationship between herself and the witness — Officer Smith — as prejudicial against the defendant and that this will have a negative impact on the state's case.

B. Saturday Night in Bunkie

In this hypothetical situation, the facts of the case are the same, except the incident took place in Bunkie, Louisiana, a town of approximately 4,500 people in Avoyelles Parish.[44] One main difference between Bunkie and New Orleans is

---

[43]MRPC Rule 1.7.

[44]Population figure according to the U.S. Census Bureau. Figures can be found on the fact sheet for Bunkie, Louisiana, *available at* http://factfinder.census.gov/servlet/ACSSAFFFacts?_event=Search&geo_id=&_geoCo ntext=&_street=&_county=bunkie&_cityTown=bunkie&_state=04000US22&_zip=&_l ang=en&_sse=on&pctxt=fph&pgsl=010. A Louisiana parish is like a "county" elsewhere.

the populations of the parishes in which the cities are located. While Orleans Parish might have ninety Assistant District Attorneys, Avoyelles Parish might have only four or five.

I. Rule 3.7

Now, the honorable Judge William Niska presiding in the 12th Judicial District for the Parish of Avoyelles has a different scenario to deal with. Prosecuting the case is ADA Dora Centanni. Judge Niska is presented with the same pleadings filed in the previous hypothetical. Judge Niska again has made the same determination that the police officer is a necessary witness. This is where the analysis between the two scenarios takes a slightly different turn. While the transfer of the case out of the hands of ADA Smith was made easy in Orleans Parish by the shear number of attorneys employed by the District Attorney's Office, the DA in Avoyelles Parish does not have that luxury. Because each of his ADAs have such a heavy caseload, it would be impossible to simply pass off the case. It would not get handled in a timely manner, and as a result, disquailfication of ADA Centanni could work substantial hardship on the case. Because the disqualification of ADA Centanni could work substantial hardship on the case, even though her husband — the police officer — is a necessary witness, ADA Smith should not be disqualified.

II. Rule 1.7

Even though ADA Centanni has not been disqualified, she should still pay attention to Model Rule 1.7. Given the setting, I believe that even if there was a conflict of interest, as long as ADA Centanni reasonably believes that she can provide competent and diligent representation to the state, she should be allowed to go forward with this case. I think it is a much fairer assumption that a jury in Avoyelles Parish could set aside the fact that a prosecutor is married to a police officer to whom she is married. Given the small size of the population, I believe that the people will be much more forgiving of this type of situation. However, I do believe that, if it is at all possible, in an effort to avoid the appearance of any impropriety, ADA Centanni should do everything in her power to withdraw from the case and let one of the other ADAs take charge.

IV. Conclusions

The relationship between a prosecutor and a witness can have a serious impact on the case. Because of this, it seems beneficial to take Model Rule 3.7 one step beyond governing the Lawyer As Witness. If the relationship is significant enough, I believe it will be hard for the witness to act in a manner where she is presenting the evidence exactly as it was, with no bias. Even if the prosecutor and witness to whom she is related can put their biases aside, I find it hard to believe that most juries could do the same. Furthermore, the prosecutor should make every effort to avoid a situation where she is forced to examine a witness with whom she holds a close relationship, so that the line between argument and evidence remains crystal clear to the jury. As one last reason to avoid this situation, the prosecutor should avoid examining someone with whom she has a relationship so that it does not appear that she is vouching for the credibility of her own witness. Each of these concerns, if brought to life, could appear to the jury and to people outside of the legal field as an impropriety.

Should an attorney avoid disqualification under the analogized version of Rule 3.7, he should also keep Rule 1.7 in mind. This rule would serve him as a general guide to conflicts of interest. It is definitely possible that an attorney could still have a potential conflict of interest, despite the fact that he has not been disqualified under Rule 3.7.

Using these two rules as a guide, it is my recommendation that a prosecuting attorney who is likely to examine a necessary witness with whom he holds a close relationship should seek to withdraw himself if at all possible.

9

Finality in "Hybridized" MDL Settlements: A Legitimate Pursuit

Raymond M. Hindieh

I. Introduction

In the years surrounding the evolution of mass tort litigation, multi-district litigation (MDL) has emerged as a litigation method of fundamental importance in the American legal system. Some five decades of class action litigation has outlined the borders and limits of the class action method, necessitating substitute methods which are either more desirable or quintessential to prospective mass tort parties. MDL cases currently constitute approximately fifteen percent of all civil litigation in federal courts.[1] As MDL cases represent a growing percentage of litigation in federal courts, the judiciary has escalated efforts to find settlement solutions for MDLs. Such efforts have led to divisions regarding ethical considerations of how MDL attorneys should conduct themselves within the confines of the attorney-client relationship. Critics of recent innovative solutions have argued that attorney-client relationships, even in MDLs, must conform to traditional pre-existing notions of the attorney-client relationship.

This article considers the position articulated by Professors Erichson and Zipursky in their 2011 article *Consent Versus Closure*[2] and by their critical compatriots, namely: that mass tort settlement in the contours of the attorney-client relationship, to be ethical, must be judicially pigeon-holed into existing models of civil litigation, either class action settlements or traditional one-on-one civil litigation.[3]

This article ultimately rejects this constructed view of the role and ethical boundaries of the attorneys involved in MDLs. Rather, this article supports the exploration of alternative mass tort settlement vehicles, such as that recently devised by Judge Eldon E. Fallon in *In re Vioxx Products Liability Litigation*,[4]

---

[1] *Panel Promotes Just and Efficient Conduct of Litigation*, The Third Branch: Newsletter of the Federal Courts, February, 2010, *available at* http://www.jpml.uscourts.gov/General_Info/Third_Branch_Interviews/The_Third_Branch_-_February-2010-Heyburn_Interview.pdf (last visited April 11, 2011).

[2] Howard M. Erichson & Benjamin C. Zipursky, *Consent Versus Closure*, 96 Cornell L. Rev. 265 (2011).

[3] *Id.*

[4] 501 F. Supp. 2d 789 (E.D. La. 2007). Eldon E. Fallon is a United States District Court Judge for the Eastern District of Louisiana; he has overseen notable recent MDLs, including *In re Vioxx Products Liability Litigation*, MDL No. 1657, and *In re Chinese-Manufactured Drywall Products Liability Litigation*, MDL No. 2047.

and in recent proposals from the American Law Institute (ALI) to amend the rules governing aggregate settlement. Such alternative methods have been dubbed "hybridization" and have been fully endorsed by Professor Richard A. Nagareda of Vanderbilt University Law School, and Professor Edward F. Sherman of Tulane University Law School, two preeminent minds in the field of mass tort litigation. Such hybrid settlement vehicles have emerged as a desirable and necessary alternative to the class action method, as a result of the limited nature of class action in regards to the fields of claims in which it can be successfully employed. This article will respond to the criticisms of "hybridization," and offers the proposition that despite the scholarly commentary critical of it,[5] the future of mass tort litigation necessitates alternative settlement methods.

II. Multi-District Litigation at a Glance

A. The Structure of MDL

The basic understanding and structure of a typical MDL, despite the complications which arise from it, is fairly straightforward. The governing body of MDLs is the Judicial Panel on Multidistrict Litigation. In 1968, Congress enacted 28 U.S.C. § 1407, which empowers the seven-member panel appointed by the Chief Justice of the United States; the original members included exceedingly accomplished jurists such as Alfred P. Murrah and John Minor Wisdom.[6] Acting under section 1407, the Panel is entrusted with broad powers to transfer groups of cases into a single district court for the purposes of conducting various pretrial proceedings without the need to satisfy the exacting requirements of personal jurisdiction and venue.[7] The Panel need only consider two issues when determining whether or not to transfer a group of cases to a single consolidated court. First, whether common issues of facts exist among the several pending civil actions such that centralization will further convenience of the parties and witnesses, and "promote the just and efficient conduct of the actions."[8] Second, which federal district and judge is the best candidate to handle the transferred and consolidated cases.[9]

Since its inception, the Panel has considered motions for the consolidation of over 1950 dockets involving more than "250,000 cases and literally millions of claims therein," encompassing varying and diverse types of litigation including: airplane crashes, train accidents, mass torts, products liability, etc.[10] In addition to the growing variety of cases, the sheer number is expanding — partly due to the dwindling availability and attractiveness of class actions

---

[5]*See infra* note 22 and accompanying text.

[6]*See* John G. Heyburn II, *A View From the Panel: Part of the Solution*, 82 Tul. L. Rev. 2225, 2226 (2008).

[7]*Id.* at 2227-28.

[8]*Id.* at 2228 (citing 28 U.S.C. §1407(a)).

[9]*Id.* (citing 28 U.S.C. §1407).

[10]*Id.*

as a method to resolve mass tort claims, given relatively recent decisions by the United States Supreme Court as well as legislation by Congress.[11] In particular, *Amchem Products, Inc. v. Windsor*[12] and *Ortiz v. Fibreboard Corp.*,[13] two asbestos cases decided by the Supreme Court in the late 1990s, made issues such as intra-class conflicts and individual characteristics of the plaintiffs a virtual death blow to class certification in many cases, leaving non-class aggregate settlements to fill the void.[14]

The purpose of MDL is to eliminate duplicative discovery in similar cases, avoid conflicting judicial rulings, and conserve valuable judicial resources.[15] Normally, the transferee court lacks authority to try actions transferred to its court, thus the Panel is also charged with the responsibility of remanding individual cases back to the transferor court from which they originated,[16] once the purposes and procedures of MDL have been accomplished.

From the perspective of the transferee district court judges who oversee these MDLs, the largest can encompass thousands of cases submitted by various attorneys.[17] Three of the largest MDLs in history were: *In re Guidant Corp. Implantable Defibrillators Products Liability Litigation*, overseen by Judge Donovan Frank; *In re Vioxx Products Liability Litigation*, overseen by Judge Eldon Fallon; and *In re Zyprexa Products Liability Litigation*, overseen by Judge Jack Weinstein.[18] Vioxx was the largest MDL in history to date; it settled for $4.85 billion.[19] Each of the district judges who oversaw these massive MDLs appointed a small number of lead attorneys to an executive committee, and a larger number to a "Plaintiff's Steering Committeee ('PSC')," and each judge also formed additional committees for different purposes, "such as conducting settlement negotiations or coordinating with attorneys handling state court cases."[20] Attorneys selected to be lead attorneys on the designated executive committee assumed complete control over the MDL from the plaintiff's perspective, including: determination and presentation of briefs and oral argument, coordination of discovery, settlement negotiations, etc.[21] By creating committees and delegating control over these tasks, the MDL can be more

---

[11]*Id.* at 2232. Notably, Congress passed the Class Action Fairness Act of 2005.

[12]521 U.S. 591 (1997).

[13]527 U.S. 815 (1999).

[14]Howard M. Erichson & Benjamin C. Zipursky, *Consent Versus Closure*, 96 Cornell L. Rev. 265, 267 (2011).

[15]John G. Heyburn II, *A View From the Panel: Part of the Solution*, 82 Tul. L. Rev. 2225, 2236 (2008).

[16]*Id.* at 2233-34.

[17]Charles Silver & Gregory P. Miller, *The Quasi-Class Action Method of Managing Multi-District Litigations: Problems and a Proposal*, 63 Vand. L. Rev. 107, 115 (2010).

[18]*Id. See* 484 F. Supp. 2d 973 (D. Minn. 2007); 501 F. Supp. 2d 789, 2005 WL 3117302 (E.D.N.Y. 2005).

[19]Charles Silver & Gregory P. Miller, *The Quasi-Class Action Method of Managing Multi-District Litigations: Problems and a Proposal*, 63 Vand. L. Rev. 107, 115 (2010).

[20]*See id.*

[21]*Id.*

succinctly organized in the hands of the selectively appointed attorneys, rather than leaving sensitive pretrial activities to a large and disorderly number of attorneys.

B. The Origins of MDL: Mass Torts and the Limits of Class Actions

In understanding MDLs, it is important to first understand the legal obstacle they were designed to address: mass torts. In his book entitled *Mass Torts in a World of Settlement*, late Professor Richard Nagareda outlined the origins of mass tort litigation and the push for developments of settlement vehicles to address the growing need.[22] In Chapter I, entitled "Origins," Nagareda identified four salient factors which arose throughout the twentieth century that were responsible for the development and expansion of mass torts: economics and market creation, evolutions in tort theory, transformations in civil procedure, and political developments.[23]

As a matter of economics, mass torts evolved in response to and in the image of industrialization, the "systematized processes for production and sale on an unprecedented scale."[24] With products marketed to consumers on a mass scale, flaws in consumer products were exposed far more widely, to far more people, necessitating a new method of redressability.[25] In response to this shift in the economic structure of the twentieth century, plaintiffs' lawyers created a new market, in which they "mass-marketed" the tortious claims of plaintiffs against products as "products" themselves, sold to defendants in the form of settlements.[26]

Developments in tort law occurred in response to the market shifts toward industrialization.[27] Mass marketing expanded the reach of products "beyond simple one-to-one contractual relationships between seller and buyer," and, as a result, by the mid-twentieth century courts had fully abandoned the concept that tort liability was founded upon the notion of contractual relationships, or "privity."[28] Consequently, consumers could now sue not only the direct supplier of the tortious product, but also manufacturers and distributors further up the chain. Producers were now susceptible to liability from not only the direct consumer, but also multitudes of other parties who came into contact with the tortious product.[29] Eventually, the Restatement (Second) of Torts in-

---

[22]Richard A. Nagareda, Mass Torts in a World of Settlement vii (2007).

[23]*Id.* at 1.

[24]*Id.*

[25]*Id.*

[26]*Id.* at 4.

[27]*Id.*

[28]*Id.* Rejection of "privity" for the tort element of duty actually began even earlier, notably in Justice Benjamin Cardozo's opinion in *MacPherson v. Buick Motor Co.*, 217 N.Y. 382, 111 N.E. 1050 (1916).

[29]Richard A. Nagareda, Mass Torts in a World of Settlement 4 (2007).

troduced the concept of "strict liability," or liability without fault.[30] Producers could now be liable for the tortious damage their products caused without requiring plaintiffs to prove the traditional tort element of fault.[31]

Transformations in civil procedure occurred in the late twentieth century as well, further creating a hospitable environment for the emergence of mass torts. First, changing attitudes concerning dispute resolution founded the widespread view that formal litigation was too expensive an option, giving way to a dominant trend in modern civil procedure to resolve litigation via settlement.[32] In addition, the introduction in 1966 of Rule 23 of the Federal Rules of Civil Procedure expanded the grounds for which certification of a class for purposes of a class action could occur.[33] Furthermore, as a reaction to the developments of products law and civil procedure, changes in plaintiff law firms occurred, transforming solo practitioners, covering various types of litigation work, into larger firms specializing in particular subjects.[34]

Finally, changes in political attitudes during the late twentieth century towards regulatory programs, in Nagareda's view, altered the preferred redress to the need for market regulation. Nagareda posited that the "dwindling of the New Deal faith in government as a source of bold solutions to social problems and the growing resistance of the public to taxation as a means to fund new government initiatives" made administrative regulation and public legislation an unsavory answer to the problems of market regulation.[35] Consequently, "tort litigation — conceived as regulation in disguise and brought in a procedural system geared to settlement — emerged as an alternative means to address the human cost of risk-taking" by manufacturers.[36]

Thus, the legal landscape of the twentieth century paved the way for mass tort litigation. However, MDL alternative settlements were not the first solution envisioned to address the new pitfalls and possibilities of mass torts. Rather, MDL settlements such as Vioxx have emerged as a consequence to the limitations inherent in existing methods, such as class actions and bankruptcy.[37] It is important to recognize the circumstances under which MDL alternative settlements came into existence, because the technical drawbacks of the class action as a vehicle to address mass torts — which are purposefully absent in the MDL

---

[30]*Id.* at 5.

[31]*Id.* Nonetheless, it is typically accepted that a plaintiff must show that the product itself was "defective" in some legally recognized way, *see* Kristine Cordier Karnezis, Annot., *Products liability: modern cases determining whether product is defectively designed*, 96 A.L.R.3d 22 (originally published in 1979).

[32]Richard A. Nagareda, Mass Torts in a World of Settlement 7 (2007).

[33]*Id.* at 8.

[34]*Id.* at 9. Solo practitioners performing personal injury practice still exist, of course, but the larger or multi-claimant litigation in torts and products liability tended to be done in, and even caused the development of, larger plaintiffs' law firms.

[35]*Id.* at 10.

[36]*Id.*

[37]*Id.* at 95.

Vioxx model — are viewed by critics of the Vioxx settlement to be the very cause of the ethical conundrum present in that settlement structure.[38]

Various factors can limit the application of class actions in a given case, such as the requirement in Rule 23(a)(3) of the Federal Rules of Civil Procedure of the typicality of harm suffered by plaintiffs,[39] or the predominance of common questions of law or fact as per Rule 23(b)(3).[40] Moreover, the notion of using Chapter 11 Reorganization in bankruptcy as a vehicle for mass tort settlement has exacerbated fears in all potential parties after the decision in *Kane v. Johns-Mansville Corp.*,[41] given that such settlement structures can lead to finite amounts of funds and delays to plaintiffs, and little-to-no remaining equity for shareholders of defendants.[42]

III. The Vioxx Settlement

Vioxx, or rofecoxib as it is referred to generically, is a member of a general class of pain relievers commonly known as non-steroidal anti-inflammatory drugs ("NSAIDs").[43] NSAIDs are used to treat chronic or acute pain and inflammation commonly "associated with osteoarthritis, rheumatoid arthritis, and other musculoskeletal conditions."[44] Adverse side effects can occur from the use of NSAIDs, most notably "gastrointestinal perforations, ulcers, and bleeds" — conditions that are exacerbated when the drug is ingested in high doses, which is often necessary to effectively manage pain and inflammation.[45] Vioxx was particularly manufactured as a "COX-2 inhibitor," designed to provide pain and inflammatory relief at a reduced risk of gastrointestinal side effects.[46] In 1999, the FDA approved the sale of Vioxx in the United States, and subsequently, the drug was widely proscribed by physicians throughout the U.S. and other markets across the world.[47]

On September 30, 2004, Merck & Company, Inc. ("Merck"), one of the major producers of Vioxx, withdrew the drug from the market following results from "a long-term, blinded, randomized placebo-controlled clinical trial" which indicated that the use of Vioxx put consumers at an increased risk of cardio-

---

[38]Richard A. Nagareda, *Embedded Aggregation in Civil Litigation*, 95 Cornell L. Rev. 1105, 1124 (2010).

[39]*In re Vioxx Products Litigation*, 239 F.R.D. 540, 560 (E.D. La. 2006). *See also James v. City of Dallas*, 254 F.3d 551, 571 (5th Cir. 2001).

[40]*In re Vioxx Products Litigation*, 239 F.R.D. at 560-63. *See also In re Bridgestone/ Firestone, Inc.*, 288 F.3d 1012, 1015 (7th Cir. 2002).

[41]843 F.2d 636 (2d Cir. 1988).

[42]Richard A. Nagareda, Mass Torts in a World of Settlement 75-76 (2007).

[43]*In re Vioxx Products Liability Litigation*, 239 F. Supp. 2d 741, 743 (E.D. La. 2006).

[44]*In re Vioxx Products Liability Litigation*, 239 F. Supp. 2d at 743.

[45]*Id.*

[46]*Id.* at 744.

[47]*Id.*

vascular complications and stroke.[48] Consequently, thousands of lawsuits were filed in both state and federal courts across the United States, and on February 16, 2005, the Judicial Panel on Multidistrict Litigation ordered that Vioxx litigation be consolidated, designated as an MDL, and assigned to the court of U.S. District Judge Eldon Fallon of the Eastern District of Louisiana.[49]

A settlement agreement between Merck and the plaintiff law firms was reached on November 9, 2007, providing that Merck pay out $4.85 billion in plaintiff claims for heart complications and stroke.[50] The settlement proposal devised by Merck which ultimately formed the terms of the settlement agreement between the parties contained two provisions that have attracted a flurry of scholarly commentary, criticism, and support. Put simply, Merck's agreement provided: (1) for a plaintiff lawyer to participate in the settlement, the lawyer was required to recommend the settlement to his eligible clients, and (2) should any of the plaintiff lawyer's clients decide to reject the settlement, the lawyer was required to withdraw from representation of those clients.[51] It is these two provisions which are the focal point of this article and the epicenter of the surrounding scholarly commentary.

IV. Criticisms of the Vioxx Settlement

As previously mentioned, a cluster of Supreme Court cases in the late 1990s, and action by Congress, have hastened the downfall of class action as a vehicle for resolving mass tort litigation through settlement due to issues of individual concern and intra-class conflict, leaving non-aggregate settlement to fill this vacuum.[52] This is the source of the ethical controversy for critics of the Vioxx settlement. In traditional one-on-one tort litigation, consent to settle is the sole possession of the client.[53] This notion is articulated in Rule 1.2(a) of the Model Rules of Professional Conduct, which states: "a lawyer shall abide by a client's decision whether to settle a matter."[54] However, exceptions are made for class actions, where "collective representation may be the only way plaintiffs in mass litigation can litigate on an even field with defendants."[55] Class actions compensate for the loss of individual consent via certification.[56] Certification of the class, through Rule 23(b)(3), "infer[s] absent class members' consent to be

---

[48] *Id.*

[49] *Id.*

[50] *See* Official Vioxx Settlement Agreement (Nov. 9, 2007), *available at* http://www.merck.com/newsroom/vioxx/pdf/settlement_agreement.pdf (last visited April 11, 2011).

[51] *Id.*

[52] *See* Howard M. Erichson & Benjamin C. Zipursky, *Consent Versus Closure*, 96 Cornell L. Rev. 265, 267 (2011).

[53] *Id.* at 283.

[54] *Id.* (citing Model Rules of Prof'l Conduct R. 1.2(a)).

[55] *Id.* at 314.

[56] Richard A. Nagareda, *Embedded Aggregation in Civil Litigation*, 95 Cornell L. Rev. 1105, 1157 (2010).

bound from the affordance of procedural protections in the nature of exit, voice and loyalty rights"[57] — or put familiarly, the ability to opt out, the opportunity to participate in proceedings given adequate notice, and an assurance of adequate representation by class counsel. These procedural guarantees are further complemented by Rule 23(e), which requires judicial review of settlement terms to ensure substantive fairness.[58] Critics view the Vioxx settlement as ethically damned because it is "legitimized neither by client consent under the rules of legal ethics nor as a class action subject to judicial oversight."[59] The Vioxx settlement is justified under neither traditional litigation approach concerning the attorney-client relationship; thus, in the view of its critics, it is susceptible to various ethical criticisms.

The criticisms of the Vioxx settlement are summarized and pointedly discussed in an article entitled *Consent Versus Closure*, written by Professors Howard Erichson and Benjamin Zipursky of Fordham Law School.[60] The article launches a scathing attack against the Vioxx deal and the concept of hybridization of mass tort aggregate settlements, and it questions the notion that global peace and closure in mass tort litigation is a legitimate concern.[61] The article also rejects a recent proposal by the ALI, which advocates advanced consent by clients in mass tort litigation as a cure to any possible ethical deficiency which may exist in hybrid deals such as Vioxx.[62]

The first structural assault Erichson and Zipursky levy against the Vioxx settlement agreement is the mandatory recommendation provision, which states in pertinent part: "Enrolling Counsel affirms that he has recommended, or ... will recommend by no later than [the deadline], to 100% of the Eligible Claimants represented by such Enrolling Counsel that such Eligible Claimants enroll in the program."[63] According to Erichson and Zipursky, this provision runs afoul of several ethics rules, most obviously Rule 1.2(a) of the Model Rules of Professional Conduct, which places the decision whether or not to settle firmly within the powers held by the client in the contours of the attorney-client relationship.[64] As they point out, "lawyers may seek court approval of settlements over the objections of class representatives, but the Vioxx personal-injury and wrongful-death litigation was not certified class action."[65] No certification of a class occurred in Vioxx which would relegate client consent powers in exchange for aggregate representation under judicial supervision. Rather, according to Erichson and Zipursky, in Vioxx the claims belonged to the in-

---

[57]*Id.*

[58]*Id.* at 1157-58.

[59]*Id.* at 1158.

[60]Howard M. Erichson & Benjamin C. Zipursky, *Consent Versus Closure*, 96 Cornell L. Rev. 265 (2011).

[61]*Id.*

[62]*Id.* at 301.

[63]*Id.* at 280 (citing The Official Vioxx Settlement Agreement, discussed *infra*).

[64]*Id.* at 283 (citing Model Rules of Prof'l Conduct R. 1.2(a)).

[65]*Id.*

dividual plaintiffs, and so did the decision as to whether to settle or have their day in court.[66]

Merck's mandatory recommendation provision gets worse for Erichson and Zipursky, given that the provision implicates the ethics rules governing an attorney's obligation to voice independent and loyal advice to his or her client.[67] Rule 1.4, which regulates attorney communications with clients, "requires lawyers to explain matters as reasonably necessary so that clients can make informed decisions."[68] Without further explanation, this requires the reader to assume that Erichson and Zipursky are insinuating that the terms and provisions of Merck's settlement proposal, including the mandatory recommendation provision, were not fully explained by the plaintiff attorneys to their clients. Moreover, Erichson and Zipursky contend the settlement agreement implicates Rule 2.1, governing the attorney's role as advisor, which requires lawyers to "exercise independent professional judgment and render candid advice."[69] Erichson and Zipursky cite these rules, and add the qualifying inquiry: How could lawyers resist the temptation to undervalue certain claims in order to enroll their clients into the settlement program with unanimity?[70]

Assuming the Vioxx plaintiffs' attorneys were bereft of some ability to independently evaluate the settlement proposal and offer candid advice to their clients regarding whether or not it was their best option, there is yet a final problem with the mandatory recommendation provision according to Erichson and Zipursky: Rule 1.7(a) expressly forbids a lawyer from representing a client if a conflict of interest exists, including where the representation of one of more clients will be materially limited by the lawyer's responsibilities to another client. According to the article's authors, this presents something of an ethical roadblock to actions like those taken by the plaintiffs' attorneys in Vioxx. This is so even though Rule 1.8(g) of the Model Rules expressly envisages aggregate settlement of mass tort claims by an attorney representing multiple clients.[71] To Erichson and Zipursky, the problem is not aggregate settlement of mass tort litigation, it is the mandatory recommendation of the proposal to a lawyer's clients, absent the blessing of class certification.[72] Taking this argument at face value, it still begs the question, is settlement of only an expressly consenting fraction of non-class mass tort claimants really aggregate settlement? That question is addressed in the next section.

Erichson and Zipursky also take aim at the second controversial provision of the Vioxx settlement agreement: the provision "requiring" mandatory withdrawal from representation of non-settling clients, which they view as violating a number of ethical rules beyond its alleged potential to undermine clients'

---

[66]*Id.*

[67]*Id.*

[68]*Id.* at 284.

[69]*Id.*

[70]*Id.*

[71]*See id.* at 304.

[72]*Id.* at 282-83.

decisions whether or not to settle.[73] Firstly, they contend that the provision violates Rule 5.6(b) of the Model Rules, which states that a "lawyer shall not participate in offering or making ... an agreement in which a restriction on the lawyer's right to practice is part of the settlement."[74] Erichson and Zipursky posit that any agreement to such a provision is a clear violation of Rule 5.6(b), citing a formal ethics opinion from the American Bar Association and a recent decision by a federal district court that agree with their contention.[75]

It is true that the Vioxx settlement agreement contains language which requires plaintiffs' lawyers to withdraw from representing non-settling claimants: The proposal provided that should any claimants disregard their attorney's recommendation for settlement, or otherwise refuse the settlement, "Enrolling Counsel shall ... to the extent permitted by the equivalents to Rules 1.16 and 5.6 of the ABA Model Rules of Professional Conduct ... disengage and withdraw from the representation" of such claimants.[76] Without more, this language would appear to violate Rule 5.6(b), but the final proposal in the Vioxx settlement also provided that "if an attorney did not withdraw from any particular case, there could be a review ultimately by the Chief Administrator (apparently including whether professional duties prevented withdrawal)."[77] Moreover, an additional clarifying proviso was included which stated, "Each Enrolling Counsel is expected to exercise his or her independent judgment in the best interest of each client individually before determining whether to recommend enrollment in the Program."[78] To Erichson and Zipursky, however, such clarifying language is not enough to combat putative "malefactors from buying off lawyers quo private attorneys general."[79]

Erichson and Zipursky further charge that in addition to placing restrictions on the plaintiff lawyer's ability to effectively practice, the Vioxx settlement agreement also violates ethical constraints governing the termination of the attorney-client relationship.[80] Rule 1.16 of the Model Rules of Professional Conduct governs mandatory and permissive withdrawal from representation of a client or clients.[81] Erichson and Zipursky stop short of contending that the Vioxx settlement required mandatory withdrawal in violation of the Rules of Professional Conduct, as per Rule 1.16.[82] This is understandable, given the American Bar Association's express endorsement of aggregate settlement in the

---

[73]*Id* at 284.

[74]*Id.*

[75]*Id.* at 284-85 (citations omitted).

[76]*Id.* at 280 (citing the Vioxx Settlement Agreement, *see supra* note 50).

[77]Edward F. Sherman, *The MDL Model for Resolving Complex Litigation if a Class Action is Not Possible*, 82 Tul. L. Rev. 2205, 2216 (2008).

[78]*Id.* (citing Vioxx settlement agreement, discussed above).

[79]Howard M. Erichson & Benjamin C. Zipursky, *Consent Versus Closure*, 96 Cornell L. Rev. 265, 285 (2011).

[80]*Id.*

[81]*Id.* at 286.

[82]*Id.* at 287.

form of Rule 1.8(g), and they take note of this.[83] Rather, what they insist is that permissive withdrawal from non-settling clients is not permitted under any of the reasons outlined in Rule 1.16(b).[84] Following Erichson and Zipursky's logic, by assuming that the Vioxx settlement *must* be justified under Rule 1.16(b) as a form of traditional tort litigation, they reason that the Vioxx plaintiff attorneys could not withdraw under 1.16(b) because the withdrawal would be materially adverse to the interests of the non-settling claimants, given that all other plaintiff attorneys were tied up in the Vioxx litigation and the exclusionary settlement proposal.[85] Thus, dropped plaintiffs would be hard pressed to find any other Vioxx attorney who would take up their case and give them their day in court.

Model Rule 1.16(b) contains several permitted reasons for withdrawal even where termination would be materially adverse to the client's interests, including where: "'(4) the client insists upon taking action ... with which the lawyer has a fundamental disagreement,' '(6) the representation will result in an unreasonable financial burden on the lawyer or has been rendered unreasonably difficult by the client,' and '(7) other good cause for withdrawal exists.'"[86] Erichson and Zipursky maintain that a plaintiff attorney attempting to justify his withdrawal under Rule 1.16(b)(4) (given a fundamental disagreement with the decision not to settle) would be difficult given an overwhelming number of cases which reject the notion that a client can be fired by his or her attorney because of a decision to decline a settlement offer.[87] For them, the clear complication is that the argument assumes that the decision to accept or decline a settlement belongs to the lawyer, despite Rule 1.2(a)'s unambiguous charge to the contrary.[88]

Furthermore, a plaintiff-attorney's argument that 1.16(b)(6) allows him or her to withdraw from representation, given that bringing a case to trial is a "highly questionable investment" on behalf of the attorney, also rings hollow.[89] This is so because, to Erichson and Zipursky, when these lawyers undertook the representation of each Vioxx claim, they were forbidden from assuming that settlement would be the ultimate conclusion to the mass tort litigation.[90] It is important to note that this argument, of course, like all of Erichson and Ziprusky's arguments, presupposes a mentality towards mass tort litigation that places it firmly within the traditional modes of tort litigation, rather than viewing it from the perspective of a private framework for administrative remedial action to mass torts.[91] Having addressed Erichson's and Ziprusky's concerns, it is time to examine mass aggregate settlement under a kinder lens.

---

[83]*Id.*

[84]*Id.*

[85]*Id.*

[86]*Id.* (quoting from Rule 1.16(b)).

[87]*Id.*

[88]*Id.*

[89]*Id.* at 289.

[90]*Id.*

[91]Richard A. Nagareda, Mass Torts in a World of Settlement 60 (2007).

V. Responses to the Critical Commentary

A. The Unthinkable: Vioxx Was Actually a Fair Settlement?

Erichson and Zipursky require their readers to begin with the supposition that closure and global peace (exclusively *defendant* goals) are illegitimate concerns to hold when evaluating an appropriate non-class mass tort settlement method.[92] This article requires no such preconceived notion; in fact, it flatly dismisses it. It was noted above that mass torts evolved as a method of non-governmental regulation of tortious conduct in markets with an *intent* to settle.[93] Mass harm to mass consumers in an industrialized economy requires mass redress,[94] and lawyers took on a pivotal role during the birth of mass torts: in a sense, "mass-marketing" the claims of consumer-plaintiffs as a "'product' that entrepreneurial plaintiffs' lawyers sell to defendants in settlements."[95] Further, the growth of mass torts, as a species of litigation, was facilitated by the trend in modern civil procedure to settle claims, at the avoidance of civil trials.[96] Indeed, modern research has substantiated the "impression that civil trial 'is a disease, not generally fatal, but serious enough to be avoided at any reasonable cost.'"[97]

It is far easier for Erichson and Zipursky to begin their article on the platform that global peace in mass torts is an entirely defendant-driven objective, completely disconnected from the legitimate pursuit of pure and unwavering individual claimant consent in mass tort settlement. This is so because if the reader begins with the presumption that any MDL which is not a certified class action is necessarily traditional tort litigation, then all the traditional Model Rules of Professional Conduct apply, without question or reference to the existence of any other method by which mass torts can and must be settled. Yet, the unfortunate fact is that absent global peace in many MDLs, including Vioxx, all the parties face a long, painful, and protracted litigation, with copious delays and costs for injury-stricken plaintiffs.[98]

Looked upon in this light, global peace becomes a legitimate pursuit not only for defendants, but for all interested parties. Taking this analysis one step further, it is useful to proceed with the opposite supposition: that the Vioxx settlement agreement was actually beneficial to plaintiffs. The underlying facts of the Vioxx settlement do not lie. In 2004, upon Merck's withdrawal of Vioxx from the market, the pharmaceutical giant openly vowed "to litigate vigorously

---

[92]Howard M. Erichson & Benjamin C. Zipursky, *Consent Versus Closure*, 96 Cornell L. Rev. 265, 282-83 (2011).

[93]Richard A. Nagareda, Mass Torts in a World of Settlement 4 (2007).

[94]*Id.*

[95]*Id.*

[96]*Id.* at 7.

[97]*Id.* (citing Samuel R. Gross & Kent D. Syverud, *Don't Try: Civil Jury Verdicts in a System Geared to Settlement*, 44 U.C.L.A. L. Rev. 1, 3 (1996)).

[98]Richard A. Nagareda, *Embedded Aggregation in Civil Litigation*, 95 Cornell L. Rev. 1105, 1152 (2010).

all cases rather than enter into peace negotiations."[99] While the scientific research conducted on Vioxx's various side effects looked promising to plaintiffs, they faced the "considerable difficulty of proving specific causation — that a given Vioxx user's heart attack or stroke is Vioxx-related and likely would not have occurred anyway," given the fact that those patient groups who use prescription-grade pain-relievers are already at a heightened risk of heart attacks and strokes because of underlying medical conditions.[100] Those concerns were justified: "Merck's studied persistence in litigation effectively bought home to plaintiffs' lawyers the difficulty — if not impossibility — of proving specific causation in individual cases, with Vioxx plaintiffs winning verdicts in only five of seventeen trials."[101]

Compounding these difficulties were the financial obstacles that lay in the plaintiffs' path. Merck had reportedly reserved $1.9 billion to fund its legal defense,[102] determined to fight off the massive and ensuing barrage of lawsuits. In contrast, plaintiffs' attorneys, retained on a contingency fee basis, were forced "to invest out of their own pockets in consolidated pretrial discovery and bellwether trials."[103] When the financial and tactical difficulties facing plaintiffs are examined closely, the $4.85 billion settlement agreement looks more like a legitimate settlement, and less like a coerced, attorney-fee frenzy. Rather, it is important to remember the purpose of MDLs, which is that "[m]ass settlements for mass torts are about unlocking and allocating the joint gains that arise from the replacement of litigation with peace."[104]

In addition to policy reasons for keeping global peace at the forefront of one's mind when evaluating non-class mass tort settlement, it is vital to bear in mind the importance of exploring alternative or "hybrid" methods of mass tort settlement. This concept stands in opposition to the general premise of Erichson and Zipursky's article. Their article claims to hold no antagonism towards mass aggregate settlement,[105] yet then admittedly offers no alternative for MDLs which cannot be certified as a class action, but are too large for traditional tort litigation.[106] These inherent inconsistencies highlight what Professor Nagareda has called the "procedural catch-22" of mass aggregate settlement.[107]

This "procedural catch-22" is a byproduct of the Supreme Court and Congress' inaction concerning mass litigation which is ineligible for class certification, following the Supreme Court's decisions in *Amchem* and *Ortiz*.[108] As a

---

[99]*Id.*

[100]*Id.*

[101]*Id.*

[102]*Id.*

[103]*Id.*

[104]*Id.* at 1148.

[105]Howard M. Erichson & Benjamin C. Zipursky, *Consent Versus Closure*, 96 Cornell L. Rev. 265, 282 (2011).

[106]*Id.* at 270.

[107]Richard A. Nagareda, Mass Torts in a World of Settlement 4 (2007).

[108]*Id.* at 73 (citing cases discussed *supra*, at notes 12 and 13).

consequence, to Erichson and Zipursky, "the Vioxx deal lies betwixt and between, legitimized neither by client consent under the rules of legal ethics nor as a class action subject to judicial oversight."[109] However, this view results from an inability to acknowledge a species of litigation which has legitimately emerged between the realms of traditionally autonomous individual litigation and class action.[110] Professor Nagareda, and many of his colleagues, have fully endorsed such a category of litigation, dubbed "hybridization."[111] The precursor to this new species of litigation is the "procedural catch-22," which refers to orphaned cases, such as Vioxx, which are procedurally damned for resembling a class action (because they lack the sanctity of certification), but which, by their nature, are incapable of being a class action.[112] Plaintiff lawyers representing this species of litigation are forced to negotiate and represent mass tort claims which resemble a class action in function and form, but which — according to Erichson and Ziprusky — lack any legitimate consent-power to negotiate on behalf of all claimants, like that provided for in a class action.[113]

B. Nagareda's "Procedural Catch-22" and Vioxx

In Professor Nagareda's article entitled *Embedded Aggregation in Civil Litigation* — seemingly written as a response to Vioxx critics such as Erichson and Zipursky — he outlined the factual scenarios in cases that give rise to the "procedural catch-22," which, in turn, necessitates innovative aggregate settlement vehicles such as Vioxx.[114] In cases involving factual scenarios such as these, "the Court ultimately limits what an individual lawsuit may do out of concern that the lawsuit would otherwise operate as a de facto class action," but at the same time, the features of each case also prevent a district court from certifying the case as a class action.[115] These cases, by their nature, demand conclusion by way of the class action method, but are deemed unacceptable for class certification.

The first decision Nagareda examines, *Taylor v. Sturgell*, involved litigation concerning the Freedom of Information Act (FOIA), wherein "two 'antique aircraft enthusiast[s],' each of whom sought disclosure by the federal government of the plans for the 'vintage' F-45 model" airplane, were initially denied by the government.[116] The first enthusiast sued in federal court in Wyoming and lost on the merits after the court ruled that such plans were exempt from

---

[109]Richard A. Nagareda, *Embedded Aggregation in Civil Litigation*, 95 Cornell L. Rev. 1105, 1158 (2010).

[110]*Id.*

[111]*Id.* at 1106.

[112]*Id.* at 1126.

[113]*Id.*

[114]*Id.* at 1121.

[115]*Id.*

[116]*Taylor v. Sturgell*, 553 U.S. 880, 884 (2008).

disclosure under the FOIA due to trade secret exemptions.[117] Subsequently, Taylor sued in federal court in Washington, D.C., only for the district court and the U.S. Court of Appeals for the D.C. Circuit to rule that such an action was precluded by the previous suit in Wyoming. The court of appeals found that the facts of the case demonstrated a "'virtual represent[ation]'" by Taylor of the prior action in Wyoming.[118] The U.S. Supreme Court unanimously reversed, however, rejecting any notion of a doctrine of "virtual representation," holding that only certain exceptions allowed for preclusion of a subsequent non-party to bring suit, one being the "class action device."[119]

The government's complications following the Supreme Court's decision in *Taylor* are clear: The government would be required to separately litigate each and every request under the FOIA for the same exact pieces of information, regardless of prior case law deeming non-disclosure correct. This leaves the government susceptible to an infinite number of lawsuits under the FOIA for each and every document it possesses, with no hope of finality. The Supreme Court explained, however, that a doctrine of virtual representation would develop a common law form of class action, authorizing "'preclusion based on identity of interests and some kind of relationship between parties and nonparties, shorn of the procedural protections prescribed in' the law of class actions"[120] — effectively creating a "de facto class action,"[121] devoid of procedural class action protections against unfair preclusion guaranteed through certification. Nagareda points out that the rationale on which the Supreme Court based its decision was such: The FOIA allows "any person" to sue for disclosure of records within the government's possession; thus, any class action to sue for release of government documents would necessitate certification of a *class* encompassing the entire world.[122] This is obviously prohibited by the current law governing class actions, since the class action device "has long been understood to contain an implicit requirement that a class must have ascertainable parameters to enable courts to tell who is within them and who is not … [t]this requirement would lose its meaning if a permissible class definition could embrace the world."[123] So, while class certification under Rule 23 is unavailable due to an unascertainable class, the Court simultaneously ruled that the preclusion of subsequent non-parties to bring identical claims is impermissible, hence the "procedural catch-22"[124] of aggregate litigation.

Similarly, in the late 1990s, the Supreme Court decided two asbestos cases: *Amchem Products, Inc. v. Windsor* and *Ortiz v. Fibreboard Corp.*, which

---

[117]Richard A. Nagareda, *Embedded Aggregation in Civil Litigation*, 95 Cornell L. Rev. 1105, 1122 (2010).

[118]*Taylor*, 553 U.S. 880.

[119]*Id.* at 896-98.

[120]*Id.* at 900.

[121]Richard A. Nagareda, *Embedded Aggregation in Civil Litigation*, 95 Cornell L. Rev. 1105, 1121 (2010).

[122]*Id.* at 1124.

[123]*Id.* at 1125-26.

[124]*Id.* at 1126.

effectively limited the types of cases a district court could certify as a class action based on concerns regarding cohesiveness of the class and conflicts of interest among class counsel.[125] In *Amchem*, the Court invalidated a district court's certification of a group of asbestos claimants, finding specifically that the group failed to meet Rule 23(b)(3)'s predominance requirement and Rule 23(a)(4)'s adequate representation requirement.[126] The asbestos claimants failed to demonstrate to the Court that common questions of fact or law pre-dominated "'over any questions affecting only individual members'"[127] because these individual claimants were exposed to different types of asbestos, at different stages, over differing periods of time, giving rise to different types of illnesses: lung cancer, mesothelioma, and asbestosis.[128] In addition, each claimant had a different history regarding cigarette smoking, further compli-cating the issues of predominance.[129] Of equal importance was the fact that some plaintiffs had only been exposed to asbestos, and were suing for the possibility of future illness, while others already manifested asbestos-related illnesses.[130] Consequently, the Court held that "certification cannot be upheld, for it rests on a conception of Rule 23(b)(3)'s predominance requirement irreconcilable with the Rule's design."[131] In the same vein, "Rule 23(a)(4)'s requirement that the named parties 'will fairly and adequately protect the interests of the class'" was not satisfied due to the fact that class representatives with differing medical conditions could not adequately represent a single class with even greater differences in illness and exposure.[132] Later, the Court would extend concerns over predominance and commonality to economic conflicts of interests between class counsel, in *Ortiz*.[133]

In the wake of these decisions, *In re Vioxx Products Liability Litigation* could not escape similar drawbacks, making it ineligible for class certifica-tion.[134] The leading arguments considered by Judge Fallon in his order refusing to certify Vioxx plaintiffs as a class included issues of typicality, adequacy of representation, and predominance.[135] As to the issues of typicality and adequa-cy of representation, Judge Fallon found that because the Vioxx claimants encompassed "a vast number of persons who took different dosages of [Vioxx], at different times, and possibly took [Vioxx] concomitantly with other pre-scription drugs," they failed to satisfy Rule 23(a)(2)'s requirement of typicality,

---

[125]Richard A. Nagareda, Mass Torts in a World of Settlement 87 (2007) (discussing cases cited *supra*, notes 12 and 13).

[126]*Amchem Products, Inc.*, 521 U.S. at 615.

[127]*Id.* at 613-15.

[128]*Id.* at 624.

[129]*Id.*

[130]*Id.*

[131]*Id.* at 625.

[132]*Id.* at 624-26.

[133]*See* Richard A. Nagareda, Mass Torts in a World of Settlement 89 (2007).

[134]*In re Vioxx Products Liability Litigation*, 239 F.R.D. 450, 459-62 (2006).

[135]*Id.*

which demands that claims at the very least "share the same essential characteristics — a similar course of conduct, or the same legal theory."[136] Claimants also failed to demonstrate the requisite adequacy of representation, given that it "overlaps with the typicality requirement because in the absence of typical claims, the class representative has no incentive to pursue the claims of the other class members."[137] Rule 23(b)(3)'s requirement of the predominance of common questions of law or fact was similarly left unsatisfied, given the differences in claims — strict liability or negligence — and the varying degrees of causation required in the individual claims, since each Vioxx-user had a unique medical history and underlying conditions.[138] Judge Fallon took note that "courts have almost invariably found that common questions of fact do not predominate in pharmaceutical drug cases," acknowledging that "[t]his case is no different."[139] Thus, Vioxx became yet another shade caught in the purgatory of the "procedural catch-22."[140] Much like *Taylor*, the inherent qualities of *In re Vioxx Products Liability Litigation* that made it a situation of "embedded aggregation, ironically, are also what would prevent overt aggregation by way of a class action."[141]

C. Acknowledging Why Mass Tort Litigation Is Often Geared for Settlement

The *Amchem* Court conceded one fundamental agreement with the petitioners it otherwise disagreed with: "Settlement is relevant to a class certification."[142] In fact, the Court singled out those cases which are filed with an eye to settle as class actions, holding that where federal courts are met "with a request for settlement-only class certification, a district court need not inquire whether the case, if tried, would present intractable management problems ... for the proposal is that there be no trial."[143] This reasoning stems from a recognition of the fact that settlement is often the best bet for recovery for an injured plaintiff. The *Amchem* Court deliberately noted that the "policy at the very core of the class action mechanism is to overcome the problem that small recoveries do not provide the incentive for any individual to bring a solo action prosecuting his or her rights," but a class action, by nature, "solves this problem by ag-

---

[136]*Id.* at 460.

[137]*Id.*

[138]*Id.* at 461-62.

[139]*Id.* at 461. *See, e.g., In re Prempro*, 230 F.R.D. at 567; *Zehel-Miller v. Astrazenaca Pharm., LP*, 223 F.R.D. 659, 663 (M.D. Fla. 2004); *In re Baycol*, 218 F.R.D. at 204; *In re Paxil Litig.*, 212 F.R.D. 539, 551 (C.D. Cal. 2003); *In re Propulsid Prods. Liab. Litig.*, 208 F.R.D. 133, 144-45 (E.D. La. 2002); *In re Rezulin Prods. Liab. Litig.*, 210 F.R.D. 61, 65-67 (S.D.N.Y. 2002).

[140]Richard A. Nagareda, *Embedded Aggregation in Civil Litigation*, 95 Cornell L. Rev. 1105, 1112 (2010).

[141]*Id.* at 1125.

[142]*Amchem Products, Inc.*, 521 U.S. at 619.

[143]*Id.* at 620.

gregating the relatively paltry potential recoveries into something worth someone's (usually an attorney's) labor."[144] But isn't this rationale equally true for an MDL caught in the purgatorial catch-22? It is.

The inherent failure in Erichson and Zipursky's arguments is that they refuse to acknowledge the natural object of mass tort litigation: settlement. As they insist: "the closure-is-necessary premise is easily refuted."[145] Judge Fallon lacked the luxury of such a sentiment — he faced an enormous MDL, including injury-stricken plaintiffs in need of paid claims, plaintiff attorneys shouldering all of the initial costs of litigation, and defendants demanding finality as to escape the infamous fate of the asbestos companies. Moreover, to properly understand mass tort litigation and class action, one must recognize the fact that finality — that is to say subsequent party preclusion — is a legitimate goal for defendants *and* plaintiffs. As Professor Nagareda put it: "the logic of Rule 23 is to marry the strategic leverage that plaintiffs derive from the threat of a class-wide trial with the prospect of an equally encompassing victory for the defendant."[146] But the great equalizing nature of Rule 23 is fundamentally altered in an MDL that has been refused class certification, since the plaintiffs continue to wield a class-wide threat, while defendants have no counter-threat of final closure should they prevail.[147] This gives an MDL defendant little choice but to try each and all MDL cases, a prospect which, by all accounts, plaintiffs could ill-afford.[148]

The importance of MDLs is recognized in unanimity, but what Nagareda (and Judge Fallon) recognize is that the "[e]xpansion in the potential scope of litigation gives rise to demands for settlement — for litigation peace — that are commensurate in their scope."[149] This is so because of the societal recognition of settlement as a generally superior outcome to trial,[150] and because "[m]ass wrongs elicit efforts at mass settlement, and, with it, a search for some vehicle through which to impose the deal on a suitably mass basis."[151] For the Vioxx parties, that vehicle was the settlement agreement proposed by Merck, and it compensated for the lack of finality traditionally provided by the class action, with its mandatory recommendation and withdrawal provisions. Thus, Vioxx accomplished via contractual relationships what could otherwise only be guaranteed through class certification: finality for all parties.

---

[144]*Id.* at 617 (citing *Mace v. Van Ru Credit Corp.*, 109 F.3d 338, 344 (7th Cir. 1997)).

[145]Howard M. Erichson & Benjamin C. Zipursky, *Consent Versus Closure*, 96 Cornell L. Rev. 265, 319 (2011).

[146]Richard A. Nagareda, *Embedded Aggregation in Civil Litigation*, 95 Cornell L. Rev. 1105, 1139 (2010).

[147]*Id.* at 1140.

[148]*Id.* at 1153.

[149]*Id.* at 1121.

[150]Richard A. Nagareda, Mass Torts in a World of Settlement 7 (2007).

[151]Richard A. Nagareda, *Embedded Aggregation in Civil Litigation*, 95 Cornell L. Rev. 1105, 1121 (2010).

D. The ALI Proposal — Legitimizing Vioxx

As Nagareda explained, the real problem with the Vioxx deal for its critics "lies not in its reliance upon client consent but in the timing for such consent."[152] Recently, the American Law Institute has proposed permitting advanced consent — that clients could agree at the outset of their representation to be bound by any aggregate settlement that is fair and reasonable after approval by a supermajority of clients — in the place of later informed consent.[153] The proposal reads: "[I]ndividual claimants may, before the receipt of a proposed settlement offer, enter into an agreement in writing through shared counsel allowing each participating claimant to be bound by a super-majority vote."[154] Erichson and Zipursky quite obviously reject the ALI proposal, arguing that it departs from the current law governing advanced consent,[155] that such consent would be inauthentic as it would never justify the imposition on traditional client rights,[156] and even if it could, it places lawyers in a non-consentable ethical dilemma by forcing them to evaluate claims of their clients against each other.[157]

But once these criticisms by Erichson and Ziprusky are examined in comparison to the rest, it is clear that these arguments once more stem from the presupposition that non-class aggregate settlements such as the Vioxx deal are not a new form of settlement, but necessarily must be pigeon-holed into existing modes of litigation. Instead, the ALI proposal should be viewed as an acceptance by the legal community of what it sees as the future of mass tort settlement that cannot be addressed with existing methods. After all, the law is meant to serve persons in the disposition of their claims, and is not bound by the theoretical criticisms of an academic few, who find innovative methods unnerving. It is, by all accounts, an express authorization of the Vioxx settlement model, with the modification of advance consent — of which Vioxx lacked the benefit. The ALI proposal is a direct recognition of this concept.

E. The Value of the Hybridized Vioxx Deal

Once it is understood that the underlying pursuit of finality in the Vioxx deal was a legitimate goal, the actual value of the settlement vehicle can be recognized in future mass tort litigation. In his article entitled *The MDL Model for Resolving Complex Litigation if a Class Action is Not Possible*, Professor Edward Sherman underlines the importance of the Vioxx model in future non-

---

[152]*Id.* at 1161.

[153]Howard M. Erichson & Benjamin C. Zipursky, *Consent Versus Closure*, 96 Cornell L. Rev. 265, 294 (2011).

[154]*Id.* at 295. (*See* "Discussion of Principles of the Law of Aggregate Litigation," 86 A.L.I. Proc. 229 (2009).)

[155]*Id.* at 297-98.

[156]*Id.* at 299-300.

[157]*Id.* at 300.

class mass tort settlements.[158] As Professor Sherman explains, in light of the difficulty of using class actions to effectively conclude modern mass tort litigation, the "MDL model, applied creatively, can be an effective alternative in certain situations to class treatment for accomplishing an aggregate or global settlement."[159] The unavailability of traditional methods has invariably left federal courts overseeing MDLs as "'the only game in town' for most multistate class actions."[160] Professor Sherman's article expressed great hope for the possible adaptation of the Vioxx deal to future litigation, explaining that the Vioxx MDL and the "global settlement could be a model for other MDL courts, especially in its use of bellwether trials and a joint federal-state court settlement that, unlike a representative proceeding like a class action, relied upon each of the plaintiffs in pending cases to choose to enroll in the settlement."[161] As to the mandatory recommendation and withdrawal provisions, Sherman concluded that the proviso which instructs each plaintiff-attorney "to exercise his or her independent judgment in the best interest of each client individually," and the ability to appeal ethical decisions to the administrator, effectively "put to rest professional responsibility concerns."[162]

VI. Conclusion

Little choice is left in mass tort settlement but to explore alternative settlement methods. Inaction by Congress and the decisions by the Supreme Court in the late 1990s have rendered the class action model all but useless for many types of mass tort litigation. This places defendants in an initially weaker bargaining position, which, in turn, leads them to the conclusion that they must litigate all cases to trial, which ultimately weakens the plaintiffs' position. If the reader can begin with the presumption that settlement is often a good thing for both parties, they must logically take the next step to agree that the Vioxx deal was a legitimate alternative settlement method, which can and should be looked to as a model for the future.

Individual autonomous client consent is a valued canon, and should be respected in all forms of traditional litigation. However, mass torts is a different animal altogether, and necessitates different methods to grant mass redress to mass plaintiffs. Such a system requires the ability to negotiate claims on a grand scale, or suffer the path of piecemeal litigation — a nightmare for all parties. Vioxx provided an answer. Professors Erichson and Zipursky have asked their readers to reject the presumption that finality in mass torts is necessary. This article has stressed the contention that such a path is not an option.

---

[158]Edward F. Sherman, *The MDL Model for Resolving Complex Litigation if a Class Action is Not Possible*, 82 Tul. L. Rev. 2205 (2008).

[159]*Id.* at 2223.

[160]*Id.*

[161]*Id.* at 2215.

[162]*Id.* at 2216.

10

Turning Back the Page: How Deregulating Information-Sharing in Negotiations Will Better Serve the Purposes of Ethical Codes

Diana C. Taylor

I. Introduction

This paper will examine the ethical obligations of negotiators. After analyzing how the current ethical obligations apply, this paper proposes that the Model Rules of Professional Conduct Rule 4.1 regarding truthfulness in statements to others should not apply in the negotiation context.[1] I will begin by reviewing the development of negotiation as an alternative to litigation, up to and including the development of the problem-solving method. I then examine the purpose of ethical codes and what ethical obligations currently apply during the negotiation process. Most importantly, and against the grain of most commentators, I propose the deregulation of negotiation ethics by eliminating the application of Rule 4.1 while maintaining the requirements of Rule 1.6 on confidentiality.[2] Instead, negotiations would retain an ethical foundation by leveraging the loss of professional reputation, existing civil law claims, and the freedom of lawyers and clients to contract if they wish to apply different ethical standards for their negotiation.

II. Negotiation as a New Dispute Resolution Forum

A. Development of Negotiation

Since 1976, the number of dispute resolution processes available to lawyers has increased dramatically.[3] Today these processes include mediation, arbitration, early neutral case evaluation, and mini-trials.[4] These processes have become

---

[1]*See generally* American Bar Ass'n, Model Rules of Prof'l Conduct R. 4.1 (2007).

[2]*See generally* American Bar Ass'n, Model Rules of Prof'l Conduct R. 1.6 (2007).

[3]*See* Deborah R. Hensler, *Our Courts, Ourselves: How the Alternative Dispute Resolution Movement is Re-Shaping Our Legal System*, 108 Penn St. L. Rev. 165, 181 (2003) (stating the processes that have developed in alternative dispute resolution since the 1980s).

[4]*E.g., id.*; Robert C. Bordone, *The Collision of Two Ideals: Legal Ethics and the World of Alternative Dispute Resolution*, 21 Ohio St. J. on Disp. Resol. 1, 6 (2005).

popular because they save time and costs.[5] Researchers have discovered that parties to arbitration felt they had been treated more fairly than those participating in the litigation system,[6] perhaps suggesting an additional reason to choose alternative dispute resolution (ADR) forums. In the federal court system, some form of ADR is required by law.[7] Many state courts require that parties attempt to resolve their disputes through ADR before they can receive a trial date.[8]

Today, litigation represents but one course of action in resolving a dispute.[9] The Model Rules of Professional Conduct, however, are designed with adjudication in mind.[10] This paper asserts it is time to acknowledge the prominent role negotiation plays in modern lawyering. If not, "adversary tendencies [will be] rewarded and reinforced" at the expense of the development of ADR.[11]

B. Styles of Negotiation

Most negotiators tend to exhibit either a problem-solving or adversarial style.[12] Problem-solving negotiators tend to seek reasonable results, maximize joint return, rely on objective standards, begin with realistic opening positions, rarely use threats or deception, and, perhaps most significantly, maximize information disclosure.[13] In problem-solving negotiation the tasks undertaken by the attorney "[range] from structuring and designing a composition of a working relationship ... to an investigation of a variety of problem solving solutions ... to listening with empathy to the client discussing her situation ... to analyzing and solving difficult legal issues...," in addition to the ability to quantify a case reasonably.[14] Questions such as "what are the underlying needs and interests of the parties?," "what is really at stake in the dispute or transaction?," and "how will the parties feel about the resolutions that are produced?" are asked during the

---

[5]Hensler, *supra* note 3, at 177; Kimberlee L. Kovach, *Lawyer Ethics Must Keep Pace with Practice: Plurality in Lawyering Roles Demands Diverse and Innovative Ethical Standards*, 39 Idaho L. Rev. 399, 405 (2003).

[6]Hensler, *supra* note 3, at 179.

[7]*Id.* at 167.

[8]*Id.*

[9]*See, e.g.*, Bordone, *supra* note 4, at 6; Kimberlee K. Kovach, *The Intersection (Collision) of Ethics, Law, and Dispute Resolution: Clashes, Crashes, No Stops, Yields or Right of Way*, 49 S. Tex. L. Rev. 789, 792 (2008) (noting some believe ADR has led to an increase in settlements and decline in trials).

[10]Bordone, *supra* note 4, at 4.

[11]Kovach, *supra* note 5, at 416.

[12]Charles B. Craver, Effective Legal Negotiation 9 (6th ed. 2009). *See generally* Kovach, *supra* note 5, at 405 (noting that when first developed the terms were cooperative or competitive). For the purposes of this paper, the author refers to the polar styles as problem-solving and adversarial unless otherwise noted.

[13]*E.g.*, Craver, *supra* note 12, at 9; Kovach, *supra* note 5, at 407.

[14]Kovach, *supra* note 5, at 409; Carrie J. Menkel-Meadow, *When Winning Isn't Everything: The Lawyer as a Problem Solver*, 20 Hofstra L. Rev. 905, 910-11 (2000).

process.[15] Recently, academics have become enamored with the problem-solving model because this approach is seen as exploring the underlying interests of the clients in attempts to "increase the overall pie" to be divided during negotiations.[16] Often this requires looking at non-monetary alternatives to compensation.

Adversarial negotiators tend to maximize their own return, focus on their own positions rather than neutral standards, use threats, be untrusting, minimize information disclosure, attempt to make minimal concessions, use deception, and manipulate opponents as they analogize negotiation to a game.[17] Many attorneys appear to believe that employing an adversarial tactic will earn them better rewards.[18] Research has contradicted this, however, showing that results obtained by problem-solving negotiators are as beneficial for clients as results obtained by adversarial negotiators.[19] The study also found lawyers who negotiated with adversarial negotiators reported they were treated in a more uncivil and less pleasant manner than those attorneys who negotiated with problem-solving negotiators.[20] This suggests that employing an adversarial tactic may negatively impact an attorney's future relationships as fellow practitioners would certainly be less willing to work with someone who has treated them uncivilly or unpleasantly in the past. It may also explain why, as this study has been replicated, there have been fewer adversarial negotiators considered effective and more considered ineffective.[21]

Other studies "demonstrate[] that it is not necessarily the style of negotiation that determine[s] effectiveness, but rather additional facets of the lawyer's conduct, such as planning, preparation, information gathering techniques, and personal characteristics that [have] a greater effect on the outcome."[22] And follow-up studies "found that more lawyers view themselves (and others) as problem-solving negotiators."[23]

Some theorists, regularly called "communitarians," believe that lawyers should not be allowed to over- or under-state how they value different terms to be exchanged, misrepresent their settlement intentions, or bluff.[24] However, other commentators have suggested:

---

[15]Menkel-Meadow, *supra* note 14, at 909-10.

[16]Craver, *supra* note 12, at 10 (describing cooperative negotiation as increasing the overall pie); *see, e.g.*, Carrie J. Menkel-Meadow, *Toward Another View of Legal Negotiation: The Structure of Problem Solving*, 31 U.C.L.A. L. Rev. 754 (1984) (discussing the benefits of the problem-solving approach and its superiority to competitive negotiation strategy); Kovach, *supra* note 5 (discussing the benefits of increasing the "overall pie").

[17]Craver, *supra* note 12, at 9.

[18]*Id.*

[19]*Id.*; *see also* Kovach, *supra* note 5, at 405-06.

[20]Craver, *supra* note 12, at 10.

[21]*Id.* at 11.

[22]Kovach, *supra* note 5, at 406.

[23]*Id.*

[24]Charles B. Craver, *Negotiation Ethics for Real World Interactions*, 25 Ohio St. J. Disp. Resol. 299, 304 (2010).

Negotiation often cannot take place if the parties must reveal the existence of a principal, their true asking price, or their intention regarding settlement throughout the bargaining process. Deception concerning value as well as deception concerning settlement point in particular are consistent with functionalism because they are recognizable as bargaining techniques and allow accurate information to be achieved through bargaining.[25]

Clearly, there are a range of opinions in regards to which tactics should be utilized by attorneys. In practice, lawyers may be called upon to employ either tactic of negotiation. The ethics of negotiation must account for both of these poles and the numerous combinations of these styles that lie in between.

III. The Application and Purpose of Ethics

A. The Ethics that Apply to Negotiation

For over one-hundred years, American lawyers have looked to ethical rules for guidance.[26] Lawyers speak of ethics and ethical standards as if all know what the standards mean and that the standards mean universally the same thing to all.[27] This is clearly not true. For years the Model Rules of Professional Conduct have been interpreted. In the negotiation context, the provisions most likely to require interpretation are Rules 4.1 and 1.6.[28] Rule 4.1 provides:

> In the course of representing a client a lawyer shall not knowingly:
>
>> (a) make a false statement of material fact or law to a third person; or (b) fail to disclose a material fact when disclosure is necessary to avoid assisting a criminal or fraudulent act by a client, unless disclosure is necessary to avoid assisting in a criminal or fraudulent act by a client....[29]

Comment 2 to Rule 4.1, in turn, clarifies:

> This rule refers to statements of fact. Whether a particular statement should be regarded as one of fact can depend on the circumstances. Under generally accepted conventions in negotiation, certain types of statements *ordinarily* are not taken as statements of material fact. Estimates of price or value placed on the subject of a transaction and a party's intention as to an acceptable settlement of a claim are ordinarily in this category, and so is the existence of an undisclosed principal except where nondisclosure of the principal would con-

---

[25]*Id.* at 307.

[26]*E.g.*, Kovach, *supra* note 9, at 808.

[27]*Id.* at 810.

[28]*See generally* Model Rules of Prof'l Conduct R. 1.6, 4.1 (2007).

[29]Model Rules of Prof'l Conduct R. 4.1 (2007).

stitute fraud. Lawyers should be mindful of their obligations under applicable law to avoid criminal and tortious misrepresentation.[30]

"Ordinarily" did not appear until the comment was amended in 2002.[31] It was added to note that in some circumstances an estimate of price or statement about settlement intention could constitute a false statement of fact in attempts to clarify the lawyer's ethical obligations in negotiations.[32] Joining Rule 4.1, the next most significant rule in negotiations is Rule 1.6 governing confidentiality.[33] In addition to the mandatory Model Rules of Professional Conduct, negotiations are subject to the Ethical Guidelines for Settlement Negotiations as drafted by the American Bar Association (ABA).[34] These guidelines serve as a permissive supplement for attorneys to model their behavior after, but are not subject to enforcement against violations as are the Model Rules (when implemented by state courts and bar associations as their own rules).

At least one commentator has suggested that "[e]thical codes should not simply limit or constrain professional behavior, acting as some kind of floor below which one's behavior is unacceptable; rather they should guide and fac-

---

[30]Model Rules of Prof'l Conduct R. 4.1 cmt. 2 (2007) (emphasis added).

[31]Center for Professional Responsibility (American Bar Association), A Legislative History: The Development of the ABA Model Rules of Professional Conduct, 1982-2005 528 (2006).

[32]*Id.*; Hilary D. Wells, *Raising the Bar in Settlement Negotiations: A Rationale for Amending Arizona's Rules of Professional Conduct*, 33 Ariz. St. L.J. 1261, 1276 (2001).

[33]*See generally* Model Rules of Prof'l Conduct R. 1.6 (2007).

> (a) A lawyer shall not reveal information relating to the representation of a client unless the client gives informed consent, the disclosure is impliedly authorized in order to carry out the representation or the disclosure is permitted by paragraph (b).
> (b) A lawyer may reveal information relating to the representation of a client to the extent the lawyer reasonably believes necessary:
>   (1) to prevent reasonably certain death or substantial bodily harm;
>   (2) to prevent the client from committing a crime or fraud that is reasonably certain to result in substantial injury to the financial interests or property of another and in furtherance of which the client has used or is using the lawyer's services;
>   (3) to prevent, mitigate or rectify substantial injury to the financial interests or property of another that is reasonably certain to result or has resulted from the client's commission of a crime or fraud in furtherance of which the client has used the lawyer's services;
>   (4) to secure legal advice about the lawyer's compliance with these Rules;
>   (5) to establish a claim or defense on behalf of the lawyer in a controversy between the lawyer and the client, to establish a defense to a criminal charge or civil claim against the lawyer based upon conduct in which the client was involved, or to respond to allegations in any proceeding concerning the lawyer's representation of the client; or
>   (6) to comply with other law or a court order.

[34]*See generally* Ethical Guidelines for Settlement Negotiations (2002), *available at* http://ocmediationconference.org/sitebuildercontent/sitebuilderfiles/settlementnegotia tions.pdf.

ilitate the performance of the established professional role."[35] In addition to ethical concerns and bar discipline, lawyers who engage in unethical behavior also risk other losses. These include a loss of trust between parties, damage to professional relationships, and impact on future relationships with both clients and fellow attorneys. These losses are not based on ethics, however, but on the professionalism that attorneys believe they owe to each other. In this regard, "[b]asic trust is essential to bargaining interactions."[36]

B. Justifications for Professional Codes

Multiple reasons exist justifying the creation of professional codes. In large part, these justifications mirror the justifications for criminal law.[37] First, codes are informational documents.[38] By reading the relevant code, lawyers know how to behave.[39] In this regard, ethical codes are used to ensure competence, as opposed to the punishment theories discussed below.[40] Ethical codes set behavioral norms.[41] Without this, a lawyer is left to innovative options.[42]

Another reason professional codes exist is to be enforced.[43] In this regard, states' implementations of the Model Rules of Professional Conduct serve as a doctrine of punishment used to penalize perpetrators for both their behavior against the profession and behavior against an individual, often the client but sometimes a fellow attorney. Although the rules are not primarily enforced for punishment purposes, the analogy to criminal law is hard to ignore.

When the violation is against a client, punishment serves the additional function of protecting both that client and future clients from unethical behavior.[44] In essence, it serves a consumer protection function. It also serves a protectionist function in fostering attorney-client relationships. The code prevents lawyers and clients from having moralistic discussions of right and wrong.[45]

---

[35]Bordone, *supra* note 4, at 10-11.

[36]Craver, *supra* note 24, at 309.

[37]*See* Fred C. Zacharias, *The Purposes of Lawyer Discipline*, 45 Wm. & Mary L. Rev. 675, 682 (2003) (comparing criminal laws to professional responsibility theories).

[38]Murray L. Schwartz, *The Professionalism and Accountability of Lawyers*, *in* What's Fair: Ethics for Negotiators 329, 335 (Carrie Menkel-Meadow & Michael Wheeler eds., 2004); *see* Zacharias, *supra* note 37, at 730 ("Some professional rules are hortatory in nature — not being intended or expected to be fully enforced, but rather serving as instruction or guidance for lawyers.").

[39]Schwartz, *supra* note 38, at 335.

[40]Zacharias, *supra* note 37, at 684.

[41]*Id.* at 687 ("Some professional rules are purely hortatory in nature, sending a signal about general aspirations for lawyer behavior but leaving implementation to lawyer discretion and good will.").

[42]Kovach, *supra* note 5, at 414.

[43]*See* Schwartz, *supra* note 38, at 335.

[44]*See* Zacharias, *supra* note 37, at 677-87.

[45]*See* Schwartz, *supra* note 38, at 335.

It also encourages information to flow freely from client to attorney under the confidentiality rule.[46] Further, clients are protected from services that do not rise to the regulated standard through restrictions like unauthorized practice of law and advertising. Unfortunately, clients are not protected from the conduct in the first place because by definition professional discipline occurs after an ethical violation.[47] Therefore, only by punishing those who are likely repeat offenders and deterring other lawyers does the code accomplish its goal of consumer protection.[48] Minimally, maintaining an ethical code helps the image of the profession in the eyes of the public.[49]

Another justification for ethical codes is consistency. The Model Rules of Professional Conduct create a normative set of standards for all lawyers to follow. In this regard, it does not matter what, specifically, the rule says. The significance of the code derives from everyone abiding by it. In articulating the standards lawyers must abide by, the code serves a signaling function of defining ethical behavior to those operating within and outside the profession. However, as one commentator notes, "professional discipline tends to take place in secret."[50] Perhaps this limits the signaling function punishment can serve, particularly to consumers.

Professional codes also serve a deterrence function, both for specific offenders and to all attorneys.[51] In this regard, the code seeks to prevent ethical violations from happening in the first place. This is general deterrence. If a violation has already occurred, the punishment theories apply, which will ideally prevent a specific offender from reoffending. This is specific deterrence.

C. Meditation and Negotiation Codes

According to the Model Standards of Conduct for Mediators, meditation gives the "opportunity for parties to define and clarify issues, understand different perspectives, identify interests, explore and assess possible solutions, and reach mutually satisfactory agreements, when desired."[52] The Preamble also indicates that the standards "might be viewed as establishing a standard of care for mediators."[53] Beyond this, the Standards themselves do not indicate why drafters viewed mediation as worthy of a separate set of ethical standards.[54] One

---

[46]*E.g., id.*; Zacharias, *supra* note 37, at 695.

[47]Zacharias, *supra* note 37, at 694.

[48]*Id.*

[49]*Id.* at 730-31 ("Still other rules are geared primarily toward maintaining the image of the bar.").

[50]*Id.* at 690.

[51]*E.g.*, Schwartz, *supra* note 38, at 335.

[52]Model Standards of Conduct for Mediators pmbl. (2005), *available at* http://www.americanbar.org/content/dam/aba/migrated/dispute/documents/model_s tandards_conduct_april2007.authcheckdam.pdf.

[53]*Id.*

[54]*See id.*

commentator has noted that the need for zealous advocacy is replaced by co-operation, collaboration, and joint problem-solving.[55] Thus, mediators and arbitrators may require separate ethical codes because of the change in lawyering skills.[56] For example, fact-finding and adjudication of fault are not required in mediation, but these skills are the core of the adversarial system.[57]

The Preamble to the Ethical Guidelines for Settlement Negotiations acknowledges that "[s]ettlement negotiations are an essential part of litigation."[58] It adds, "[t]he settlement process necessarily implicates many ethical issues. Resolving these issues and determining a lawyer's professional responsibilities are important aspects of the settlement process and justify special attention to lawyers' ethical duties as they relate to negotiation of settlements."[59] The Guidelines also state they are "intended to be a practical, user-friendly guide for lawyers who seek advice on ethical issues arising in settlement negotiations" and "suggest best practices and aspirational goals."[60]

Some commentators suggest the guidelines are not mandatory because credence must be given to the appropriateness of certain bargaining tactics, the distribution among the bargainers of value created by agreement, and the possible effects of negotiation on those not at the table.[61] In essence, attorneys need to maintain freedom to choose their tactic and strategy during negotiations. Perhaps another reason the negotiation ethical code is not mandatory is "the profession's conception of the lawyer as adversarial advocate."[62] In essence, the lawyer's primary role is advocate, and hence those ethical rules are mandatory, while a potential secondary role is negotiator, so those rules are permissive in case of a conflict with the advocate rules.

IV. Negotiation Ethics Proposal

Thus far this paper has discussed the tactics of negotiation, what ethical obligations are imposed in negotiations by the Model Rules of Professional Conduct, and the purpose of ethics. This section will examine the problems of fitting adversarial-based ethics into a non-adversarial setting, such as a negotiation, and how to cure this conflict. Instead of forcing adversarial ethics, the bar should apply the confidentiality rule, currently Rule 1.6 of the Model Rules

---

[55]Bordone, *supra* note 4, at 2.

[56]*Id.*

[57]Kovach, *supra* note 5, at 404-05.

[58]Ethical Guidelines for Settlement Negotiations pmbl. (2002), *available at* http://ocmediationconference.org/sitebuildercontent/sitebuilderfiles/settlementnegotiations.pdf.

[59]*Id.*

[60]*Id.*

[61]David A. Lax & James K. Sebenius, *Three Ethical Issues in Negotiation, in* What's Fair: Ethics for Negotiators 5, 7 (Carrie Menkel-Meadow & Michael Wheeler eds., 2004).

[62]Scott R. Peppet, *Lawyers' Bargaining Ethics, Contract, and Collaboration: The End of the Legal Profession and the Beginning of Professional Pluralism*, 90 Iowa L. Rev. 475, 480 (2005).

of Professional Conduct, but rules relating to bluffing and information sharing, currently Rule 4.1, should not be applied in the non-adversarial setting. Additionally, proposals from other commentators, such as rules regarding fairness, should not be applied. Instead I propose that "ethics" will come from the moral obligations of professionals to guard the profession, the desire to protect their professional reputation, existing laws such as fraud and criminal law,[63] and the ability of attorneys to contractually enhance their ethical obligations through private contracts if they desire. The ABA may draft the clauses to be included in these contracts if it sees fit.[64] Using this avenue would mean there would be a civil breach of contract action and disciplinary proceedings by the bar as possible remedies for unethical conduct. There are several reasons why my proposal would advance the justifications of the ethical code, to be discussed in turn.

A. Reporting

There are numerous problems in reporting ethical violations in negotiations that do not exist in the adversarial setting. First, enforcement must take place in a private forum without a public record.[65] This creates both evidentiary problems and places the burden of reporting on the honest party. As to the first, when disciplinary proceedings begin, there is no record, such as a court transcript, to substantiate the claims and verify what the parties said. Second, placing the burden on the honest party is problematic because "if one negotiator lies to another, only by happenstance will the other discover the lie."[66] But, if there is no reporting, the bar would appear weak and unable to enforce its code. As one commentator put it, "it is better to have no rule at all than one that is not subject to ready enforcement."[67]

The proposal of eliminating information sharing and fairness ethics, while allowing professional reputation damage, existing law, and private contract law theories to prevail, solves these problems. At the most basic level, if there are no ethics there can be no ethical violations and hence there is no need for reporting. Others may argue that the realm of negotiation cannot be entirely unregulated. This is likely true. But the proposal does not leave victims of questionable conduct without recourse. Practitioners who believe they have been taken advantage of can find relief in private laws. To file a claim, one must only have a claim with enough merit that it is not frivolous. Once a claim is filed, the plaintiff, or victim, is entitled to discovery assuming the claim passes a motion

---

[63]*See* Wells, *supra* note 32, at 1276.

[64]*See* Peppet, *supra* note 62, at 514 (discussing a contract-based theory of ethics under which the bar would draft a menu of options for lawyers to select from).

[65]Wells, *supra* note 32, at 1286; *see* Paul Rosenberger, *Laissez-"Fair": An Argument for the Status Quo Ethical Constraints on Lawyers as Negotiators*, 13 Ohio St. J. on Disp. Resol. 611, 626 (1998) (discussing the difficulties of monitoring unethical behavior in negotiations because it is non-public).

[66]Craver, *supra* note 24, at 307; *see also* Rosenberger, *supra* note 65, at 627 ("[O]nly by chance will the other discover the deception.").

[67]Wells, *supra* note 32, at 1286.

for summary judgment. Therefore, the plaintiff need not have all of the facts at the time of filing because investigation procedures are significantly more prevalent in civil claims than ethical violations. The flaws of reporting in the negotiation are drastically decreased by acknowledging the privacy in which settlements take place. Under this proposal, lawsuits filed by victimized attorneys shift the burden from disciplinary committees to outside law. By making the unethical conduct more public, the proposal serves a stronger deterrence and signaling function than if the information remained solely with the disciplinary board. Further, the opinion issued from the proceedings, whether fraud, breach of contract, or another claim, will serve both as a model or guideline for other attorneys' behavior and as an informative document.

The most likely ethical violation in a negotiation would be misrepresentation of a material fact. Because of the non-public forum that disciplinary proceedings take place in, and the non-public forum that negotiations take place in with exchanging information pertinent to a client's case, the goals of the ethical code would be not be served in enforcement of that code. Imposed subjective standards, like fairness, would require examining the actual results of the negotiation.[68] Examining the actual results of negotiation in a private setting would not give attorneys much information upon which to model their behavior, one goal of the ethics rules. By making the information more accessible and the standards objective, lawyers will be better able to model their behavior under the proposal.

B. Enforcement

Rule 4.1 and ethics that have been proposed to apply to negotiations contain language that lacks definition and may be too vague to enforce, particularly with consistency. For example, one of the earliest proposals was from the 1980 Kutak Commission, which proposed an addition to the Model Rules of Professional Conduct entitled "Fairness to Other Participants."[69] The addition would have required that "in conducting negotiations a lawyer shall be fair in dealing with other participants."[70] Other numerous proposals by commentators include requirements of honesty, competency, trust, and respect.[71]

But, what is fairness? As one critic of the addition noted, "notions of 'fairness' are relative and may change according to the circumstances of the negotiation and the personalities of the negotiators."[72] Notions of fairness may also change over time and in different parts of the nation. Other critics have suggested that notions of fairness are vague, unconscionable, unjust, or all of the above, and worry that this will lead to arbitrary enforcement, if not lack of enforcement entirely.[73] They caution this could lead to "discrimination against

---

[68]Rosenberger, *supra* note 65, at 627.

[69]Wells, *supra* note 32, at 1277.

[70]*Id.*

[71]*See* Kovach, *supra* note 5, at 418-29.

[72]Wells, *supra* note 32, at 1277.

[73]*See* Schwartz, *supra* note 38, at 333-34 (summarizing various critics' views).

lawyers who represent unpopular causes or oppressed persons, or who them-selves are for personal, political, or other reasons personae non gratae at the bar."[74]

Similar to reporting, the proposal of this paper cures the current enforce-ment defects because it does not require interpretation of arbitrary and vague language. Instead, conduct would be enforced according to private remedies, like fraud, with clear guidelines articulated through common law. On the other hand, as professionals operate with an implicit notion of fairness, damage to one's professional reputation would cure the problem in borderline cases. Instead of having to interpret language, information on reputations would spread. The amount of damage to one's reputation directly correlates to the severity of the alleged action. In borderline cases, where conduct is arguably improper, reputational damage would be minor. The disciplinary proceedings procedure currently used has a harsher effect on a lawyer's ability to practice in the future, when disciplining on the basis of vague standards, than would the more flexible standard of damage to the reputation. And the stronger standard of private remedies would only be applicable in accordance with stringent stan-dards.

C. Drafting

In drafting an ethical code for negotiation, difficulties will inevitably present themselves in defining when the negotiation starts and stops, which correlates to when the negotiation ethical obligations start and stop. Many may still view negotiation not as an individual process itself but as part of litigation.[75] In fact, many lawyers often negotiate in a manner that contemplates litigation.[76] Some lawyers, like transactional attorneys, would not be confronted with this prob-lem because of the settings they negotiate in.[77] It is true that litigation often involves negotiation over the dispute at some point, or at least there is a time when parties exchange offers and demands in an effort to settle the dispute, but the "goals of negotiation are substantially different from those of litigation."[78] Some commentators have addressed the issue of when negotiation begins and ends, proposing that negotiation would be presumed before the filing of a com-plaint; during litigation, litigation would be presumed and changes would re-quire the filing of a notice of process change; or the client could utilize settle-ment and litigation counsel.[79] Clearly this issue is no small task for drafters.

Drafters will also encounter problems based on the sheer volume of dis-putes that are negotiated and their range in contexts.[80] Negotiation takes place in

---

[74]*Id.* at 334.

[75]Bordone, *supra* note 4, at 38.

[76]Rosenberger, *supra* note 65, at 622.

[77]Bordone, *supra* note 4, at 39.

[78]*Id.* at 22.

[79]*Id.* at 38-39.

[80]Rosenberger, *supra* note 65, at 627.

multiple settings, which must be contemplated by the ethical standards. Much of negotiation takes place without lawyers even realizing it, such as short phone calls or email exchanges.[81] On the other hand, negotiation can be very formal and take place before a tribunal.[82] Negotiations can occur in the presence of a third-party mediator or may simply take place between the two parties and their lawyers. When formal negotiations occur, more stringent ethical standards apply because of the duty of disclosure to the tribunal.[83] The variety of contexts would require either rules targeted to specific contexts or, more likely, rules of great generality.[84] Further, the potential expansion of negotiation must be considered.[85] One commentator has suggested that the international scope and effect of the internet would need to be considered in drafting.[86]

The drafting benefit of my proposal is that it is not a sweeping change; it does not require the imposition of new ethical standards. In fact, it is a minimalist strategy. Many commentators have proposed sweeping changes such as the requirement of fairness or good faith. These terms would be new to disciplinary committees, making it difficult to get the ethical obligation adopted and enforced. Further, the proposal of this paper does not choose a negotiation tactic that lawyers must follow. As others have noted:

> Commentators who have examined the Model Rules with respect to their appropriateness for problem-solving negotiation agree that, rather than helping to create the conditions that enable or facilitate a good outcome in negotiation, the rules tend to do just the opposite: they tend to encourage dissembling behavior that borders on lying, inviting distrust, bluffing, and puffery into the negotiation process.[87]

The proposed fairness and good faith standards are meant to encourage problem-solving negotiation. But adoption of these standards would force adversarial bargainers to change their tactics or engage in unethical negotiations. By eliminating fairness, good faith, and bluffing standards, the proposal seeks to leave the decision on how to negotiate with the client and attorney. This is consistent with Model Rule 1.2 on the allocation of authority between client and lawyer, which leaves the choice of "objectives of representation" with the client.[88] The decision of tactic and strategy in negotiation and objectives of representation in litigation are similar because both require consideration of the client's goals.

---

[81]Craver, *supra* note 12, at 371.

[82]*See* Wells, *supra* note 32, at 1261-62 (discussing the differences when negotiations take place before a tribunal).

[83]*Id.* at 1262, 1268.

[84]*Id.*; *see also supra* Part IV.B.

[85]*See* Kovach, *supra* note 9, at 822.

[86]*See id.* ("As dispute resolution processes move across oceans and cyberspace, it is doubtful that the same rules, guidelines, or principles used in our national or state matters will be appropriate in international cases and translate to other cultures as well.").

[87]Bordone, *supra* note 4, at 21-22.

[88]*See generally* Model Rules of Prof'l Conduct R. 1.2 (2007).

Clearly, the problems of drafting are eliminated under the proposal as no drafting is required. Even more so, by not requiring drafting the ethical purpose of deterrence is increased as attorneys will operate under the fear of reputational damage. Because attorneys will not know what others might find offensive, they will operate with heightened awareness of their actions and be deterred from borderline conduct. Additionally, the proposal serves the ethical purpose of consumer protection because it leaves with the client the choice of which negotiation strategy to adopt after consultation with his or her lawyer.

D. Misuse of Ethics as Inappropriate Leverage

Commentator Mark Young has suggested that what he calls sharks and saints negotiators, which we are referring to as adversarial and problem-solving negotiators, both use ethics as leverage/power in negotiations.[89] The sharks use ethics to gain an advantage by appealing to fairness standards and making the opponent trust them.[90] A saint negotiator will not only "pay lip service" to ethics but also abide by them to protect their reputation for future dealings.[91] But ethics are not meant to be trading chips amongst lawyers nor are they meant to bring power as a by-product.[92]

Unfortunately, this is one area where if ethics are removed, and reputation is the major asset, few changes would result. The sharks will instead use reputation as their asset. For them, this is likely to fall apart over time as people realize they are not trustworthy. The saints, however, who currently operate with ethical reputation as the chief asset, will have that replaced with professional reputation as the chief asset. Therefore, the proposal of this paper will only bring to light the adversarial negotiators but not change anything for problem-solvers. What the proposal does do is make professional reputation the traded asset, meaning ethics will no longer be used as a bargaining chip. Clearly, this protects the image of the profession and the public's view of lawyers' ethics.

E. Lack of a Neutral Arbitrator

Negotiations almost always take place in a non-adversarial setting.[93] The exception is when the negotiation is required by a tribunal and subject to judicial approval.[94] Each stage of private settlement, however, "lacks at least

---

[89]Mark Young, *Sharks, Saints, and Samurai: The Power of Ethics in Negotiation*, 24 Negot. J. 145, 147 (2008).

[90]*Id.* at 148.

[91]*Id.*

[92]*Id.* at 150.

[93]Schwartz, *supra* note 38, at 331.

[94]*Id.*

one essential element of the adversary system: the impartial arbiter."[95] The question is whether this renders the principles of the adversary inapplicable to the negotiation context.[96] The presence of an impartial arbiter ensures that only one part of the system has the responsibility of reaching the correct legal determination and places the burden on the parties to present the issues, evidence, and arguments of their side.[97] The arbiter creates and administers the rules of competition to determine who has prevailed.[98] The attorneys who are participating in a procedure with a neutral arbiter "are justified in using methods and seeking results with which they may personally disagree because of faith in the ability of the arbiter to reach a correct decision."[99] But "[t]he advocate in negotiation presents his facts and arguments to the other party for agreement, rather than to a tribunal for a decision."[100] In reality, negotiations are not even limited to the same remedies available in the court system.[101]

One commentator has compared the difference in a proceeding with an arbiter, and one without, to an officiated versus pick-up basketball game.[102] In a pick-up basketball game, each side must minimize tangential disputes, such as debating fouls, in order to ensure that the primary objective, playing basketball, continues. In a formal basketball game, the official can determine the winner of the tangential disputes to ensure the game progresses. Because the official will determine the merits of tangential disputes, each side can argue adamantly why they believe, for example, a foul was or was not committed. Not only does this make for better facial expressions from players in televised games, but also for a better presentation of the issues.[103] Without the referee, there is no longer anyone to point to for the ultimate resolution of disputes, and impartiality is removed from the decision making process.[104] As with basketball, the behavioral differences for a lawyer acting before an arbiter and a lawyer who is not are so stark that it renders the forums worthy of different ethical codes.

One may argue that clients' expectations do not change when the attorney acts as an advocate versus non-advocate.[105] Thus, some believe that the ethics

---

[95]*Id.*; *see* Menkel-Meadow, *supra* note 16, at 791-92 ("[T]here is no third party adjudicator in most negotiations.").

[96]Schwartz, *supra* note 38, at 331.

[97]*Id.* at 332.

[98]*Id.*

[99]*Id.*

[100]Rosenberger, *supra* note 65, at 623.

[101]*See* Menkel-Meadow, *supra* note 16, at 789 ("The assumption that only limited items are available in dispute resolution occurs because negotiation takes place in the shadow of the courts.").

[102]Schwartz, *supra* note 38, at 332.

[103]*Id.*

[104]*Id.*

[105]*Id.*

for a non-advocate should closely track those of advocates.[106] In essence, it is the client expectations, not the forum, that determine whether differences are so stark as to warrant using separate ethical codes for each forum. Yet while client expectations are certainly worthy of merit as consumer protection is one purpose of creating ethical standards, it is not sufficient to overcome the differences in the environment.

The proposal accommodates the lack of a neutral arbiter by distinguishing the two forums. In doing so, consumer protection is increased. As it currently stands, clients will always believe that their attorney will zealously advocate on their behalf. This is untrue, however. In the case of negotiation, if a lawyer advocates too zealously, the deal may crumble. This likely will result in the lawyer failing to meet the goals of the client. Instead, the proposal seeks to distinguish the two forums. The attorney will have to explain to the client the differences in arbiter and no-arbiter forums so the client can make an informed decision on which forum to choose.

F. Non-Attorney Negotiators

A final reason for adoption of the proposal is to level the playing field between lawyers and non-lawyers who participate in negotiation. There are many fields where one can participate in negotiations without having graduated from law school or passed the bar exam. Take, for example, sports agency. In this profession, there is no governing body that regulates all agents. ABA and state-imposed ethical obligations apply to lawyer-agents, increasing their ethical obligations to the athletes they represent, but not to non-lawyer agents.[107] It has been argued by many commentators that these ethical obligations place attorney-agents at a competitive disadvantage because young, naïve athletes care more about the promises an agent makes them than about the agents' ethical obligations.[108] Because of their ethical restrictions, attorney-agents make fewer puffery promises, leading athletes to those who are unregulated and promising them more rewards during their careers.

In just this one field, representative of other lines of work where lawyers and non-lawyers commingle, it is clear that attorneys are at a disadvantage in getting clients. They are also at a heightened risk of sanction for their actions during negotiation. The proposal of deregulating ethics would help these attorney-agents compete with their non-attorney counterparts and subject all to equal risk for wrong behavior. In doing so, the proposal would advance the lawyer protection justification of the code by allowing those subject to the ethical obligations to compete with those not subject to ethical obligations.

---

[106]*Id.*

[107]Stacey B. Evans, *Sports Agents: Ethical Representatives or Overly Aggressive Adversaries?*, 17 Vill. Sports & Ent. L.J. 91, 93 (2010) ("[A]ttorney-agent is held to a strict code of ethics.").

[108]*See id.* ("Unfortunately, players are often swayed by agents who claim they can obtain the most lucrative deal for a client rather than paying attention to who is the most qualified to negotiate.").

V. Conclusion

It has been suggested by commentator Robert Bordone:

> The more reluctant lawyers are to embrace negotiation fully as a separate academic discipline and a separate process-choice for dispute resolution, the more the legal profession is likely to be supplanted by conflict management consultants, public policy analysts, businesspeople, and those from other related professions who have the skill-set and training to use negotiation as an independent problem-solving process to find integrating outcomes for their clients.[109]

To embrace the negotiation process as part of the legal profession and fortify negotiation in the profession so non-attorneys do not dominate, ethics need to be defined. Ethical obligations are the core of a profession as they create normative behavior and provide substance to the professional leader, in this case the American Bar Association. To this point, however, only academics have been willing to acknowledge the conflict between the effective problem-solving negotiation style and the adversarial ethical obligations of the Model Rules of Professional Conduct.

This paper has proposed a cure to this conflict by suggesting that only Rule 1.6 on confidentiality should apply to negotiations. This would mean that Rule 4.1 on information-sharing and other proposed role ethics, like good faith and fairness, would not apply. Instead, if practitioners felt a violation had occurred and the violation lived up to the standards of a private remedy like fraud or criminal law, practitioners could pursue this remedy. If an adequate remedy at common law did not exist, the damage that would ensue would be to the violator's reputation. If attorneys wanted, they could agree to a standard of information-sharing through a private contract, which would create a breach of contract action if violated. This proposal is a necessary result of the problems in reporting, enforcement, drafting, utilizing ethics as bargaining chips, the lack of a neutral arbiter in negotiations, and the unlevel playing field for jobs where lawyers regularly negotiate with non-lawyers.

---

[109]Bordone, *supra* note 4, at 14.

PART THREE

Disciplinary Concerns

11

The Scope of Attorney Discipline: Analyzing the Conflicts and Concerns in Non-Professional Roles

Sanford J. Roth

In 1998, politician and attorney William J. Clinton became the second President of the United States to be impeached.[1] Clinton's impeachment followed charges of perjury and obstruction of justice relating to his testimony before a federal grand jury regarding alleged sexual misconduct while serving in political office.[2] Despite being impeached by the House of Representatives, Clinton was acquitted three months later by the Senate on both counts and was retained in office as the President.[3] Following Congress' acquittal, the Arkansas Supreme Court's Committee on Professional Conduct began disbarment proceedings on the same charges against Clinton who was a licensed attorney in the state.[4] Instead of facing permanent disbarment from Arkansas, Clinton agreed to have his law license revoked for a period of five years and subsequently resigned from the United States Supreme Court bar.[5]

Despite being deemed fit enough to continue serving as President of the United States, Clinton was deemed unfit to continue serving as an attorney in the State of Arkansas. The dichotomy of punishments seems particularly ironic when it is considered in light of the fact that Clinton's charges arose from conduct he undertook while acting as a politician, not as an attorney. Regardless, Arkansas believed that there was a sufficient enough nexus between his charges and fitness to practice law to commence disbarment proceedings against him which culminated in his suspension.

The impeachment saga of former President Clinton prompts several legal ethics questions which are not easily determinable. First, do the American Bar Association's ("ABA") Model Rules of Professional Conduct ("Model Rules"), and the state replications thereof, apply only to the misconduct of lawyers acting in their professional legal capacities? Or do the rules extend to conduct in an attorney's personal life as well? Second, if the Model Rules do apply to conduct outside of an attorney's professional role, which types of conduct are

---

[1]H.R. Res. 611, 105th Cong. (1998).

[2]*Id.*

[3]On the grand jury perjury charge, the Senate voted 55-45 in favor of acquittal. On the obstruction of justice charge, the Senate voted 50-50. *See* 145 Cong. Rec. S1458-59 (daily ed. Feb. 12, 1999).

[4]John King, *President's Law License Suspended for 5 Years*, January 19, 2001, *available at* http://archives.cnn.com/2001/ALLPOLITICS/stories/01/19/clinton.lewinsky (last visited Apr. 17, 2011).

[5]*Id.*

sufficient to warrant discipline? Do the Model Rules lend any guidance? Third, would such far-reaching regulations over an attorney's personal life conflict or coincide with the general goals of the ABA in furthering the legal community?

President Clinton's suspension from the Arkansas Bar is an example which helps illustrate the difficulties that the states have in disciplining attorneys for non-legal conduct. Although Clinton's charge of perjury stemmed from a courtroom setting, he was not acting as an attorney but instead as a litigant responding to a charge of misconduct while in political office. Disciplinary proceedings against attorneys in similar circumstances highlight the conflict that the state courts have: in suspending or disbarring an attorney for conduct unrelated to his professional legal role, the state's legal community loses an attorney who did not abuse his position and is otherwise entirely fit to practice the law, yet progresses in maintaining a respected and dignified profession.

I. The Scope of Attorney Discipline

A. Problems and Contemporary Reasoning for Expanding Reach

The length of the Model Rules' reach into the non-legal conduct of an attorney is far from axiomatic. The rules themselves seem to be at odds with its own determined scope of application. According to the ABA, the Model Rules "should be interpreted with reference to the purposes of legal representation and of the law itself."[6] Furthermore, the rules "simply provide a framework for the ethical practice of law."[7] Rule 8.4(c), however, broadens the scope of the rules beyond purposes of what occurs only during legal representation by allowing an attorney to be censured for any dishonest, fraudulent, deceitful or misrepresenting conduct whatsoever.[8] Punishable conduct, then, may be completely unrelated to an attorney's lack of actual legal fitness.

The state courts have widely accepted the ABA's stance that lawyer discipline may be given for misconduct undertaken outside of the professional role.[9] The Maryland Supreme Court, for example, has reasoned that "unlike matters relating to competency, diligence, and the like, intentional dishonest conduct is closely entwined with the most important matters of basic character to such a degree as to make intentional dishonest conduct by a lawyer almost beyond excuse."[10] Although this reasoning parallels the intentions of Rule 8.4 in

---

[6]American Bar Association, Model Rules of Prof'l Conduct: Scope cmt. 14 (2010).

[7]Model Rules of Prof'l Conduct: Scope cmt. 16 (2010).

[8]Model Rules of Prof'l Conduct R. 8.4(c) (2010) ("It is professional misconduct for a lawyer to engage in conduct involving dishonesty, fraud, deceit or misrepresentation.").

[9]*See, e.g., State ex rel. Oklahoma Bar Ass'n v. Gassaway*, 196 P.3d 495, 504 (Okla. 2008) ("[T]his Court has recognized that discipline may be imposed for occurrences outside the attorney-client relationship."); *In re Disciplinary Proceeding Against Day*, 173 P.3d 915, 920 (Wash. 2007) ("[T]his court has held that an attorney may be sanctioned for conduct that occurs outside the practice of law.").

[10]*Attorney Grievance Com'n of Maryland v. Webster*, 402 Md. 448, 474 (Md. 2007).

maintaining the personal integrity of lawyers, it does not draw any bright line as to exactly what dishonest conduct is worthy of discipline. Rule 8.4, by itself, essentially leaves lawyers susceptible to punishment for conduct which they might not themselves believe to be "dishonest," while a court may disagree. The issue is magnified when it is considered that lawyers who are licensed in multiple jurisdictions are usually required to alert the other jurisdictions in which they are admitted that they have been disciplined.[11]

B. The History of Determining Attorney Misconduct

One of the earliest interpretations on the scope of punishable conduct for attorneys came from the United States Supreme Court in 1883.[12] In *Ex Parte Wall*, an attorney was stripped of his law license after he organized and encouraged a crowd to remove an inmate from a jail and unlawfully hang him to death.[13] Justice Joseph Bradley, writing for the majority, reasoned that the attorney's role in the murder was so "in defiance and contempt of all law and justice [that he has] shown himself unfitted to longer retain the position of attorney in any court."[14] Justice Bradley further concluded that an attorney's right to practice law should be rescinded "for conduct gravely affecting his professional character."[15] The Court's holding thus established a discretionary test; in determining when to penalize an attorney for misconduct outside of his legal role, anything a court deems to be compromising to the attorney's professional character is enough to warrant professional discipline.

The Supreme Court's decision in *Wall* eventually became the twentieth century paradigm in the gradual sculpting of a set of criteria to determine the discipline assessed to an attorney for misconduct outside of his professional role. The lower courts' interpretations and responses to *Wall* would eventually evolve into the "moral turpitude standard" which provides that any conduct which a court determines to be of "moral turpitude" is subject to professional discipline. Moral turpitude does not always need to be discovered as a separate and distinct element of the conduct for which the disciplinary proceedings are being brought.[16] Gauging the conduct's level of moral turpitude, though, became the guiding factor throughout the twentieth century in determining attorney discipline — and still remains a prevalent factor today. Difficulty lies, however, in deciding what conduct exactly falls under the umbrella of moral turpitude.

The states have established their own definitions of moral turpitude through both common law and legislatively enacted statutes. The most widespread and commonly used definition has stood for over a hundred years and is

---

[11]James R. Devine, Problems, Cases and Materials in Professional Responsibility 90 (3d ed. 2004).

[12]*Ex parte Wall*, 107 U.S. 265 (1883).

[13]*Id.* at 290.

[14]*Id.* at 295.

[15]*Id.*

[16]7A C.J.S. Attorney and Client § 68 (2011).

described as "an act of baseness, vileness, or depravity in the private and social duties which a man owes to his fellow men or to society in general."[17] Some jurisdictions, however, have made small changes to the definition. New York classifies moral turpitude as "the quality of a crime involving grave infringement of the moral sentiment of the community."[18] The District of Columbia uses three overlapping definitions which include the common baseness standard, "conduct which offends the generally accepted moral code of mankind," and "conduct contrary to justice, honesty, modesty, or good morals."[19] Most courts recognize that the moral turpitude standard is largely elusive and cannot be defined with any precision.[20]

The comments to Rule 8.4 make mention of the moral turpitude standard but only lay out a few specific examples of what are considered violations.[21] Violence, dishonesty, breach of trust, and serious interference with the administration of justice are the only *per se* violations to be within the category.[22] Besides those specific examples, the Model Rules leave a large amount of discretion to the courts in deciding exactly what conduct is misconduct under the standard. The comments cast a broad net of what may be considered misconduct, establishing even adultery as grounds for attorney discipline.[23] The comments to Rule 8.4 raise an indirect question which is left unanswered; if even adultery is considered grounds for attorney discipline, how far away from the legal profession and into an attorney's personal life are the courts and bar associations able to go to discipline an attorney professionally?

C. Determining Punishment

Over time, the state courts have developed a largely uniform set of criteria in determining the level of punishment against an attorney for unethical conduct

---

[17]*Holloway v. Holloway*, 126 Ga. 459 (Ga. 1906).

[18]*People v. Furguson*, 286 N.Y.S.2d 976, 981 (N.Y. Sup. Ct. 1968).

[19]*In re Sneed*, 673 A.2d 591, 594 (D.C. 1996).

[20]*See, e.g., In re Lesansky*,25 Cal.4th 11, 16 (Cal. 2001) ("As we have in the past, we acknowledge here that the term 'cannot be defined with precision.'"); *United States ex rel. Manzella v. Zimmerman*, 71 F. Supp. 534, 537 (E.D. Pa. 1947) (describing moral turpitude as "a phrase so lacking in legal precision and, therefore so likely to result in a judge applying to the case before him his own personal views as to the mores of the community.").

[21]Model Rules of Prof'l Conduct R. 8.4 cmt. 2 ("Traditionally, the distinction was drawn in terms of offenses involving 'moral turpitude.' That concept can be construed to include offenses concerning some matters of personal morality, such as adultery and comparable offenses that have no specific connection to fitness for the practice of law. Offenses involving violence, dishonesty, breach of trust, or serious interference with the administration of justice are in that category. A pattern of repeated offenses, even ones of minor significance when considered separately, can indicate indifference to legal obligation.").

[22]*Id.*

[23]*See id.*

once a violation of moral turpitude has been found.[24] First, the punishment must be fair to society both in protecting the public from an attorney's unethical conduct, and not denying the public the services of a qualified lawyer as a result of undue harshness in penalty.[25] Second, the punishment must be fair to the attorney, both in terms of punishing the attorney's breach of ethics and encouraging reformation and rehabilitation.[26] Third, the punishment must be severe enough to deter others who might be prone or tempted to become involved in like violations.[27] In disciplining an attorney, the primary objective of the courts is not to punish the offender.[28] Instead, its basic purpose is to protect the public against an attorney who cannot or will not measure up to the high standards of responsibility required of every member of the profession.[29]

Attorneys often hold the misconception that a conviction of a felony will serve as the basis for automatic disbarment. While this was true historically, most jurisdictions in recent years have changed their outlook on automatic disbarment.[30] Until 1940, nearly 30 jurisdictions had automatic disbarment statutes for attorneys convicted of felonies.[31] Today, only New York, Mississippi, the District of Columbia, and Puerto Rico still retain traditional automatic disbarment statutes.[32] California allows for "summary disbarment," a standard which will automatically disbar an attorney only if he is both convicted of a felony and the felony is one which involves moral turpitude.[33] The remaining states, instead, largely follow a case-by-case approach gauging the moral turpitude of the conduct, as well as the lawyer's mental state, extent of disrespect for the law, victim, injury, and pattern of criminal conduct.[34]

---

[24]*See, e.g., The Florida Bar v. Lord*, 433 So.2d 983, 986 (Fla. 1983); *Jackson v. State Bar*, 23 Cal.3d 509, 514 (Cal. 1979); *In re Steele*, 630 A.2d 196, 200 (D.C. 1993); *In re Petition for Disciplinary Action Against De Rycke*, 707 N.W.2d 370, 373 (Minn. 2006).

[25]*See The Florida Bar v. Behm*, 41 So.3d 136, 150 (Fla. 2010).

[26]*Id.*

[27]*Id.*

[28]*See Matter of Stout*, 75 N.J. 321, 325 (N.J. 1978).

[29]*Id.*

[30]Rhonda Richardson Caviedes, *Remnants of an Attorney Disciplinary Sanction: Which Jurisdictions Impose Automatic Disbarment? What Offenses Warrant the Imposition of an Automatic Disciplinary Sanction?*, 26 J. Legal Prof. 195, 197 (2002).

[31]*Id.*

[32]*Id.*

[33]*Id.* at 206.

[34]*See In re Conduct of White*, 815 P.2d 1257, 1265 (Or. 1991) ("Each [disciplinary] case must be decided on its own facts."); *In re Finneran*, 919 N.E.2d 698, 704 (Mass. 2010) ("In bar disciplinary cases ... we review the matter and 'reach our own conclusion.'"); *State ex rel. Counsel for Discipline of Neb. Supreme Court v. Wintroub*, 765 N.W.2d 482, 494 (Neb. 2009) ("The determination of an appropriate penalty to be imposed on an attorney in a disciplinary proceeding requires the consideration of any aggravating or mitigating factors. Each attorney discipline case must be evaluated individually in light of its particular facts and circumstances.").

In a case-by-case analysis under the criminal context, the lower courts have great discretion and walk a very fine line in determining which criminal conduct is sufficient for discipline. For example, Louisiana has suspended an attorney for operating a motor vehicle while intoxicated,[35] but did not issue discipline to an attorney who failed to address her responsibility for an automobile accident and unlawfully failed to carry motor vehicle insurance coverage.[36] Similarly, in non-criminal contexts, the state courts have wide discretion in determining which conduct is punishable as well. Some examples where courts have professionally disciplined attorneys for non-criminal conduct include the failure to pay child support,[37] misrepresenting a letter of recommendation in an application for employment,[38] lying about downloading pornographic images on a work computer,[39] plagiarism,[40] and faking one's death.[41] In those examples where discipline was issued, each court found that the attorney displayed enough through his non-professional conduct to be deemed unfit to practice law. But upon examining these examples, does an attorney's misconduct in his personal life truly affect his ability to be a sufficient legal advisor, representative, or zealous advocate?

According to the ABA, "a lawyer should be professionally answerable only for offenses that indicate lack of those characteristics relevant to law practice."[42] Without an attorney's misconduct stemming from his professional duties, it can be argued that suspending or disbarring an attorney simply removes an otherwise capable legal mind from the profession who could have had the ability to help someone in legal need. Furthermore, it could serve to discourage prospective attorneys from pursuing a career in law as they might prefer the right to a private life over profession, or at least value the distinct partition of each. On the other hand, holding such a high standard for an attorney's personal conduct may be essential to keeping the law a learned and respected profession. Additionally, the amount of responsibility that an attorney owes to her client is of unmistakable importance; it may leave no room for an immoral fault in character because of what could possibly be at stake for the client.

D. Constitutional Concerns

Further issues arise from the disciplining of attorneys for non-professional misconduct when it is evaluated in respect to the Constitution of the United

---

[35]*In re Baer*, 21 So.3d 941, 944 (La. 2009).

[36]*In re Parks*, 9 So.3d 106, 112 (La. 2009).

[37]*See Cincinnati Bar Ass'n v. Heisler*, 895 N.E.2d 839 (Ohio 2008); *Disciplinary Counsel v. Curry*, 858 N.E.2d 392 (Ohio 2006); *Disciplinary Counsel v. Geer*, 858 N.E.2d 388 (Ohio 2006).

[38]*Attorney Grievance Com'n v. Floyd*, 929 A.2d 61 (Md. 2007).

[39]*In re Disciplinary Proceedings Against Beatse*, 722 N.W.2d 385 (Wis. 2006).

[40]*In re Lamberis*, 443 N.E.2d 549 (Ill. 1982).

[41]*Matter of Bock*, 607 A.2d 1307 (N.J. 1992).

[42]Model Rules of Prof'l Conduct R. 8.4 cmt. 2 (2010).

States. Do attorneys receive proper due process of law as required by the Fourteenth Amendment[43] when a state court has nearly full discretion in determining what attorney conduct is of moral turpitude and thus punishable? This question and those similar to it have been a major source of litigation at both the state and federal levels.

The United States Supreme Court has held that attorney disciplinary proceedings are adversarial in nature and quasi-criminal, and that the attorney party at such a proceeding is entitled to due process of law under the Fourteenth Amendment.[44] Furthermore, in order to satisfy the due process clause therein, a penal statute must define an offense with sufficient definiteness so that ordinary people can understand what conduct is prohibited and in a manner that does not encourage arbitrary or discriminatory enforcement.[45] This is referred to as the "void for vagueness" doctrine.[46]

Many state courts have expressed their inability to define moral turpitude with any sort of precision, as discussed above. Without elaborate guidance from the Model Rules or a state statute as to exactly what non-professional conduct is considered punishable, moral turpitude is inherently an extremely vague term. Furthermore, the American Bar Association's *Standards for Imposing Lawyer Sanctions* comments on and encourages due process claims which could arise out of reciprocal discipline in other jurisdictions because of the variability of the term.[47] Although the U.S. Supreme Court has yet to address the constitutionality of the moral turpitude standard, some of the states have had the opportunity to do so.

In *Matter of Rabideau*, the Wisconsin Supreme Court recognized the inherent generality and indefiniteness in the moral turpitude standard but nonetheless upheld it as constitutional.[48] The court reasoned that the generality of the concept did not render it meaningless or constitutionally infirm as to adequacy of notice because lawyers have a heightened awareness of the law and responsibility to respect it.[49] The court went on to describe the difficulty of creating a fixed list of "turpitudinous" conduct because the "differing moral quality of criminal behavior in various situations necessitates a flexible approach to the assessment of discipline."[50]

---

[43]U.S. Const. amend. XIV, § 1. ("No State shall make or enforce any law which shall abridge the privileges or immunities of citizens of the United States; nor shall any State deprive any person of life, liberty, or property, without due process of law.").

[44]*In re Ruffalo*, 390 U.S. 544, 551 (1968).

[45]*Skilling v. United States*, 130 S. Ct. 2896, 2904 (2010).

[46]*Id.*

[47]American Bar Association, Standards for Imposing Lawyer Sanctions (1992) (Commentary to Section 2.9: "Reciprocal discipline can be imposed without a hearing, but the court should provide the lawyer with an opportunity to raise a due process challenge or to show that a sanction different from the sanction imposed in the other jurisdiction is warranted.").

[48]*Matter of Rabideau*, 102 Wis.2d 16, 24 (Wis. 1981).

[49]*Id.*

[50]*Id.* at 25.

The Ohio Court of Appeals similarly found the moral turpitude standard descriptive enough to be constitutionally sufficient, comparing it to the "reasonable doubt" standard used in criminal law.[51] The court reasoned that creating a verbose definition of moral turpitude would not improve its clarity because of the amount of inconsistency there would be between courts as to what exactly moral turpitude is.[52]

The United States Court of Appeals for the Ninth Circuit, in *Rosenthal v. Justices of the Supreme Court of California*, rejected a challenge by an attorney who claimed that aspects of California's attorney disciplinary procedure violated several integral rights protected by the U.S. Constitution.[53] The court first distinguished how an attorney disciplinary proceeding is not a criminal proceeding and that the normal protections afforded to a criminal defendant do not apply.[54] This seems to be a narrowing interpretation of the Supreme Court's holding in *In re Ruffalo*, where the Court held that attorney disciplinary proceedings were quasi-criminal and entitled to nearly all of the same constitutional rights.[55] The Ninth Circuit dismissed several procedural rights for attorneys in disciplinary proceedings such as the presumption of innocence, the standard of proof of "beyond a reasonable doubt," and the Confrontation Clause.[56] Despite these dismissals, the court did ultimately agree with the Supreme Court that a lawyer is still entitled to some procedural due process including the right to notice and opportunity to be heard.[57] The court held that California's procedures provided attorneys in disciplinary proceedings constitutionally sufficient procedural due process because the procedures place the burden on the state to establish the culpability of the lawyer and allow an accused lawyer the opportunity to call witnesses and cross-examine them.[58]

It is difficult to determine whether or not the Supreme Court would find the moral turpitude standard constitutional. The justices have indirectly shined a bit of light through several other related cases on how it would rule if the issue did in fact come before them. In *Spevack v. Klein*, the Court held that the Fifth Amendment's protection against self-incrimination cannot be curtailed against attorney invocation in disciplinary proceedings.[59] The Court overturned an order for disbarment based on the attorney's refusal to produce demanded financial records at a judicial inquiry when he believed producing them may have incriminated him.[60] Justice William Douglas rejected the argument that the privilege against self-incrimination should not be extended to attorneys be-

---

[51]*In re Prentice*, 132 N.E.2d 634, 643 (Ohio App. 1953).

[52]*Id.*

[53]910 F.2d 561, 566 (9th Cir. 1990).

[54]*Id.* at 564.

[55]*In re Ruffalo*, 390 U.S. 544, 551 (1968).

[56]*Id.*

[57]*Id.* at 564.

[58]*Id.*

[59]385 U.S. 511, 516 (1967).

[60]*Id* at 519.

cause of their particular professional nature, and held that the Fifth Amendment applies to lawyers and all other individuals alike. Justice Douglas's reasoning in *Spevack* seems to conflict with the reasoning in *Rabideau*, where the Wisconsin Supreme Court found that an attorney is less demanding of due process because of his heightened awareness of the law.

Moreover, in *In re Ruffalo,* the Supreme Court overturned an order of disbarment against an attorney who had no notice of his disciplinary violation and testified in legal proceedings against disbarment without still fully knowing.[61] There, the attorney did not have knowledge that his employment of a certain person would subject him to disbarment.[62] Instead, the attorney testified about all of the material facts pertaining to the employment of this person and was given no opportunity to expunge his statements after the violation was made known to the attorney.[63] The Court held that the attorney's procedural due process rights were violated, reasoning that "notice should be given to the attorney of the charges made and opportunity afforded him for explanation and defense."[64] Furthermore, the Court found that "such a procedural violation of due process would never pass muster in any normal civil or criminal litigation."[65] In light of the decisions in *Spevack* and *Ruffalo*, it is difficult to imagine that the Court would hold the constitutional mandates of due process any less applicable to attorneys in disciplinary proceedings. Instead, it seems as though the moral turpitude standard may be vague enough to not adequately put attorneys on notice for what conduct is prohibited and which is not.

II. Unauthorized Practice of Law

A. Problems with Defining "Practice of Law"

In order to grasp just how far the Model Rules extend their scope beyond the conduct of attorneys in their professional roles, it is helpful to first understand what conduct is even considered to be professional practice. Many of the same problems and ambiguities that plague the moral turpitude standard are also present in defining the "practice of law." Furthermore, it is another area which highlights an expansion of the Model Rules beyond simply attorneys acting in their professional roles; instead, the ABA and the courts have allowed for non-attorneys who are engaged in the "unauthorized" practice of law to be disciplined as well under Rule 5.5. At the heart of both the moral turpitude standard and Rule 5.5 is the goal of protecting the public from the potential danger and injury that could result from unfit legal practice.[66] Particularly, the unauthorized practice of law is regulated to protect the public from the severe con-

---

[61]*In re Ruffalo,* 390 U.S. 544, 552 (1968).

[62]*Id.* at 544.

[63]*Id.*

[64]*Id.* at 550.

[65]*Id.* at 551.

[66]*See, e.g., The Florida Bar v. Schramek,* 616 So.2d 979, 983 (Fla. 1993). [Further analysis of "the practice of law" and the difficulty of defining it is found in Chapter 1.]

sequences that might arise from receiving incompetent advice or preparations from unqualified persons.[67] Despite these laudable purposes, the courts have had great difficulty in determining exactly what conduct is punishable when done by non-attorneys. The Model Rules provide little guidance on the matter and the state courts are again left with full discretion in their disciplinary determinations.

Rule 5.5 and its comments regarding the unauthorized practice of law mostly deal with lawyers who attempt to practice law outside of a jurisdiction in which they are permitted.[68] The comments to Rule 5.5 make passing mention to the regulation of non-attorneys practicing law, only reiterating the importance of curtailing unqualified persons from acting in a legal capacity for the reasons discussed above.[69] The comments also discuss the wide variance in what is considered the "practice of law" because the definition changes from jurisdiction to jurisdiction.

Because the courts are invested with the authority to regulate the practice of law, they inherently have a power which encompasses the unauthorized practice of law.[70] As Massachusetts' highest state court recently stated, "[w]hile the judicial department is necessarily the sole arbiter of what constitutes the practice of law, the task of doing so is not easy and, in most cases, will depend on the facts of each case."[71] Generally, the "practice of law" is defined as the performance of services in any matter pending in a court of justice throughout its various stages and in conformity with the adopted rules of procedure.[72] In a larger sense, however, it includes legal advice, counsel, and the preparation of legal instruments and contracts by which legal rights are secured although such matters may or may not be pending in a court.[73] Many states have differing definitions and tests for defining the practice of law. For example, Arizona uses a "traditional custom" test where only acts which attorneys have customarily carried on throughout the centuries can constitute "practice of law."[74] Other states use the "affecting legal rights" test where the practice of law will be found if the non-attorney's conduct affects the legal rights of her client.[75]

---

[67]*See, e.g., Charter One Mortg. Corp. v. Condra*, 865 N.E.2d 602, 605 (Ind. 2007).

[68]*See* Model Rules of Prof'l Conduct R. 5.5.

[69]Model Rules of Prof'l Conduct R. 5.5 cmt. 2 ("The definition of the practice of law is established by law and varies from one jurisdiction to another. Whatever the definition, limiting the practice of law to members of the bar protects the public against rendition of legal services by unqualified persons. This Rule does not prohibit a lawyer from employing the services of paraprofessionals and delegating functions to them, so long as the lawyer supervises the delegated work and retains responsibility for their work.").

[70]*See, e.g., Banks v. United States*, 926 A.2d 158, 165 (D.C. 2007); *Kentucky Bar Ass'n v. Brooks*, 325 S.W.3d 283, 286 (Ky. 2010).

[71]*Superadio LP v. Winstar Radio Prod., LLC*, 844 N.E.2d 246, 250 (Mass. 2006).

[72]7 Am. Jur. 2d, Attorneys at Law § 119.

[73]*In re Utz*, 769 P.2d 417, 425 (Cal. 1989).

[74]*See State Bar of Ariz. v. Arizona Land Title & Trust Co.*, 366 P.2d 1, 9 (Ariz. 1961).

[75]*Palmer v. Unauthorized Practice Committee of State Bar*, 438 S.W.2d 374, 376 (Tex. Civ. App. 1969).

In disciplining non-attorneys for the unauthorized practice of law, a state bar association or one of its committees may be authorized to commence contempt proceedings against a person accused.[76] The complications which arise from the lack of consistency in what is considered "practice of law" are magnified when contempt proceedings against someone for unlawful practice of law are criminal in nature.[77]

B. Complications with Growing Technology

As technology has progressed over recent years, so have the growing complications in courts attempting to delineate what conduct is considered practice of law and what is not. In *Office of Disciplinary Counsel v. Palmer*, the Ohio Board of Commissioners on the Unauthorized Practice of Law was unwilling to find that a non-lawyer owner of a website advertising free legal advice was practicing law.[78] Despite the owner's statements on the website urging visitors to email him regarding any questions they have on specific legal matters, the Board found that the website was similar to books, magazine articles, and pamphlets which similarly alert readers to their legal rights. "The practice of law involves the rendering of legal advice to an individual, and legal publications offering general advice or opinions do not purport to customize the advice to the particularized needs of the reader."[79] There was no evidence that the owner actually helped anyone individually as only the content of his website was challenged.

Furthermore, websites such as LegalZoom[80] offer legal forms and kits for purchase in which users only need to enter their relevant personal information to create a working legal document. Courts typically have drawn the line for unauthorized practice of law in these circumstances where companies offer specific advice to users on the documents as opposed to simply just selling them.[81] By offering advice specific to the user concerning the forms, the companies are participating in unauthorized practice; if they simply sell the forms, they are not.

The rise in technology, as evidenced by the growth of legal websites and do-it-yourself kits, helps illustrate the continuing complications that courts have in determining what exactly "practice of law" is. Courts are continuously trying to play catch-up with the different nuances and advances of non-traditional legal settings. The courts have no choice but to simply devise common law along the way without any grounding or base from the Model Rules as to

---

[76] 7 C.J.S. Attorney and Client § 38 (2011).

[77] *Id.*

[78] 761 N.E.2d 716, 718-20 (Bd. Unauth. Prac. 2001).

[79] *Id.*

[80] LegalZoom is a website specializing in "online legal document services" which allows users to purchase fill-in legal forms to start up businesses, draw wills and trusts, handle divorces, and a plethora of other legal services; *available at* http://www.legalzoom.com (last visited Apr. 17, 2011). [*See* Chapter 1 of this book.]

[81] *See, e.g.*, *People v. Landlords Prof'l Servs.*, 215 Cal.App.3d 1599, 1607 (1989).

what the practice of law is considered to be in the first place. As time and technology have progressed, these questions have continued to become more and more difficult.

C. The ABA's Proposed Model Rule

In an attempt to add consistency to the term "practice of law," the American Bar Association proposed in 2002 that an additional rule be added to the Model Rules which specifically outlines the conduct which would be considered to fall under the term.[82] The proposed rule classified the general practice of law as "the application of legal principles and judgment with regard to the circumstances or objectives of a person that require the knowledge and skill of a person trained in the law."[83] The rule would specifically prohibit non-attorneys from giving advice to persons as to their legal rights or responsibilities, the drafting of legal documents or agreements that affect the legal rights of a person, the representing of a person before an adjudicative body, and the negotiating of legal rights or responsibilities on behalf of a person.[84] The proposed rule also explicitly laid out exceptions to the unauthorized practice of law, including *pro se* representation, serving as mediator or arbitrator, providing services under the supervision of a lawyer in compliance with the Model Rules, and practicing with a limited license.[85]

Opponents of the proposed rule contended that if the rule were enacted, it would be akin to an antitrust violation in that it would prohibit competition between lawyers and non-lawyers for many services.[86] The basis of antitrust law comes from the idea that society will usually be disadvantaged when there is a prohibition of competition because it will usually lead to fewer options and higher prices for services.[87] Any agreement or law made which potentially inhibits competition may be considered an antitrust violation and unlawful.[88] Opponents of the rule argue that services such as real estate closings, drawing of wills, trusts, and estates and other services which are routinely performed by non-lawyers will be prohibited except to licensed attorneys and therefore consumers will be hurt by less availability of services, lower quality, and higher prices.[89] Additionally, they believe that there may be a less restrictive alter-

---

[82]American Bar Association, "Group Floats Model Rule That Would Define Practice of Law," 19 ABA/BNA Lawyers' Manual on Professional Conduct 620, 621 (2002).

[83]*Id.*

[84]*Id.*

[85]*Id.*

[86]Letter from Federal Trade Commission and the Department of Justice to the Task Force on the Model Definition of the Practice of Law, American Bar Association (Dec. 20, 2002), *available at* http://www.justice.gov/atr/public/comments/200604.htm (last visited Apr. 17, 2011).

[87]*See* United States v. Topco Associates, Inc., 405 U.S. 596, 608 (1972).

[88]*See* Sherman Antitrust Act, 15 U.S.C. § 1 (2010).

native rather than passing the proposed rule, such as mandating the issuance of warnings to those involved in real estate dealings, or the like, of the risks involved of proceeding without an attorney.[90] These opposing arguments to the rule were central to why the proposed rule was never enacted.

III. Conclusion

In an attempt to protect society from the unfit practice of law, the ABA and state courts have expanded their traditional reach of authority to conduct of lawyers in their non-professional roles and to non-lawyers engaged in the unauthorized practice of law. In doing this, however, the Model Rules provide very little guidance as to the circumstances, process, and extent which discipline should be issued. The states courts, in an attempt to develop a grounded basis of law to interpret their disciplinary functions, have only been able to develop ambiguous rules of law which vary from jurisdiction to jurisdiction and from court to court. Because of this, there are large areas of grey which leave attorneys and non-attorneys alike subject to discipline for which they may have never been given proper notice.

Although discipline for unauthorized practice of law and non-professional misconduct may be necessary for the preservation of the legal field, it may be better served if clearly articulated by the Model Rules like all other attorney ethics regulations. Otherwise, it is difficult to decide whether the integrity of the legal profession outweighs the private lives and due process rights of attorneys and non-attorneys alike.

---

[89]Letter from Federal Trade Commission and the Department of Justice to the Task Force on the Model Definition of the Practice of Law, American Bar Association (Dec. 20, 2002), *available at* http://www.justice.gov/atr/public/comments/200604.htm (last visited Apr. 17, 2011).

[90]*Id.*

12

Tempest in a Tea-Party: The Ethical Ramifications of Justice Scalia's Remarks to the Conservative Constitutional Seminar

Stuart R. Breaux

I. Introduction

Much ink was spilled during the first quarter of 2011 in the debate over the propriety of Justice Antonin Scalia's speech to the Tea Party's first Conservative Constitutional Seminar. The meeting at which the speech took place, arranged by Minnesota Republican Congresswoman Michelle Bachmann, was a closed-door seminar open to all members of Congress, regardless of party affiliation.[1] It attracted fifty members of the House of Representatives, including four Democrats.[2] By all accounts, the discussion itself was largely apolitical and uncontroversial.[3] According to one report, Scalia's message to members of Congress was to "[b]e as specific as possible when writing legislation, and watch the boundaries set out by the Constitution."[4] In response to questions from the audience, "Scalia restated his longstanding willingness to overturn *Roe v. Wade* and reiterated his view that a line-item veto could be constitutional."[5] Rep. Jan Schakowsky, a Democrat from Illinois who was in attendance, described the seminar as "pretty dry" and "perfectly suited for a bipartisan audience."[6] Another Democrat, Rep. Jerrold Nadler of New York, affirmed Schakowsky's assessment: "There was nothing partisan here."[7]

---

[1] Posting of Ashby Jones to Wall Street Journal Law Blog, *Scalia to Congress: Mind Your Constitutional Ps and Qs*, http://blogs.wsj.com/law/2011/01/25/scalia-to-congress-mind-your-constitutional-ps-and-qs/ (Jan. 25, 2011, 11:18 AM EST) (last visited Apr. 16, 2011). Congresswoman Bachmann has been described as "[a]n intensely ideological female politician closely identified with the Christian Right and with the Tea Party movement, someone liberals love to hate." Ed Kilgore, *Springtime for Bachmann: Why She's a Serious Contender for 2012*, The New Republic, Mar. 17, 2011, *available at* http://tnr.com/article/the-permanent-campaign/85365/michele-bachmann-2012-gop-presidential-nominee (last visited Apr. 16, 2011). With her polarizing persona, Rep. Bachmann's connection to the event likely complicated matters for Justice Scalia.

[2] Jones, *supra* note 1.

[3] *Id.*

[4] *Id.*

[5] *Id.*

[6] *Id.*

[7] *Id.*

Despite the seemingly bland tenor and scope of Justice Scalia's lecture, the event set off a firestorm of criticism. Jonathan Turley, a professor of law at The George Washington University, penned an editorial for *The Washington Post* entitled "The Price of Scalia's Political Stardom: On Why the High Court Doesn't Need Celebrity Justices," arguing that by educating newly elected Congresspersons under the auspices of a Tea Party seminar, Scalia compromised "the principle of judicial neutrality."[8] *The New York Times* Editorial Board proclaimed that "it was a bad idea" for Justice Scalia to accept the invitation of the Tea Party Caucus because "[b]y meeting behind closed doors .... and by presiding over a seminar, implying give and take, the justice would give the impression that he was joining the throng .... The ideological nature of the group and the seminar would eclipse the justice's independence and leave him looking rash and biased."[9] By presiding over the seminar, "Justice Scalia would provide strong reasons to doubt his impartiality when he ruled later on any topic discussed there."[10] The thrust of the debate surrounding Justice Scalia's actions centered on competing notions of the role of judges and the limits of extrajudicial political speech. More specifically, to his detractors, Scalia's participation in the Conservative Constitutional Seminar called into question his impartiality and was improper, or at least appeared improper.[11]

Scalia is hardly the first Justice to engender debate over the propriety of certain extrajudicial activities. The history of the American judiciary, indeed the Supreme Court itself, is littered with examples of potentially dubious extrajudicial conduct, depending on how one delimits the bounds of judicial propriety.[12] This paper attempts to analyze Justice Scalia's recent controversial actions by examining the history of extrajudicial speech by Supreme Court Justices, investigating the history and scope of the ABA Model Code of Judicial Conduct, and by exploring two competing schools of thought regarding extrajudicial behavior — those who believe that the public has a right to know a judge's thoughts on political issues of the day and those who believe that judges should lead essentially cloistered lives and whose public role should therefore be strictly limited.[13]

II. A History of the Extrajudicial Political Activities of Supreme Court Justices

When Justice Scalia took the stage at the Conservative Constitutional Seminar, he was hardly breaking new ground with regard to extrajudicial political ac-

---

[8]Jonathan R. Turley, *The Price of Scalia's Political Stardom: On Why the High Court Doesn't Need Celebrity Justices*, Washington Post, Jan. 23, 2011, at B03.

[9]Editorial, *Justice Scalia and the Tea Party*, N.Y. Times, Dec. 19, 2010, at WK7.

[10]*Id.*

[11]*Id.*

[12]*See, e.g.,* Emily Field Van Tassel, *Resignations and Removals: A History of Federal Judicial Service—And Disservice—1789-1992*, 142 U. Pa. L. Rev. 333 (1993).

[13]*See, e.g.,* Jon C. Blue, *A Well-Tuned Cymbal? Extrajudicial Political Activity*, 18 Geo. J. Legal Ethics 1 (2004).

tivity. From the outset, Supreme Court Justices not only engaged in extrajudicial political activities, but even assumed high profile roles within coordinate branches of government.[14] John Jay, the first Chief Justice of the United States, served both in that role and as Secretary of State for Foreign Affairs.[15] John Marshall, the fourth Chief Justice, served concurrently as Chief Justice and Secretary of State.[16] In both cases, the period of concomitant service lasted only a few months, but the dual roles played by Marshall and Jay "provide dramatic evidence that extrajudicial activity by judges was not considered unthinkable in the nation's early years, even when that activity included holding cabinet-level executive rank."[17] In addition to serving as Secretary of State for Foreign Affairs, Jay ran for Governor of New York while serving as Chief Justice and served as Ambassador to Great Britain.[18] Justice Oliver Ellsworth similarly accepted the position of Ambassador to France.[19] Jay, upon returning from Great Britain, resigned to become Governor of New York, a position to which he was elected in his absence.[20] In addition, Jay provided informal advice to President Washington throughout his term as Chief Justice.[21]

Beyond accepting high ranking positions in the executive branch, Justices engaged in a wide variety of extrajudicial conduct, from academic lectures to legislative lobbying.[22] Justice James Wilson gave a series of lectures on the nature of law, government, and the Constitution.[23] Justice James Iredell lobbied the President to urge Congress to change certain policies regarding circuit courts.[24] Justices Bushrod Washington and William Paterson drafted and submitted a bill to the House Judiciary Committee.[25] John Jay was not the only founding-era Justice to seek elected office: Justice William Cushing ran for Governor of Massachusetts in 1794.[26] Moreover, Justices actively campaigned for favored candidates: Justice Washington campaigned for Charles Pickney, and Justice Samuel Chase made speeches on behalf of John Adams.[27]

---

[14]*Id.* at 36.

[15]*Id.*

[16]*Id.*

[17]*Id.*

[18]Leslie B. Dubeck, Note, *Understanding "Judicial Lockjaw": The Debate Over Extrajudicial Activity*, 82 N.Y.U. L. Rev. 569, 589 (2007). Justice Jay engaged in minimal active campaigning for the Governorship. *Id.*

[19]*Id.*

[20]Blue, *supra* note 13, at 37.

[21]Dubeck, *supra* note 18, at 590.

[22]*Id.*

[23]*Id.*

[24]*Id.*

[25]*Id.*

[26]*Id.*

[27]*Id.*

Some scholars point to another episode involving Justice Chase as transforming the role of the judiciary with regard to extrajudicial political activities and speech.[28] In 1803, Justice Chase issued a charge to a grand jury which included pointed criticism of federal legislation abolishing circuit judgeships.[29] The actions of Chase, himself aligned with the Federalist Party, angered Republican Thomas Jefferson, who subsequently encouraged his congressional allies to impeach the Justice.[30] "Impeachment," the Republicans reasoned, "must be considered a means of keeping the Courts in reasonable harmony with the will of the Nation."[31] It has been posited that Chase's impeachment had a chilling effect on extrajudicial political speech, and that the Republicans "succeeded in changing expectations of what constituted proper judicial behavior, thereby excluding overt partisan political activity."[32]

Supreme Court Justices did not, however, retreat into judicial monasteries.[33] Justices spoke publicly on the highly charged issues of slavery and nullification, defended themselves against criticisms of their decisions by publishing articles in newspapers, and continued to involve themselves in the politics and policies of the coordinate branches of government.[34] Justice John McLean, for instance, "aspired to the presidency at every four-year interval from 1832 until 1860."[35] While it is widely accepted that the Chase impeachment forced Justices to cease using their positions to pursue partisan ends, convincing evidence exists tending to show that the Justices continued to be involved in politics, especially in the form of extrajudicial political speech.[36]

Extrajudicial political speech is not a phenomenon that is unique to the founding-era Justices. Justice Oliver Wendell Holmes, Jr. was "a noted critic of laws."[37] Chief Justice Taft not only endorsed Calvin Coolidge's 1924 bid for the Presidency, but actively supported him, sounding out his rivals and packing an important committee at the Republican Convention.[38] In 1929, following an Arab attack on Jews in the Middle East, Justice Louis Brandeis addressed an

---

[28]Keith E. Whittington, *Reconstructing the Federal Judiciary: The Chase Impeachment and the Constitution*, 9 Stud. Am. Pol. Dev. 5, 112 (1995).

[29]Talbot D'Alemberte, *Searching for the Limits of Judicial Free Speech*, 61 Tul. L. Rev. 611, 626-27 (1987).

[30]Dubeck, *supra* note 18, at 591-92.

[31]*Id.* at 592.

[32]Whittington, *supra* note 28, at 112. Professor Whittington contends that "[t]he Republicans successfully held Chase up as an exemplar of the partisan judiciary and made him pay for the sins of his brethren," and as a result "[f]uture conduct of a like nature was ... effectively proscribed." *Id.* at 92-93.

[33]Dubeck, *supra* note 18, at 593-94.

[34]*Id.*

[35]*Id.* at 594.

[36]*Id.*

[37]D'Alemberte, *supra* note 29, at 623.

[38]Peter A. Bell, *Extrajudicial Activity of Supreme Court Justices*, 22 Stan. L. Rev. 587, 593 (1970).

emergency conference of Washington businessmen.[39] He lauded the Zionist movement and remarked that he saw nothing wrong with Jewish immigration into Palestine, despite British objections.[40] Justices Douglas, Brennan, Jackson, and Black were all outspoken commentators in their day, contributing to an "explosion of frank out-of-Court commentary."[41] Justice Potter Stewart praised media coverage of the Watergate scandal.[42] Justice Blackmun discussed his decision in an abortion case as well as his personal stance on the death penalty.[43] Justice John Paul Stevens criticized the media's reaction to the exclusion of a reporter from a pretrial criminal hearing.[44] Justice Sandra Day O'Connor also criticized the death penalty.[45]

Members of the current Supreme Court have raised eyebrows with their extrajudicial statements as well.[46] Justice Thomas is on record as denouncing "our society's 'focus on rights.'"[47] Justice Alito spoke at a fundraiser for the conservative Intercollegiate Studies Institute.[48] Justices Scalia, Thomas, Alito and Chief Justice Roberts have spoken to or been honored by the conservative Federalist Society, while Justice Ginsberg and Breyer have spoken to similar liberal groups, such as the American Constitution Society.[49] Of all the current Justices, Justice Scalia has drawn the most attention, speaking, along with Justice Thomas, at events funded by wealthy conservatives David and Charles Koch.[50] After he remarked in Switzerland that detainees at Guantánamo Bay should be denied access to federal court, critics asserted that Scalia should recuse himself from the upcoming case of *Hamdan v. Rumsfeld*, which was to address the very same issue.[51]

---

[39]*Id.* at 601.

[40]*Id. See also* Bruce Allen Murphy, The Brandeis/Frankfurter Connection: The Secret Political Activities of Two Supreme Court Justices (1982) (exploring the political activities of two well-regarded Justices).

[41]Bell, *supra* note 38, at 601.

[42]D'Alemberte, *supra* note 29, at 623.

[43]*Id.* at 624.

[44]*Id.*

[45]Editorial, *supra* note 9.

[46]*Id.*

[47]*Id.*

[48]*Id.*

[49]*Id.*

[50]*Id. See* Jane Mayer, *Covert Operations: The Billionaire Brothers Who Are Waging War Against Obama*, The New Yorker, Aug. 30, 2010, at 44, for an exhaustive description of the controversial Koch brothers and their political activities.

[51]Charles Lane, *Scalia's Recusal Sought in Key Detainee Case*, Washington Post, Mar. 28, 2006, at A06. The case was eventually reported at 548 U.S. 557 (2006), *superseded by statute*, Military Commissions Act of 2006, Pub. L. No. 109-366, 120 Stat. 2006, *as recognized in* Al Maqaleh v. Gates, 605 F.3d 84 (D.C. Cir. 2010); and in fact Justice Scalia participated, 548 U.S. at 655 (Scalia, J., dissenting).

III. The Development and Application of the Model Code of Judicial Conduct

The Model Code of Judicial Conduct (hereafter "Code") "establishes standards for the ethical conduct of judges and judicial candidates.... It is intended to provide guidance and assist judges in maintaining the highest standards of judicial and personal conduct, and to provide a basis for regulating their conduct through disciplinary agencies."[52] The Code was crafted under the auspices of the American Bar Association ("ABA") and has been adopted, in some form, by forty-nine states and by the federal government.[53] While it is not binding on the United States Supreme Court, the history of the Code suggests that Justices are bound, at least hortatively, to adhere to the principles therein.[54]

In 1924, the ABA promulgated the first general code of judicial conduct, the Canons of Judicial Ethics.[55] The impetus behind the 1924 Canons was the outrage among members of the bar over Judge Kenesaw Mountain Landis' dual role as federal district judge and commissioner of Major League Baseball.[56] Judge Landis was appointed the first commissioner of Major League Baseball "in order to combat gambling and bribery influences that many thought were corrupting the national pastime."[57] He gained fame and the adulation of the nation after permanently barring from the league eight Chicago White Sox team members who stood accused of fixing the 1919 World Series.[58] Despite his status as a national hero, many of his fellow legal professionals charged that he had "tarnish[ed] the image of the judiciary by retaining his federal judgeship while serving as Commissioner."[59] In the end, the Attorney General of the United States reported that there was no law prohibiting a judge from receiving compensation for extrajudicial employment.[60] Nonetheless, the ABA issued a resolution censuring Landis for maintaining dual employment, deeming that such activities give rise to the appearance of impropriety.[61]

---

[52]American Bar Association, Model Code of Judicial Conduct Preamble (2007).

[53]Tobin A. Sparling, *Keeping Up Appearances: The Constitutionality of the Model Code of Judicial Conduct's Prohibition of Extrajudicial Speech Creating the Appearance of Bias*, 19 Geo. J. Legal Ethics 441, 451 (2006). "Because the Judicial Model Code is simply that, a model, no state or jurisdiction is required to adhere to it or to adopt it. To date, however, forty-nine states and the District of Columbia have adopted and follow the Judicial Model Code in some iteration, Montana being the single holdout." *Id.* Federal judges are regulated by their own version of the Model Code. Dubeck, *supra* note 18, at 570 n.3.

[54]Bell, *supra* note 38, at 606; Dubeck, *supra* note 18, at 570 n.3.

[55]Raymond J. McKoski, *Judicial Discipline and the Appearance of Impropriety: What the Public Sees is What the Judge Gets*, 94 Minn. L. Rev. 1914, 1925 (2010).

[56]*Id.* at 1921-22.

[57]*Id.* at 1922.

[58]*Id.* at 1922-23.

[59]*Id.* at 1923.

[60]*Id.*

[61]*Id.*

In light of its concerns over the Landis affair, the ABA began work on drafting a judicial code of ethics.[62] The finished product was a purely hortatory code, "a model for judges and an indicator of 'what the people have a right to expect from them.'"[63] The focus of the 1924 Canons was "public impressions, perceptions, and suspicions."[64] Throughout the code, judges were warned against activities creating the appearance of impropriety and "reminded that a judge's life should be 'beyond reproach.'"[65] Pertinently, Canons 28 and 30 warned against engaging in political speech.[66] "Plainly, the traditional principles of judicial independence had begun to clash with the goals of judicial accountability."[67] Forty-three states adopted the 1924 Canons, and even though they carried "only an aspirational message, many jurisdictions began to view them as a mediating influence...."[68]

It was not until 1969, and another judicial scandal, that the ABA revisited the 1924 Canons.[69] The malfeasance prompting what would later become the 1972 Code of Judicial Conduct involved Supreme Court Justice Abe Fortas, who accepted a $20,000 fee as compensation for his help in planning the charitable, educational, and civil rights activities of the Wolfson Family Foundation.[70] Louis Wolfson, the foundation's director, was under investigation by the Securities and Exchange Commission at the time Fortas accepted the fee, and was eventually indicted.[71] Upon Wolfson's indictment, Fortas returned the fee and cancelled his agreement with the foundation, but the damage had been done.[72] He was censured by the ABA, which cited him as violating eight of the Canons.[73] "[M]ost forcefully cited" was Canon Four, which commanded that "a judge's official conduct should be free from impropriety and the appearance of impropriety."[74] Fortas resigned from the Supreme Court on May 16, 1969.[75]

---

[62]*Id.* at 1924. Interestingly enough, the 1924 Canons of Judicial Ethics did not prohibit judges from receiving compensation for extrajudicial employment. In fact, the Canons specifically permitted judges to serve in dual roles as long as the extrajudicial activities did not interfere with the performance of judicial duties. *Id.*

[63]Sparling, *supra* note 53, at 450.

[64]McKoski, *supra* note 55, at 1925.

[65]*Id.* at 1926.

[66]Sparling, *supra* note 53, at 450.

[67]*Id.*

[68]*Id.*

[69]McKoski, *supra* note 55, at 1926.

[70]*Id.* at 1926-27.

[71]*Id.* at 1927.

[72]*Id.* at 1927.

[73]*Id.* at 1928.

[74]*Id.*

[75]*Id.*

Appointed to replace Justice Fortas was Clement Haynsworth, Chief Judge of the Fourth Circuit Court of Appeals.[76] Already sensitive to the issue of extra-judicial activities giving rise to an appearance of impropriety, the Senate voted against Haynsworth's nomination after it became known that he ruled in favor of a customer of a company in which he held a one-seventh share.[77] Haynsworth also owned stock in multiple corporations that appeared before him as litigants.[78] Coupled with the Fortas scandal, "Haynsworth's perceived impropriety in presiding over matters in which he had a de minimis or indirect financial interest helped persuade [the ABA Committee] to drastically overhaul the judicial disqualification rules of the 1924 Canons."[79]

The 1972 Model Code of Judicial Conduct replaced the aspirational 1924 Canons with a mandatory and enforceable set of rules.[80] "Underlying the entire Judicial Model Code is the admonition that judicial independence depends upon public confidence in the judicial system."[81] It is important to note that neither Justice Fortas nor Judge Haynsworth engaged in any illegal activity; the chief transgression of each man was giving off the appearance of impropriety.[82] Thus, under the 1972 Model Code of Judicial Conduct, "appearances governed a judge's personal and official behavior.... Appearances officially became, and would continue to be, the heart of judicial ethics."[83] In 1990, the Model Code of Judicial Conduct was again revised, and the appearance of impropriety rule was "considerably amplified."[84] "Shall" replaced "should" with regard to avoiding the appearance of impropriety, eliminating "any lingering doubt about the nature of the prohibition."[85] Additionally, a reasonable person standard was applied to the rule, making the test "whether the conduct would create in reasonable minds a perception that the judge's ability to carry out judicial responsibilities with integrity, impartiality, and competence is impaired."[86] Furthermore, avoiding the appearance of impropriety now applied both to a judge's judicial role as well as his or her extrajudicial activities.[87]

The Model Code of Judicial Conduct was last revised in 2007.[88] The 2007 Model Code of Judicial Conduct (hereafter "Code") includes the same proscription on conduct giving an appearance of impropriety, despite a draft version

---

[76]*Id.* at 1929.

[77]*Id.*

[78]*Id.*

[79]*Id.*

[80]Jeffrey M. Shaman, *The Impartial Judge: Detachment or Passion*, 45 DePaul L. Rev. 605, 607 (1996).

[81]Sparling, *supra* note 53, at 451.

[82]McKoski, *supra* note 55, at 1927, 1929.

[83]*Id.* at 1930.

[84]*Id.* at 1931.

[85]*Id.*

[86]*Id.*

[87]*Id.*

[88]*Id.* at 1931.

excluding the appearance standard from the black letter rules.[89] This draft version spurred a wave of criticism from judges, committee members, and the media.[90] The Code was subsequently amended to reincorporate the rule.[91]

Several provisions of the Code raise potential problems with regard to Justice Scalia's participation in the Conservative Constitutional Seminar. Canon 1 provides: "A judge shall uphold and promote the independence, integrity, and impartiality of the judiciary, and shall avoid impropriety and the appearance of impropriety."[92] Rule 1.2, entitled "Promoting Confidence in the Judiciary," requires that "[a] judge shall act at all times in a manner that promotes public confidence in the independence, integrity, and impartiality of the judiciary, and shall avoid impropriety and the appearance of impropriety."[93] The comments to Rule 1.2, which are not in themselves binding or enforceable, clarify somewhat the obligations of a judge with regard to avoiding the appearance of impropriety.[94] The test for the appearance of impropriety is "whether the conduct would create in reasonable minds a perception that the judge violated this Code or engaged in other conduct that reflects adversely on the judge's honesty, temperament, or fitness to serve as judge."[95] On the other hand, a judge is encouraged to "initiate and participate in community outreach activities for the purpose of promoting public understanding of and confidence in the administration of justice."[96]

Similarly, Canon 3 states: "A judge shall conduct the judge's personal and extrajudicial activities to minimize the risk of conflict with the obligations of judicial office."[97] Under Rule 3.1, "Extrajudicial Activities in General," a judge is forbidden from participating "in activities that would appear to a reasonable person to undermine the judge's independence, integrity, or impartiality."[98] Given their unique qualifications "to engage in extrajudicial activities that concern the law, the legal system, and the administration of justice," judges are encouraged to speak, write, teach, and participate in scholarly research projects involving such concerns. Judges are also allowed and encouraged to engage in "educational, religious, charitable, fraternal and civil extrajudicial activities not conducted for profit."[99] Moreover, Rule 3.2 offers the following proscription:

---

[89]*Id.* at 1931-32.

[90]*Id.* at 1934-35.

[91]*Id.*

[92]Model Code of Judicial Conduct Canon 1 (2007).

[93]Model Code of Judicial Conduct R. 1.2 (2007). Impropriety is defined as including "conduct that violates the law, court rules, or provisions of this Code, and conduct that undermines a judge's independence, integrity, or impartiality." Model Code of Judicial Conduct Terminology (2007).

[94]Model Code of Judicial Conduct Scope (2007).

[95]Model Code of Judicial Conduct R. 1.2, cmt. 5 (2007).

[96]Model Code of Judicial Conduct R. 1.2, cmt. 6 (2007).

[97]Model Code of Judicial Conduct Canon 3 (2007).

[98]Model Code of Judicial Conduct R. 3.1 (2007).

[99]Model Code of Judicial Conduct R. 3.1, cmt. 1 (2007).

A judge shall not appear voluntarily at a public hearing before, or otherwise consult with, an executive or a legislative body or official, except:

(A) in connection with matters concerning the law, the legal system, or the administration of justice;

(B) in connection with matters about which the judge acquired knowledge or expertise in the course of the judge's judicial duties; or

(C) when the judge is acting pro se in a matter involving the judge's legal or economic interests, or when the judge is acting in a fiduciary capacity.[100]

Recognizing the "special expertise" of judges "in matters of law, the legal system, and the administration of justice," judges are allowed to "share that expertise with governmental bodies and executive or legislative branch officials."[101] Judges are cautioned in comments, however, to avoid using the prestige of their office to advance personal interests, to refrain from commenting on pending and impending matters, and "from engaging in extrajudicial activities that would appear to a reasonable person to undermine the judge's independence, integrity, or impartiality."[102]

Finally, Canon 4 allows that "[a] judge or candidate for judicial office shall not engage in political or campaign activity that is inconsistent with the independence, integrity, or impartiality of the judiciary."[103] Rule 4.1 prohibits, among other things, a judge from making speeches "on behalf of a political organization," and "attend[ing] or purchas[ing] tickets for dinners or other events sponsored by a political organization or a candidate for political office."[104] Additionally, a judge shall not "make any statement that would reasonably be expected to affect the outcome or impair the fairness of a matter pending or impending in any court."[105]

IV. The Debate Over Extrajudicial Activity: Judicial Monasticism Versus An Increased Public Persona For The Judiciary

It is widely held among commentators that a crisis of confidence exists in the American judiciary.[106] The public's level of confidence in judges is low — a by-product of unethical conduct on the part of judges, both on and off the bench.[107]

---

[100]Model Code of Judicial Conduct R. 3.2 (2007).

[101]Model Code of Judicial Conduct R. 3.2, cmt. 1 (2007).

[102]Model Code of Judicial Conduct R. 3.2, cmt. 2 (2007).

[103]Model Code of Judicial Conduct Canon 4 (2007).

[104]Model Code of Judicial Conduct R 4.1(5) (2007).

[105]Model Code of Judicial Conduct R. 4.1(12) (2007).

[106]Roger J. Miner, *Judicial Ethics in the Twenty First Century: Tracing the Trends*, 32 Hofstra L. Rev. 1107, 1107-08 (2004).

[107]*Id.*

Depending on whom one asks, the solution to the purported crisis might be a reassertion of the concept of judicial monasticism.[108] Conversely, one might hear that confidence in the judiciary can be restored only by stripping away the conventions and regulations that situate judges as a class apart.[109] While proponents of each idea have valid points, neither can claim to be in sole possession of the solution.[110] The complexity of the responsibilities facing judges, especially Supreme Court Justices, cannot be so neatly confined to one end of the spectrum.[111] Nevertheless, it is helpful to examine these competing philosophies in order to better understand the strengths and weaknesses of each.

"The Chief Justice goes into a monastery and confines himself to his judicial work," said William Howard Taft, himself Chief Justice of the United States.[112] "If you put on the black sheet," another commentator stated, "you have withdrawn your right to talk about politics and indeed to think about politics."[113] Adherents to this line of thinking believe that extrajudicial political activities and out-of-court commentary threaten "the independence, strength, and decisional quality of the Court."[114] They are idealists, and their "guiding light" is Alexander Hamilton.[115]

In *The Federalist Number 78*, Hamilton conceived of a judiciary above the whims of a populace given to excess and a legislature given to tyranny.[116] The independence and moderation of the judiciary, Hamilton argued, are the very qualities that allow the courts to serve "as the bulwarks of a limited constitution against legislative encroachments" and "to guard the constitution and the rights of individuals from the effects of those ill humours which the arts of designing men ... sometimes disseminate among the people themselves."[117] Hamilton, beyond stressing the essentiality of independence and moderation of judges, noted that judges must also be paragons of knowledge and virtue:

> It has been frequently remarked, with great propriety, that a voluminous code of laws is one of the inconveniences necessarily connected with the advantages of a free government. To avoid an arbitrary discretion in the courts, it is indispensable that they should be bound down by strict rules and precedents, which serve to define and point out their duty in every particular case that comes before them; and it will readily be conceived from the variety of controversies which grow

---

[108]*See, e.g.*, Bell, *supra* note 38, at 603-05.

[109]*See, e.g.*, Dubeck, *supra* note 18, at 572.

[110]William G. Ross, *Extrajudicial Speech: Charting the Boundaries of Propriety*, 2 Geo. J. Legal Ethics 589, 641-42 (1989).

[111]Sparling, *supra* note 53, at 485.

[112]Bell, *supra* note 38, at 603. This is an altogether ironic quote given that "Taft was the most extrajudicially active Justice of [the twentieth] century." *Id.* at 604.

[113]Blue, *supra* note 13, at 27-28.

[114]Bell, *supra* note 38, at 616.

[115]Sparling, *supra* note 53, at 445-46.

[116]The Federalist No. 78 (Alexander Hamilton) (Jacob E. Cooke ed., 1961).

[117]*Id.*

out of the folly and wickedness of mankind, that the records of those precedents must unavoidably swell to a very considerable bulk, and must demand long and laborious study to acquire a competent knowledge of them. Hence it is, that there can be but few men in the society who will have sufficient skill in the laws to qualify them for the stations of judges. And making the proper deductions for the ordinary depravity of human nature, the number must be still smaller of those who unite the requisite integrity with the requisite knowledge.[118]

Although no one would read the above and confuse Hamilton with an idealist as regards human nature, *The Federalist Number 78* evinces a great deal of idealism with regard to the nature and character of judges. Hamilton views them as a class apart, and contemporary adherents to judicial monasticism expect judges to remain that way.[119]

The ostensible dangers to judges who venture outside of the cloister are (1) participation in extrajudicial activities to such an extent that such participation consumes so much time and energy that it detracts from the judge's ability to perform his or her judicial duties; (2) giving off the appearance of bias or prejudice; and (3) impairing the dignity and esteem of the court.[120] The appearance of impropriety factors heavily into these concerns, hence the concern over public confidence.[121] It is largely uncontested that public faith in the integrity of the judiciary is essential to the functioning of any legal system, but one in favor of judicial monasticism believes that this can be achieved only where judges are disconnected, at least in part, from the "real world."[122]

On the other hand, advocates of an increased public persona for the judiciary counter that judges have a great deal to offer society.[123] "Judges have no monopoly on wisdom, but they nevertheless have something to say.... The experience of listening to the stories and problems of persons representing the entire spectrum of humanity and resolving those problems (or at least attempting to do so) in principled ways" is a perspective uncommon to those not privileged to serve as judges.[124] The fact that there can be no assurances that a judge engaging in extrajudicial speech will positively contribute to society, it is argued, "is to miss the point entirely."[125] Not only is such a standard unthinkable in almost any other context, there is a "strong possibility" that a judge's

---

[118]*Id.*

[119]Sparling, *supra* note 53, at 445-46.

[120]Robert B. McKay, *The Judiciary and Nonjudicial Activities*, 35 Law & Contemp. Probs. 9, 12 (1970).

[121]Dubeck, *supra* note 18, at 582.

[122]Blue, *supra* note 13, at 17; McKay, *supra* note 120, at 12. *See also* Republican Party of Minnesota v. White, 536 U.S. 765, 818 (2002) (Ginsberg, J., dissenting).

[123]Blue, *supra* note 13, at 33.

[124]*Id.*

[125]Dubeck, *supra* note 18, at 572.

extrajudicial conduct "will make uniquely valuable contributions to the public discourse."[126]

Moreover, the argument goes, justifications employed by supporters of judicial monasticism are historically inaccurate.[127] Judges have not traditionally lived cloistered lives. From Chief Justice Jay through Justice Scalia, judges have been active extrajudicially.[128] Opponents of judicial monasticism also dispute the notion that modern standards require increased reticence.[129] While it is not uncommon to open up a newspaper and find an editorial lambasting a member of the judiciary for his or her extrajudicial activities, this is not a modern phenomenon.[130] Chief Justice Jay's appointment as Ambassador to Great Britain, for instance, was publicly decried as violating the separation of powers and being "contrary to the spirit and meaning of the constitution."[131]

Ultimately, neither side may claim sole possession of the truth with regard to extrajudicial speech.[132] With technological advances increasing the transparency of the judicial system, details about the personal lives of judges, and their personal views, will inevitably escape the cloister and wind up on the information superhighway.[133] The illusion that a judge's mind is a blank slate has been shattered and members of the public likely want to know a judge's personal views, even if only for their edification.[134] Then again, the noble ideals of judicial monasticism are largely shared by the public.[135] Confidence in the judiciary and the judicial system are based on notions of fairness and impartiality, and the public's opinion of the judiciary will rise and fall in relation to how well judges measure up to those ideals.[136] Although extrajudicial speech can be useful, the prudent judge should temper such speech with a high level of circumspection.

Pertinently, however, there is wide agreement across the spectrum that a judge has a right and even a duty to engage in quasi-judicial activity, defined as "activities that are not part of their assigned duties but are related to the judicial branch through efforts to improve judicial administration, or to inform other judges, lawyers, or the general public about the nature of law or the substance of its component parts."[137] Judges should nevertheless take caution that quasi-judicial activities not give rise to bias or the appearance of impropri-

---

[126]*Id.*

[127]*Id.* at 588.

[128]*See supra* Part II.

[129]Dubeck, *supra* note 18, at 596.

[130]*Id.* at 571, 596.

[131]*Id.* at 596-97 nn. 150-52.

[132]Sparling, *supra* note 53, at 486.

[133]*Id.* at 485.

[134]*Id.*

[135]*Id.* at 486.

[136]*Id.*

[137]McKay, *supra* note 120, at 21. "No one is better qualified to speak on law reform and questions of improvement in judicial administration than judges." *Id.*

ety.[138] The 1973 Reporter's Notes to the Code of Judicial Conduct offer an example:

> There is a significant difference between the statement, "I will grant all divorce actions that come before me — whatever the strength of the evidence to support the statutory ground for divorce — because I believe that persons who no longer live in harmony should be divorced," and the statement, "I believe that limited statutory grounds for divorce are not in the public interest. The law should be changed to allow persons who no longer live in harmony to obtain a divorce." The latter does not compromise a judge's capacity to apply impartially the law as written, although it clearly states his position about in [sic] the law.[139]

Care must also be taken to ensure that the forum in which the judge is speaking will not give rise to charges of bias, or an appearance of impropriety.[140] Bar groups and law schools are preferable, but a non-controversial speech delivered to a special interest group could be similarly unproblematic "if that talk could not be interpreted as addressing or alluding to any issue that is on the [group's] partisan agenda."[141] Addressing groups whose very purpose is legal change (e.g., pro-choice or pro-life groups), would be inappropriate.[142] Thus, quasi-judicial activity affords a judge a great deal more latitude than does extra-judicial activity, but it is not without limits.

V. Did Justice Scalia Violate His Ethical Duties by Speaking at the Conservative Constitutional Seminar?

In 2006, the *New York Times* — continuing in its decades-long effort to sound the alarm about the overnight explosion of controversial extrajudicial activity — opined that "speeches by Supreme Court justices are usually sleepy civics lessons studded with references to the Federalist Papers and the majesty of the law. That seems to be changing."[143] If this is the standard for judicial ethics, Justice Scalia is unequivocally innocent of any ethical violations with regard to his participation in the Conservative Constitutional Seminar. The speech was described by one Democrat in the audience as "pretty dry," and included a suggestion by Scalia that "everyone read the Federalist Papers ... and underline and dog ear them."[144] The Editors of the *New York Times*, however, excoriated

---

[138]Ross, *supra* note 110, at 615.

[139]*Id.* at 615 (quoting E.W. Thode, Reporter's Notes to Code of Judicial Conduct 74 (1973)).

[140]*Id.* at 618.

[141]*Id.*

[142]*Id.*

[143]Dubeck, *supra* note 18, at 587 (citing Adam Liptak, *Public Comments by Justices Veer Toward the Political*, N.Y. Times, Mar. 19, 2006, §1 at 22).

[144]*Scalia Holds 'Conversational' Session with House Tea Partiers*, CNN, Jan. 24, 2011, http://articles.cnn.com/2011-01-24/politics/scalia.tea.party_1_scalia-tea-party-caucus-constitution?_s=PM:POLITICS (last visited Apr. 16, 2011).

Scalia for agreeing to make the speech — cautioning that speaking before members of the Tea Party Caucus would erode public confidence in the Justice's impartiality — and the *Times* was not alone in that opinion.[145] Professor Lucas A. Powe, a law professor at the University of Texas, opined that Scalia's participation in the seminar was one of many examples of the Justice "taking partisanship to levels not seen in over half a century."[146] The greater weight of scholarly opinion, however, seemed to take the opposite opinion, especially in light of the fact that Scalia has spoken to liberal groups as well.[147]

Although no transcript of the speech is available to the public, because the seminar was open only to members of Congress and their aides, it appears from limited reports that Justice Scalia's comments fell within the scope of quasi-judicial activity. Tailored to educate new members of Congress about passing legislation that will pass constitutional muster, Scalia's remarks were, by and large, devoid of references to hot-button political issues. Scholars of legal ethics approve, in seemingly unanimous fashion, of judicial speech that serves to inform not only legal professionals but all members of the public of the nature and substance of the law.[148] Additionally, the Code specifically allows judges to share their "special expertise" with the legislative branch "in connection with matters about which the judge acquired knowledge or expertise in the course of the judge's judicial duties."[149]

Faced with questions from the audience about abortion and the line-item veto, Justice Scalia answered frankly but also appropriately. According to reports, Scalia said that he was *willing* to overturn *Roe v. Wade*, and believed the line-item veto *could* be constitutional.[150] This comports with the principle that a judge may give his opinion on specific legal issues, but may not speak in such a manner that would "compromise [the] judge's capacity to apply impartially the law as written."[151] If the reports are accurate, Scalia did just that. A willingness to overturn a prior decision, or openness to the possibility that legislation deemed unconstitutional in one instance may be constitutional in another, is not committing oneself to a course of action. Moreover, the remarks, if accurately reported, only reiterate what Scalia already stated in several judicial opinions.[152]

---

[145]*See supra* Part I.

[146]Kathleen B. Hennessey & David Savage, *Scalia Appears at 'Tea Party' House Meeting*, L.A. Times, Jan. 24, 2011, http://articles.latimes.com/2011/jan/24/nation/la-na-scalia-tea-party-20110125 (last visited Apr. 16, 2011).

[147]Steve Inskeep, *Justice Scalia Speaks to Tea Party Caucus, Democrats*, Morning Edition (NPR radio broadcast Jan. 25, 2011).

[148]*See supra* Part IV.

[149]*See supra* Part III.

[150]*See supra* Part I.

[151]Ross, *supra* note 110, at 615 (quoting E.W. Thode, Reporter's Notes to Code of Judicial Conduct, 74 (1973)).

[152]*See, e.g.,* Clinton v. City of New York, 524 U.S. 417, 453 (Scalia, J., dissenting) (asserting that the line-item veto is in accord with the Constitution); Planned Parenthood v. Casey, 505 U.S. 833, 983 (Scalia, J., dissenting) (stating that *Roe v. Wade*

Given that his actual remarks create no apparent conflict with the Code or with general ethical principles, the issue becomes whether Scalia created an appearance of impropriety, bias, or lack of independence. An argument can be made that by agreeing to speak at a seminar sponsored by the Tea Party Caucus, a controversial group in contemporary American politics, Scalia at least raised questions about his neutrality and created the appearance of impropriety.[153] Noting that he has garnered the moniker "the Justice from the Tea Party," the *New York Times* blasted Scalia for participating in what it deemed to be a partisan affair.[154] Although it is clear from the reports of those Congresspersons who attended that the subject matter of the seminar was not partisan, it is equally clear from the media reaction that Scalia's participation was viewed as political. If the aim of the Code, and its emphasis on avoiding the appearance of impropriety, is to ensure public confidence in the judicial system, it follows that anything tending to erode such confidence violates the Code, at least in spirit.[155] At the same time, the test for whether a judge's conduct gives rise to an appearance of impropriety is whether such conduct "would create in reasonable minds a perception that the judge violated [the] Code or engaged in other conduct that reflects adversely on the judge's honesty, temperament, or fitness to serve as judge."[156] While the controversial nature of the group sponsoring the Conservative Constitutional Seminar cannot be denied, it is also true that the seminar was tailored to a non-partisan audience and that Scalia's speech was merely instructional. Thus, could reasonable minds really perceive that the speech reflected adversely on Justice Scalia's honesty, temperament, or fitness to serve as judge?

Regardless of whether it was inappropriate to address a seminar sponsored by a controversial political group, those who espouse judicial monasticism would rightly note that pointed editorials in *The New York Times* and *The Washington Post* do contribute to the impairment of the dignity and independence of the judiciary, even if a judge's behavior was not outside the bounds of propriety. Moreover, while speaking to a gathering of Tea Party Caucus members might not, in and of itself, give rise to an appearance of impropriety, Scalia's speech was just one in a long line of extrajudicial activities that have

---

was wrongly decided); Webster v. Reproductive Health Servs., 492 U.S. 490, 537 (Scalia, J., concurring) (discussing the need to re-examine *Roe v. Wade*).

[153]Recent national opinion polls have shown that 29% of Americans view the Tea Party unfavorably, with 23% viewing it favorably. Posting of Stephanie Condon to CBS News Political Hotsheet, *Tea Party Supported by One in Five in New CBS News/NYT Poll*, http://www.cbsnews.com/8301-503544_162-20016526-503544.html (Sept. 15, 2010) (last visited Apr. 16, 2011). Another poll showed 37% of Americans reporting a favorable impression of the Tea Party and 40% reporting an unfavorable impression. Lydia Saad, *Tea Partiers are Fairly Mainstream in their Demographics*, Apr. 5, 2010, http://gallup.com/poll/127181/tea-partiers-fairly-mainstream-demographics.aspx#1 (last visited Apr. 16, 2011).

[154]Editorial, *Politics and the Court*, N.Y. Times, Feb. 5, 2011, at A16.

[155]Sparling, *supra* note 53, at 451.

[156]Model Code of Judicial Conduct R. 1.2, cmt. 5 (2007).

raised eyebrows.[157] Scalia's history of questionable extrajudicial activity gives commentators and critics cause to look at any extrajudicial venture cynically.

VI. Conclusion

In sum, Justice Scalia's actions appear to have been in line with the Code of Judicial Conduct. One might even venture to say that Scalia deserves praise for volunteering to educate new members of Congress on the process of creating constitutional legislation. This particular example of extrajudicial activity comports with the history of the extrajudicial activity of other Supreme Court Justices. No reasoned argument can be made that the activity itself was aberrant. Moreover, the general consensus among legal ethics scholars is that Scalia's behavior was ethical.[158]

Perhaps the most fitting assessment proffered was that of legal ethics expert and Northwestern Law School professor Steven Lubet, who noted that, despite being controversial, the speech was more a question of prudence than of ethics.[159] As such, perhaps Scalia should have considered the travails of Chief Justice Harlan Fiske Stone. A day after giving "an innocuous speech on the legal profession" at Georgetown Law School, Stone awoke "to find newspaper reports that he had told the gathering he agreed with most of the administration's program to curb monopolies."[160]

Prudence might not require a judge to retreat into the monastery, but in consideration of public confidence in the judiciary it is necessary for judges to exercise a high degree of circumspection. While the content of his speech cannot be considered improper, a simple Google search evidences the reality that, as with Justice Stone, Scalia's participation in the Conservative Constitutional Seminar came with a price.

---

[157]*See supra* Part II.

[158]*See supra* Part V.

[159]Inskeep, *supra* note 147.

[160]Bell, *supra* note 38, at 601.

PART FOUR

Social and Philosophical Concerns

13

Training Culturally Competent Lawyers: What Can Law Learn From Medicine?

Kimberly Mills

Introduction

Sociocultural differences between client and attorney influence communication, trustworthiness, and a client's perception of the justice system as a whole. Attorney-client communication and related attributes of the relationship are directly linked to an attorney's ability to secure a favorable outcome for his or her client.[1] Therefore, the delivery of competent and effective legal counsel mandates an understanding of the sociocultural backgrounds of clients, their families, and the environments in which they live. Cultivating an understanding of culture allows for attorneys to make better decisions and recognize the importance of developing effective communication and problem-solving techniques, and highlights the impact that culture has on an attorney's ability to build trust with her client.[2] Attorneys also need to be aware of how their own assumptions, values, and beliefs influence the provision of legal services.[3]

Cultural competence, which is defined as the ability to recognize and respect diversity of background and opportunity, language, culture, and way of life, is increasingly recognized as a specialized communication skill that allows for a more effective attorney-client encounter.[4] It is critically important to prepare lawyers to communicate in a culturally competent manner with clients in order to meet the needs of a growing diverse population, to improve attorney-client communication, to build trust within the attorney-client relationship, and to change clients' perceptions of the justice system.[5]

Despite this growing recognition of the value of cultural competence in the provision of legal services, it is largely ignored in traditional legal education. Unlike the legal profession, the medical profession has consistently recog-

---

[1]Shani M. King, *Race, Identity, and Professional Responsibility: Why Legal Services Organizations Need African American Staff Attorneys*, 18 Cornell J.L. & Pub. Pol'y 1, 1 (2008). *See generally* Austin Sarat & William L.F. Felstiner, *Law and Strategy in the Divorce Lawyer's Office* in *Lawyers: A Critical Reader* 45, 46-54 (Richard L. Abel ed., 1997) (explaining an early study showing that better outcomes result from trust and communication between attorneys and clients in divorce proceedings rather than lawyer paternalism).

[2]Susan Bryant, *The Five Habits: Building Cross-Cultural Competence in Lawyers*, 8 Clinical L. Rev. 33, 34 (2001).

[3]Sylvia E. Stevens, *Is There an Ethical Duty?*, 69 Or. State Bar Bulletin 9, 9 (2009).

[4]Bryant, *supra* note 2, at 39-40; Stevens, *supra* note 3, at 9.

[5]Bryant, *supra* note 2, at 38, 39.

nized the importance of training culturally competent physicians. The medical profession understands that when a patient and physician do not share the same culture, barriers to effective communication can arise and may result in diagnostic errors, adverse drug reactions as a result of patients employing traditional indigenous and Western medicine and treatment, and lack of patient adherence to treatment plans.[6] Physicians who have undergone cultural competence training are believed to be better able to break down barriers within culturally discordant patient-provider relationships.[7] Through accrediting bodies, national policy, and federal and statewide legislation, the medical profession has made a strong commitment to training culturally competent medical professionals.

In this paper, I argue that legal education has largely failed to introduce a cultural competence curriculum into professional development training — and as a result, lawyers are not prepared to effectively uphold their duty to provide effective and competent legal services to clients in culturally discordant attorney-client relationships. Part I introduces healthcare disparities among minorities and White Americans, discusses the impact culture has on the quality of care a patient receives, and finally looks at the effect cultural competence has on the patient-provider relationship. Part II explores the nature of the attorney-client relationship, the ethnic and racial disparities within the criminal justice system, and the barriers to cultivating trusting interactions and successful outcomes in culturally discordant attorney-client relationships.

Part III discusses how the medical field has made efforts, through formal integration of cultural competency curriculum into medical education, to prepare healthcare professionals to work in societies that are increasingly culturally and ethnically diverse. Additionally, Part III discusses how medical schools train students to be culturally competent and addresses proposed methods of integrating cultural competency education into law schools. Finally, this paper recommends what legal institutions can learn from medical institutions to move from being aware of attorneys' inability to provide effective legal counsel in culturally discordant attorney-client relationships, to taking action in addressing the issue.

Definition of Cultural Competence

The concept of culture is a fundamental anthropologic construct. The role of a particular culture is to ensure the survival and well-being of its members and to facilitate interactions among its members.[8] Culture is a dynamic shared system of beliefs, values and learned patterns of behavior that are shaped by factors such as proximity, education, gender, age, and sexual preference. Culture manifests as different languages, levels of acculturation, and socioeconomic

---

[6]*E.g.*, Darci L. Graves et al., *Legislation as Intervention: A Survey of Cultural Competence Policy in Health Care*, 10 J. Health Care L. & Pol'y 339, 345 (2007).

[7]*Id.*

[8]Marjorie Kagawa-Singer & Shaheen Kassim-Lakha, *A Strategy to Reduce Cross-cultural Miscommunication and Increase the Likelihood of Improving Health Outcomes*, 78 Academic Medicine 577, 578 (2003).

status.[9]

Most often culture is thought to be synonymous with race or used to describe people who are phenotypically similar and thus assumed to have the same shared beliefs and values. But culture is not race; it does not designate racial or ethnic categories.[10] Each member of a particular ethnic or racial group may have varying levels of acculturation and assimilation that dictates differential expression of culture. Variations in age, education, income, family structure, gender, and country of origin influence the degree to which one's culture affects one's beliefs and practices. The use of culture as synonymous with race or ethnicity leads to stereotyping and misconceptions.

Cultural competence is a "set of congruent behaviors, attitudes, and policies that come together in a system, agency, or among professionals and enable that system, agency or those professionals to work effectively in cross-cultural situations."[11] Accordingly, culturally competent individuals have a heightened sense of awareness of their own culture, identity, and personal biases while also maintaining an enhanced consciousness of the fact that people of different cultures will react differently to various situations and will hold different values, traditions, and assumptions.[12] In essence, cultural competence refers to an individual or organization's ability to function effectively within the context of differing cultural beliefs, practices, and needs of individuals or communities.[13]

I. The Patient-Physician Relationship

Healthcare Disparities and the Patient-Physician Relationship

Estimates suggest that by 2030 more than 40% of the U.S. population will be members of minority races and by 2050 that number will be approximately 50%.[14] Currently, however, African American physicians account for less than

---

[9]Emilio J. Carrillo, Alexander R. Green & Joseph R. Betancourt, *Cross-Cultural Primary Care: A Patient-Based Approach*, 130 Annals of Internal Medicine 829, 829 (1999).

[10]Kagawa-Singer & Kassim-Lakha, *supra* note 8, at 579.

[11]Jessica Jean Kastner, *Beyond the Bench: Solutions to Reduce the Disproportionate Number of Minority Youth in the Family and Criminal Courts System*, 15 J.L. & Pol'y 941, 944 (2007); Carolyn Copps Hartley & Carrie J. Petrucci, *Practicing Culturally Competent Therapeutic Jurisprudence: A Collaboration Between Social Work and Law*, 14 Wash. U.J.L. & Pol'y 133, 171 (2004).

[12]Stevens, *supra* note 3, at 9.

[13]*Cultural Competence Education for Medical Students* (Association of American Medical Colleges, 2005), *available at* https://www.aamc.org/download/54338/data/culturalcomped.pdf.

[14]2004 American Community Survey: Data Profile Highlights (U.S. Bureau of the Census, 2004), *available at* http://www.census.gov/population/www/projections/usinterimproj/natprojtab01a.pdf [hereinafter U.S. Census] (last visited Apr. 10, 2011).

five percent of the physician population.[15] Even though the number of minorities in the U.S. is steadily growing, the minority physician population is unable to mirror the number of minority patients.[16] Numerous studies have been conducted that indicate that the significant health-related disparities that exist between minorities and White Americans can be attributed to factors which limit an individual's access to healthcare and factors which affect the quality of healthcare an individual receives. Factors which limit access to healthcare include high cost of comprehensive healthcare plans, lack of health insurance, limited access to specialty care, high cost of access to private physician care, transportation to facilities that provide care, and long wait times.[17] Factors which affect the quality of healthcare include physician bias or prejudice against minorities (as a result of a patient's age, sex, gender, race, ethnicity, education and healthcare literacy, socioeconomic status, and primary language), a physician's limited understanding of patients' cultural behaviors and beliefs, and physician-patient discordance.[18] As a result of the unequal treatment that minorities face from the healthcare system and providers, minorities are much more likely to have poorer health, earlier disability, earlier death, and fewer healthcare resources, and are less satisfied with the care they receive, than are White Americans.[19]

The Influence of Race and Ethnicity on the Quality of the Patient-Physician Relationship

Evidence suggests that ethnic and racial minorities receive lower-quality healthcare than the majority White population.[20] When patients and providers are engaged in a culturally discordant relationship, the quality of the healthcare that the patient receives is lower than if the patient and provider are in a culturally concordant relationship.[21] African Americans, Asians and Latinos were more likely than White Americans to report that they believe that they would

---

[15]Somnath Saha, Miriam Komaromy, Thomas D. Koepsell & Andrew B. Bindman, *Patient-Physician Racial Concordance and the Perceived Quality and Use of Health Care*, 159 Archive of Internal Medicine 997, 1000 (1999).

[16]The term 'disparity' refers to "different groups having different probabilities for a particular outcome due to their group status." Hartley & Petrucci, *supra* note 11, at 147. The presence of disparity "does not necessarily mean that racial and ethnic discrimination exists." *Id.*

[17]Saha et al., *supra* note 15, at 998-99; *Unequal Treatment: What Healthcare Providers Need to Know About Racial and Ethnic Disparities in Healthcare* (Institute of Medicine, 2002) [hereinafter *Unequal Treatment*]. Patient access to healthcare is beyond the scope of this paper.

[18]Saha et al., *supra* note 15, at 998-99; *Unequal Treatment*, *supra* note 17, at 2-3.

[19]A. Noah, *A Prescription for Racial Equality in Medicine*, 40 Conn. L. Rev. 675, 683 (2008); Saha et al., *supra* note 15, at 997.

[20]Somnath Saha, Jose Arbelaez & Lisa A. Cooper, *Patient-Physician Relationships and Racial Disparities in the Quality of Health Care*, 93 American Journal of Public Health 1713, 1713 (2003).

[21]Saha et al., *supra* note 15, at 999.

receive a higher quality of healthcare if they had been of a different race or ethnicity.[22] Patients in racially concordant physician-provider relationships have indicated that they had better communication and had a significantly greater participatory role in the decisions affecting their healthcare than in racially discordant relationships.[23]

The ability of a patient and provider to effectively communicate during the clinical encounter influences patient satisfaction and patient adherence to physician recommendations.[24] Respect, spending adequate time with patients, adequate listening, and participatory decision-making all effect patient satisfaction.[25] African Americans were more likely than other minority groups to report that physicians would disrespect them in a clinical encounter and would exhibit the disrespect by addressing them in a rude manner, talking down to them, and ignoring them.[26] Asians were the most likely to feel that their doctor did not understand their background and values and that their doctor looked down on them.[27]

Individuals in racially concordant patient-provider relationships gave higher ratings to their physicians on treating them with respect, explaining medical problems, and listening to their concerns.[28] African American patients in a racially concordant patient-provider relationships gave their physicians excellent ratings in providing healthcare and in being accessible.[29] Generally, minorities were more satisfied with the overall healthcare they received from physicians of their same race or ethnicity as opposed to White physicians.[30]

Healthcare provider prejudice or bias towards patients of a different race or ethnicity contributes to the physicians' diagnostic and treatment decisions and feelings towards the patient.[31] Considerable empirical evidence suggests that White Americans sometimes "demonstrate unconscious implicit negative

---

[22]*Minority Americans Lag Behind Whites on Nearly Every Measure of Health Care Quality* (The Commonwealth Fund, 2002) [hereinafter The Commonwealth Fund] *available at* http://www.commonwealthfund.org/Content/News/News-Releases/2002/Mar/Minority-Americans-Lag-Behind-Whites-On-Nearly-Every-Measure-Of-Health-Care-Quality.aspx.

[23]Lisa Cooper-Patrick et al., *Race, Gender, and Partnership in the Patient-Physician Relationship*, 282 Journal of the American Medical Association 583, 587 (1999).

[24]Carol M. Ashton et al., *Racial and ethnic disparities in the use of health services: bias, preferences, or poor communication?*, 18 Journal of General Internal Medicine 146, 147 (2003).

[25]Cooper-Patrick et al., *supra* note 23, at 587-88.

[26]The Commonwealth Fund, *supra* note 22.

[27]*Id.*

[28]Saha et al., *supra* note 15, at 998.

[29]*Id.*

[30]*Id.* at 998-99.

[31]*Unequal Treatment*, *supra* note 17, at 4.

racial attitudes and stereotypes."[32] A recent study found that physicians "rated black patients as less intelligent, less educated, more likely to abuse drugs and alcohol, more likely to fail to comply with medical advice, [and] more likely to lack social support ... even after patients' income, education, and personality characteristics were taken into account."[33]

The Effect of Cultural Competence on the Patient-Physician Relationship

Physicians are treating patients that are increasingly culturally and ethnically diverse and the patient-physician relationship is extremely important in determining the quality of care the patient receives.[34] In order for the physician to provide a patient with a high quality of care, it is essential for the physician to understand that in every patient-provider encounter, there will be an interaction between the culture of the physician and the culture of the patient.[35] Thus, it is important for the physician to recognize that when he or she first enters into a clinical encounter with a patient, the physician will depend on his or her own inferences and observations about the needs of the patient, and those inference and observations will be influenced by the patient's age, gender, socioeconomic status, and race or ethnicity.[36] A physician's sense of her own self-awareness is the first step in becoming a physician with the ability to provide patients with a higher quality of care. Additionally, a physician who seeks to provide a high quality of care for his or her patients must also recognize that the culture of the patient will influence the patient's ability to communicate effectively with a physician, the patient's perception of the success of the clinical encounter, the patient's ability and willingness to adhere to regimens, and the patient's overall health outcome.[37] In essence, ensuring a physician's ability to provide the highest quality of care for his or her patients requires the physician to be culturally competent.

When the patient and provider are engaged in a culturally discordant relationship, communication can be a significant barrier to a successful clinical encounter. The inability of the patient to effectively communicate with his physician can adversely affect the physician's ability to diagnose and treat the patient.[38] Arguably, the most obvious communication barriers are discordant languages or dialects. However, even in racially concordant patient-provider rela-

---

[32]*Id.* For the purposes of this paper, a stereotype is defined as "the process by which people use social categories in acquiring, processing, and recalling information about others." *Id.*

[33]*Id.* at 4-5.

[34]U.S. Census, *supra* note 14.

[35]Nahid Azad, Barbara Power, Janet Dollin & Sandra Chery, *Cultural Sensitivity Training in Canadian Medical Schools,* 77 Academic Medicine 222, 226 (2002).

[36]*Unequal Treatment, supra* note 17, at 3.

[37]John M. Eisenberg, *Sociologic Influences on Medical Decision-Making by Clinicians,* 90 Annals of Internal Medicine 957 passim (1979).

[38]Cooper-Patrick et al., *supra* note 23, at 583.

tionships where the patient and provider speak the same language, the use of terms, idioms, and metaphors — used by either patient or physician — may interfere with effective communication.[39] Furthermore, ineffective communication between patient and provider in racially discordant relationships is partly attributable to the fact that African Americans and White Americans interact within a "unique historical and sociopolitical context that influences the ... sense of balance, power, and trust" between individuals of both races.[40]

Communication is verbal and nonverbal; thus, it is essential for the physician to not only be able to verbally communicate in a cross-cultural patient-provider relationship, but it is also imperative for the physician to be able to effectively read body language and maintain a heightened sense of awareness regarding other forms of non-verbal communication when treating culturally diverse patients.[41] With regard to verbal communication, a patient's ability to provide a health narrative, ask questions, express concerns, and be assertive all influence a physician's ability, effectiveness, and willingness to communicate with his or her patient.[42] However, it is important to note that a patient's propensity to ask questions, express concerns, or be assertive in a clinical encounter is influenced by the patient's culture.[43] Additionally, the health narrative provided by the patient will be influenced by the patient's cultural norms, beliefs, and customs; thus, a patient might fail to disclose all information pertaining to her health that a physician would deem necessary to provide quality healthcare.[44]

Patients might feel more respected and satisfied in racially or culturally concordant patient-provider relationships because physicians of the same race, ethnicity, or culture might share similar experiences that promote trust and mutual understanding.[45] The culture of the patient and provider influence one another reciprocally; however, the physician shoulders the responsibility of heightening his or her awareness regarding the variability of cultural expectations the patients will bring to the clinical encounter.[46]

II. The Attorney-Client Relationship

Disparities Within the Criminal Justice System and the Attorney-Client Relationship

Currently, people of color and new immigrants are disproportionately repre-

---

[39] Ashton, *supra* note 24, at 148.

[40] *Id.*

[41] Cooper-Patrick et al., *supra* note 23, at 588.

[42] Ashton, *supra* note 24, at 150.

[43] *Id.*

[44] *Id.*

[45] Saha et al., *supra* note 15, at 1001.

[46] Carillo et al., *supra* note 9, at 830; *Unequal Treatment*, *supra* note 17, at 5.

sented in the criminal justice system as victims and perpetrators of crime.[47] Statistics indicate that an African American is eleven times more likely to be shot dead and nine times more likely to be murdered than a White American.[48] Further, almost one in three African American males between the ages of twenty and twenty-nine is either in prison, on probation, or on parole on any given day.[49] The high rates of African Americans and other minorities in the criminal justice system is partly attributable to the fact that certain crimes that are most often perpetrated by Black offenders have harsher sentences than crimes most often committed by non-Black or White Americans.[50] For example, harsher sentences are given for possession of crack cocaine, a crime most often committed by African Americans, than for possession of powder cocaine, a crime more often committed by White Americans.[51]

African Americans and other minorities have not received the same quality of legal services, representation and treatment as White Americans.[52] Asian Americans are often devalued in comparison to White Americans when they are the victims and perpetrators of crime.[53] Black violence against White victims is considered to be the most serious offense in American society and this is evidenced by the severe racial disparity in imposing the death penalty on guilty offenders.[54] Factors which affect the quality of legal services, representation, and treatment that an individual receives include bias or prejudice held by law enforcement, attorneys, judges and other actors in the criminal justice system, an attorney's limited understanding of clients' cultural behaviors and beliefs, and attorney-client discordance.[55] Additionally, attorneys are a part of a profession where communication is the cornerstone of the relationship she will form with a client.[56] Therefore, the capacity of attorneys to effectively identify culturally relevant behaviors of diverse populations and to communicate across

---

[47]Shelia A. Bedi, *The Constructed Identities of Asian and African Americans: A Story of Two Races and the Criminal Justice System*, 19 Harv. BlackLetter L.J. 181, 182 (2003).

[48]*Id.* at 184.

[49]Mary Maxwell Thomas, *The African American Male: Communication Gap Converts Justice Into "Just Us" System*, 13 Harv. BlackLetter L.J. 1, 2 (1997).

[50]*Id.*

[51]*Id.*

[52]Bedi, *supra* note 47, at 182; Thomas, *supra* note 49, at 3.

[53]Bedi, *supra* note 47, at 189.

[54]Dorothy E. Roberts, *Crime, Race, and Reproduction*, 67 Tul. L. Rev. 1945, 1959 (1993). In California, a study was conducted and revealed that defendants who killed White Americans were over three times more likely to be sentenced to death than defendants who killed African Americans and over four times more likely than those who killed Latinos. *Facts About the Death Penalty* (Death Penalty Information Center, 2011), *available at* http://www.deathpenaltyinfo.org/documents/FactSheet.pdf.

[55] Thomas, *supra* note 49, at 2-3.

[56]Eli Wald, *Taking Attorney-Client Communications (and Therefore Clients) Seriously*, 42 U.S.F. L. Rev. 747, 747 (2008).

cultural and language barriers are essential characteristics of an attorney and necessary to provide a higher quality of legal services to a client.[57]

The Influence of Race and Ethnicity on the Quality of the Attorney-Client Relationship

Many attorneys are unaware of the impact of culture and race on the practice of law.[58] Often, individuals unconsciously employ bias, prejudice, and stereotypes when making assessments and judgments about people of different races and ethnicities.[59] In order to effectively address the influence of race and ethnicity on the quality of the attorney-client relationship, it is essential for attorneys to endure the uncomfortable process of breaking down their biases, prejudices and stereotypes.[60] This process is important because the attorneys' "preconceived cultural notions will impact both the lawyer's expectations of the client as well as the lawyer's interpretation and understanding of the client's actions and ultimate objectives."[61] Once an attorney has an understanding of how he or she perceives the others, the attorney will likely be better able to develop cross-cultural communication skills and engage with the client in an appropriate and culturally sensitive manner.

A. The Attorney-Client Relationship and Race-Concordance

Individuals who share a cultural identity will likely be able to cultivate a relationship founded upon certain mutual understandings regarding behavior, beliefs, and communication. As a result, it is unsurprising that African American clients often prefer African American attorneys because they believe that they are less likely to be judged "based on the color of their skin, the way they walk, or the way they talk."[62] Empirical evidence suggests that in race-concordant attorney-client relationships, attorneys are more likely to gain the trust of their client and communicate effectively with their client; however, most attorney-client relationships are discordant.[63] The gross underrepresentation of minorities in law school greatly contributes to the fact that most attorney-client relationships are racially discordant.[64]

---

[57]Stevens, *supra* note 3, at 9.

[58]Majorie A. Silver, *Emotional Competence, Multicultural Lawyering and Race*, 3 Florida Coastal L.J. 219, 220 (2002).

[59]*Id.* at 231.

[60]*Id.* at 230.

[61]Michelle S. Jacobs, *People from the Footnotes: The Missing Element in Client-Centered Counseling*, 27 Golden Gate U.L. Rev. 345, 378 (1997).

[62]King, *supra* note 1, at 16.

[63]*Id.* at 4.

[64]David B. Wilkins & G. Mitu Gulati, *Why Are There So Few Black Lawyers in Corporate Law Firms? An Institutional Analysis*, in Lawyers: A Critical Reader 101, 101 (Richard L. Abel ed., 1997). In death penalty states, ninety-eight percent of the chief district attorneys are White Americans while only one percent are African American.

African American clients and African American attorneys share a common experience: being Black in America. As a result of this experience, Black clients often feel like a Black attorney will maintain the same worldview, "identify with their historical and current struggle in this country as Black Americans," and understand the widely held perception by African Americans that the criminal justice system is racist.[65] Kenneth P. Troccoli, in "'I Want a Black Lawyer to Represent Me': Addressing a Black Defendant's Concerns with Being Assigned a White Court-Appointed Lawyer," discusses a Black defendant's preference for a racially concordant attorney-client relationship. Troccoli offers three reasons why an African American will likely prefer a Black attorney. First, Troccoli suggests that a Black defendant might see a White attorney a part of the 'racist criminal justice system.'[66] Second, Troccoli suggests that an attorney who does not share a racial identity with the client is unable to appreciate the impact of the client's race on the present legal issue.[67] Third, Troccoli suggests that an African American client does not want to shoulder the burden of getting his White attorney "up to speed" on the impact of the client's race on the existing legal issue.[68]

It is important to reinforce the fact that culture is not race and as a result individuals who share a racial identity may not share the same cultural values and beliefs. Sometimes, a Black client may not want a Black attorney because the client believes the attorney is "not black enough."[69] A Black client may develop the perception of a Black attorney as "not being black enough" because of the lawyer's "skin color, hair texture, wealth, academic success, social status or speech."[70] As a result, the Black attorney that is "not black enough" will encounter many of the same barriers to fostering a successful and trusting attorney-client relationship as a non-Black attorney.

B. The Attorney-Client Relationship and Communication

The attorney-client relationship is reflective of an agency-principal relationship where the attorney, as the agent, is expected to serve the interest of the client.[71] Therefore, in order for there to be a successful attorney-client encounter, the client must effectively communicate to the attorney her goals and objectives and necessary and relevant information for the attorney to successfully provide

---

Facts About the Death Penalty (Death Penalty Information Center, 2011), *available at* http://www.deathpenaltyinfo.org/documents/FactSheet.pdf.

[65]King, *supra* note 1, at 4, 16.

[66]Kenneth P. Troccoli, *"I Want a Black Lawyer to Represent Me": Addressing a Black Defendant's Concerns with Being Assigned a White Court-Appointed Lawyer*, 20 Law & Ineq. 1, 17 (2002).

[67]*Id.* at 25.

[68]*Id.*

[69]King, *supra* note 1, at 43.

[70]*Id.*

[71]Wald, *supra* note 56, at 748.

counsel.[72]

A client's ability to effectively communicate with an attorney is influenced by the client's race and ethnicity. When an attorney does not share the same culture as his client, certain phrases and idioms used by the client to express information the attorney needs to know, to adequately represent the client, might be misunderstood. For example, "hood" can mean (1) head covering, (2) hoodlum, or (3) neighborhood.[73] Other words that carry at least three meanings include, but are not limited to, "honey," "house," "fresh," "fly," "dope," and "dis."[74] Thus, it is imperative for an attorney to develop an understanding of various cultures and the ways in which members of different cultures express themselves in order to close communication gaps within the attorney-client relationship. Moreover, developing cross-cultural communication skills affords attorneys the ability to make more informed and fair decisions involving their clients.[75]

Language minorities face significant communication challenges within the attorney-client relationship. In 2000, over one-fourth of the U.S. population reported that they spoke a language other than English in their home, and over twenty-one million people in the U.S. reported they had difficulty speaking English.[76] The number of Spanish-speaking American lawyers is too low to meet the demands of Spanish-speaking litigants, and it is likely that the demand for attorneys who speak other languages (excluding English and Spanish) is also unmet.[77] While the passage of the Court Interpreters Act of 1978 was an important step in beginning to narrow the communication gap between English-speaking attorneys and non-English-speaking litigants, language barriers still remain.[78]

The Current Effect of Cultural Competence on the Attorney-Client Relationship

Cultural competence is recognized as an important factor in the attorney-client relationship.[79] Knowledge of cultural practices allows attorneys to more effectively manage client expectations, more effectively communicate with clients, build trust with the client, and address client perspectives about the justice sys-

---

[72]*Id.*

[73]Thomas, *supra* note 49, at 34.

[74]*Id.*

[75]*Id.* at 4.

[76]Daniel J. Rearick, *Reaching Out to the Most Insular Minorities: A Proposal for Improving Latino Access to the American Legal System*, 39 Harv. C.R.-C.L. L. Rev. 543, 546 (2004).

[77]*Id.* at 553.

[78]*Id.* at 553-54. The Court Interpreters Act, 28 U.S.C. § 1837 (1978), applies in Federal court and grants non-English speaking litigants a right to an interpreter in criminal trials and in civil cases when the non-English speaking defendant is being sued by the government. *Id.* at 553.

[79]Hartley & Petrucci, *supra* note 11, at 165.

tem — and can prevent an attorney from being insensitive to a client's cultural taboos, family norms, and conflict-management styles.[80] While it is not possible to be completely knowledgeable about all cultures, the awareness of the fact that different cultures have different expectations and different rules of appropriate behavior is an important first step in fostering a stronger relationship between attorney and client.[81] However, it is time for the legal profession to move past recognition and awareness of the importance of training culturally competent attorneys, and into action.

III. Training Culturally Competent Lawyers

The Formal Integration of Cultural Competence Curriculum into Medical Education

The seemingly ever-present healthcare disparities that plague minorities have alarmed the medical profession. As a result, the medical profession now requires that cultural competence training be integrated into medical education. Through national policy, federal and statewide legislation, and healthcare accrediting bodies in the United States, the medical profession has taken the necessary steps to ensure that all physicians have undergone cultural competence training.

A. Federal and State Legislation

At the federal level, the Office of Minority Health in the Department of Health and Human Services oversees the National Standards on Culturally and Linguistically Appropriate Services, or CLAS standards. The CLAS standards were initially designed for healthcare organizations but physicians are also encouraged to abide by the standards.[82] The CLAS standards were established to establish "(1) common and consistent terminology for culturally and linguistically appropriate services, and (2) practical guidelines for healthcare organizations with regard to service delivery and infrastructure needed to best serve diverse patient populations."[83] In 2010, the federal government reinforced its commitment to work towards ensuring that all patients receive culturally competence care, by issuing the *Healthy People 2010* report.[84] The *Healthy People 2010* report states that "every person in every community across the nation deserves equal access to comprehensive, culturally competent, community-based healthcare systems that are committed to serving the needs of the individual and pro-

---

[80]Stevens, *supra* note 3, at 10.

[81]*Id.* at 9.

[82]Maria B.J. Chun, *Cultural Competency Compliance Issues in Health Care*, 11 J. Health Care Compliance 27, 29 (2009).

[83]*Id.*

[84]Graves et al., *supra* note 6, at 345.

moting community health."[85] As a result of efforts made at the federal level to ensure that patients receive culturally competent care, states began to mirror the federal government and implement statewide legislation requiring cultural competence training as part of medical education and/or licensure and accreditation.[86]

States have enacted a plethora of laws addressing language access in healthcare and cultural competence training. State motivation behind enacting language access laws stems from the concept of "linguistic competence," an outgrowth of cultural competence. Linguistic competence is the ability to effectively communicate "information that may be easily understood by any given patient population — including, but not limited to, persons of limited English proficiency, those who have low literacy skill or are not literate, and individuals with disabilities."[87] The implementation of language access laws promoting linguistic competence has manifested in physician use of trained interpreters to effectively communicate with patients.[88]

In 2005, New Jersey was the first state to pass legislation that requires cultural competence training for all medical students as a licensure requirement.[89] Shortly after, California and Washington echoed New Jersey by passing laws that require cultural competency training for licensure and accreditation or as a part of medical education.[90] Additional states have attempted to pass legislation pertaining to cultural competence training, but the legislation has either been vetoed, failed to make it out of committee, or is still pending.[91] Those states include Arizona, Colorado, Georgia, Illinois, New Mexico, New York, and Ohio.[92]

B. Healthcare Accrediting Bodies

Medical education accrediting bodies, such as the Liaison Committee on Medical Education (LCME), the Association of American Medical Colleges (AAMC), and the Accreditation Council for Graduate Medical Education (ACGME), have outlined a series of requirements to which medical schools must adhere related to cultural competence training.[93] Further, at the organizational level,

---

[85]*Id.* (citing *Healthy People 2010* (2010)).

[86]*Id.* at 350-51.

[87]*Id.* at 346.

[88]*Id.*

[89]Chun, *supra* note 82, at 29; Graves, *supra* note 6, at 349.

[90]Graves, *supra* note 6, at 394.

[91]*Id.* at 349, 350.

[92]*Id.* at 349.

[93]Chun, *supra* note 83, at 29. The LCME "expects that both faculty and students have the ability to deal with diverse patient populations by understanding the impact of culture with regard to symptoms, diseases, and treatments." *Id.* The AAMC has "recognized that, in order to communicate effectively with patients, physicians will need to understand how a person's spirituality and culture affect how they perceive health and illness, and particularly their desires regarding end of life care." Graves, *supra* note 6, at

accrediting bodies, such as the Joint Commission on the Accreditation of Health-care Organizations (now Joint Commission) and the National Committee for Quality Assurance, have also demonstrated a commitment to providing culturally competent healthcare services.[94]

In addition to accrediting bodies, numerous professional associations have pledged support for cultural competence training.[95] Such associations include the American College of Physicians, the National Medical Association, the American Board of Internal Medicine, the American Academy of Pediatrics, the American Nurses Association, and the American Pharmacists Association.[96]

Training Culturally Competent Physicians: Instructional Methodologies

Medical schools have implemented various ways to integrate the cultural competence curriculum into medical education. Generally, medical schools have integrated cultural competency education into required courses; often those courses are taken during the first and second years of medical school.[97] Medical schools have trained students through cultural immersion, didactic and small group sessions, language skills acquisition programs, and through the use of standardized patients.

Most American medical schools use case-based instruction and/or didactic sessions to train their students to be culturally competent.[98] Some medical schools have implemented language skills acquisition programs that afford medical students the opportunity to learn another language in an effort to serve

---

353-54. Furthermore, the AAMC generated the Tool for Assessing Cultural Competency Training (TACCT) which articulates the standards for the knowledge, skills and attitudes that should be part of the instruction in cultural competence training. Association of American Medical Colleges, Tool for Assessing Cultural Competence Training (TACCT), https://www.aamc.org/initiatives/tacct/ (last visited Apr. 17, 2011). The ACGME "specifies professionalism and interpersonal and communication skills as two of six competencies it requires for resident training [and] cultural competency falls under both of those competencies, requiring residents to demonstrate the ability to effectively care for diverse patient populations." Chun, *supra* note 82, at 29.

[94]Chun, *supra* note 82, at 29. The Joint Commission stated, "It is well recognized that the individual's involvement in care decisions is not only an identified right, but is a necessary source of accurate assessment and treatment information." *Id.* The Joint Commission has several standards that support the provision of care, treatment, and services in a manner that is conducive to the cultural, language, literacy, and learning needs of individuals. *Id.*

[95]Graves, *supra* note 6, at 356.

[96]*Id.* at 357.

[97]Nisha Dogra, Sylvia Reitmanova & Olivia Carter-Pokras, *Teaching Cultural Diversity: Current Status in U.K., U.S., and Canadian Medical Schools*, 25 Journal of General Internal Medicine 164, 165 (2009).

[98]Glenn Flores, Denise Gee & Beth Kastner, *The Teaching of Cultural Issues in U.S. and Canadian Medical Schools*, 75 Academic Medicine 451, 452 (2000).

language minorities better.[99] The University of California, San Diego School of Medicine implemented a language skills acquisition program in response to difficulties that their medical students faced when communicating with Latino patients, approximately twenty-five percent of the population in San Diego.[100] The objective of the program extended beyond learning how to speak Spanish by also focusing on training students to develop a heightened sense of awareness and understanding of Latino and other cultures.[101]

Medical schools have also adopted cultural immersion programs as a means of training students to be culturally competent. The University of Massachusetts Medical School implemented a cultural immersion program that allowed students to actively engage with multicultural populations during the first two years of medical school.[102] Students participating in the cultural immersion program work with local families of various cultures to learn about the family's culture, health beliefs, healthcare experiences in the U.S., and linguistic and cultural barriers to obtaining services in the U.S.[103] Furthermore, students complete a six-week language and cultural immersion program during the summer before their second year, begin a community service project that serves culturally diverse populations, and attend seminars that focus on cultural issues that will arise within the patient-provider relationship.[104]

The final method of training medical students to be culturally competent is through the use of standardized patients. A standardized patient is a well individual who has been trained to simulate a patient's illness or a patient problem in an unvarying way so that each student participating in an exercise with the "actor" will have the same experience.[105] The "role-play" that takes place between a medical student and a standardized patient affords the student an opportunity to practice taking the medical history of a patient, conducting a physical examination, and developing communication skills.[106]

Barriers to Training Law Students to Be Culturally Competent Lawyers

The deficiency of cultural competence training for law students is apparent. Despite the fact that cross-cultural lawyering theorists have argued that lawyers

---

[99]Teresa Gonzalez-Lee & Harold J. Simon, *Teaching Spanish and Cross-Cultural Sensitivity to Medical Students*, 146 Western Journal of Medicine 502, 502 (1987).

[100]*Id.*

[101]*Id.*

[102]Michael A. Godkin & Judith A. Savageau, *The Effect of a Global Multiculturalism Track on Cultural Competence of Preclinical Medical Students*, 33 Family Medicine 178, 178 (2001).

[103]*Id.*

[104]*Id.* at 179.

[105]Howard S. Barrows, *An Overview of the Uses of Standardized Patients for Teaching and Evaluating Clinical Skills*, 68 Academic Medicine 443, 444 (1993).

[106]Amitai Ziv et al., *Simulation-Based Medical Education: An Ethical Imperative*, 78 Academic Medicine 783, 785 (2003).

and law students must develop an understanding of the role culture plays in the attorney-client relationship, little has been done to train lawyers to be culturally competent.[107] The lack of cultural competence curriculum in legal education can be attributed to the emphasis on neutrality in teaching client-centered counseling, an already overburdened law school curriculum, and a resistance to institutional change.

Neutrality is assumed to be the cornerstone of the justice system's ability to impartially apply the law.[108] Society expects neutral judges to apply the law regardless of a party's personal identity, and the justice system relies on juries to objectively perform their civic duty; however, training law students to apply "neutrality" to the attorney-client relationship can result in unfavorable consequences.

A more radical view of the role neutrality should play in law schools advocates that "law school can sufficiently retrain individuals to apply their talents regardless of personal identity.... Therefore ... race not only should not be a factor in the attorney-client relationship, but it absolutely is not a factor if law school has done its job."[109] However, a more likely view of how neutrality and law school interact would reveal that legal education, specifically clinical legal education, fails to question how "lawyer neutrality," ignoring or not ade-quately addressing cultural differences between attorneys and clients, or "standardizing clients," seeing all clients as exactly the same, hinders one's ability to serve clients effectively.[110]

A majority of law schools teach client-centered counseling as the normative framework for the attorney-client relationship.[111] Client-centered models focus on empowering the client, preserving the autonomy of client as the decision-maker, and ensuring that lawyers abide by the Model Rules of Professional Conduct.[112] Despite the noble goals of client-centered counseling, many clinical programs teach law students how to appropriately interact with clients

---

[107]Elizabeth Tobin Tyler, *Allies Not Adversaries: Teaching Collaboration to the Next Generation of Doctors and Lawyers to Address Social Inequality*, 11 J. Health Care L. & Pol'y 249, 269.

[108]Roland Acevedo, Edward Hosp & Rachel Pomerantz, *Race and Representation: A Study of Legal Aid Attorneys and Their Perceptions of the Significance of Race*, 18 Buff. Pub. Int. L.J. 1, 7 (2000).

[109]*Id.* at 11.

[110]Tyler, *supra* note 107, at 269.

[111]Jacobs, *supra* note 61, at 350.

[112]*Id.* at 348. Rule 1.2(a) states "Subject to paragraphs (c) and (d), a lawyer shall abide by a client's decisions concerning the objectives of representation and, as required by Rule 1.4, shall consult with the client as to the means by which they are to be pursued. A lawyer may take such action on behalf of the client as is impliedly authorized to carry out the representation. A lawyer shall abide by a client's decision whether to settle a matter. In a criminal case, the lawyer shall abide by the client's decision, after consultation with the lawyer, as to a plea to be entered, whether to waive jury trial and whether the client will testify." American Bar Ass'n, Model Rules of Prof'l Conduct R. 1.2 (2011), *available at* http://www.americanbar.org/groups/professional_responsibility/publications/model_rules_of_professional_conduct/rule_1_2_scope_of_representation_allocation_of_aut hority_between_client_lawyer.html.

by standardizing the client or by assuming the role of the "neutral lawyer."[113] In standardizing the client or approaching the attorney-client relationship from a neutral vantage point, law students do not acquire the requisite skills to effectively engage in attorney-client relationships where the client does not reflect the "standardized client." Thus, the ever-presence of neutrality in legal education serves a huge roadblock in law schools' ability to produce culturally competent attorneys because the application of neutrality to the attorney-client relationship directly undermines the purpose of cultural competence training.

In addition to neutrality serving as a huge barrier to law schools' ability to produce culturally competent attorneys, integrating a cultural competence curriculum into legal education faces other challenges. Law schools are tasked with preparing students to pass state bar exams. As a result, law schools have implemented curricula that are rigorous but necessary for ensuring that students will pass the bar and be competent attorneys. Given the vast number of courses students may take and requirements students must meet, the idea of adding an additional requirement to students' already heavy load might be undesirable for many law schools.

Integrating a cultural competence curriculum not only requires administrators and faculty to recognize and appreciate the importance of training culturally competent students but also requires institutional changes.[114] In order for a law school to effectively teach cultural competency, the school — the institution itself — must become more culturally competent.[115] A culturally competent institution has five essential characteristics, and an institution seeking to teach cultural competency must adopt the following five characteristics.[116] First, the institution must recognize and respect the value of diversity.[117] If the institution were a law school, the application of this first characteristic would manifest as the school's accepting "that its faculty, students and the clients the students will ultimately serve come from very different backgrounds and will make different choices based on their culture."[118] Second, the institution must undergo a "cultural self-assessment."[119] In essence, a law school, for example, "must have a sense of its own culture, how the school is shaped by that culture, and how that culture influences the school's interactions with other cultures."[120] Third, an institution must have the capacity to manage the dynamics of difference.[121] A law school "would need to be aware of how [its] culture influences [its] position on client advocacy and how [it] might perceive" another professional or graduate school's different perspectives on client advocacy.[122]

---

[113]Jacobs, *supra* note 61, at 351.

[114]Hartley & Petrucci, *supra* note 11, at 171.

[115]*Id.* at 172.

[116]*Id.*

[117]*Id.*

[118]*Id.*

[119]*Id.*

[120]*Id.*

[121]*Id.*

[122]*Id.*

The fourth element of institutional cultural competence requires the institution to "develop ways of integrating knowledge about cultures in to the institution that live beyond the individuals that make up the institution."[123] Fifth, and finally, the institution must "modify its organizational policies and structures to reflect a commitment to cultural competency."[124] All of these necessary institutional characteristics require an institution to make serious changes that are likely to meet resistance.

The final main hurdle to training law students to be culturally competent lawyers is the physical development and implementation of a cultural competence curriculum. The successful development and implementation of such a curriculum requires individuals with strong cultural competence skills to generate the curriculum, developers to design training methods that are conducive to legal education, and a willingness of the administration to foster an environment in which the cultural competence curriculum will thrive.

Proposed Method for Training Law Students to Be Culturally Competent Lawyers

Evidenced by medical schools' approach to teaching cultural competency, there are multiple ways to train students to be culturally competent professionals. However, within the legal field, there is one dominant model often referenced as the best way to train law students to be culturally competent lawyers. This model, the "Five Habits of Cross-Cultural Lawyering," outlines five professional habits for developing cross-cultural skills. The five professional habits are: (1) recognizing "degrees of separation and connection" with clients, (2) understanding the "rings of similarity and difference" among lawyers, clients, and decision-makers, (3) "parallel universe," i.e., different motivations for client behavior, (4) understanding "pitfalls, red flags, and remedies" regarding cultural differences communication, and (5) "the camel's back," involving self-evaluation of one's own cultural biases and stereotypes.[125]

The Five Habits

The "Five Habits of Cross-Cultural Lawyering" model seeks to train students to acknowledge the role racism, privilege, power, stereotypes and bias play within the attorney-client relationship and gives students the resources and tools necessary to lessen the effect of these destructive influences.[126] Furthermore, this model establishes a framework within which law students are afforded opportunities to look at potential differences and similarities that might arise within the attorney-client relationship, to gain an understanding of why individuals employ ethnocentric thinking, and to develop cross-cultural lawyering skills that include (1) intercultural communication skills (i.e., deep listening skills,

---

[123]*Id.* at 172-73.

[124]*Id.* at 173.

[125]Bryant, *supra* note 2, *passim.*

[126]Bryant, *supra* note 2, at 55.

the ability to focus on what is being said rather than how something is said and the capacity to understand non-verbal communication), (2) non-judgmental thinking, and (3) the ability to reflect and debrief while developing cross-cultural skills.[127] A critical element of this model is the effort it makes to eliminate issues that sometimes arise in diversity training.[128] Thus, this model makes a conscious effort to not (1) exclusively train White American students, (2) place an unfair burden on students of color to educate other students, and (3) impose judgment on students for holding certain biases and stereotypes.[129]

This model is founded on the assumption that if students develop five specific habits, students' cross-cultural competence will increase.[130] The first "habit" of the model is titled "Degrees of Separation and Connection."[131] This habit is designed to give students "a framework within which to analyze these questions regarding how similarities and differences between the lawyer and client may influence lawyer-client interactions, especially information gathering."[132] In order to do this, students are asked to list and diagram all the differences and similarities that they see between themselves and their clients.[133] Students who indicate that they have many similarities with clients are encouraged to reflect on their conclusion of similarities and make sure they are not overlooking differences because inaccurate assumptions of similarity can lead to gross misunderstandings.[134] Ultimately, developers of this model reason that if students develop this habit, students will have the requisite skills to conduct more effective interviews with clients and mitigate negative judgments about clients.[135]

The second habit of the model, "The Three Rings," trains students to develop the capacity to "identify and analyze the possible effects of similarities and differences on the interaction between the client, the legal decision-maker and the lawyer," and then use that information to think about the ways culture may influence the attorney-client relationship.[136] The model advocates that students be taught how to develop this habit through the use of simulations.[137] Once students have developed this habit, students are expected to have gained perspective on why certain issues may be relevant to a client that seem, at first glance, miniscule and irrelevant to the student, or why some clients will resist attorney advice and harbor mistrust for the legal system.[138] Furthermore, stu-

---

[127]*Id.* at 55-56.

[128]*Id.* at 57.

[129]*Id.* at 57-58.

[130]*Id.* at 34.

[131]*Id.* at 64.

[132]*Id.*

[133]*Id.*

[134]*Id.* at 65-66.

[135]*Id.* at 88, 93.

[136]*Id.* at 68-69.

[137]*Id.* at 88.

[138]*Id.* at 70.

dents who have developed habit two are also expected to be able to better serve her client by reexamining case strategies and by thinking of other options that take into account the concerns and viewpoints of the client.[139]

The third habit, "Parallel Universe," teaches students "a method for exploring alternative explanations for clients' behaviors."[140] The purpose of developing this habit is to encourage students to think about the plethora of possibilities that might explain certain client behavior and prevent students from making assumptions regarding client behavior.[141] Developers of the model believe that the most effective way to teach students this habit is to show videos of scenarios where a client's behavior can be misinterpreted and then engage the students in discussion.[142]

Unlike the first three habits which focus on developing different ways of approaching the attorney-client relationship, habit four, "Pitfalls, Red Flags and Remedies," focuses on developing cross-cultural communication skills, "identifying tasks in the normal attorney-client interaction that may be particularly problematic in cross-cultural encounters as well as alerting students to signs of communication problems."[143] The developers of this model suggest that the way to teach this habit to students is through "watching and interpreting videotapes, conducting simulated role play in class, ... engaging in reflection," and having students participate in supervised meetings with actual clients.[144] The developers believe that through these teaching methods, students will be able to better understand why it is important to (1) develop multiple ways to talk to clients about confidentiality, the legal system, and other issues pertinent to the client, (2) pay attention to a client's introductory rituals, (3) acquire active listening skills and develop ways to gain feedback from the client which indicates that the client understands the attorney, and (4) cultivate a heightened sense of awareness regarding communication "red flags" (i.e. indications that the client is angry, frustrated, confused, etc.) and ways to address the "red flags" immediately.[145]

The fifth and final habit, "The Camel's Back," encourages students to engage in a self-evaluation of one's own cultural biases and stereotypes.[146] Development of this habit will allow students to prevent bias and stereotypes from adversely affecting the attorney-client relationship in addition to encouraging students to abandon their own biases and stereotypes.[147] The model suggests teaching this habit to students via in-depth conversations in which the students

---

[139]*Id.*

[140]*Id.*

[141]*Id.* at 71.

[142]*Id.* at 90.

[143]*Id.* at 72.

[144]*Id.* at 94.

[145]*Id.* at 76.

[146]*Id.* at 77.

[147]*Id.*

are asked to talk about how their own behavior or thinking changes in relation to different clients.[148]

What the Legal Profession Can Learn from the Medical Profession

The medical profession has discovered an abundance of ways to train students to become culturally competent physicians, and the legal profession can learn how to effectively train law students to be culturally competent lawyers by mirroring the medical profession. Similar to the medical profession, the legal profession can utilize federal and state legislation and accrediting bodies as support for the development and implementation of instructional methodologies with the capacity to effectively train law students to be culturally competent attorneys.

State and Federal Legislation and Accrediting Bodies

If the appropriate federal agencies and offices supported cultural competence training for licensure and accreditation or as part of legal education, then the potential for states to adopt legislation mandating the integration of cultural competence curriculum would greatly increase. However, even if the legal profession did not find support on the federal level for the integration of a cultural competence curriculum into legal education, support on the state level would still make an enormous difference and ignite positive change in legal education.

Licensure and accrediting requirements are powerful tools at the disposal of the legal profession that have the ability to modify legal education. Currently, in most states, individuals seeking to obtain a license to practice law must pass the Multistate Professional Responsibility Exam (MPRE). Thus, incorporating a few questions that have the capacity to determine whether a student has undergone cultural competence training would be an ideal way to ensure that cultural competence training became a part of legal education.

Accrediting bodies, such as the American Bar Association (ABA) and state accrediting agencies, have the ability to impact legal education by implementing requirements. Accrediting bodies also have the capability to address and mitigate some of the barriers to the integration of the cultural competence curriculum into legal education. All ABA-accredited law schools must follow accrediting standards; thus, if the ABA required cultural competence training as part of legal training, then law schools would begin to train their students to be culturally competent. Accrediting standards also effectively eliminate resistance to institutional change because the alternative to not adopting accrediting standards will likely result in gross consequences law schools are often unwilling to assume. An advantage of an accrediting body's executing a requirement for cultural competence training is the notion of fairness. If the ABA were to impose a cultural competence training requirement on law schools, any arguments from the schools articulating the above concern that the law school cur-

---

[148]*Id.* at 89.

riculum is already overburdened would be ameliorated by noting that the burden would rest on the shoulders of all law schools. Additionally, if cultural competence training is required for licensure either through states adopting legislation or through the MPRE, there is no guarantee that all law students in all states will receive cultural competence training.

Development and Implementation of Cultural Competence Curriculum in Legal Education

The biggest challenge the legal profession faces with regard to the development of cultural competence curriculum is the fact that law school faculty have not been trained to be culturally competent lawyers. Thus, it is essential for law school faculty to acquire cultural competence training from the few legal professionals who are well-versed in cultural competence education, the medical profession, and other professions that have implemented cultural competence training curriculum into their educational programs. Once the law faculty has the knowledge and skills necessary to develop and implement a cultural competence curriculum into legal education, law schools can adapt the instructional methodologies of cultural competence training in medical education (i.e., cultural immersion, didactic and small group discussions, language skills acquisition, and standardized patients) or the proposed "Five Habits" method of teaching cultural competence curriculum to legal education.

Law schools already afford students opportunities to interact with clients through pro bono programs, clinics, and externships, and these opportunities serve as perfect venues to train students to be culturally competent. In clinics, externships, and pro bono placements, students gain insight into the attorney-client relationship and the importance of creating a trusting environment and the necessity of being able to effectively communicate with a client. Any law school faculty member who advises and teaches students how to interact with clients when students are participating in externships, pro bono placements, or clinics should strongly consider abandoning teaching neutrality in client-centered counseling. Instead, faculty should focus on teaching students to recognize cultural similarities with, and differences between, themselves and clients in addition to communication "red flags," through group discussions, exercises, and simulations or role-play. When students are not participating in clinics, externships, or pro bono placements, law faculty should mirror the concept of the "standardized patient" in medical education and use a "standardized client" to train students to build upon their cultural competence. The use of the "standardized client" to enhance law students' cultural competence training might fit well into legal profession or professional responsibility courses and courses which focus on issues of individual rights and criminal procedure.

Currently, two law schools, Hamline University School of Law and Thomas M. Cooley Law School, have integrated cultural competence training into their curricula. Thomas M. Cooley Law School has designed an elective course entitled "Cultural Competence and the Law" that gives students an opportunity to "examine the impact of culture on diverse users of the civil and criminal justice systems."[149] Students also have a chance to "develop their own cultural awareness as they being to recognize the importance for them as future lawyers and judges" to maintain a heightened sense of awareness of the impact culture has on the ability to ensure justice.[150]

Hamline University Law School recognizes the importance of teaching students how to effectively communicate in cross-cultural settings.[151] In the Trial Practice clinic, the clinic director devotes time to "exploring how culture, race and gender differences affect the attorney-client relationship and how to confront race and gender bias in representation."[152] Students must prepare to discuss the effect of culture on the attorney-client relationship and bias in representation, and thus are asked to "define culture, describe their own cultural background and how it shapes their world view, and to discuss how understanding culture and cultural differences can assist attorneys."[153] Furthermore, students are encouraged to engage in a self-assessment of how their own culture or perspective might lead them to make false assumptions or appear disrespectful to a client. In the clinic, students are trained in how to conduct a cross-cultural interview which requires students to "ask open-ended questions, take plenty of time in interviews, ask follow-up questions, attempt to learn the context as well as the facts, ask clients how they feel about the situation and what they would like to see happen."[154]

Hamline University School of Law and Thomas M. Cooley Law School have been successful in implementing cultural competency instruction into their curricula. Ideally, other schools would look to both law schools for inspiration and guidance on how to successfully implement cultural competency training into their curriculum.

IV. Conclusion

Cynthia Enloe, in *The Curious Feminist*, suggests that everyone wears "lenses," whether knowingly or unconsciously; and the "lenses" that we all wear shape how one looks at situations and how one views the world and environments that we find ourselves in. The time is ripe for law students, like medical students, to consciously wear a pair "cultural lenses." Law students need to understand that culture is a dynamic shared system of beliefs, values, and learned patterns of behavior that are shaped by factors such as proximity, education, gender, age, and sexual preference. Law students need to understand that culture manifests as different languages, levels of acculturation, and socioeconomic status. Most importantly, law students need to understand that culture

---

[149]Cynthia M. Ward, *The Role of Law Schools in Shaping Culturally Competent Lawyers*, 89 Michigan B.J. 16, 18 (2010).

[150]*Id.*

[151]Angela McCaffrey, *Hamline University School of Law Clinics: Teaching Students to Become Ethical and Competent Lawyers for Twenty-Five Years*, 24 Hamline J. Pub. L & Pol'y 1, 57 (2002).

[152]*Id.*

[153]*Id.*

[154]*Id.* at 58.

impacts all relationships — and how not understanding culture will limit one's ability to effectively serve as a trusted professional and advocate for the best interests of a client. However, law students cannot develop the requisite skills to have success in cross-cultural attorney-client relationships on their own; law students need the support of legal institutions.

Law schools must recognize the imperative nature of heightening students' awareness of issues such as the inequality in the application of the law to persons of color — and how divergent expectations of success for minorities in education impacts the legal system and racially discordant attorney-client relationships. Law schools need to recognize that they need to train students to develop solutions that would mitigate the adverse effects of racially discordant attorney-client relationships. Once a law student becomes an attorney, she should not enter attorney-client relationships and feel limited by her agency. If law students are taught to consciously wear a pair of cultural lenses, to be culturally competent, they will become attorneys that have a heightened sense of awareness of the cultural issues that may plague the attorney-client relationship, in addition to acquiring the skill set necessary to successfully overcome cultural barriers.

14

The Ethics of False Guilty Pleas Under Modern Moral Philosophies

Clinton H. Smith

I. Introduction

James Ochoa, an innocent man later exonerated by DNA evidence, voluntarily pled guilty to a crime he did not commit.[1] Ochoa had just been released from prison after serving a six-month sentence for drug possession. Shortly after his release, he was arrested and accused of armed robbery and carjacking. Police officers and the district attorney alleged that Ochoa had robbed two men with a pellet gun and stolen their car. After pleading guilty, Ochoa was sentenced to two years in prison.

Some of the circumstances surrounding the crime certainly indicated that Ochoa may have been involved. Police officers recovered the stolen car close to Ochoa's home, and the stolen car contained the clothes worn by the robber. In addition, the pellet gun used during the crime fell from the rear bumper when the car was towed. Both victims, to a varying extent, identified Ochoa as the perpetrator of the crime. However, other evidence suggested that Ochoa was not involved. Police officers recovered DNA from the clothes in the stolen vehicle, but it was linked to another individual. Furthermore, Ochoa persistently claimed his innocence throughout interrogation and investigation.

Prior to trial, the prosecutor offered Ochoa two years in state prison in exchange for a guilty plea. Ochoa initially turned down the prosecutor's offer, believing he could prove his innocence at trial. Prior to the trial, the presiding judge informed Ochoa that an additional conviction would make him a repeat offender and that Ochoa would face a life sentence if convicted. Ochoa was forced to reweigh his options. His attorney, so convinced of his innocence, offered to represent Ochoa for free if he would reject the plea deal. Although he knew he was innocent, Ochoa rejected his attorney's offer and accepted the guilty plea — "he was afraid of what would happen if the jury found him guilty."[2] Fortunately, Ochoa was freed ten months later; he was cleared by the DNA evidence recovered from the crime scene.

Although Ochoa accepted the guilty plea against his attorney's advice, this is not always the case. Some attorneys who know their client is innocent advise their client to accept the offer, and never disclose their knowledge to the court.[3]

---

[1]H.G. Reza, *Innocent Man Grabs His Freedom and Leaves Town*, L.A. Times, Nov. 2, 2006, *available at* http://articles.latimes.com/2006/nov/02/local/me-wrong2 (last visited April 12, 2011). Further details set out below are from this news report.

[2]*Id.*

[3]*See infra* Part II.

However, those actions are contrary to the American Bar Association's Model Rules of Professional Conduct ("Model Rules") because they require the attorney to make misrepresentations to the court.[4] It is unlikely that those attorneys are seeking to behave unethically. Rather, the attorneys likely believe they are acting ethically and that the Model Rules are simply wrong.

After analyzing the proper behavior under applicable standards of legal ethics, this Comment explores whether those attorneys' typical actions are considered moral or ethical under modern moral philosophies. Part II explores false guilty pleas, Part III analyzes false guilty pleas under the Model Rules, and Part IV provides an analysis under modern moral philosophies. Part V concludes that, although Model Rule 3.3 creates hardship on the particular attorney and defendant, the attorney's required disclosure brings the ethical issue out into the open, which could lead to reform that eliminates the problem at its source.

II. Plea Bargaining and False Guilty Pleas

Plea bargaining is generally an agreement between a defendant, a prosecutor, and a judge in which the defendant pleads guilty to a lesser crime or a reduced sentence compared to what the defendant would face if found guilty at trial.[5] Plea bargaining is a common occurrence in American criminal law. The percentage of criminal defendants who plead guilty in the United States is approximately 95 percent[6] — almost one defendant every two seconds.[7] Plea bargaining has both proponents[8] and critics.[9]

---

[4]*See infra* Part III.

[5]Michael W. Smith, *Making the Innocent Guilty: Plea Bargaining and the False Plea Convictions of the Innocent*, 46 No. 5 Crim. L. Bulletin Art. 4 (2010).

[6]*Id.*; *see also* Timothy Lynch, *The Case Against Plea Bargaining*, Regulation, Fall 2003, *available at* http://www.cato.org/pubs/regulation/regv26n3/v26n3-7.pdf ("Fewer than 10 percent of the criminal cases brought by the federal government each year are actually tried before juries.... More than 90 percent of the criminal cases in America are never tired, much less proven, to juries."). In comparison, Italy's overall guilty plea rate is 8%, while Germany has a plea rate of 20-30%. Smith, *supra* note 5.

[7]Allison D. Redlich, *The Susceptibility of Juveniles to False Confessions and False Guilty Pleas*, 62 Rutgers L. Rev 943, 944 (2010).

[8]Proponents of plea bargaining often argue that it is in the defendant's best interest because it provides a choice of surrendering the right to go to trial in exchange for rights the defendant values more. *See* Smith, *supra* note 5. Other proponents argue that it promotes efficiency and reduces the costs of the criminal justice system, allows public defenders to concentrate on the more serious crimes, provides certainty to defendants, is easier on witnesses, and that the negotiation process promotes justice. *Id.*

[9]*See, e.g.*, Lynch, *supra* note 6 (arguing that the practice of plea bargaining should be abolished as unconstitutional). Critics of plea bargaining argue that the process is inherently flawed because *Brady* materials, which prosecutors must turn over before trial, do not have to be turned over prior to the defendant's deadline to plea — therefore the defendant does not truly know the information necessary for an informed plea. Smith, *supra* note 5. Additionally, critics also claim that plea bargaining permits prosecutors and judges to abuse their power, reduces investigation by defense attorneys, permits

The typical plea bargain involves an exchange of words between the judge, the prosecutor, the defendant, and the defendant's attorney. Although the exact dialogue may differ according to local rules, the substance is consistent. The judge will ask the defendant a series of questions to verify that the defendant is fully aware of the charges and the effect of his guilty plea. The judge will also ask whether the defendant is tendering the guilty plea because he is in fact guilty. Furthermore, the judge will ask the defendant's attorney whether there is any reason that the defendant should not plead guilty.

Although there is little research available on false guilty pleas, various studies confirm they do occur.[10] The data also indicates that false guilty pleas are not limited to susceptible classes of individuals such as juveniles[11] or the mentally disabled.[12] Recent evidence on DNA exonerations provides some insight into the frequency of false guilty pleas. One study showed that of 214 adults exonerated by DNA evidence, roughly 8% had pled guilty.[13] Another study verified similar results and found that of 340 exonerated individuals, roughly 6% had pled guilty.[14] Some scholars also believe that false guilty pleas are more prevalent than false confessions[15] — which occurred in 15% of exonerations between 1989 through 2003[16] — because guilty pleas account for a majority of convictions, defendants pleading guilty often waive numerous rights including the right to appeal, and because the weakest evidentiary cases are the most

---

truly guilty defendants to receive more lenient sentences, and "induces innocent defendants to commit perjury by falsely stating they committed the crime." *Id.*

[10]*See* Allison D. Redlich et al., *Self-Reported False Confessions and False Guilty Pleas Among Offenders with Mental Illness*, 34 Law & Hum. Behav. 79, 80 (2010) [hereinafter *Self-Reported False Confessions*] ("[L]ittle research has been done on [false guilty pleas].").

[11]*See* Joshua A. Tepfer et al., *Arresting Development: Convictions of Innocent Youth*, 62 Rutgers L. Rev. 887, 914 (2010) (finding that youth DNA exonerees pled guilty at lower rate than adult DNA exonerees).

[12]*See Self-Reported False Confessions*, *supra* note 10, at 89 (estimating a 7.7% false guilty plea rate for offenders cycling through the criminal justice system and with mental illness, and ultimately concluding that false confessions and false guilty pleas "are not unfortunate anomalies in the criminal justice system but rather are unfortunately common").

[13]Tepfer et al., *supra* note 11, at 914.

[14]Samuel L. Gross et al., *Exonerations in the United States 1989 Through 2003*, 95 J. Crim. L. & Criminology 523, 536 (2005).

[15]A false confession generally occurs at the investigation stage and is not the equivalent of a conviction. A false guilty plea occurs before a court and is an admittance of guilt. There is some relation between the two, with false confessions likely increasing the possibility of a false guilty plea. *See, e.g.,* Peter A. Joy, *Brady and Jailhouse Informants: Responding to Injustice*, 57 Case W. Res. L. Rev. 619, 627 (2007) ("In a more recent study, research documented fourteen false guilty pleas out of 125 proven false confessions — eleven percent of their sample.") (citing Steven Drizin, *False Guilty Pleas: DNA Clears Man in Carjacking Case*, Bluhm Blog (Nov. 4, 2006, 8:29 PM), http://blog.law.northwestern.edu/bluhm/2006/11/false_guilty_pl.html).

[16]Gross et al., *supra* note 14, at 544.

likely to end with a guilty plea.[17] Since criminal defendants facing a prison sentence have a constitutional right to counsel,[18] the vast majority of innocent defendants pleading guilty are represented by attorneys.

Initially, it is difficult to understand why a defendant would consciously plead guilty and accept a prison sentence for a crime he knew he did not commit.[19] However, there are multiple plausible and logical explanations. A defendant's loss of faith in the criminal justice system provides one explanation for false guilty pleas. As illustrated by Melanie D. Wilson:

> [I]t makes sense that a defendant would lose confidence that the system would exonerate him, if police are willing to lie to make the evidence look as though he is guilty. If the police are telling lies about the defendant's criminal involvement and the amount or strength of the evidence, it is not irrational to think that they will continue to lie and lie convincingly to a jury, resulting in conviction and a severe sentence. If police, who have access to, and control over, all of the trial evidence, are willing to lie to convict a defendant, there is little incentive to fight the lies, even if the defendant is innocent. If the result — a conviction — is inevitable, then the logical action to take is to seek the most lenient sentencing solution available.[20]

However, not all explanations are based upon subjective fears or losing faith in the criminal justice system. It may actually be in an innocent defendant's best interest to plead guilty when the risks of trial are perceived as more severe than the maximum sentence through a guilty plea.[21] Similar to Ochoa's

---

[17] *See Self-Reported False Confessions*, supra note 10, at 80; *see also* Gross et al., *supra* note 14, at 536.

[18] The United States Supreme Court has held that in all federal cases, counsel must be appointed to defendants who lack the financial resources to hire their own. Johnson v. Zerbst, 304 U.S. 458 (1938). A similar rule applies to defendants in state court — defendants who cannot afford counsel and are either facing a felony charge or any charge resulting in imprisonment have a constitutional right to counsel. *See* Scott v. Illinois, 440 U.S. 367 (1979); Argersinger v. Hamlin, 407 U.S. 25 (1972).

[19] The definition of "false guilty plea" could encompass a variety of situations. For example, it could extend as far as when the defendant is guilty of one crime, but pleads to a lesser crime for which she is innocent. This Comment primarily addresses defendants not guilty of any crimes but when there is some factual basis for the charges. I will refer to that client as the innocent client or innocent defendant. The ethics issues raised in this Comment are more acute when the defendant is wholly innocent but are also similarly problematic in other forms of false pleas. In addition, this Comment does not consider, but may be relevant to, false pleas induced by delusion or mental impairment.

[20] Melanie D. Wilson, *An Exclusionary Rule for Police Lies*, 47 Am. Crim. L. Rev. 1, 21 (2010).

[21] Kent Roach, *Wrongful Convictions: Adversarial and Inquisitorial Themes*, 35 N.C. J. Int'l L. & Com. Reg. 387, 397 (2010) ("The guilty plea sentencing reduction that characterizes Anglo-American systems presents a particular risk that innocent people who fear receiving a higher sentence if convicted at trial will plead guilty in order to receive a more lenient sentence."); *see also* Redlich, *supra* note 7, at 943 (describing defendants' decisions to plead guilty as "based on numerous factors, including their understanding of the law, the perceived strength of evidence against them, the probability of conviction at trial, the value of the plea offer (the distance between the sentence if convicted at trial

case, the defendant may rather accept the certainty of a short sentence than risk the chance of a much longer sentence — even though he knows he is innocent.[22]

Additional explanations surround the practice of detaining defendants prior to trial. If the defendant has been at a correctional facility awaiting his trial and the prosecutor offers a plea deal with time served, resulting in his immediate release, he would not likely turn down the offer and spend another six months in jail to prove his innocence at trial — risking additional jail time if found guilty.[23] In some of these cases, it would be hard to argue that it is not in the defendant's best interest to plead guilty. Since an attorney has the responsibility of providing the defendant with all information necessary for an informed decision, these facts are presumably disclosed to defendants and form the basis of their decisions.[24]

III. False Guilty Pleas and the American Bar Association's Model Rules of Professional Conduct

Although false guilty pleas overwhelmingly affect the individual defendant as she is the one serving any prison sentence, false guilty pleas also implicate a lawyer's ethical duties. As a representative of her client, the attorney must consider her client's best interests and represent those interests zealously.[25] However, an attorney's duties extend beyond just the client that she is representing.[26] An attorney also owes a duty of honesty toward tribunals as an officer of the court and a representative of the justice system.[27] When an attorney believes it is in her innocent client's best interests to plead guilty, she is placed in the position of choosing between being a zealous advocate and an officer of the court: the attorney's duty of honesty towards the court does not allow counseling acceptance and remaining silent while the innocent defendant pleads guilty, but the duty to zealously represent her client suggests that she should. Similar to any conflict or ethical question, the Model Rules promulgated by the American Bar Association and influential in state bars and courts are the first place to look for an answer.[28]

---

and the proposed plea sentence), the advice and perceived effectiveness of attorneys, perceptions of procedural justice, etc.").

[22]Joy, *supra* note 15, at 625 ("[S]ome innocent defendants plead guilty in order to secure a certain short sentence or avoid the possibility of a death sentence."); *see also* Reza, *supra* note 1.

[23]Smith, *supra* note 5.

[24]American Bar Association, Model Rules of Prof'l Conduct R. 1.4(b) (2010).

[25]Model Rules of Prof'l Conduct, Preamble (2010).

[26]"A lawyer, as a member of the legal profession, is a representative of clients, an officer of the legal system and a public citizen having special responsibility for the quality of justice." *Id.*

[27]*Id.*; *see also* Model Rules of Prof'l Conduct R. 3.3 (2010).

[28]The Model Rules are intended to be a guide for states implementing their own code of legal ethics. Approximately forty-three jurisdictions have adopted the Model Rules in full or in part. Richard Zitrin et al., Legal Ethics: Rules, Statutes, and Comparisons x

Several of the Model Rules and its comments are applicable. Model Rule 1.2(a) provides that "a lawyer shall abide by a client's decisions concerning the objectives of representation."[29] Model Rule 1.2(a) further provides that "[i]n a criminal case, the lawyer shall abide by the client's decision, after consultation with the lawyer, as to a plea to be entered...."[30] At first glance, these rules appear to indicate that the client has the ultimate authority to falsely plead guilty and that the attorney has no means of recourse. However, comment 1 to Model Rule 1.2 clarifies that the purpose of the above rules "confers upon the client the ultimate authority to determine the purposes to be served by legal representation, within the limits imposed by law and the lawyer's professional obligations."[31]

The limits imposed by law and the lawyer's professional obligations are found in later rules. Rule 3.3(a)(1) provides that "a lawyer shall not knowingly .... make a false statement of fact or law to a tribunal or fail to correct a false statement of material fact or law previously made to the tribunal by the lawyer." Furthermore, an attorney cannot "offer evidence that the lawyer knows to be false. If ... the lawyer's client ... has offered material evidence and the lawyer comes to know of its falsity, the lawyer shall take reasonable remedial measures."[32]

During a guilty plea, the court will ask the defendant whether she is in fact guilty, and ask the attorney whether there is any reason why the defendant should not plead guilty. Under the Model Rules, the lawyer cannot testify that she knows no reason why her client should not plead guilty. Furthermore, the attorney cannot remain silent while her client admits guilt; she knows the statement is false, and a failure to make a corrective disclosure is likely treated as an affirmative misrepresentation.[33] Failing to remedy the false testimony makes the attorney a party cooperating to deceive the court and subvert "the truth finding process which the adversary system is designed to implement."[34] Therefore, when the attorney's duties to represent the best interests of her client conflict with her duty of candor toward the tribunal, the Model Rules find the latter more important.[35]

(2010). Since some form of the Model Rules is applicable in a large majority of the states, they will form the basis of the ethical rules in this Comment. In addition, the rules of truthfulness and zealous advocacy are similar in all jurisdictions, even those not directly applying a version of the Model Rules.

[29]Model Rules of Prof'l Conduct R. 1.2(a) (2010).

[30]*Id.* [Rule 1.2(a), and the problem of client autonomy and paternalism, are also discussed, in a different context, in Chapter 6.]

[31]Model Rules of Prof'l Conduct R. 1.2 cmt. 1 (2010).

[32]Model Rules of Prof'l Conduct R. 3.3(a)(2) (2010).

[33]Model Rules of Prof'l Conduct R. 3.3 cmt. 3 (2010).

[34]Model Rules of Prof'l Conduct R. 3.3 cmt. 11 (2010).

[35]*See* Model Rules of Prof'l Conduct R. 3.3 cmt. 2 (2010) ("Performance of [the duty to act as an advocate] is qualified by the advocate's duty of candor to the tribunal.... [T]he lawyer must not allow the tribunal to be mislead false statement of law or fact or evidence that the lawyer knows to be false."). The rules apply in full force to criminal

Not only do the Model Rules find the latter more important, the rules suggest a variety of corrective measures that should be taken.[36] There are different courses of action depending upon whether the false statement has already been made or if it is about to be made. Scholars generally agree that if the client has not yet offered false evidence, the lawyer should first attempt to persuade her client not to make the false statements.[37] If unsuccessful, and the false statement has not yet occurred, the lawyer should generally refuse to offer the testimony.[38] However, criminal cases are unique. The right to accept or reject a guilty plea is a constitutional right belonging to the defendant.[39]

When the defendant has a constitutional right to testify and accept a guilty plea, a harmonious reading of the Model Rules provides a rough guideline for remedial steps the attorney should take.[40] If persuading the client is unsuccessful, the attorney may seek to withdraw from representation.[41] But a court may not permit withdrawal if it would be prejudicial to the client.[42] If withdrawal is not permitted, the lawyer should likely wait and see whether her client actually offers a false guilty plea before prematurely disclosing confidential information and impacting the defendant's constitutional rights.[43] If the innocent client later accepts the guilty plea or if the attorney comes to know that the guilty plea was in fact false, the attorney has further obligations to the

---

defense attorneys, even though the situation implicates constitutional rights. *See* Model Rules of Prof'l Conduct R. 3.3 cmt. 7 (2010).

[36]Model Rules of Prof'l Conduct R. 3.3(b) (2010) ("[A] lawyer who represents a client in an adjudicative proceeding and who knows that a person intends to engage, is engaging or has engaged in criminal or fraudulent conduct related to the proceeding shall take reasonable remedial measures, including, if necessary, disclosure to the tribunal.").

[37]Model Rules of Prof'l Conduct R. 3.3 cmt. 6 (2010); *see also* Donald Liskov, *Criminal Defendant Perjury: A Lawyer's Choice Between Ethics, the Constitution, and the Truth,* 28 New Eng. L. Rev. 881, 900 (1994).

[38]Model Rules of Prof'l Conduct R. 3.3 cmt. 6 (2010).

[39]Jenia Iontcheva Turner, *Legal Ethics in International Criminal Defense,* 10 Chi. J. Int'l L. 685, 730-31 (2010) (citing *Jones v. Barnes,* 463 U.S. 745, 751 (1983)). It is often said that while a criminal defendant has a right to testify and the right to effective assistance, there is no constitutional right to commit perjury. *See* Brian Slipakoff & Roshini Thayaparan, *The Criminal Defense Attorney Facing Prospective Client Perjury,* 15 Geo. J. Legal Ethics 935, 950 (2002) (citing *Nix v. Whiteside,* 475 U.S. 157, 173 (1986)).

[40]*See* Slipakoff & Thayaparan, *supra* note 39, at 947-55 (discussing the different remedial methods that can be used when an attorney knows of perspective client perjury); *see also* Liskov, *supra* note 37, at 899-907.

[41]Model Rules of Prof'l Conduct R. 3.3 cmt. 10 (2010). Some scholars criticize this as an alternative as it likely just passes the problem on to the next lawyer. *See* Slipakoff & Thayaparan, *supra* note 39, at 953 (citing Norman Lefstein, *Client Perjury in Criminal Cases: Still in Search of an Answer,* 1 Geo. J. Legal Ethics 520, 538 (1988)).

[42]Model Rules of Prof'l Conduct R. 1.16(c) (2010).

[43]*See* Orange County Bar Association Ethics and Professionalism Committee, *Formal Opinion 2003-01—Client Perjury and the Criminal Defense Attorney,* Orange County Lawyer, Jan. 2004, at 24 [hereinafter Orange County] ("Disclosure to the court regarding the client's intention to testify is another disfavored option.").

tribunal. The attorney must again counsel with her client about her duty of honesty towards the tribunal and attempt to persuade her client to remedy the false statement.[44] If unsuccessful, the attorney must disclose to the tribunal the amount of information "reasonably necessary to remedy the situation," even if that information is confidential.[45]

The only flexibility comes through the narrow definition of knows, known, or knowingly.[46] The Model Rules only apply as a mandatory matter when a lawyer *knowingly* makes a false statement, *knows* that her client will be making a false statement, or *knows* that her client has made a false statement.[47] A reasonable belief is not enough to trigger the obligations,[48] as the definition of knows, knowingly, or known "denotes actual knowledge of the fact in question."[49] Furthermore, any doubts regarding whether the information is false should be resolved in favor of the client.[50]

However, not all states follow the definition of knowledge contained in the Model Rules. Most jurisdictions find that "'knowledge' means something less than 'actual knowledge.'"[51] The states' definitions fall along a spectrum[52] and include a good cause belief, compelling support, knowledge beyond a reasonable basis, a factual basis, a firm factual basis, or a good faith determination.[53] Given the states' various definitions of knowledge, it is realistic to believe that there are in fact situations where an attorney knows, under the definition of knowledge in her jurisdiction, that her client is innocent.[54] Therefore, attorneys

---

[44]Model Rules of Prof'l Conduct R 3.3 cmt. 10 (2010).

[45]Model Rules of Prof'l Conduct R. 3.3 cmt. 7 (2010).

[46]*See* Monroe H. Freedman, Lawyer's Ethics in an Adversary System 57 (1975) (concluding that the American Bar Association's standard of knowledge places the lawyer "under an apparent, but really nonexistent, obligation to violate the client's trust").

[47]Model Rules of Prof'l Conduct R. 3.3(a)(1), (3) (2010) (emphasis added).

[48]Model Rules of Prof'l Conduct R. 3.3 cmt. 8 (2010). The Model Rules are triggered upon actual knowledge, and the comments make it clear that an attorney can present evidence to the trier of fact that he reasonably believes to be false. *Id.*

[49]Model Rules of Prof'l Conduct R. 1.0(f) (2010).

[50]Model Rules of Prof'l Conduct R. 3.3 cmt. 8 (2010).

[51]Erin K. Jaskot & Christopher J. Mulligan, *Witness Testimony and the Knowledge Requirement: An Atypical Approach to Defining Knowledge and its Effect on the Lawyer as an Officer of the Court*, 17 Geo. J. Legal Ethics 845, 862 (2004).

[52]*Id.* at 847; Slipakoff & Thayaparan, *supra* note 39, at 942-46 (2002) ("Knowledge may be represented along a spectrum."); Susan E. Thrower, *How Can I Confuse Thee: Let Me Count the Ways: An Argument for a Due Process-Based Reality in the Ethics Rules Governing Lawyer Confidentiality and Candor*, 34 J. Legal Prof. 329, 347 (2010) ("[N]o consensus exists across jurisdictions as to when a lawyer has knowledge.").

[53]*See* Thrower, *supra* note 52, at 347-49 (listing nine different standards of knowledge); Orange County, *supra* note 43, at 22 (noting the variation in the definition of knowledge); *see generally* Jaskot & Mulligan, *supra* note 51 (discussing some of the differing standards of knowledge and its impact upon Model Rule 3.3).

[54]Turner, *supra* note 39, at 729 (explaining how an attorney would know that his client is innocent when there is "a corroborated alibi that the client now unconvincingly claims is false"). It could also occur when the client actually tells the lawyer that he intends to

have likely confronted this ethical conflict in practice — and the evidence indicates that some have allowed their innocent client to plead guilty.

IV. Searching Beyond: An Analysis of False Guilty Pleas Under Modern Moral Philosophies

It is unlikely that these attorneys are affirmatively seeking to act unethically when counseling acceptance of the guilty plea and standing by silently as their client admits guilt. Rather, the attorneys likely believe that in such a situation the true ethical choice is to allow the innocent defendant to plead guilty. The following section seeks to provide an attorney's analysis and outcome if he decided to consult modern moral philosophy, rather than the Model Rules, to decide the issue.

The two moral philosophies analyzed in the following section are utilitarianism and the categorical imperative. Utilitarianism and the categorical imperative represent two different schools of thought in modern moral philosophy. Utilitarianism is a consequentialist theory, meaning that decisions are ethical based upon their consequences to others.[55] The categorical imperative is a deontological theory, which means that an act is either good or bad regardless of the consequences of the action — whether it is ethical is based upon the reason and rationality of the act.[56]

A. Utilitarianism

Utilitarianism is an ethical philosophy proposed by David Hume and refined by both Jeremy Bentham and John Stuart Mill.[57] It arose during periods of mass change in social structure and in "the new 'ideas of liberty, equality, [and] fraternity.'"[58] Accordingly, its consequentialist roots are apparent since it was as much targeted toward social reform as an abstract idea in thought.[59]

In essence, the classic version of the theory— *act utilitarianism* — states that morality or an ethical decision is nothing more than a choice that creates the most amount of pleasure or happiness.[60] The theory "requires that whenever we have a choice between alternative actions or social policies, we must choose the one that has the best overall consequences for everyone con-

---

accept the guilty plea because he views it as less risky than going to trial. *See* Orange County, *supra* note 43, at 22; *see also* Reza, *supra* note 1.

[55]Henry R. West, Mill's Utilitarianism 3 (2007).

[56]*Id.* at 4.

[57]James Rachels, The Elements of Moral Philosophy 79 (1986).

[58]*Id.* at 79.

[59]*Id.* at 81.

[60]J. S. Mill, Utilitarianism 55 (Roger Crisp, ed. 1998) ("The creed which accepts as the foundation of morals, Utility, or the Greatest Happiness Principle, holds that actions are right in proportion as they tend to promote happiness, wrong as they tend to produce the reverse of happiness."); *see also* Rachels, supra note 57, at 80.

cerned."[61] Happiness and pleasure is the only thing that matters,[62] but there are different levels of happiness — intellectual pleasures such as feelings and emotions are qualitatively better than mere physical satisfaction.[63] No individual's happiness is given more weight than any other individual, and it is not solely the actor's happiness that matters, but that of society in general.[64] The ends *always* justify the means, but the end is *always* the greatest amount of pleasure or happiness for society.[65]

An attorney using act utilitarianism would therefore have to determine whether counseling the defendant to accept the plea and remaining silent during acceptance creates the most amount of happiness.[66] The attorney's first step in the process would be to determine whom is affected by his choice. This would include himself, the defendant, the judge, and the prosecutor. However, utilitarianism requires the attorney to consider the broader implications of society as well.

Second, the attorney would have to determine how the particular parties would be affected. The following paragraphs illustrate the impact that the attorney might consider for each party. Beginning with the defendant, the attorney would attempt to analyze what decision creates the most amount of satisfaction or pleasure for each party. Assuming there is a high possibility of conviction at trial, the defendant should be happier with the attorney's guidance

---

[61]Rachels, *supra* note 57, at 80.

[62]Mill, *supra* note 60, at 55 ("[P]leasure, and freedom from pain, are the only things desirable as ends...."); *see also* Rachels, *supra* note 57, at 90.

[63]Mill, *supra* note 60, at 56 ("It is quite compatible with the principle of utility to recognise the fact, that some *kinds* of pleasure are more desirable and more valuable than others.") (emphasis in original); *see also* West, *supra* note 55, at 43 (noting Mill's description of intellectual, emotional, and imaginative pleasures as having higher value than mere sensations).

[64]Mill, *supra* note 60, at 59 ("[T]hat standard is not the agent's own greatest happiness, but the greatest amount of happiness altogether...."); *see also* Rachels, *supra* note 57, at 90.

[65]Mill, *supra* note 60, at 55 ("[P]leasure, and freedom from pain, are the only things desirable as ends...."); *see also* Rachels, *supra* note 57, at 90 (citing John Stuart Mill, Utilitarianism (1861)). Critics challenged the traditional idea of act utilitarianism on several grounds, including that it could label decisions as "ethical" when it is counterintuitive to our own common sense of justice. *Id.* For example, torturing an individual could be thought of as an ethical choice if it brought more happiness to the general public than the harm caused to the person tortured. *Id.* Additionally, the idea of "happiness" being discoverable, static, and independent from personal preferences posed problems. *Id.* As a result, *rule utilitarianism* was developed. *Id.* Rule utilitarianism takes the same general premise — that decisions should maximize happiness, but focuses on general principles rather than the consequences of any particular act. *Id.* Since rule utilitarianism is more of a deontological theory, which is addressed with the categorical imperative, I do not analyze the result under rule utilitarianism.

[66]There is no question that the situation is not ideal for any party involved. However, utilitarianism does not change the past — that the decision in the particular instance has to be made. Dissatisfaction generated from competing choices must be distinguished from disappointment from being forced to make the decision. It is only the former, and not the latter, that utilitarianism is concerned with.

and choice to remain silent because any alternative would likely jeopardize the guilty plea and may result in an increased sentence. Furthermore, the defendant could escape the emotional and financial consequences of a trial by accepting the guilty plea. In addition, assuming there is a real possibility of conviction, the innocent defendant is likely to face less emotional distress because the plea deal should result in reduced prison time.

The attorney would also have to consider the impact of his decision upon himself. The attorney who believed it was in his client's best interest to accept the guilty plea would also generate some happiness for the same reason as the defendant — he views it as less risky and the best outcome. Since he is remaining silent, there is no chance that disclosing information to the court will jeopardize the defendant's guilty plea and he would generate some pleasure. However, the attorney may have some dissatisfaction with the choice of counseling and remaining silent. If the state bar authorities discover his actions, he would likely be disciplined for violating the code of ethics.

The attorney would also have to consider the impact on the prosecutor. Assuming the prosecutor would pursue the case at trial regardless of any disclosure, the prosecutor might be more satisfied with the attorney's counseling and silence because it would consume fewer resources and allow the prosecutor to focus on other cases. However, the attorney's disclosure may cause the prosecutor to re-evaluate the case. If the attorney's disclosure would cause the prosecutor to re-evaluate the case, conduct further investigation, and gather more evidence, the prosecutor may drop the charges. If so, the prosecutor would likely generate more happiness if the attorney disclosed his knowledge because the prosecutor would not then participate in sending an innocent person to prison. Either way, the prosecutor would likely want to know whether the attorney truly believed his client was innocent so disclosure may generate more happiness for the prosecutor than remaining silent.

Next, the attorney would have to consider the happiness of the court and sentencing judge. The court may spend less time and work on the case with a plea deal, but a judge would likely largely be dissatisfied with the attorney's choice to remain silent. First, the judge would likely feel that he was denied a chance to investigate into the merits of the case and possibly prevent an innocent person from serving prison time.[67] Second, the judge is likely to feel deceived by the attorney since the attorney has an obligation under the Model Rules to disclose his knowledge to the court and the court is likely relying upon the attorney's statements. Therefore, the judge would appear to be dissatisfied with the attorney's choice to remain silent rather than to disclose his knowledge.

Finally, the attorney would need to consider the impact on society. If there is a real risk of conviction and the defendant is innocent, society may be happier with imprisoning the innocent defendant for the least amount of time possible, and this result is most likely to occur through a guilty plea.[68] Disclo-

---

[67]Model Rules of Prof'l Conduct R. 3.3 cmt. 10 (2010) ("It is for the tribunal then to determine what should be done....").

[68]David Luban, *The Adversary System Excuse* (1984), *in* Lawyers: A Critical Reader 5 (Richard Abel, ed., 1997) (quoting the old adage "[b]etter, we say, that a hundred criminals go free than that one person be wrongly convicted.").

sure by the attorney may put the issue in the spotlight for reform, but it is unlikely that a *single* disclosure would have that effect. On the other hand, if the client accepts the guilty plea, the real criminal remains free to potentially harm society with future crimes. It would appear that disclosure may lead to further investigation and possibly apprehension of the true perpetrator, which society would likely value highly.

To determine whether counseling acceptance and remaining silent is ethical, the attorney would have to compare the *quality* and *quantity* of happiness for the competing choices. The ethical result would be the choice that creates the greatest amount of pleasure and the least amount of pain, taking into consideration both quantity and quality. This task is likely impossible. The first difficulty the attorney would face would be attempting to quantify the happiness that each party receives. Even if that were possible, the attorney would have to compare that quantity to another as if it were simple math. But the analysis would not end there. The attorney would have to consider a qualitative dimension as well. Given the difficulty of the task,[69] it is unlikely utilitarianism conclusively decides that one choice is more ethical than the other, or provides any alternative ethical decision-making model.

B. The Categorical Imperative

Immanuel Kant created the categorical imperative.[70] The categorical imperative is a rule of maxims or absolutes — rules that must always be followed regardless of the likely or perceived consequences.[71] Kant himself expressed the categorical imperative as "[a]ct only on that maxim through which you can at the same time will that it should become a universal law."[72] Therefore when deciding between choices, one must determine what maxim she is following and ask whether she could desire it to be a universal rule that every person must use in that situation.[73] If she can logically or rationally will such a uni-

---

[69]The above paragraphs simply describe some of the factors that an attorney might consider when attempting to apply utilitarianism to the decision to remain silent. It would be impossible to provide a conclusive list given that it would be impossible for an attorney to actually know the consequences of disclosing his knowledge to the court. Furthermore, the specific feelings of each party are likely to change with underlying facts.

[70]Rachels, *supra* note 57, at 104.

[71]*See* Immanuel Kant, Groundwork of the Metaphysic of Morals 84 (H.J. Patton, trans., 1964) ("[W]hat is essentially good in the action consists in the mental disposition, let the consequences be what they may."). The term imperative refers to a command or an order to act in a particular way. *Id.* at 81. Kant said that "[a]ll imperatives command either hypothetically or categorically." *Id.* at 82. "If the action would be good solely as a means to something else, the imperative is hypothetical; if the action is represented as good in itself and therefore as necessary, in virtue of its principle, for a will which of itself accords with reason, then the imperative is categorical." *Id.*

[72]Kant, *supra* note 71, at 88; *see also* Rachels, *supra* note 57, at 106 ("Act only according to that maxim by which you can at the same time will that it should become a universal law.").

[73]Rachels, *supra* note 57, at 106.

versal rule, then the choice is an ethical one; if not, the choice is unethical.[74] Essentially, she is asking whether it is logically possible to do what she desires if everyone did the same.

For example, if a person was seeking to borrow money, but the lender would only lend with a promise to repay, the prospective borrower may contemplate lying if she knows she is unable to repay in the future.[75] In determining whether her actions were ethical, she must first determine the maxim. In such a case, it would be "[w]henever I believe myself short of money, I will borrow money and promise to pay it back, though I know that this will never be done."[76] Then, she must determine the consequences if her maxim became a universal law.[77] According to Kant's reasoning, the answer is straightforward. One could not wish that it become a universal law because it would be self-defeating.[78] No lenders would lend money because in the past they had relied upon a promise that turned out to be false. Therefore, lying in that situation is unethical because it is irrational and illogical — one cannot wish that her particular act becomes a universal law because it would defeat the very act she seeks to carry out.[79] Kant, who developed the theory, thought that no one should lie for any reason, ever.[80]

Immanuel Kant also expressed the rule in another way.[81] Additionally, he stated that the categorical imperative requires a person to "[a]ct in such a way that you always treat humanity, whether in your own person or in the person of any other, never simply as a means, but always at the same time as an end."[82] The foundation is Kant's belief in human dignity compared to that of other objects. Kant viewed humans as having intrinsic worth because humans were unique as "rational agents capable of making their own decisions, setting their own goals, and guiding their conduct by reason."[83] Kant believed that only humans were capable of reason and that all other objects, including non-human animals, lacked the consciousness or capacity to use reason and logic.[84]

This difference between humans and all other objects was extremely important to Kant. He concluded that non-human objects only have value in their use to humans — it is their use as a means to a human end that gives them

---

[74]Kant, *supra* note 71, at 84; *see also* Rachels, *supra* note 57, at 106.

[75]Kant, *supra* note 71, at 90.

[76]*Id.* at 91.

[77]*See id.* at 91; Rachels, *supra* note 57, at 106.

[78]Kant, *supra* note 71, at 91; Rachels, *supra* note 57, at 107.

[79]*See* Kant, *supra* note 71, at 91 ("I then see straight away that this maxim can never rank as a universal law of nature and be self-consistent, but must necessarily contradict itself.").

[80]*See* Rachels, *supra* note 57, at 107.

[81]There is debate on whether these two rules express the same idea. *Id.* at 115.

[82]Kant, *supra* note 71, at 96; Rachels, *supra* note 57, at 115.

[83]Rachels, *supra* note 57, at 115-16; *see* Kant, *supra* note 71, at 95.

[84]Rachels, *supra* note 57, at 115.

value.[85] Human beings, who have special dignity, could not be treated like mere objects because it would irrationally ignore the fact that humans *themselves* are "the beings for whom mere 'things' have value."[86] To Kant it was unethical to regard rational humans "as one kind of valuable things among others" as it would not respect the distinction between humans and objects.[87] An ethical decision, according to Kant, never uses a human being as only a means to an end.[88]

Analyzing the attorney's situation under the first statement of the rule arguably provides a conclusion. Under the first expression of Kant's theory, an ethical decision occurs when one acts "only on that maxim through which [one] can at the same time will that it should become a universal law."[89] The first step is to determine the maxim. If the attorney views her actions as a lie to the court,[90] then the analysis is clear — it is unethical because attorneys cannot rationally will that everyone should lie to a court while still expecting the court to believe her statement. Her own lie would become self-defeating if she wishes that everyone lie. Courts would not accept the truth of anyone's statement, including testimony in the course of a guilty plea. Therefore, the attorney is not using reason when she lies, and since ethical decisions are those that are logical, the decision is unethical.[91]

The attorney may also choose to analyze the dilemma under the alternative statement of the categorical imperative. The alternative statement, phrased as "[a]ct in such a way that you always treat humanity, whether in your own person or in the person of any other, never simply as a means, but always at the same time as an end" makes the rule more difficult to apply.[92] For the rule to make sense in application, the attorney must test it against her *reasons* for remaining silent or disclosing information to the tribunal. It is hard to see how the attorney would be using her client as a means to an end when remaining silent while her client accepts a false guilty plea — she may be counseling her client to do so because she believes it is in her client's best interest. The attorney is not using her client as a mere object or a means to an end. However, the same cannot be said for the courts and the prosecutors. The attorney would be using the prosecutor, and her plea bargain, as merely a means for securing a reduced sentence for her client and disregarding that the prosecutor is a human

---

[85]Kant, *supra* note 71, at 95-96 ("All the objects of inclination have only a conditioned value; for if there were not these inclinations these inclinations and the needs grounded on them, their object would be valueless."); Rachels, *supra* note 57, at 114-15.

[86]Rachels, *supra* note 57, at 116; *see also* Kant, *supra* note 71, at 96.

[87]Rachels, *supra* note 57, at 116; *see also* Kant, *supra* note 71, at 96.

[88]*See* Kant, *supra* note 71, at 96.

[89]*Id.* at 88.

[90]One of the criticisms of the categorical imperative is that maxims may be stated in many ways, and perhaps in a way to compel a specific result. *See* Rachels, *supra* note 57, at 108. For example, the maxim might be stated as "break Model Rule 3.3 to reduce an innocent person's prison time." In such a case, the result may be different.

[91]Rachels, *supra* note 57, at 112.

[92]Kant, *supra* note 71, at 96; Rachels, *supra* note 57, at 115.

capable of reason, and who might, after reviewing the facts further, decide this is not a case ethical to prosecute. Additionally, the attorney would likely be using the court and its reliance on the attorney's statements as a means to securing more favorable treatment for her client and disregarding the fact that the judge, who is a human capable of reason, might be able to resolve the issue better than the attorney.

The categorical imperative offers a clearer conclusion than utilitarianism. If the attorney's actions are viewed as a simple lie, it is unethical because guilty pleas or any other statement to the tribunal would no longer be sufficient to accept a guilty plea — courts would not believe anything defendants or attorneys said. However, it is likely possible to state the maxim in a way to conclude the opposite. Under Kant's alternative statement of the rule, it appears that the defense attorney is treating the prosecutor and judge as a means to her client's end and ignoring the fact that courts and prosecutors are rational agents capable of fulfilling their own moral actions through the attorney's disclosure. But the above analysis completely disregards the hardship that a defendant may face if the attorney discloses the information. Although the categorical imperative, as a deontological theory, is intended to disregard consequences, it would be extremely difficult for an attorney to do in practice — when the particular human defendant she is representing, communicates with on an ongoing basis, and comes to know is the most tangible form of the ethical dilemma.

V. Conclusion

Unfortunately, plea bargaining can create situations when it is more favorable for an innocent defendant to accept a guilty plea than risk proving his innocence at trial. When this occurs, the defense attorney's dual capacity as a representative of his client and an officer of the court conflict. As a zealous representative of his client, the attorney owes a duty to pursue his client's best interests, which would appear, in many situations, to do whatever is necessary for the defendant to accept the guilty plea. However, counseling that course of action conflicts with the attorney's duty of candor towards the tribunal because it requires the attorney to make misrepresentations to the court.

The Model Rules answer this conflict and conclude that an attorney's duty towards the court outweighs the attorney's duty towards any particular client. The Model Rules find that when an attorney knows that his client is innocent, the attorney cannot counsel his client to accept a guilty plea and cannot remain silent while his defendant admits his guilt to a court. Rather, the attorney is required to take a series of corrective steps, up to and including disclosure to the court. But given the multiple definitions of knowledge as enacted by the various states and the evidence on false guilty pleas, attorneys are not always following their obligations under the Model Rules. The attorneys likely believe that the Model Rules simply call for the wrong result and that the ethical choice is to allow the defendant to accept the guilty plea.

This Comment explored whether those attorneys' actions could be explained under the modern moral philosophies of utilitarianism and the categorical imperative. Under utilitarianism, there is no clear answer. Applying utilitarianism would be an overwhelmingly difficult task for attorneys. Therefore, it does not conclusively indicate that attorneys are acting ethically. At the other end of the spectrum is the categorical imperative. The categorical imperative lends support to Model Rule 3.3 and suggests that remaining silent is unethical, but the conclusion could be easily manipulated. Additionally, it would be hard to strictly follow in real practice given that the categorical imperative requires an attorney to disregard any impact upon the defendant. Therefore, neither of the theories clearly proves that one option is more ethical than the other.

Perhaps the failings of utilitarianism and the categorical imperative provide additional insight to Model Rule 3.3. Model Rule 3.3, unlike utilitarianism and the categorical imperative, is more than an abstract exercise in thought. Model Rule 3.3 exists out of necessity because attorneys *will* face ethical dilemmas in practice. Therefore, unlike utilitarianism and the categorical imperative, the Model Rules must draw a line and provide a workable resolution. Otherwise, ethical dilemmas would be left to the subjective personal feelings and moral positions of the representing attorney.

Model Rule 3.3 has provided a workable solution by requiring an attorney faced with the ethical dilemma discussed in this Comment to take corrective action up to and including disclosure to the tribunal. But just like any rule that is forced to take a position, there are winners and losers. The losers under Model Rule 3.3 may be the particular attorney and defendant before the court. Perhaps some attorneys like Ochoa's recognize the hardship and offer free representation in an attempt to help their distressed clients.

But there are also winners with Model Rule 3.3. Attorneys benefit by having a rule that is usable. More importantly, when disclosure is required, the ethical dilemma is placed in the spotlight for reform and improvement. After becoming more aware of the problem, courts can adjust their practices and pressure prosecutors to change their practices as well. Judges, who are among the most influential law reformers, could push for legislative reform or a change in the Model Rules. The input of defense attorneys on how to fix the problem would become more influential as well. Therefore, if all attorneys followed Model Rule 3.3, their disclosure may lead to changes in the criminal justice system that target the problem's sources rather than symptoms. The same cannot be said if Model Rule 3.3 allowed them to remain silent. Although the particular defendant and attorney may feel they benefit by remaining silent, remaining silent does nothing to fix the system that creates the problem. Attorneys are all public citizens with a responsibility to seek improvement of the law, and disclosure seems to be more of a step towards improvement than does the practice of remaining silent.

qp

Visit us at *www.quidprobooks.com.*

www.ingramcontent.com/pod-product-compliance
Lightning Source LLC
Chambersburg PA
CBHW070307200326
41518CB00010B/1919